Senses of Tradition

SENSES OF TRADITION

Continuity and Development
in Catholic Faith

John E. Thiel

UNIVERSITY PRESS

2000

OXFORD
UNIVERSITY PRESS

Oxford   New York
Athens   Auckland   Bangkok   Bogotá   Bombay   Buenos Aires
Calcutta   Cape Town   Chennai   Dar es Salaam   Delhi   Florence   Hong Kong
Istanbul   Karachi   Kuala Lumpur   Madras   Madrid   Melbourne
Mexico City   Nairobi   Paris   Singapore   Taipei   Tokyo   Toronto
and associated companies in
Berlin   Ibadan

Copyright © 2000 by John E. Thiel

Published by Oxford University Press, Inc.
198 Madison Avenue, New York, New York 10016

Oxford is a registered trademark of Oxford University Press.

Library of Congress Cataloging-in-Publication Data
Thiel, John E.
Senses of tradition : continuity and development in Catholic faith
John E. Thiel
p.   cm.
Includes index.
ISBN 0-19-513726-4
1. Tradition (Theology) 2. Catholic Church—Doctrines.   I. Title.
BT90.T45   2000
231'.042—dc21   99-047480

Grateful acknowledgment for permission
to use the following material:

"Pluralism in Theological Truth," in *Why Theology?*
(Concilium/Fundamental Theology: 1994/6), ed. C. Geffré and
W. Jeanrond (London: SCM Press/Maryknoll, NY: Orbis Books, 1994):
57–69; "Responsibility to the Spirit: Authority in the
Catholic Tradition," *New Theology Review* 8 (August 1995): 53–68;
"Tradition and Authoritative Reasoning:
A Nonfoundationalist Perspective," *Theological Studies* 56
(December 1995): 627–51; "Perspectives on Tradition,"
*The Catholic Theological Society of America: Proceedings of the
Fifty-Fourth Annual Convention*, vol. 54, ed. M. Downey (1999): 1–18.

1 3 5 7 9 8 6 4 2

Printed in the United States of America
on acid-free paper

For
Dorothea,
David,
and Benjamin

Preface

In his 1903 essay *History and Dogma*, the French philosopher and religious thinker Maurice Blondel articulated the Scylla and Charybdis of a modern understanding of tradition. Tradition is poorly conceived, he argued, when it is portrayed in the manner of extrinsicism, which cannot truly take account of the facts of history in its explanation of continuity, or historicism, which reduces tradition to the phenomenal flow of events in time. Nearly one hundred years later, a contemporary systematic theology of tradition faces these same interpretive pitfalls. In this regard, the problem for a systematic theology of tradition on the cusp of the twenty-first century is the same as that faced by theologians throughout the nineteenth and twentieth centuries: how to speak well of tradition's continuity in light of the real development (often a religious euphemism for "change") that all things historical undergo, while respecting the facts of historical research.

The often troubled relationship between traditional continuity and traditional development is the focus of this monograph. In the course of its pages, I attempt to show that previous understandings of traditional continuity have labored under an assumption that cannot effectively be reconciled with the critical investigation of the history that Christians call their tradition. I sketch a theory of tradition unburdened by this assumption, a theory that accounts for continuity in a manner different from premodern and modern explanations. For constructive use in understanding the workings of tradition, the theory retrieves an important resource in the history of Catholic exegesis: the fourfold senses of scripture. It attempts to explain not only how the old in tradition endures but also how the old becomes new, how the new becomes old, and how the old occasionally ceases to be valued traditionally.

The theory proposed herein is developed and illustrated with particular reference to the Roman Catholic tradition, though it could be applied, mutatis mutandis, to understand the workings of any Christian community that prizes theological tradition in some way. The judgment of whether this theory is better than current understandings of tradition, I leave to the reader. I would state at the outset, however, that in my own judgment a good theory upholds two values. It is faithful to a Catholic understanding of authoritative tradition, and it is faithful in the face of the historical-critical evidence.

All biblical citations are from the New Revised Standard Version. Unless otherwise noted, all translations are my own.

As this project comes to publication, I must express extensive gratitude.

Fairfield University has been more than generous in support of this work. A 1995 Fairfield University Research Committee Summer Stipend grant enabled me to write an article, later published in *Theological Studies*, that became the cornerstone of this work; it appears herein as the substance of chapter 3. In addition, the university granted me a sabbatical during the 1997–1998 academic year, during which I completed much of the writing of this book. My sabbatical year was also funded by a National Endowment for the Humanities (NEH) Fellowship for College Teachers and Independent Scholars (#FB-34000). I am extremely grateful to the NEH for supporting my work a second time. I am also happy to acknowledge Orin Grossman, Academic Vice-President at Fairfield University, who offered me encouragement on numerous occasions. Cynthia Read, my editor at Oxford University Press, was both supportive and gracious in guiding the manuscript to publication, as was her assistant, Theo Calderara. Joan Vidal proved to be a superb copyeditor and Jennifer Rozgonyi an expert production editor.

Brian Gerrish, David Kelsey, and Francis Schüssler Fiorenza were generous in their willingness to write to various funding agencies in support of the project. In this last regard, I must single out especially the help offered by Margaret Farley, to whom I owe much for her support and encouragement in this and so many other respects. I am grateful to Cyril O'Regan, Tony Godzieba, Kathy Tanner, and Simon Harak for their critical readings of parts of the work in progress, and to Brad Hinze, Paul Lakeland, Randy Sachs, and Nancy Dallavalle, who took the time to read the whole manuscript and to offer many suggestions for improvement. Gregory Schopen read none of this book along the way but remained a source of inspiration during the time of its writing, as he has during the time of our long friendship.

Finally, I thank Dorothea Cook Thiel and our sons, David and Benjamin, for much in this book that is not readily visible here and for much more beyond its covers that is. I dedicate these pages to them.

June 1999   J.E.T.
Fairfield, Connecticut

Contents

Senses of Tradition

Introduction

SENSES OF SCRIPTURE AND TRADITION

It is a distinctive Roman Catholic teaching that, in the words of the Second Vatican Council's "Dogmatic Constitution on Divine Revelation," "[s]acred Tradition and sacred Scripture make up a single sacred deposit of the Word of God, which is entrusted to the Church."[1] In this one divine Word, God speaks the promise of salvation. Catholic Christians believe that one finds this Word of promise both in the writings of biblical scripture and in tradition— in the ways that scripture informs and is informed by the authentic teachings of the Church; age-old Christian practice; liturgical devotion; the compelling lives of the saints; the writings of great Catholic thinkers; and God's recognized sacramental presence to holy times, places, and events. This Word is one, issuing as it does from the one divine Speaker and conveying the message of the one Word, unique Son, spoken by God before the saved world was created (John 1:1). And yet because this one divine Word is communicated in both scripture and tradition, it is communicated in a mediated plurality that extends further still to scripture's many words and to tradition's many more words, actions, persons, times, places, and happenings. Certainly, this teaching of the Church is among its most important, for it articulates where and how the Christian community encounters the truthful promise of eternal life and the ecclesially embraced narrative of how God has gracefully brought this promise to fulfillment. A doctrine so basic to the claims of the faith that it professes both the source and means of God's revelation to humanity cannot help but shape the understanding of every other Catholic belief, doctrine, and practice.

Although all Christian confessions proclaim scripture as the revelatory Word of God, only Roman Catholicism accords to tradition, in such an explicit way, the authority of the Word. The teaching of the Second Vatican Council (1962–1965) on scripture and tradition can be found in some incipient form in the earliest years of the emerging Great Church of the fourth and fifth centuries and, earlier still, in the writings of the apologists and in selected testimonies of the New Testament witness. This teaching, however, began to achieve its present-day definition in the controversial setting of sixteenth-century Reformation polemics. Rejecting the Roman ascription of authority to ecclesial tradition, the Protestant Reformers defended instead the sole authority of the Bible as divine revelation. Against the Protestant watchword *sola scriptura*, Catholic theologians insisted upon a belief that was defined with unprecedented clarity at the Council of Trent (1545–1563): the communi-

3

cation of God's revelation in both scripture *and* tradition. Though understood and even expressed in different ways since the sixteenth century, this formulation has come to carry not only the authority of an orthodox understanding of God's inspired Word but also, by virtue of its particularity and controversial history, much of the identity of Roman Catholicism in the Tridentine and post-Tridentine periods.

The contrapuntal character of this Catholic doctrine—defined as it is by its explicit rejection of the Protestant scripture principle—has done much to solidify the distinctiveness of Catholic belief on the means of divine revelation. And yet, aside from this formal clarity, much ambiguity remains about this teaching in the belief and practice of the Church. Even though the Council of Trent had offered a definitive teaching four hundred years earlier, the Second Vatican Council struggled to find the right language to convey the Church's authentic teaching on scripture and tradition as the conveyance of God's inspired Word. Theologians have continued to grapple, far short of consensus, with such questions as how scripture and tradition are related to each other; how each measures and complements the truth of the other; and where, within this complement, the weight of authority is to be placed in judging the meaning of the divine Word. Frequent teachings of the magisterium on controverted issues, and the seeming inability of such teachings to quell controversy in the Church, testify to the ambiguity that attends the community's judgment on tradition's faithfulness to scripture and scripture's right traditional understanding. Indeed, one might understand the persistence of authority issues in the postconciliar Church to derive from an abiding ambiguity about the force of the conjunction in the Catholic formula "scripture and tradition." To the degree that this formula remains distinctively Catholic, its conjunctive ambiguity extends to Catholic identity in the contemporary Church itself.

This ambiguity, in both the "scripture and tradition" formula and the Catholic identity it informs, draws its ambivalent resonance from the hermeneutical issues inherent in the Christian belief in a God who reveals—and more, in a God who reveals in scripture and tradition. God's revelation is the unfolding of the divine promise of salvation in a way that avails what otherwise would be inaccessible to human understanding. And yet this manifestation of the promise in revelation's inspired Word remains immersed in the divine mystery it communicates, a mystery as incomprehensible as it is paradoxically articulate in the revealed Word. Inexhaustibly hidden, the mystery beckons believers to inexhaustible interpretation. Whether interpretation takes place in the systematic order of theological reflection or in the utterly unselfconscious efforts of any believer to understand faith more fully, its task can never be brought to unambiguous closure as long as it respects the mystery it seeks. The ambiguity of interpretation is rooted not only in its inevitable inadequacy to its object but also in the plurality of the means by which God reveals, in both scripture *and* tradition; in the plurality of meanings that Christians have found and continue to find in scripture, tradition, and, to an even greater degree in the mutually informative ways that scripture and tradition together present God's inspired Word. The plurality of both these sacred means and the meanings they offer the faithful imagination becomes more plural and, as a result, more ambiguous still when set in the vast spectrum of possible experience in which scripture and tradition are encountered, their meanings are sought, and their mystery is interpreted.

In this plurality of scripture *and* tradition *and* experience, in the plurality of meanings that each offers, and in the many meanings that proceed from their interpretive intersection, one meets a complex source of the ambiguity that, in the judgment of some, vexes modern Catholic identity. Given the plurality of interpretation, which understanding of the inspired Word is true? Does not the scriptural Sermon on the Mount stand at odds with the tradition's teaching on the possibility of a just war? Are not the magisterium's more recent social teachings on the dignity and freedom of the human person a clearer and more faithful rendition of the inspired Word than are magisterial teachings from the earlier tradition or the rather scattered scriptural account of the human person before God? Does not the human experience of justice in the post-Enlightenment age cast new light on the traditional practice of excluding women from priestly ordination? For many in the Church, such questions prove troublesome in principle, since the interpretive pluralism they expose seems to conflict with Christian expectations about the unity of God's inspired Word. Admittedly, this interpretive pluralism does cause consternation in the Church. But one would be shortsighted not to see a more resourceful and productive side to this ambiguity, for if, in the midst of divine revelation and its ecclesial affirmation, pluralism occasions doubt, it also marks the interpretive richness that scripture, tradition, experience, and the many possibilities of their hermeneutical encounter offer to the believing community as avenues to the mystery of God's revelation.

Beyond the Literal Sense

Acknowledging the interpretive richness of scripture, tradition, and experience should not suggest that there are no limits to interpretive possibilities in the range of Catholic judgment. Catholic belief accords the authority of revelation to scripture and tradition but not to experience. Even when the authority of experience seems irresistibly veridical, it still must be weighed, valued, and judged by the ecclesially acknowledged authority of the revealed Word. The truthfulness of the divine mystery is ingrained in the reflective intersections between and among scripture, tradition, and experience that shape a particular understanding. The relative adequacy of any interpretation, whether presented in the published ideas of a professional theologian or occasioned by an illiterate believer's creative reflection on a gospel parable, lies in the interpreter's grasp of these meaningful intersections—in the ability of a graced insight to identify dimensions of the Word and dimensions of experience that appropriately clarify, appreciate, renew, enact, criticize, and correct each other and, in so doing, manifest their faithfulness to the truth of God. Although such interpretation strives to appreciate the one divine mystery through the unity of the revealed Word, it can and usually does draw its insights, evidence, and conclusions from a vast array of meaningful nuance proffered by experience and the Word. The possibilities for Catholic interpretation are appropriately limited by the authority accorded to scripture and tradition and, finally, by the self-sustaining truth of the divine reality that scripture and tradition reveal. Even within this thankfully narrower range of possibilities, however, scripture, tradition, and experience provide expansive and fertile fields for interpretive cultivation.[2]

This last point can readily be appreciated with regard to experience and scripture, for both seem to admit of a hermeneutical "more" of nuanced meanings that transcend initial, commonplace judgments on their significance. In the history of the interpretation of scripture, the commonplace understanding of biblical meaning has been known as its literal sense, a term that one can extend, metaphorically at least, to commonplace meaning as such. The literal sense that one might attribute to experience and the literal sense that believers affirm in their communal reading of scripture function as a baseline for understanding that serves to check and limit the proliferation of interpretation. And yet, in both cases, the literal sense not only allows for but also encourages supplements to its meaning, thus promoting an interpretive richness whenever its own limitations as a particular sort of meaning are conceded.

The claim that experience is interpretively rich is hardly surprising. Experience in time and culture possesses an extraordinary pluralism of interpretive senses that seems to grow with the actual determinacy of experience in moment and place. Indeed, experience is so open to the possible, the new, and the contingent that its meaningful yield can often seem centerless and infinitely proliferated. Even if Christian sensibilities would be unwilling to follow the hermeneutical logic of deconstruction to its indeterminate conclusions, most who have had occasion have learned from poststructuralist criticism that experience, however textually encoded, offers more generous bounds for interpretive play than might at first be imagined. From this perspective, it has become difficult to speak of an experiential literal sense that is universal in some neutral or context-free fashion. A commonality of experience so widely measured would collapse interpretive pluralism and the breadth of experience from which it proceeds into something capriciously fixed and familiar, a fundamentalist construction bearing little resemblance to actual experience and the multiple possibilities for its interpretation.

Clearly, though, appeals to "common sense" or the rhetoric of "everybody" or culturally understood forms of civil behavior and discourse between strangers are all examples of an experiential literal sense that limits interpretive possibilities by reining in the proliferation of which experience and its meaning are capable. This literal sense provides a basic stock of uncontroversially interpreted experience whose meaningfulness can be taken for granted by its matter-of-fact interpreters. If appropriately self-aware, claims for this literal sense acknowledge that its common meaningfulness already presupposes a restriction on its latitude. However grandly an experiential literal sense may imagine its commonality, it is always this or that literal sense, held in common by a large or small—but in any case particular—group that finds meaning in a certain spectrum of shared experience. The experiential literal sense can be distinguished as a specific sort of meaning to the degree that it represents this particular commonality but also because its own specificity opens a space for a hermeneutical "more" of other interpretive senses. Experience remains so susceptible to a plurality of interpretive senses that claims for a common or "literal" sense inescapably join the ranks of the interpretive multitude that their own commonplace meaning highlights and even fosters.

Modern or postmodern sensibilities would find scripture's meaningful range to be no less extensive than the interpretive spectrum offered by experience. Indeed, as these sensibilities are crafted in the analytic precision of theory, they seem to expect an interpretive pluralism so unbounded that a discrete literal sense is taken up into other interpretive senses or even disappears entirely. For hermeneutical theory, a simple distinction between the literal and other interpretive senses of a text seems naïve in its suggestion that a hypostatized truth dwells in words or their grammatical relations, as though truth in history could stand on its own, impervious to interpretation. "Ostensible" meanings, in this perspective, are not textually given in some neutral manner available to all. Rather, claims for the meaning of a literal sense immediately suggest a context that is laden with values, interests, and commitments, that can be identified by asking for whom, when, where, and to whose end a particular literal sense is meaningful. Because modern and postmodern hermeneutical theories typically presuppose the interpretive malleability of the text to the broad spectrum of experiential possibilities already considered here, reference to the literal sense of a text (and perhaps even the act of reference itself) requires justification.

Whether one accounts for the susceptibility of the text to interpretation as Hans-Georg Gadamer does by speaking of its effective mediation from past to present by historical consciousness, as Paul Ricoeur does by speaking of critical understanding shaped in the passage from a first to a second naïveté, or as Wolfgang Iser does by speaking of the presence of the text in the readings of its audiences[3]—these approaches all tend to speak of textual meaning as a function of interpretation and not as a commonly available sense distinguishable from its interpretation. In this hermeneutics of sublation, no textual meaning is affirmed in its own right as though it possessed intrinsic worth; it is affirmed only in another, "higher" meaning constituted by the act of understanding in its full historicity. A deconstructive approach to writing does not merely sublate the literal in the interpretive; it even erases any sublated integrity that might be attributed to the literal sense. Jacques Derrida, for example, is eager to show how quickly the supposed literal meaning of a text unravels, as its closer scrutiny exposes the arbitrary privilege accorded it in the assumptions of writer and readers. Ambiguity in the face of infinitely possible readings, not the clarity of an artificial literal sense, is all that any text has to offer its readers. In such a hermeneutics of erasure, hopes placed in a writing's literal meaning are seen to be grounded indirectly in claims for the Bible's literal sense. Since Derrida's deconstructive criticism regards any claim for the stability of meaning as logocentric—as an alternate expression of the belief in God's inspired presence to the Bible's literal sense—its judgment on the arbitrariness of any literal sense extends finally, and most of all, to the supposed ostensible meaning of the biblical page. The fate of the Bible's literal sense is the fate of all literal senses, for all books promulgate the assumptions of the Book.[4]

These hermeneutical stances are frequently seen as threats to the Christian belief in a literal sense of scripture as God's Word, for their affirmation of a hermeneutical "more" beyond any literal sense is so complete that the literal seems to evaporate. The hermeneutical "more," one might say, becomes a hermeneutical "only," with no point of departure or reference other than the infinite plurality of interpretation. The hermeneutics of sublation, to be sure the lesser of the threats and an interpretive approach often put to theological use, holds that whatever stability textual meaning might possess is always immersed in the unstable historicity of the human imagination that reconstructs it. This is a position whose anthropological orientation, in the judgment of some, diminishes the priority that Christians rightly should accord to an available biblical meaning of divine origin. The hermeneutics of erasure argues that textual meaning is utterly unstable because there is no literal sense, no authorial intention, and so—in a manner of speaking—no author. This is a position that, in the judgment of many denies not only the authorship but also the existence of the God who speaks in the scriptural Word and thus the created worth of the Word's human hearer. As influential as these hermeneutical theories have been, and as theologically instructive as they may be, there is no reason to accept their judgments on the nature or viability of literal meaning in general, or on the biblical literal sense in particular, as the final word.

To the degree that the hermeneutics of sublation and the hermeneutics of erasure both stress the historicity of interpretation, both would grant that interpretation takes place within the full spectrum of historicity's conditions, which includes the social character of human existence. Like all human endeavors, interpretation is social and occurs in communities of interpretation. In these communities, interpretive assumptions are held, insights occur, values are shaped, judgments are made, and readings are enacted. These activities and their results do not issue from the work of solitary interpreters but take place in a shared setting defined by the commitments of its interpreters. An interpretive community might be understood as broadly as those educated in the intellectual culture of Western classics (Gadamer), or as ephemerally as those who form a shifting audience of a text's sphere of influence (Iser), or as narrowly as those who have recognized the end of the logocentric epoch (Derrida). Although these communities may seem, in comparison to others, rather highbrow, disparate, or lonely, their existence is a reminder that interpretation is the practice of particular, shared beliefs whose meaningfulness is recognized within, but not necessarily outside, their respective communities.

Claims for the sublation or erasure of the literal sense are examples of such communal belief, as is the belief in the literal sense of scripture that Christians have affirmed throughout the centuries. Each flourishes in a determinate context of meaning from the perspective of which it assesses the meaning of other claims. As each belief encounters another, it may discover one that is a close or distant relative. Or one belief may judge another to be a hostile stranger, to express a meaning incommensurable with its own. Each must be appreciated in its respective particularities, and none has the power of consummate judgment over the others, unless of course that judgment itself is made as a particular claim expressing the values of the claimant. Contemporary interpretive theories, then, though critical of the Christian belief in the literal sense of scripture, should not be credited with or blamed for the undermining of that belief, as though the hermeneutics of sublation and erasure had demonstrated objectively the untenability of the Christian belief.

The believing Church is the community in which the plain sense of scripture is valued as a literal footing for Christian insight and understanding. The literal sense is a point of departure for ecclesial appreciation of the inspired Word of God that the Church believes scripture to be. If the literal sense presents scripture's ostensible meaning, then its ostensibility requires believers' eyes and a vision already shaped by faithful commitment. Within the panoply of interpretations, the literal sense remains a touchstone for adjudicating the nuanced readings of scripture that have always been advanced in believing communities throughout the Christian tradition. And yet it is important to recognize that the Christian affirmation of a literal sense of scripture has not threatened scripture's interpretive richness. This is especially true in the Catholic tradition, which throughout its history has spoken of senses of scripture beyond the literal sense.

Drawing on Jewish interpretive assumptions and Hellenistic rhetorical practice, early Christian exegetes read the Hebrew scriptures, and eventually the writings of their own Bible, in ways that recognized interpretive senses beyond the literal sense.[5] Typological readings of the Hebrew scriptures, which found the Christ and his meaning in the story of Israel, were the first Christian forays beyond a literal sense. The third-century Alexandrian School, through the work of Clement and Origen, began to systematize the allegorical method of interpretation—an exegetical practice committed to an explicit distinction between a writing's literal sense and its deeper, interpretive meanings. In his greatest theological work, *On First Principles*, Origen took pains to delineate three senses of scripture—the literal, the moral, and the mystical—which he identified respectively as scripture's body, soul, and spirit.[6] Such influential Christian interpreters as Tyconius and Augustine followed Origen's lead by detailing rules for reading scripture that amounted to multiple interpretive senses—seven in the Donatist Tyconius's listing, for which Augustine, his erstwhile opponent in matters of doctrine, had the utmost respect.[7] The fifth-century monastic writer John Cassian catalogued the senses of scripture into a fourfold schema—the literal, allegorical, tropological, and the anagogical—that endured throughout the medieval period as the accepted ecclesial understanding of scripture's interpretive richness. In Cassian's schema, the literal sense portrayed the events of history, the allegorical sense portrayed the mystery of the divine life and its dispensation, the tropological sense portrayed moral guidance for Christian comportment, and the anagogical sense portrayed the eschatological fulfillment of Christian hope in God's heavenly consummation of earthly life.[8]

The Christian belief that scripture offers a plurality of inspired meanings beyond the literal sense did not diminish the importance of the literal sense. Third-and fourth-century representatives of the so-called Antiochene School, such as Diodore of Tarsus and Theodore of Mopsuestia, defended the authority of scripture's literal meaning against what they judged to be the excesses of Alexandrian allegory. Augustine so valued the literal sense that he sought multiple meanings *within* it by distinguishing between its unedifying and edifying dimensions, setting the latter as the normative goal of exegesis.[9] The respect accorded the literal sense by the twelfth-century Victorines Hugh and Andrew became the common regard of the High Middle Ages[10]—one that Thomas Aquinas expressed in the first question of the *Summa Theologiae* by noting that the literal sense, as the intended Word of the divine author, is itself the productive source of multiple meanings.[11]

The acknowledged meaningfulness of the literal sense in medieval exegesis has endured to the present day in Catholic belief, as has the medieval affirmation of scripture's allegorical, tropological, and anagogical meanings. Scripture's plurality of interpretive senses has come under attack by the sixteenth-century Reformers, who insisted on exegetical devotion to the plain sense; and more recently, by reductive proponents of the historical-critical method, who measure scripture's real meanings by their correspondence to nature, history, or some construction of Enlightened reason; and, more recently still, by twentieth-century deconstructionists, whose eclipse of the inspired literal sense undercuts the spiritual significance, and wildly proliferates the number, of scripture's interpretive senses. In the face of each attack, Catholic faith has held fast to the assumption that scripture possesses an interpretive richness that unfolds in a communally affirmed literal sense and in a hermeneutical "more" of interpretive senses beyond the literal, all together ways of appreciating the mystery of God's revelation communicated through the biblical page.

Beyond the Literal Sense of Tradition?

Now, in light of the Catholic belief that scripture and tradition make up a single deposit of divine revelation, one might think that scripture's interpretive richness would extend to tradition. I argue, in the course of this book, that it does. The need for this argument stems from the prevalent assumption that tradition does not offer a hermeneutical "more" beyond what might be called its literal sense—that tradition, by its very nature, is not susceptible to inter-pretive possibilities as experience and scripture clearly are. The Catholic belief in a single deposit of divine revelation would seem to require that tradition admit of the same sort of hermeneutical range that characterizes scripture. It is well worth noting, however, that Catholic theology has never spoken of a plurality of interpretive senses of tradition comparable to the senses of scrip-ture. If there are not such senses of tradition, then it would seem that tradition possesses only a literal meaning, at least metaphorically in its unwritten di-mensions, and therefore an inspiration interpretively more restricted in scope than that of scripture. No teaching of the Church, however, suggests that an interpretive differential separates God's revelation in scripture and tradition or that tradition does not offer a wealth of meaning ever capable of appreci-ation in a plurality of ways. There are a number of historical and theological reasons for the absence of interpretive senses of tradition that deserve our attention.

The status of "tradition" as a dimension of divine revelation identifiable in its own right and distinguishable from "scripture" is a more recent develop-ment in Catholic belief, dating from the later Middle Ages. Its arrival occurred at the contentious threshold of Reformation polemics, where its affirmation or denial was taken to be the mark of true or false faith. Since the sixteenth century—when the Council of Trent's 1546 *Decretum de libris sacris et de traditionibus recipiendis* raised a distinguishable "tradition" to the authority of a conciliar teaching—theologians (and to some extent the magisterium too) have struggled with the problem of defining tradition's relationship to scrip-ture and thus the authority scripture and tradition hold as media of God's inspired Word. Ecclesial reflection on tradition, then, has been preoccupied with the more basic questions and ad hoc concerns of its identity, its place in and as divine revelation, and the nature of its authority—formal issues that do not address the more material concern of tradition's interpretive rich-ness.

One can also account for the absence of interpretive senses of tradition by noting that tradition has served as a limitation on the interpretive possibilities of scripture. Tradition—especially in its written forms, such as the teachings of ecumenical councils or papal encyclicals—has often functioned as an au-thoritative reading of scripture occasioned by ecclesial ambiguity in the face of conflicting claims about scripture's literal sense. Tradition here is oriented much more toward the unity of scripture's literal sense than toward the plu-rality of scripture's other interpretive senses. Indeed, the authority accorded to tradition often seems to be exercised by narrowing the interpretive plural-ism of scripture, a tendency that would seem, a fortiori, to resist any efforts to interpret tradition's own clarifications of scripture more widely. If the doc-trinal tradition further "literalizes" the literal sense of scripture by paring the scope of its hermeneutical possibilities, then the specificity of its representation of the Word would seem not susceptible to, and in principle suspicious of, senses of its own meaning beyond the literal.

Another important reason for the absence of interpretive senses of tradition is that the Catholic belief in a distinguishable tradition within the deposit of revelation developed at the same time as, and in connection with, the Catholic belief in papal infallibility. With the definition of the dogma of papal infallibility in the First Vatican Council's 1870 *Pastor Aeternus*, the authority of tradition came to be most closely linked with the authority of the magisterium and particularly with the exercise of that extraordinary papal prerogative. The development of the belief in the ordinary universal magisterium in the nineteenth and twentieth centuries together with the increasingly frequent exercise of the ordinary magisterium in modern times have done much to promote the idea that the magisterium's authenticity as the teacher of the Church, by which it is the rightful and most authoritative interpreter of divine revelation, naturally carries with it the truthful guarantee of infallibility. And to the extent that authentic magisterial teaching promulgates tradition, tradition so understood seems, in turn, to radiate an aura of infallibility that makes the need for interpretive senses superfluous. The ascription of infallibility to tradition encourages a univocal understanding of its meaning and thus the expectation that its literal sense exhausts its meaning.

These reasons help to explain why Catholic belief has not made claims for interpretive "senses" of tradition that function in a manner comparable to the senses of scripture. Multiple senses of tradition would presuppose a flexibility to its meaning that the very notion of tradition as it has developed in Catholic belief often seems to deny. Tradition in this perspective seems to inscribe the literal itself. Tradition, I argue, does have a literal sense, which, like the literal senses of experience and scripture, conveys a valued and communally held meaning. Commitment to this literal sense has become increasingly important in a postmodern age whose delight in relativity presents a strong challenge to faith in an inspired and thus infallible Word of God. The religious desire for the literal is theologically appropriate, expressing as it does belief in the clarity of the inspired Word and acknowledging as it does that there are, in fact, proper limits on tradition's interpretation. But the desire for the literal can, and often does, devolve into a complacent literalism—a fundamentalism that takes ecclesial tradition to be an uninterpretable presentation of a revelatory Word whose inspiration lies only at the level of the letter and before which interpretation is reduced to repetition. Although Catholic sensibilities resist such fundamentalism when encountering the Word in scripture, they have often been inclined toward an ecclesiastical fundamentalism defined by the literalism of tradition.

My project in this book is to counter this tendency toward ecclesiastical fundamentalism by exploring the susceptibility of tradition to a plurality of interpretations, to a hermeneutical "more" beyond its literal sense. I do so by showing that one can speak productively of "senses" of tradition that are comparable to the senses of scripture, by delineating each in turn, by considering how they are discerned by believers, and by showing how their perspectives are represented in different styles of contemporary theology. Before proceeding to the next four chapters, which examine of each of the senses of tradition in turn, it is essential to explore further the Catholic understanding of tradition, especially the historical circumstances of its development that make the need for a hermeneutics of tradition so pressing.

The Integrity of Tradition

Although Trent and Vatican II taught that God's inspired Word is communicated in scripture and tradition, these councils did not elaborate on what tradition *is*. There is no teaching of the Church on the substance of tradition akin to Trent's precise and authoritative listing of the inspired books of holy scripture.[12] "Tradition" as a noun names persons, places, and things. Yet this nominal form must be appreciated initially through its verbal meaning. *Traditio* in Catholic understanding is an ongoing event, a *tradere* in which the faith is "handed down" from generation to generation. But what is it that is handed down? Scripture is the first and most explicit answer. Tradition is the handing down of the Bible, and, more specifically, its interpretation, throughout the Christian centuries. This first response to the question of what tradition is, although it properly accentuates the close connection between scripture and tradition on which Catholic belief insists, is also acceptable to Protestant assumptions so long as tradition is oriented completely to the biblical text.[13] Catholic belief, however, regards the handing down of scripture as involving interpretive possibilities that extend beyond scripture's literal and figurative parameters—beyond its fourfold, text-oriented sense, to the time-honored faith and practice of the Church.

To repeat and fill out the examples noted earlier, the substance of tradition can be found in such authentic teachings of the Church as the complete divinity and humanity of Christ, the Immaculate Conception, and papal affirmations of the dignity of the worker and workers' rights; age-old Christian practice, such as the care of the poor and the sign of the cross; liturgical devotion ritualized in the enduring rubrics of the mass or devotions, such as benediction and the novena; the compelling lives of the saints and the veneration of their relics; the writings of great Catholic thinkers whether such speculative theologians as Bonaventure or such spiritual counselors as Catherine of Siena; and God's recognized sacramental presence to holy times, such as Advent, Lent, Christmas, and Easter; such places as Jerusalem, Lourdes, St. Peter's Basilica, and local shrines; and such events as Francis of Assisi's embrace of the leper, John XXIII's surprising call for a council, and the religiously meaningful life of any believer. Although one could find scriptural justification, or evidence of scriptural faithfulness, for all these examples, there is a real sense in which these beliefs, doctrines, and practices present the inspired Word in words, events, and actions that cannot be reduced simply to the biblical words.[14] This nonreducibility of tradition to scripture is perhaps the most formal way of distinguishing between scripture and tradition within their Catholic unity. Another, less minimalist, way would be to highlight tradition's own peculiar richness in offering God's revelation to the believing community in words, events, and actions that faithfully complement, as well as interpret, biblical meaning.

If tradition cannot be reduced to scripture, and yet does not present a truth different from biblical revelation, then tradition possesses an integrity, a meaningful richness of its own—however much bound to scripture's—that must be respected if tradition is to be interpreted well. This integrity of tradition makes talk about interpretive senses of tradition possible, for if tradition had no integrity of its own, its interpretation would be merely a function of the interpretation of scripture. A tradition that was only the history of the interpretation of scripture would require no regional hermeneutics to respect the particularity of its own interpretable substance. The Catholic teaching on the integrity of tradition reached conciliar definition for the first time at the sixteenth-century Council of Trent. In order to appreciate its implications for a hermeneutics of tradition, this distinctively Catholic teaching must be placed in the history that preceded it and in the teaching's subsequent development to our own time. By way of anticipation, consider at this point that the narrative of tradition's increasing integrity is a narrative of tradition's presumed limitation to a literal sense not itself susceptible to a broader interpretive range.

Modern scriptural studies have shown that the proclamation of the gospel—"that Christ died for our sins, in accordance with the scriptures; that he was buried; that he was raised to life on the third day, according to the scriptures; and that he appeared to Cephas, and afterwards to the Twelve" (1 Corinthinans 15:3–5)—did not begin to take written form until the second half of the first century, first in the letters of Paul and then in the narratives of the evangelists and the contributions of the other New Testament authors. And yet, as this passage from Paul evinces, there never was a time in which the early Christian churches were without scripture. The first Christians experienced and proclaimed the resurrection of Jesus as the fulfillment of God's covenant with Israel revealed in the Hebrew scriptures. The authority, indeed the real meaning, of the Christian kerygma is that the events of salvation through Christ have taken place "according to the scriptures," and only so measured can they be recognized as the consistent work of God in history. Although there was a time when the earliest Church lacked the writings that came to be regarded as the New Testament, there never was a time when the Christian proclamation lacked a revealed and written Word, even though that proclamation obviously believed in the Word in light of the risen Lord.

The kerygma that took shape in the writings of the New Testament was first proclaimed in the faith, hope, and joy of the earliest Christians. In their stories of Jesus, their liturgical prayers, their testimonies of conversion, and their exhortations to discipleship, the first Christians at once formulated the claims that would receive written and revelatory shape in the many genres of the New Testament and initiated the "handing down" of the faith in the very acts of voicing, enacting, and relating those claims. Paul himself, on the cusp between the unwritten and written proclamation, introduced the "good news" to the Corinthians in the previously quoted passage by noting, "I handed on to you the facts which had been imparted to me" (1 Corinthians 15:3). Later New Testament writings, such as Jude (3) and 2 Peter (2: 21), portray these imparted facts as a *paradosis*—that is, the content of the saving knowledge of Jesus Christ "handed down" from believer to believer.[15]

That these testimonies to the process and content of an oral tradition began to be made in writing did not mark the end of an oral tradition of Christian confession any more than the existence of books precludes the act of conversing. The Christian biblical writings became an expression and—with the formation of the New Testament canon by the beginning of the third century—the most authoritative expression[16] of the *paradosis*. God's revelation in the Bible, both Old and New Testaments, was what tradition preeminently handed down. And yet early Church fathers such as Irenaeus, Tertullian, Clement of Alexandria, Origen, Cyprian, and Basil continued to affirm the authority of an extrabiblical tradition of right Christian practice and belief. The words of the baptismal formula, the form of the eucharistic celebration, the commemoration of the martyr's anniversary, the keeping of the Sabbath on Sunday, and the making of the sign of the cross are all examples of Christian practice not found in the Bible that the fathers cite as constituents of the apostolic tradition.[17] Credal recitations of the essentials of faith, committed to memory in an age in which literacy was a rare commodity, proved to be valuable measures of the orthodoxy Christians believed to be handed down by the apostles themselves. This extrabiblical tradition possessed an authority in the early Church that complemented scripture at the same time that it provided a context in which scripture was read, lived, and handed down to the next generation of believers. Scripture and tradition, then, represented not different avenues to the truth of Jesus Christ but rather truthful authorities mediated in a common ecclesial life. This integration of scripture and tradition can be seen even more clearly in the early development of an explicitly extrabiblical scriptural tradition in the apologetics and polemics of the early Church.

Second- and third-century apologists such as Irenaeus, Tertullian, and Origen struggled to define Christian orthodoxy against the spiritualizing and dualistic interpretations of scripture offered by the Gnostics. For the Gnostics, the God of the Old Testament who created the world was really Satan; physical existence was Satan's domain; and Christ, the emissary of the true and hidden God, was the liberator of the Gnostic's spirit from its imprisonment in an unsalvageable bodily bondage. Against the Gnostics, the apologists brought belief to written expression in what they called the "rule of faith." The second-century bishop Irenaeus of Lyons, for example, formulated the rule as belief in the one creator God, in God's son Jesus Christ the incarnate savior, and in the resurrection of the flesh[18]—all professions of faith that counter the Gnostic disparagement of the goodness of God's creation. To the degree that the rule of faith catalogues the mainstays of Christian faith, it might be understood as a brief compendium of doctrine or as a basic creed. Since the emergence of the Christian biblical canon, however, the genres of doctrine and creed do not stand on their own as alternatives to this authoritative ecclesial genre. The Christian tradition of doctrine and creed first and foremost hands down the Word of God revealed in the Bible. For this reason, the *regula fidei* is best understood as an interpretive profession of faith governing the right understanding of the Christian narrative. It is entirely reasonable to assume that the rule of faith in one form or another was handed down verbally from believer to believer from the time of the earliest Christian communities. In the days of the apologists, though, it became a scriptural criterion of faith regulating the right reading of the biblical story.

The rule of faith, then, is one important illustration of the beginnings of an extrabiblical *scriptural* tradition—that is, writings that expressed an apostolic oral tradition and that were valued in the Church for their capacity to convey and clarify the truth of God's revelation. A second, even more important, example in early Christian history is the teachings of ecumenical councils. By the late fourth century, the Council of Nicea (325) was accorded an unprecedented authority among the many local councils called in the first Christian centuries to adjudicate disputes in Christian belief, doctrine, and practice. Although any number of sociological, political, or ecclesiastical factors might shed light on Nicea's unique authority, no adequate explanation could overlook the effect of the council's principal teaching on the life of the Church. The extraordinary authority of Nicea gradually came to be acknowledged as its teaching on the eternity of the Son of God won acceptance among a majority—and eventually a significant majority—of believers as the proper way to interpret scripture. Indeed, so fundamental to the faith was the teaching of the council that its work was considered by many ancient Christian authorities to be inspired by God—a belief that, through the paradigmatic regard in which Nicea was held evermore, came to be extended to the teaching and work of subsequent ecumenical councils.[19]

A third example of the beginnings of an extrabiblical scriptural tradition is the authority attributed first to ancient and later to medieval Christian writers whose literary work was judged to be so extraordinarily representative of the apostolic tradition as to be its promulgation. In the ancient Church, the work of such writers as Cyprian, Athanasius, the Cappadocians, Ambrose, Jerome, and Augustine and, in the medieval Church, the work of such writers as Dionysius, Damascene, Anselm, Aquinas, and Bonaventure was considered to possess special authority that reflected their unquestioned orthodoxy. To this list of theological authors, whose literary corpus as a whole was typically accorded authority, it is important to add those popes whose occasional writings presented a teaching on some particular and usually disputed matter of faith and practice. The measure of the orthodoxy of these writers remained the biblical text and, in the case of any particular writer, the previously established and recognized apostolic tradition. Ancient and medieval Christians conceived the authority of these authors in terms of the *auctoritas* of God. Theological and papal writings entered the authoritative tradition if they were judged to represent faithfully the biblical words of the divine author and the received tradition of authors whose words reiterated and so reflected the revelatory Word.[20]

Scripture and the extrabiblical scriptural tradition, whether in profession, conciliar decree, or theological writing, are not equatable. The canonical status of the biblical writings distinguishes them from all others, if only by virtue of the authority they possess. Yet a remarkable consistency abides between the Bible and the extrabiblical scriptural tradition. Commenting on the teaching of the Gelasian Decree (495), which authorized an extrabiblical scriptural tradition, George Tavard made this point well:

> Holy Writ, in the proper sense, ensures the basis of the Church, being dependent on Jesus himself. However, a superstructure rises from this basis. In view of it, the Church in Rome does not object to "receiving," besides the self-authenticated Holy Writ, other scriptures. . . . In other words, the scriptural charism spreads, to a certain extent, outside of the inspired [biblical] writers and reaches to many post-apostolic men. Christians write. Their works cannot claim the value of the New Testament, since the latter is sacramentally identical with the Word. Yet the fact that they speak well of him gives them a place next to Holy Writ. They are not the Sacred Scriptures; but they are the "other scriptures." They may also be received in Church. They may be read liturgically and may provide the occasion of another experience of the powerful Word of God.[21]

For Tavard, what has in more recent times been called "tradition" and distinguished more clearly from "scripture" had no such nominal identity in the ancient and medieval Church, in which a greater emphasis was placed upon a true "Holy Writ"—biblical and extrabiblical—handed down from the days of the apostles.[22] Although the great theologians of the medieval Church, like those of the ancient Church, continued to recognize a nonscriptural *paradosis*, they tended to conceive of the authentic tradition in terms of the writings of *auctoritates* and thus included the fathers, the canons of ecumenical councils, papal decretals, and the works of the most honored theologians under the rubric *Scriptura sacra* or *Divina Pagina*.[23]

This classical unity of scripture and tradition that, in the striking formula of the fifth-century monk Vincent of Lerins, conveyed what has been believed "everywhere, always, by all" was challenged dramatically by the Reformers of the sixteenth century. As Tavard has shown, the fissure in Holy Writ that was affirmed in the Reformation formula *sola scriptura* did not originate utterly with the Reformers' rejection of the authority of ecclesial tradition. Henry of Ghent, commenting on Peter Lombard's *Sentences* between 1276 and 1292, suggested the disjunctive possibilities within *Scriptura sacra* by posing the question "Must we rather believe the authorities of this doctrine [i.e., Sacred Scripture] than those of the Church, or the other way round?" Henry answers the question not by positing a separation between scripture and Church but by imagining that the teaching Church that claims to be true may in fact be false, a pretender usurping the authority of the apostolic tradition. Henry's distinction between a false church of the majority and a true, minority Church implicitly made biblical scripture more reliably true than the ecclesially sanctioned extrabiblical scriptural tradition—an assumption that was accepted by William of Ockham and the later conciliarists and that paved the way for the *sola scriptura* stance of the Reformers.[24]

Martin Luther's claim that all saving knowledge of God is found in "scripture alone" was not simply a theological catchphrase but, along with the watchwords *sola fide* and *sola gratia*, also an expression of a consistent doctrinal position that attributed the realization of the divine promise of eternal life utterly to the gracious power of God. In Luther's view, just as no human action merits salvation and, apart from divine grace, can be counted only as a deadly sin, so, too, no human action to which the Church ascribes the authority of "tradition" can be anything but a perversion of the fecund knowledge of God offered in scripture alone. Biblical revelation brooks no rival or complement. Although he was willing to concede a juridical value to councils, Luther firmly denied a council's "power to establish new articles of faith, even though the Holy Spirit is present," for the Spirit of God sanctifies the Church "through his holy word."[25] In his early treatise "To the Christian Nobility of the German Nation," Luther linked his attack on tradition to what was to be a career-long assault on the authority of the papacy, an institution he increasingly identified with the Antichrist. The "Romanist" claim, he chided, "that only the pope may interpret Scripture is an outrageous fancied fable."[26] Even the doctrines of the saints are "uncertain" and pale in comparison to the certainty and clarity of the words of Christ.[27] The "holy fathers," Luther lamented, "wanted to lead us to the Scriptures by their writings, but we use their works to get away from the Scriptures. Nevertheless, the Scripture alone is our vineyard in which we must all labor and toil."[28] Having rejected the scriptures, popes and theologians "took the license to transform dreams and human vanities into articles of faith" and, having done so, "found no measure or end of articles." According to Luther, evangelical liberty, the liberty of grace in and through the Word, is freedom from "the filth of traditions and human opinions."[29]

Like Huldrych Zwingli and John Calvin, Luther recognized an apostolic tradition that communicates sacred truth from generation to generation, and whose witness can be found to some degree in the councils and the fathers. These Reformers all agreed, however, that the content of scripture exhausts this tradition's testimony. Measured against the biblical Word, so much of what the Roman Church invests with authority in the fathers, the councils, and customs shows itself to be a tradition of human corruption, the promulgation of original sin and not the Spirit of truth revealed so clearly in scripture's plain sense.[30]

As one might expect, the Reformers' attack on the medieval understanding of *Scriptura sacra* engendered a variety of Catholic responses: from Sylvester Prierias's strong defense of an autonomous traditional authority, exercised especially in the prerogatives of the Roman Pontiff, to Johann Cochläus's more classical view of ecclesial tradition bound to and authoritatively interpreting scripture, to Kaspar Schatzgeyer's expectation that authentic tradition is evinced in scripture.[31] Wherever a particular apologist for the Church (and polemicist against the Reformers) chose to place the accent within the homogeneous authority of *Scriptura sacra*, each esteemed the bible as God's revelation and yet assumed, contrary to Luther, that the clarity of revelation is not found in scripture alone but shines through in an apostolic tradition articulated in the Bible and continued in the fathers, councils, papal teachings, and ecclesial customs. In many respects, the Reformation challenge of *sola scriptura* to the medieval unity of *Scriptura sacra* had the effect of providing "tradition" with an authoritative identity in its own right that it had not possessed before Luther raised his critical voice—an identity that was shaped as much in the defense of the Catholic apologists as it was in the criticism of the Protestant Reformers. Indeed, the first book-length treatise on the topic of scripture and tradition—*De Ecclesiasticis Scripturis et Dogmatibus* (1533), by the Louvain theologian Johannes Driedo—appeared in this apologetical ferment. Perhaps it was this "novelty" of the status of "tradition" in the life of the Church, as much as the threat of the Protestant scripture principle, that accounts for the discussion and definition of this matter at the fourth session of the Council of Trent.

On April 8, 1546, the council fathers approved a teaching on scripture and the apostolic tradition, the full text of which follows:

> The holy, ecumenical, and general Council of Trent, which has lawfully assembled in the Holy Spirit . . . has always as its purpose to remove error and preserve in the Church the purity of the gospel [*Evangelii*] that was originally promised by the prophets in Sacred Scripture [*Scripturis sanctis*] and first promulgated by the Son of God himself, our Lord Jesus Christ. He, in turn, ordered his apostles, who are the source [*fontem*] of all saving truth and moral teaching, to preach it to every creature (*Mark* 16:15). The Council is aware that this truth and teaching are contained in written books [*libris scriptis*] and in the unwritten traditions [*sine scripto traditionibus*] that the apostles received from Christ himself or that were handed on, as it were from hand to hand, from the apostles under the inspiration of the Holy Spirit, and so have come down to us. The council follows the example of the orthodox Fathers and with the same sense of devotion and reverence [*pari pietatis affectu ac reverentia*] with which it accepts and venerates all the books both of the Old and the New Testament, since one God is the author of both, it also accepts and venerates traditions concerned with faith and morals [*tum ad fidem, tum ad mores pertinentes*] as having been received orally from Christ or inspired by the Holy Spirit and continuously preserved in the Catholic Church.[32]

The debates and process of draft revision that led to this final text make for an interesting chapter in the history of the categories of scripture and tradition, one that is often cited in the attempt to understand the purport of Trent's teaching.

The council's Fourth Session had two principal concerns—the nature and number of the canonical books of the bible and the authority of tradition—issues pressed to the point of controversy by the Protestant scripture principle. After some debate on the first matter, the Tridentine fathers affirmed the enumeration of the Catholic canon defined at the Council of Florence in 1442 and decided not to settle definitively the disputed question of the existence of different degrees and types of authority among the canonical books.[33] The second matter, the authority of tradition and its relation to the Bible, received far more attention.

The council fathers were intent on refuting the attack on ecclesial authority expressed in the theology of *sola scriptura*, but they struggled to find a common language that conveyed the faith of the Church. In a February 12, 1546 speech, Cardinal Giovanni Maria del Monte spoke of the task at hand by noting that divine revelation "is transmitted by the Church partly [*partim*] by virtue of scriptures which are in the Old and New Testament, and partly [*partim*] by the simple tradition from hand to hand." He continued by urging the council's agenda to address in turn the "sacred scriptures," "ecclesiastical traditions," and finally the "abuses" associated with them.[34] Del Monte's portrayal of traditions as "ecclesiastical" immediately met with dissatisfaction among those who preferred to speak of "apostolic traditions"—a formulation that at once placed the discussion of tradition in the earliest lineage of the faith, sidestepped the difficulty of enumerating the aspects of such a tradition (e.g., ecumenical councils, customs, and ecclesiastical canons), and avoided the more controversial issue of papal authority. Within days of del Monte's address, talk in the council chambers gravitated much more toward "apostolic traditions" in written and unwritten forms.

The Cardinal's understanding of a divine revelation imparted partly in scriptures and partly in traditions clearly expresses Catholic dissatisfaction with the restriction of revelation to the Bible alone and had enough of a supportive constituency to make its way into the Fourth Session's draft document, which spoke of an apostolic truth "partly [*partim*] contained in written books, partly [*partim*] in unwritten traditions."[35] Debates on the draft, however, saw vocal opposition to the conceptualization of revelation suggested by the *partim . . . partim* formula, especially in the concerns raised by Augustino Bonuccio, the general of the Servites. In his view, the *partim . . . partim* formula wrongly suggested that all truth is not contained in Holy Writ, as though biblical revelation were in some way incomplete. For Bonuccio, as for Bishop Giacomo Nacchianti, scripture cannot be deficient as a source of revelation. Its truth is not partial, a position intimated, in their view, by the language of *partim . . . partim*[36] Many of the council fathers were yet attracted to the formula, which had something of a history in sixteenth-century Catholic theology and which expressed so clearly the Catholic understanding of an apostolic tradition not exhausted in the biblical writings.[37] Nevertheless, criticism was telling enough that the draft language of *partim . . . partim* was changed to *et* in the council's final and official teaching: "[T]his truth and teaching are contained in written books [*libris scriptis*] and [*et*] in the unwritten traditions [*sine scripto traditionibus*] that the apostles received from Christ himself." If the substitution of the conjunction for the adverbs suggested to the proponents of *partim . . . partim* a diminution of the authority of traditions, their concerns were mitigated by the force of the final document's confession that these "traditions of faith and morals" were to be accepted and venerated "with the same sense of devotion and reverence" as the Bible.

What was the significance of this change for the fathers at Trent? As Josef Rupert Geiselmann has observed, no definitive answer is possible based on the minutes of the council.[38] Although it is tempting to think that the substitution of *et* for *partim . . . partim* evinces majority support for Bonuccio's and Nacchianti's concern that scriptural truth not be judged a partial presentation of the gospel, it is also possible that the revision offers only a language of compromise that avoided any specific doctrinal stance. Granting the elusiveness of the fathers' intentions, what still of the significance of the change in the aftermath of Trent? Edmond Ortigues has argued that the suppression of the *partim* language had the effect "of affirming that the two witnesses [written books, unwritten traditions], taken in conjunction, allow our faith to find support in its principle or source"—that is, the gospel handed down by the apostles.[39] Certainly, and with an intentional pun, it can be acknowledged that Ortigues is partly right to note Trent's emphasis on a single source (the final document uses the singular *fontem*) for the truth of the apostolic tradition in the gospel of Jesus Christ, a truth to which the written books and unwritten traditions bear witness. Yet he may not be entirely correct in his view that these words can be identified with their effects in Catholic tradition. Yves Congar, among others, has observed that Catholic controversialists writing in the aftermath of Trent—such as Martin Perez de Ayala, Peter Canisius, and Robert Bellarmine—typically invoked a *partim . . . partim* understanding of the council's teaching and that this sense of scripture and tradition has flourished throughout the nineteenth century to our own day.[40] Aware of these interpretive possibilities and wary of claims for the completeness of any one explanation, I offer several observations on the council's teaching and its effects.

First, Trent teaches that there is at once a unity to the truth of revelation and a plurality in its communication and reception. There is but one truth of Jesus Christ, the Savior, handed down in one apostolic tradition. And yet that inspired truth knows two modes of communication. Second, Catholic belief in the authority of these two modes of communication—written books and unwritten traditions—stands in opposition to and condemns the Protestant belief in *sola scriptura*. The two modes of communication thus define a belief in what constitutes the apostolic tradition that differs from the Protestant understanding of an apostolic tradition communicated only in the Bible. Congar described this difference well by speaking of the Reformers' commitment to "the *purity* of the apostolic *witness*," and the Church's commitment to "the *plenitude* of the apostolic *heritage*."[41] Third, the council expresses the modes of apostolic communication in a manner that has since developed in the language of the Church. Whereas Trent speaks of the truth of the gospel in "written books and unwritten traditions," Vatican II speaks of "sacred Tradition and sacred Scripture" making up a single sacred deposit of the Word of God. Accustomed to the more recent language of "scripture and tradition," a modern reader of the Tridentine decree might assume too quickly that the newer and older language are interchangeable ways of expressing the two modes of communication, as though the Tridentine "written books" refers to the biblical scriptures and the Tridentine "unwritten traditions" refers to a "tradition" distinguishable from biblical "scripture." This assumption, however, would be wrong on two counts. It would overlook the extent to which the fathers at Trent were still committed in their teaching to a tradition of *sacra scriptura* that included both the biblical books and other writings judged to be inspired. The phrase "written books" refers not only to the Bible but also to the writings of the fathers, the decrees of the councils, and papal teachings that represent the apostolic tradition. The phrase "written books," one might say, is itself a refutation of the Protestant principle *sola scriptura*, which identified *scriptura* with the Bible. The assumption that the newer and older language are interchangeable might also relegate what the later language calls "Tradition" to the "unwritten," since the Tridentine Decree speaks of "traditions" specifically as "unwritten" conveyors of the apostolic faith. What the language of Vatican II calls "Tradition," however, comprises both the written and the unwritten in the terminology of Trent, and these oral and literary means, together with the biblical books, present the one truth of Jesus Christ.

Our capacity to understand the language of Trent in the language of Vatican II and vice versa testifies to the real consistency in the faith taught by these more recent councils. An appreciation for the unity of Catholic belief, however, should not lead one to overlook a particular shape that the Catholic understanding of tradition has taken in the modern period. In its naming of "written books" and "unwritten traditions" as the modes by which the apostolic faith is communicated, and in its assumption that the literary dimension of this communication includes both biblical and extrabiblical writings, the Tridentine Decree expresses the medieval understanding of *sacra doctrina* as the way in which God reveals. This integrated understanding was affirmed by the Second Vatican Council to the degree that its teaching on this matter insisted on the same perichoretic relationship between scripture and tradition taught by Trent. Indeed, an earlier draft of the "Dogmatic Constitution on Divine Revelation" had proposed that scripture and tradition be portrayed as two "sources" of divine revelation, a twentieth-century version of the *partim . . . partim* conceptualization that was rejected in the document's final version. And yet, though faithful to Trent, Vatican II's "scripture and tradition" formula voices a distinction between the Bible and an extrabiblical tradition that was not framed in quite this way at Trent and that expresses a development in Catholic thought and practice that took place in the aftermath of the sixteenth-century council.

Several reasons can be identified for this somewhat sharper distinction between scripture, now understood as the bible, and an extrabiblical tradition, though one committed to handing down the biblical message. First, Catholic identity since Trent has been defined, for the most part, along the lines of interconfessional polemics. Although Catholics and Protestants have shared belief in scripture as divine revelation, Catholics alone have been willing to count tradition as another revelational mode, however inseparable from scripture. This difference in Catholic belief has had the effect of highlighting the distinctiveness of tradition in the life of the Church. Second, Geiselmann has proposed the interesting, though speculative, explanation that the world view of the Baroque, as appropriated in Tridentine Catholic experience, encouraged the distinguishability of scripture and tradition. Its imagination dominated by spatial categories, the Baroque mentality followed Nominalism in breaking the medieval unity of the natural and the supernatural, inventing the idea of a supernatural "beyond" and compartmentalizing dimensions of human intercourse with the divine "here below." For Geiselmann, Baroque intuition, whether in art or scholasticism, was inclined to portray reality as parts extended in space, a conceptualization that "had no motive to reject the '*partim . . . partim*' " understanding of scripture and tradition.[42] Third, the practice of the magisterium since the eighteenth century, if only in the frequent promulgation of encyclical letters, has contributed through its ongoing activity to a heightened appreciation for the integrity of tradition alongside scripture.[43] Fourth, nineteenth-century currents in the theology of the magisterium carried in their sweep a theology in which tradition was accorded an authority commensurable with the growing authority of the magisterium. Indeed, the theology of the magisterium in this period—especially in the work of the nineteenth-century Roman School; the Gregorian professor and later cardinal Johannes Baptist Franzelin; and influential Neo-Scholastic theologians, such as Ludovico Billot, Jean Vincent Bainvel, and August Deneffe—tended to identify tradition with the magisterium.[44] This identification extended to tradition the visible, institutional authority of the papal office and its recently defined prerogative of infallibility, thereby accentuating the distinguishability—and in this case even the separability—of tradition from scripture.

Despite the fact that Trent had clearly taught that revelation had only one source, these developments—which contributed to an increasing regard for the integrity of tradition in the centuries after Trent—made the representation of scripture and tradition as two sources of revelation a serious option in discussions of the draft of the Second Vatican Council's "Dogmatic Constitution on Divine Revelation."[45] Whereas *Dei verbum* insists that "[s]acred Tradition and sacred Scripture . . . are bound closely together, and communicate one with the other," that they flow "from the same divine well-spring, [and] come together in some fashion to form one thing," and that tradition "transmits in its entirety the Word of God," there is still a sense in which tradition possesses an integrity that keeps it from being reduced to the process of handing down scripture. Vatican II's use of the formula "scripture and tradition," which particularizes the language of Trent, itself manifests the assumptions of the Tridentine theology of tradition. Moreover, the most recent council specifically affirms the integrity of tradition by teaching that "it comes about that the Church does not draw her certainty about all revealed truths from the holy Scriptures alone" but rather from tradition too.[46]

From the eve of the Second Vatican Council to the present, any number of theologians have attempted to negotiate the relationship between the modes of revelation by mitigating tradition's distinguishability from scripture. Geiselmann, for example, has claimed that the teaching of Trent implies the material sufficiency of scripture for the revelation of the divine Word, a sufficiency that makes scripture the basis of tradition.[47] Following Geiselmann's lead, Karl Rahner has argued that there is no Catholic reason to accept "a constitutive material function of tradition that goes beyond the testimony of the nature of scripture" and, more, that there is a genuinely Catholic understanding of the *sola scriptura* principle.[48] More recently, David Tracy has suggested the formula "Scripture in tradition" as a better conceptual alternative to the "older Roman Catholic 'Scripture *and* tradition' " or "the Reformation's 'Scripture alone.' "[49] Proposals such as these possess merit not only for their ecumenical sensitivity but also for their commitment to the unity of scripture and tradition affirmed in Catholic belief. But perhaps such proposals also express a measure of distrust in the way the integrity of tradition has come to be formulated in the history of Catholicism since Trent, as a "separable" and thus authoritarian tradition and not as one rightly "distinguishable" from scripture. The teaching of the Second Vatican Council, understood as a promulgation of the Tridentine heritage, certainly would seem to invalidate any reduction of tradition to the magisterium or a "constitutive" understanding of a tradition not even implicit in scripture.[50] Yet tradition does possess an integrity in its relation to scripture that the conjunction "and" in the didactic formulas of Trent and Vatican II preserves well, that by now has a long-standing history in Catholic belief, and that Catholic theologians should be reluctant to leave behind.

A Catholic understanding of revelation needs to affirm the distinctiveness of the Church's dogmatic teaching on scripture and tradition—and in a manner that truly recognizes the integrity that tradition possesses by virtue of its conjunctive relationship to scripture. Belief in the integrity of tradition is an important dimension of Catholic identity, a belief forsaken at the cost of tradition's loss. This doctrine, and no other, does justice to the actual ways that the revelation of Jesus Christ to the apostles and the Church has been received in the course of Catholic tradition. The affirmation of tradition's integrity may always run the risk of a false conception of its separability from scripture and a resulting ecclesiastical fundamentalism in which tradition is reduced to ossified categories and formulas that diminish rather than highlight the mystery of divine revelation. But such a narrow understanding of tradition must be ascribed to human fault. Its risk need not inevitably lead to the distortion of tradition's proper integrity but remains, instead, a resistible temptation.

Theological efforts to negotiate the scripture-tradition relationship by diminishing the integrity of tradition stem, in no small part, from hermeneutical concerns, from a recognition of the need to interpret tradition so that its truth can be adequate to the mystery of divine revelation and to the facts of its unfolding history. Aligning tradition so closely with scripture that its integrity is mitigated brings tradition into the ambit of scripture's long-acknowledged susceptibility to interpretation and, in turn, diminishes the risk of a falsely hypostatized tradition of literal authority resistant to interpretation. There is legitimate motive in pressing for a tradition open to interpretation. If God's inspired Word is communicated in both scripture and tradition, then there is a consistency in the expectation that both scripture and tradition would be susceptible to interpretation fostering a richer appreciation of the Word. Indeed, affirming the interpretive richness of scripture but *not* of tradition might well convey a hermeneutical version of *sola scriptura* or a *partim . . . partim* disjunction between scripture and tradition, with revelation partly interpretable in one of its modes and partly not in the other.[51] But however important a hermeneutics of tradition is to a richer appreciation of God's revelation, it cannot fail to respect the integrity of tradition that is one of the mainstays of Catholic belief.

Here again, though, it is difficult to strike a balance between the need for a hermeneutics of tradition and the affirmation of tradition's integrity. The only traditionally acknowledged hermeneutics at one's disposal is the fourfold senses of scripture. Understanding tradition only as the handing down of scripture would allow the senses of scripture to extend to tradition, thus providing a hermeneutics of tradition in the long-established practice of spiritual exegesis. Such a hermeneutics, however, would come at the cost of tradition's integrity. A tradition of acknowledged integrity, though, would elude the scope of the scriptural hermeneutic whose interpretive senses beyond the literal—the allegorical, tropological, and anagogical—would apply poorly to tradition, which offers beliefs, doctrines, practices, and historical process as objects of interpretation quite different from the biblical page. Interpreting a tradition faithful to the classical conciliar formula "scripture and tradition" requires a hermeneutic particular to tradition, one that can do justice to the integrity of its workings in time and place, to the manner in which God's revelation is received in a history claimed by believers as religiously significant. My task in the pages to come is to give an account of such a hermeneutics of tradition. And, to do so, I begin with an orientation to the study, which delimits some of its assumptions.

Orientation and Assumptions

My goal is to sketch an interpretive theory of tradition that acknowledges a hermeneutical "more" beyond tradition's literal sense. In its use of categories, this theory follows the lead of the senses of scripture. I speak of four interpretive possibilities for appreciating tradition's meaningfulness as "senses," even if the literal sense of tradition is the only one of the four that possesses a direct counterpart among the classical senses of scripture. This construction of interpretive senses of tradition beyond the literal takes a historical point of departure in its appeal to, and proposed revision of, the by now accepted understanding of how tradition occurs—as a development through time and culture. Modern theology has recognized the prospect for a nonliteral, interpretive sense (in the singular) of tradition in the idea of the development of doctrine. A product of the same nineteenth-century thought world that gave rise to historical consciousness, the expectation of technological advance, and conceptions of biological and social evolution, this principle—broadly understood—regards tradition as the belief, doctrine, and practice of the whole Church that experiences, expresses, and enacts the Holy Spirit's eventful presence to history. Although the idea of doctrinal development met with much ambivalence on the part of the Church's teaching authority throughout most of the twentieth century, it has gradually gained acceptance in Roman Catholic belief and has even received formal recognition on the part of the magisterium since the Second Vatican Council.

Even though the historical fact of doctrinal development has become an axiom of modern theological understanding, the development of doctrine as a hermeneutical principle has not offered a sufficient interpretive range to account for the plurality of tradition or for the complexity of tradition's historical workings. The claim that a particular belief, doctrine, or practice is developing certainly opens a space for a richer meaning beyond a literal sense. But since a modern understanding of development has been narrowly conceived as a *single* meaningful alternative to an established literal meaning, tradition seems to offer itself to reflection only as a hermeneutical "either-or" in which the interpreter may choose between a tradition past and fixed or a tradition developing in an unspecified, amorphous fashion. Typically in this conceptualization, a currently meaningful sense of developing tradition is distinguished from some past and, now from the current perspective, undeveloped sense. Or a meaningful claim for a developing tradition finds itself criticized by a contemporaneous claim for literal meaning that denies the developing status of the belief, doctrine, or practice in question. In both cases, the possibilities for interpreting tradition are restrictively disjunctive. In the first example, tradition is judged to be either more or less meaningful in the course of its development; in the second, tradition is judged to be either meaningfully developing or not developing at all and thus meaningfully fixed. Tradition in this modern paradigm is therefore reduced to what was and still is or to what once was but has since become. Narrowly conceived, tradition can now only narrowly be interpreted, its hermeneutical options restricted to judgments about whether tradition has or has not developed or whether tradition is or is not developing.

By distinguishing several respects in which the development of belief, doctrine, and practice might be understood, the following chapters consider a wider range of interpretive senses of tradition. In addition to the literal sense, development-in-continuity, dramatic development, and incipient development are discussed as senses of tradition. The literal sense of tradition is the Church's judgment on the stability of belief, doctrine, and practice in its uncontroverted plain meaning. The sense of development-in-continuity is the Church's appreciation of how tradition's constancy is ever renewed in the present historical moment. The sense of dramatic development claims to discern a loss of authority in what had heretofore been regarded as tradition's literal sense. And the sense of incipient development claims to discern in unauthoritative beliefs and practices the authoritative and yet only recently recognized constancy of tradition. Together these senses attempt to name how tradition abides (the literal sense) and how tradition changes (the three developing senses) through the ages and in the present moment. If this task is successful, the wider interpretive latitude offered by the four senses of tradition will enable a greater appreciation for the workings of tradition—for their often elusive dynamics of continuity and change and for their significance in relating the presence of the Spirit to history.

This theory of tradition, like any theory, offers its insights against the backdrop of previous theoretical explanation. Since the Council of Trent, and especially since the First and Second Vatican Councils, much theological reflection has been devoted to the nature and workings of tradition. This intellectual history has produced a host of categories, concepts, and distinctions that strive to account for the complexity of tradition. An examination of this nomenclature allows the articulation of some of the assumptions of this study.

Neo-Scholastic theology has distinguished between "passive" and "active" tradition—the former a label for the material communicated in tradition, the latter a label for the process of handing down tradition's objects.[52] Although this distinction possesses some formal value and has already been invoked in so many words earlier in this introduction, one would distort any description of tradition by pressing the difference between the "passive" and the "active" too ardently. Traditional objects, by virtue of their historicity, are always being handed down, just as the traditioning process always takes place in an objective world of things. Any confidence in the abstract meaningfulness of either traditional process or traditional objects would founder on the shoals of hermeneutical naïveté. The four senses presented in the following chapters at times apply to what previous theology has called passive or active tradition, without any attempt along the way to distinguish between the two, since each—one must presuppose—is always integrally related to the other.

Another common distinction in twentieth-century theology draws a conceptual line between apostolic and ecclesiastical traditions—the former conveying the truth of the revelation of Jesus Christ handed down to the apostles and through them to the Church of the ages; the latter a repository of beliefs, doctrines, and practices that may have a long or short history in the life of the Church but that lack the authority of revelation and, as such, may be dispensable. This distinction attempts to name what is infallibly and what is contingently true in tradition and in this regard may be invoked in any theory of tradition interested, like the present one, in speaking about different kinds of truth. The mutual relationships among the four senses in this theory, however, show that the traditioning process is one in which the community of faith is constantly making judgments about the path of apostolic truth through time and culture, in the course of which the apostolic tradition is always being identified and reidentified as perceptions of infallible and contingent truths are modified. Any judgment on how apostolic and ecclesiastical traditions stand in the entire narrative of tradition, then, cannot be a priori but only a posteriori, subject to revision, and as open-ended as tradition itself before the eschaton.

This study advances a theory of tradition that takes seriously the authoritative teachings of Trent and Vatican II. Although a preponderance of examples offered in these pages are drawn from traditional writings for the reasons of their marked influence on Catholic history and their accessibility as interpretive objects, the importance of what Trent called "unwritten traditions" is not overlooked in this theoretical account. Indeed, as this study proceeds, it is important to recall the judgment of Maurice Bévenot that Trent's "unwritten traditions" refer as much to the enactment of Christian practice as they do to the oral words of the faithful.[53] This study assumes, as it has already argued, that the notion of a literal sense can extend metaphorically beyond texts to experience, to the spoken word, and to deeds. The metaphorical extension of a literal sense to these dimensions of tradition means, as well, that they can and do possess interpretive senses beyond the literal sense that this theory of tradition delineates.

This hermeneutics of tradition rarely employs the language of Scholasticism to speak of tradition—assuming, as it does, that a premodern conception of tradition is no longer adequate. Moreover, the study shows itself to be suspicious of modern configurations of tradition as "developing" in the manner of Romantic theories of the nineteenth and twentieth centuries. If this approach can be labeled tersely, then it can, in a sense, be described as "postmodern," though it risks with that designation a multitude of prejudices and misunderstandings. How the theory is postmodern, and is postmodern to the benefit of a Catholic understanding of tradition, must to be explained in detail as the study unfolds. Suffice it to say at this point that its aim is an account of tradition that is both faithful to the teaching of the Church and in accord with the historical record of how what the Church calls tradition has appeared in and moved through time and culture. Let the reader judge whether this intention has been realized in act.

Finally, this study draws on philosophical insights in an ad hoc fashion in order to elucidate the mystery of Christian tradition, assuming that no philosophy finally can do justice to that mystery. As helpful as philosophies might be in the search for Christian understanding, they take their direction from faith and properly follow faith's guidance. If a particular philosophical perspective is represented with some measure of consistency in these pages, it is the perspective of pragmatism—specifically enlisted in chapter 2, where Donald Davidson's understanding of metaphor informs an understanding of tradition, and in chapter 3, where the epistemological reflections of such pragmatists as Wilfrid Sellars and Willard Van Orman Quine are invoked to appreciate the importance of ecclesial argumentation. But throughout the study, the complex interrelationships of traditional claims are clarified by appeal to pragmatism's regard for the holism of knowledge. According to this perspective, what is called knowledge takes shape in an integrated network of revisable claims. The network does not stand or fall through any one claim, as though a single claim provides a "foundation," as it were, for the edifice of the network or as though the invalidation of any of the network's claims would undercut the integrity of the whole. A holistic regard for knowledge, and for tradition as a holistic network of beliefs, doctrines, and practices, appreciates the real boundedness of seemingly separable claims to each other, however more or less basic to the whole network they may be. A holistic regard for knowledge appreciates, too, how this meaningful whole is enmeshed in time and culture, ever aligning its interrelated claims for meaning to the circumstances in which knowledge—and faith—is practiced.

With these observations in mind, let us turn to the delineation of this study's theory of tradition, beginning with the first of the four senses—the literal sense of tradition.

1

The Literal Sense of Tradition

This chapter begins this study's effort to sketch a hermeneutics of tradition. As we have seen, the four senses of scripture—the literal, the allegorical, the moral, and the anagogical—had a long history in medieval exegetical theory and practice. The senses of tradition expounded here and in the following chapters are fourfold as well. That consistency in number with the medieval interpretive schema, however, should not suggest a parallel between the content of all four classical senses of scripture and that of the interpretive senses of tradition proposed herein. "Development-in-continuity," "dramatic development," and "incipient development," the interpretive senses of tradition to be elucidated in the following chapters, do not correspond directly to the ancient interpretive senses of scripture: the allegorical, the tropological, and the anagogical, respectively. The first interpretive sense of tradition and the first interpretive sense of scripture do, nevertheless, resemble each other in their shared commitment to a stable meaning connected closely with the "letter" of tradition or the "letter" of scripture. To the degree that both scripture and tradition present their teaching in writing, they possess a literal sense that acts as a gravitational field for the other interpretive senses. Whether some of the other interpretive senses are attracted inexorably to the literal sense's center of gravity or ardently resist its pull, they all nonetheless fall within the sphere of its influence. The literal sense of tradition is the concern of this chapter.

It is important to begin by distinguishing clearly between the "literal sense," on one hand, and what I call "literality," on the other. One cannot speak of a scripture, a writing, without acknowledging its literality. In the most basic of ways, a writing comes to be in the actual marks that offer the visible relief of script against the backdrop of an otherwise ordinary and un-committed surface. Whether one can name a writing's inscribed marks in a jingle of letters learned in the earliest days of schooling; or, by the strokes of its characters, identify as Chinese the language one cannot read; or, having made a remarkable archaeological find, recognize in bizarre etchings the possibility of an untranslatable writing in a language previously unknown to contemporaries, it is the "letter" that is the most elementary fact of a scripture's existence. The physicality of its marks manifests the scripture in all sorts of ways. The marks define the space they inhabit as, literally or figuratively, a page. Their positioning on the page poses a scriptural geography that may alert the reader to the expectations of genre in the form, say, of a lyrical poem, a novel, an editorial, or a creed. Their number through the pages sets forth a scriptural time measured in the sequence of the already read and the yet to be read. In their totality and in their completedness, the marks present the substance of a scripture that abides and that cannot be other than it is, so long as the marks elude the corruption of physical things or—if they are more fortunate—are preserved by human care.

If writings are defined by their literality at their most elementary level, then certainly the writings that make up Catholic tradition—ancient creeds, decrees of ecumenical councils, and papal encyclicals, for example—are also configured most starkly by what Nicholas Lash has described as "a set of black marks on white paper."[1] Tradition in its written form exists as the bare facticity of letter. By analogy, at least, one might say the same of the unwritten traditions that Trent teaches have been handed down in the Church since the time of the apostles and under the inspiration of the Holy Spirit. Unwritten traditions, by definition, do not possess a literality. But they possess something of the facticity, the givenness, and the stability of the "letter" in the physicality of the objects around which they are centered (such as the relics of the saints), in the bodily movements by which they are enacted (such as those required to make the sign of the cross), and in the repetitive constancy of a central practice (as in the celebration of the liturgy). The prevalence of not just one but all these "lettered" qualities, and undoubtedly more, in each of these examples of unwritten traditions suggests that the character of literality appears—and appears strongly—throughout the expanse of Catholic tradition, explicitly in traditional writings and implicitly in unwritten traditions communicated by objects, words, and behaviors.

Understood simply as sign, this literality of marks offers a patterned contrast to the page, to other objects, and to other practices, a contrast in which the possibility of meaning is announced. This possibility may become an actuality under conditions favorable to understanding in which interpretation can actually take place. The actual meaningfulness of inscribed, physical, or enacted marks, however, often lies beyond the comprehension of the one who encounters them. The black marks on a white page may proclaim their semiotic value, but that value escapes the one for whom they remain a foreign language. The marked literality of a repeated behavior may be recognized as a ritual among other more random behaviors, but the observer may be a stranger to the cultural system in which it flourishes and thus incapable of sharing in its meaning. And even when actual meaningfulness is so closely associated with literality that the two cannot be distinguished in experience— when one is at home, so to speak, in a system of physical marks—the inescapability of illiteracy of one sort or another even within one's broad culture allows one to distinguish, if only by abstraction, between the fact of literality and its associated meaningfulness.

Literality, then, stands at the threshold of meaning but is not yet meaning. It marks the fact of writing but not the value of sense. This is an important point to make at the start of the discussion of the first sense of tradition, for the notions of "letter" and the "literal" are polyvalent and easily misunderstood. As just described, literality denotes the bare existence of inscription, the givenness of the letter (or the character or the hieroglyph) that offers an obstacle to intelligibility as much as it does an opportunity for meaning. For those within a semiotic system encountering long familiar inscriptions or practices, literality often goes unnoticed since it is already taken up into interpretation and so dwells at the level of meaning. And yet, even within a semiotic system, disputes among interpretations corrode the authority of the claims in conflict, accentuating their ambiguity and exposing—if only as a shadow cast by the disputed meaning—the otherwise unperceived opaqueness of the letter. Any talk of the literal sense of tradition does well to distinguish between tradition's literal sense and tradition's "letter" or literality. Whereas tradition's literality is presented in the physical marks that inscribe its pages or in the physicality of its objects or practices, tradition's literal sense already offers an interpretation. The literality of tradition may declare the possibility of meaning by its very existence, but it is in tradition's literal sense that meaning becomes actual. A literal sense cannot be identified with the letter of tradition or scripture, for as a sense it has already passed beyond the letter into the ambit of meaning.

As an interpretive stance, the literal sense has much more in common with the other interpretive senses that ancient Christianity found in scripture—and that are found in tradition, as the pages that follow demonstrate—than it does with literality. And yet the literal sense has more in common with literality than do the other ancient and latter-day interpretive senses that extend beyond the first sense. Like literality, the literal sense is resistant to change and development. If the literal sense presents an interpretation, it is one that abides for long periods of time and elicits a relatively clear and common recognition on the part of those who share its meaning. Like literality, then, the literal sense possesses a stability, although, unlike literality, the literal sense is characterized by a constancy of value and not by a constancy of fact.

For those who are accustomed to identifying the literal sense of any text with what is written and thus with the text's literality, this distinction between "letter" and literal sense can be disconcerting. The inescapability of interpretation in the realm of meaning seems to suggest that no enduring meaning lies within the text. And if the texts of scripture and tradition can be so utterly shifting in their meaning that even their literality can meaningfully appear only as interpretation, as a "sense" for the letter, then no authority seems capable of halting the infinitely possible interpretations that the text might engender.[2] This fear of interpretive possibility wrongly postulates a meaningful literality and thus conflates the fact of inscription with its value. Those who would invest literality with sense expect too much of the letter—at least that, as inscription, it provide a *meaningful* common denominator for a community of interpreters and at most that it present an interpretive certainty capable of quelling the conflict of claims. And such high expectations of the fact of the letter cannot help but be accompanied by a low esteem for "sense" that finds its interpretive value to be compromised at least by a relativistic pluralism and at most by wild caprice. These judgments fail to appreciate the ability of the literal sense, even as interpretation, to provide a touchstone for a community of interpreters that brings unity, stability, and concreteness to their understanding and practice. Moreover, the literal sense, even as interpretation, powerfully conveys an abiding authority by which an interpretive community's understanding and practice are measured and shaped. One can appreciate these qualities of the literal sense as they apply to tradition by exploring the recent efforts of scholars to speak of the literal sense of scripture as its "plain sense."

The Plain Sense of Tradition

As the previous chapter discussed, Christian interpretation of scripture took its most basic assumptions from Jewish exegesis. Like their Jewish forebears and counterparts, early Christian exegetes affirmed the biblical word as God's and defined their vocational responsibility as faithfulness in interpretation to scripture's revelation of God's biblical promise. And like their Jewish forebears and counterparts, early Christian exegetes recognized that biblical interpretation could move in ordinary or extraordinary directions, either by remaining close to an ostensible meaning of the words recognized as a matter of course by those who value them or by moving beyond their literal sense to fathom less obvious interpretive meanings.

In both traditions, the very notion of a text's less than obvious, or even hidden, meanings encourages a distinction between the literal sense of scripture, on one hand, and the extraordinary senses of scripture, on the other. In this perspective, the Jewish tradition's *peshat* and the Christian tradition's *sensus literalis* serve as points of departure for allegorical flight, or as ballast and keel for interpretive navigation, but do not themselves represent interpretation. The literal sense in this conceptualization offers a stability that grounds the possible vagaries of interpretation, and this stability is attributed precisely to what is assumed to be the literal sense's difference from the extraordinary senses: its preinterpretive literality. This conflation of the literal sense and literality is common among not only scriptural fundamentalists but also most members of any scripturally based religious tradition who would be inclined to value ordinary readings of the authoritative writing over extraordinary readings. At its best (even though still in error), the conflation of the literal sense and literality expresses the legitimate conservative commitments at work in any religious community that treasures its past, including those consistent readings of scripture honored over time. At its worst, however, this conflation fosters the illusion that the literal sense escapes interpretation, as though this were possible or even desirable, and thus promotes the false view that authority lies only in the literal to which the interpretive is but a superficial gloss. The discussion of the notion of the "plain sense" of scripture in the work of Raphael Loewe, Brevard S. Childs, and Kathryn E. Tanner can help to sort out the important distinctions that must be made between scripture's "letter" and what might be described as its interpretive literal sense.

In the Jewish tradition, *peshat* is the ordinary meaning of scripture that one would expect any believer to garner from its reading. But what, Loewe has asked, did early Jewish exegesis understand by *peshat*, by the plain or simple meaning of scripture? "Did it constitute, for the early exegete, a positive concept the definition of which he could without difficulty adduce?" Or was it an "essentially negative" concept invoked in polemical argument to defeat a particular interpretation, an applied sense, with which the invoker of the plain sense disagreed?[3] Loewe's close studies of a number of Talmudic-period writers have led him to give an affirmative answer to the second question much more readily than to the first. He has concluded that the "plain sense" serves an author's judgments about what constitutes an authoritative reading of the text and what does not, both in the author's own mind and in the collective expectations of the author's audience. Although Loewe's analysis recognizes that the plain sense might be defined by what lies in the text itself, as the "simple exegesis which corresponds to the totality of the meaning(s) intended by the writer,"[4] it considers such a definition to be decidedly at odds with the ways rabbinic interpreters actually interpreted the scriptural words. The plain sense, in other words, at least from a perspective that respects actual exegetical performance, does not refer to "plain meaning" but to the "*traditional, familiar,* and hence *authoritative* meaning of the text.*"[5] To the degree that the traditional, the familiar, and the authoritative within the scriptural text are measured not only by the exegete but also, and even more, by the community in which the exegete flourishes, the plain sense in Loewe's analysis seems to be more the product of communal sensibilities than it is the product of individual insight.

Loewe's functional consideration of the plain sense of scripture can do much to explain the workings of Christian exegesis. In a study that charts the changing fortunes of the literal sense from ancient to modern times,[6] Childs called attention to the various ways in which the literal sense has been conceived and valued. From Origen's minimizing of the literal sense, to the increasing authority ascribed to the literal sense in the medieval Christian tradition from Augustine through the Victorines to Aquinas and Nicholas of Lyra, to the centrality accorded the *sensus literalis* in the Reformers, and finally to the remarkable reconceptualization of the literal sense in post-Enlightenment exegesis as the historical reference of the biblical words to a natural and not a biblical world, the construal of the literal sense has changed dramatically over the ages—and in ways that seem to defy any theoretical definition of the literal sense that is common to all times and places. Childs's view, like Loewe's, is that the literal sense is not inherent in scripture itself but shaped by the authority of a community of belief as it responds to the needs of the time.

Childs's constructive commendations along these lines reflect his judgment that the rise of the historical-critical method in post-Enlightenment exegesis destroyed "the significance, integrity, and confidence in the literal sense of the text."[7] The literal sense, now understood as the *sensus originalis*, was ripped from the setting of the biblical narrative, which it properly represented, and made to refer to a secular history and a Newtonian universe, which it could only fail to do at every important juncture. Although Childs's work gives no indication that he is willing to jettison the historical-critical interpretation of scripture, it stands firmly against every effort to elevate the assumptions of modern over traditional exegesis, in which "the study of the [biblical] text cannot be separated from its reality."[8] Understood as a sacred scripture, the Bible is fittingly read, believed, and treasured by a community of faith. Childs has observed that

> [t]he authority of the canon of Scripture is not a claim of objective truth apart from the community of faith but it is a commitment to a particular perspective from which the reality of God is viewed. The literal sense is the plain sense witnessed to by the community of faith. It makes no claim for being the original sense, or even of being the best. Rather, the literal sense of the canonical Scriptures offers a critical theological norm for the community of faith on how the tradition functions authoritatively for future generations of the faithful.[9]

The literal sense, thus understood as the plain sense witnessed to by the community, is not immediately presented in the words on the page but is sought by the Christian community in its belief and practice. Indeed, Childs has gone so far as to propose that the literal sense, so commonly misconceived as the givenness of literality available to all, actually requires a "discernment" by and within the believing community in order to be brought to clarity.[10]

For Tanner, as for Loewe and Childs, the plain sense of scripture is not an obvious meaning inscribed in the text but the religious community's witness to scripture's authoritative meaning. Tanner, though, more than Loewe and Childs, has called attention to the community-forming power of the plain sense. The plain sense, she has insisted, "is not a property of those texts that happen to function as scripture for the Christian community." Rather, it is "a function of communal use; it is the obvious or direct sense of the text according to a *usus loquendi* established by the community in question."[11] And yet this perspective, from which the plain sense seems to be only the result of communal practice, is a partial one. The plain sense is "the sense of the text that establishes group identity." Itself the "traditional distillate of communal practice," the plain sense "becomes the norm governing the ongoing practice of using such a text to shape, nurture, and reform community life: the product of traditional practice norms its further operation."[12] Tanner's analysis recognizes that this intratextual, and so intracommunal, conception of the plain sense appears insular to some, as though the plain sense understood in this way could do no more than reiterate and reinforce scriptural meaning held as authoritative at one moment in the tradition's past. The plain sense, she has conceded, could conceivably issue from and at the same time shape the ongoing tradition in a repressive or hegemonic way. It is important to note, however, that the plain sense is not a formal principle but a functional practice that could just as easily serve a self-critical, reforming use of scripture. Moreover, Tanner's understanding of the plain sense as interpretation distinguishable from the biblical words seems to undercut efforts to hypostatize the plain sense and make its meaning resistant to change.[13]

In the work of Loewe, Childs, and Tanner there is agreement that what the Jewish and Christian traditions have called *peshat* or the *sensus literalis* of scripture cannot be identified with the words of the biblical text or even with what is judged to be the text's objective meaning. This is not to say, of course, that these commonplace understandings of the literal sense do not appear in the Jewish and Christian traditions. Indeed, both traditions provide ample evidence of the literal sense's characterization as the words on the page or as the obvious meaning of the words, conspicuous as expressions of the author's intention and, finally, of the divine author's purpose. But if one looks more at the practical workings of the literal sense than at its theoretical conceptualization, then the literal sense seems to behave much more as what Loewe, Childs, and Tanner have called the plain sense of scripture. Distinguishing between the literal sense and the plain sense, as these commentators have done, has the advantage of inscribing in the "plain sense" the interpretive character of what traditionally has been called the literal sense. Tanner has made this point well by noting that the "plain sense is itself a product of the interpretive tradition; the distinction between what is and is not the plain sense of a text becomes, therefore, a relative distinction between different sorts of communal uses of a text. Because the plain sense of a text is a functional reality—a function of a community's practice of appealing to a text—it is also a function of all the rest of the interpretive conventions constituting such a practice."[14] Understanding the literal sense as the interpretive plain sense, then, militates against any reductionist perspective on the authority of the biblical words and serves as a reminder to those who value the words that their meaning is a product of a tradition shaped by both elements of constancy and elements of renewal.

The efforts here to speak of the literal sense of tradition must take into account this notion of the literal sense as the plain sense. At first glance, an understanding of the literal sense as the plain sense might seem to undercut the stability of more traditional conceptions of the literal sense and might thus seem to set interpretation adrift, loosed as it were from its lettered moorings. But the particular contribution to this study's hermeneutics of tradition that the notion of the plain sense might make stems from its regard for interpretation as a practice contextually bound to the religious tradition in which it flourishes. Although this perspective represents a shift in the understanding of the literal sense, its capacity to explain the actual workings of more traditional, and various, notions of the literal sense justifies its consideration here. Let us examine, then, the ways in which the contextuality of the plain sense might elucidate an understanding of Catholic tradition.

One might be tempted to understand the literal sense of tradition as the literality of a conciliar decree, a papal encyclical, or an infallible pronouncement of the magisterium—or, analogously, as the bodily movements that inscribe a liturgical or devotional practice. A more adequate understanding of the literal sense, however, would resist the seductive power of such a fundamentalist view and recognize the extent to which the literal sense is indeed very much a "sense" whose interpretive value has already transcended the "letter" of inscriptive fact. And although one might be tempted to understand the plain sense as a meaning blatantly ingrained in the words and practices of tradition, a more adequate understanding of the plain sense would recognize that the obviousness of its meaning is itself an interpretive stance that is defined in the context of the believing community and that shifts occasionally in the larger sweep of ecclesial history. To the degree that the plain sense of scripture and tradition is not an individual but a communal meaning, its sense might better be described as a sensibility, as a shared awareness or responsiveness to a particular state of affairs—in this case, to the meaning of scripture and tradition in the Church.

Conceiving the plain sense as a shared sensibility on the part of the Church achieves a deeper theological significance when informed by the Catholic understanding of the *sensus fidei*. According to the teaching of the Second Vatican Council, the sense of the faith is the subjective disposition of the "whole body of the faithful who have an anointing that comes from the holy one" and in which they "cannot err in matters of belief." This appreciation of the faith, "aroused and sustained by the Spirit of truth," dwells in the whole people of God when " 'from the bishops to the last of the faithful' they manifest a universal consent in matters of faith and morals."[15] From a Catholic perspective, the plain sense of tradition would be an authoritative meaning that derives from the sensibility for the faith that is formed in believers by the Holy Spirit at work in history, guiding the Church and maintaining it in the truth. A functionalist approach to the plain sense might explain the unity of its interpretive power from a sociological point of view in which common readings and understandings within communities achieve an authority that is largely uncontested. As informative as this sociological account of the plain sense is—and as helpful as it might be as a reminder that the plain sense is indeed an interpretive sense—it remains insufficient for the present purposes if it is not, in turn, informed by a theological account of the Spirit's role in effecting the authority of the plain sense in the community of the Church as it extends from time to time and place to place.

An interpretive sensibility attuned to the workings of the Spirit in the Church that believers call "tradition" will be naturally (or better, gracefully) aware of the unpredictable, inspired movement of tradition that any adequate notion of the plain sense takes for granted. Yet, though it remains interpretation subject to revision, the plain sense of tradition is more typically resistant to change and is characterized by understandings that have garnered community support for longer periods of time. Like the plain sense of scripture, the plain sense of tradition represents an interpretive stance that has typically held currency in the Church for generations or even for centuries. The Council of Chalcedon's teaching on the unity of the divine and human natures in the person of the incarnate Christ offers a good example of this enduring character of the plain sense.

The comparison can be expanded by noting that the plain sense of tradition is even clearer, more stable, and more authoritative than the plain sense of scripture. Because tradition is largely the interpretation of scripture, it offers an interpretive field narrower than the plain sense of scripture. The plain sense of Chalcedon's teaching on the person of Christ, for example, is even plainer than scripture's plain sense on the person of Christ, for Chalcedon itself circumscribes the possible interpretations of the scriptural evidence. This plain sense of tradition includes what such commentators as Loewe, Childs, and Tanner have called the plain sense of scripture. And yet the plain sense of tradition has a standing in its own right—one that, though inseparable from the plain sense of scripture, has its own integrity. To the degree that tradition in Catholic belief is a distinguishable mode of revelation that cannot simply be reduced to scripture, one can speak of tradition's own plain sense, even when that plain sense in many cases can also be understood as the plain sense of scripture. Historical study usually shows that the unity, stability, and concreteness of tradition emerged from a history of interpretive ambiguity, disagreement, and conflict. And yet, in spite of this history and perhaps even because of it, tradition manifests an abiding plain sense, the clarity of an ecclesial consensus that perdures in Christian communities and serves as an authoritative measure for Catholic belief, doctrine, and practice.

Understanding the literal sense of tradition as tradition's plain sense, then, allows one to conceive the constancy of Catholic belief, doctrine, and practice not as a static inscription on page, object, or body but as the interpretive vitality of the faith preserved in the ecclesial sensibility of all the faithful by the Holy Spirit and manifested clearly in the historical life of the Church. This understanding also brings with it the advantage of representing the particularity of Catholic belief on the authority of tradition, while avoiding an ecclesiastical fundamentalism that reduces tradition to the letter of doctrine and practice. The literal sense of tradition, understood as its plain sense, serves as a constant reminder to the Church that the abiding stability of faith associated with the text of a conciliar decree, the recited words of the Nicene Creed, or the pattern of liturgy lies as much in the ongoing testimony of the community whose sense for the literal raises the "letter" of writing and behavior to the universality of ecclesial meaning.

The Canon of Tradition

If the literal sense of tradition is best understood as tradition's plain sense, then it is important to consider in greater detail how the plain sense garners its authority. How does a particular teaching of the Church come to be regarded as authentic tradition? How does a particular practice become normative Christian behavior? How does tradition's literal sense claim the

Church's recognition? These questions have already been answered from sociological and theological perspectives through the insights gained from the
workings of the plain sense of scripture. Like the plain sense of scripture, the
plain sense of tradition is an understanding of belief, doctrine, and practice
that is community-forming. Consensus about the plain sense solidifies the
bonds of community, and the unitive power of the plain sense reflects the
same bonds. From a theological point of view, the unity of meaning that
makes for the plain sense of tradition rests on the common sensibility of the
Church for the truth of the Holy Spirit. As illuminating as these perspectives
might be, their attention to particular expressive instances of tradition (for
example, *this* conciliar decree, *this* credal statement, or *this* liturgical rite)
limits their capacity to explain how the plain sense of tradition flourishes
among the multitude of teachings and practices that make up tradition. How
can one speak of the plain sense not of this or that teaching or practice but
of all the teachings and practices that are invested with authority and to
which Catholics refer as a "deposit" of tradition that along with scripture
presents the Word of God itself? Although the sociological and theological
perspectives that have served this study might be understood more comprehensively than they have been thus far and as such enlisted to answer this
question, a more fruitful approach would turn to scripture to find once again
an analogue for the authority of tradition. The idea of a scriptural canon can
aid these efforts to appreciate the literal sense of tradition in a larger context.

Understood in the broadest way, a canon is a collection of authoritative
writings. However this collection is defined, its meaning, worth, and normativity—all synonymns for "authority"—are affirmed by those who read or
hear its words and who, in that affirmation, acknowledge as a whole the
integrity of the various writings that make up the canonical collection. We
have become accustomed in recent times to considering the issue of canonicity with regard to secular literature, especially as nineteenth- and early
twentieth-century assumptions about the authority of the traditional Western
canon of literature have been challenged vigorously by postmodern critics.
But traditionally, canonicity is a religious value and represents a communal
judgment about the literary sacred and, concomitantly, the literary profane.
Greek in its origins and etymologically a reference to a measuring stick, the
word "canon" appears only a few times in the Septuagint and in the New
Testament, usually as a metaphor for a boundary and for a rule. In Clement
of Rome, "canon" refers to a rule for right preaching and living, and, for
Irenaeus of Lyons, it is a way of naming the "rule" of faith that distinguishes
Christian from heretical belief. The teachings of the Council of Nicea were
referred to as canons, disciplinary rules for the Church to live by. Athanasius
of Alexandria seems to be the first Christian writer to apply what became the
customary use of the word "canon." In his thirty-ninth festal letter, written
in 367, Athanasius distinguished between "the books included in the Canon,
and handed down, and accredited as Divine" and "other books . . . called
apocryphal" that beguile and mislead the faithful.[16]

Although this typical use of the word "canon" first appears in a fourth-century C.E. Christian setting to name the authoritative books of the Christian Bible, the actual delimiting of the collection of authoritative writings and thus the concrete process of canon formation took place earlier and occurred in both the Jewish and Christian traditions. In post-Exilic Israelite religion, the authority of canon was measured by the Torah, which shaped and preserved the identity of Israel.[17] This Torah-formed identity became especially important in the formative Judaism of the early years of the Diaspora. And in the course of the late first to second century, this identity was definitively linked to a fixed collection of writings that has been recognized ever since as the closed canon of Judaism. New Testament writers accepted the Hebrew scriptures as a divine revelation they believed to be completed in the events of Jesus' life, death, and resurrection. Gradually, first- and second-century Christians came to judge their epistolary, historical, and narrative accounts of Jesus the Christ as themselves revelatory along with the Hebrew scriptures. Through the practices of preaching, citation, exegesis, and polemics, the New Testament canon took definitive shape by the early third century C.E.[18] And like its Jewish counterpart, the Christian canon came to possess authority as a revelatory collection of writings that was fixed once and for all.

One can only speculate why Judaism and Christianity formed canons at all, and, moreover, canons that eventually were closed. Among the many traits that might account for the fact and status of the Jewish and Christian collections, three in particular are important to consider here: canonical authority, identity, and permanence. The authority of canon in the Jewish and Christian traditions lies in their shared belief in a revealing God whose words are found in the biblical writings. Even though these writings include different genres, historical settings, characters, and even, seemingly, messages, the belief that their truth is inspired by the one revealing God—that God is the sole author of the writings, making them indeed a single writing—is the basis of the authority attributed to the canon by believers. Canonical identity, like all the canonical traits, offers a perspective on the authority of the inspired canon. At once a narrative quality and a subjective disposition, canonical identity is a judgment of faith that the power of inspiration flourishes only in *these* stories that together form a single story that in turn determines the personal and communal identities of believers committed to the story's truth.[19] Identities, whether narrative or psychological, are formed both positively and negatively, and in this latter regard competition between Judaism and Christianity for the right understanding of the story of Israel undoubtedly played some role in their respective and yet mutual histories of canon formation. One cannot overlook the fact that the Jewish and Christian canons together moved toward and achieved closure early in the Common Era, no doubt as important moments in Jewish and Christian self-definition that were in each case both affirming and exclusionary.

Canonical permanence expresses the belief that God's inspired speech has been spoken fully in the tradition's past, that the canon is closed because

God's story has been completely narrated. Although one might argue that permanence is not an essential trait of canonicity, since some canons, such as the canon of Western literature, remain open and (in the judgment of many) even revisable, one would do better to see canonical permanence in the Jewish and Christian traditions as an expression of their most basic religious claims. The common Jewish and Christian belief in the one God who reveals in the law and through the prophets suggests the need for canonical closure as itself a monotheistic reflection of Jewish and Christian unwillingness to brook textual rivals—once, of course, a consensus has been reached on the narrative unity of a certain number of writings that can claim canonical status. Christian experience added its belief in the uniqueness of the Christ event to the value of monotheism and, by doing so, only heightened the need for determinate unity and closure.[20]

These three traits—authority, identity, and permanence—can be understood together as the coherence of canon. The plain sense of scripture is a function of canonical coherence, the capacity of the scriptural narrative—singly configured as the once-and-for-all spoken divine Word—to shape the biblical identity of the religious community. Scripture's plain sense is achieved not as the community agrees on the meaning of this or that scriptural passage in isolation from others but as the community understands biblical events, persons, books, and passages coherently in their relation to each other finally as expressions of the same divine voice.[21] Historical criticism presupposes that biblical books written earlier in the time of canon formation often are indispensable resources for understanding books written later but that the opposite is never true. And certainly in the process of canon formation prior to closure, a sensibility for the literal is cultivated retrospectively as more recent texts are measured for their revelatory value against accepted, authoritative writings. Since the closure of the canon, however, the plain sense of scripture issues from a sensibility that assumes the coherence of the canon, that readily reads canonical parts as mutually informative, and that regards each canonical part—irrespective of chronology, setting, and criticism—as an expression of the canonical whole.

Even though Judaism and Christianity closed their biblical canons early in the Common Era, it is interesting to note that both religions began at the same time to produce authoritative textual supplements to their respective canons that attempted to clarify canonical coherence, adjudicate biblical ambiguities, and address issues that did not seem to be definitively treated within the canon's boundaries. For Judaism, the supplement to the canon took the form of the Talmud; for Christianity, the supplement to the canon took the form of an apostolic tradition communicated from generation to generation along with the Old and New Testaments. As we have seen, an important dimension of this tradition took the form of an extrabiblical scripture that comprised the writings of orthodox Christians, the decrees of ecumenical councils, and eventually certain papal teachings. Although this extrabiblical scriptural tradition might be understood as an authoritative supplement to the canon that negotiated its coherence in one way or another, there is another sense in which it, and by analogy the nonscriptural tradition too, was elevated to the status of canon in Catholic belief.

The early Christian claim that the decrees of ecumenical councils are inspired by the Holy Spirit, the medieval understanding of a *sacra doctrina* in which the bible and the extrabiblical scriptural tradition were intertwined, and the teachings of Trent and the Vatican Councils on the communication of the divine Word in scripture and tradition all suggest that tradition functions in Catholic belief not merely as a supplement to the biblical canon but also with the biblical canon as a mode of revelation. And yet, since the biblical canon possesses boundaries as definite as a listing of its authoritative books, one can distinguish clearly between the biblical canon and what might be called the canonical properties of tradition. These canonical properties can be named in the same ways as those of the biblical canon, though in some important respects the canonical properties of tradition behave differently from their biblical counterparts.

The authority of tradition lies in the Catholic belief that the Spirit of God preserves the Church in a saving truth that has been handed down from the time of the apostles and that it is through this sacred tradition that the Holy Spirit "leads believers to the full truth, and makes the Word of Christ dwell in them in all its richness."[22] The authority of tradition, then, is the authority of inspiration whose source is the same divine author of scripture. In the words of Vatican II's "Dogmatic Constitution on Divine Revelation":

> Sacred Tradition and sacred Scripture . . . are bound closely together, and communicate one with the other. For both of them, flowing out of the same divine well-spring, come together in some fashion to form one thing, and move towards the same goal. Sacred scripture is the speech of God as it is put down in writing under the breath of the Holy Spirit. And Tradition transmits the Word of God which has been entrusted to the apostles by Christ the Lord and the Holy Spirit. It transmits it to the successors of the apostles so that, enlightened by the Spirit of truth, they may faithfully preserve, expound and spread it abroad by their preaching.[23]

One might understand the canonical authority of tradition simply to be a function of the canonical authority of the biblical books. The "Dogmatic Constitution on Divine Revelation" seems to support this view in its teaching that "[b]y means of the same Tradition the full canon of the sacred books is known to the Church and the holy Scriptures themselves are more thoroughly understood and constantly actualized in the Church."[24] Yet the same document insists that "the Church does not draw her certainty about all revealed truths from holy Scriptures alone" but from both scripture and tradition, which "must be accepted and honored with equal feelings of devotion and reverence."[25] And if there is some sense in which Catholic tradition does possess an integrity of its own, then by analogy one might speak of tradition's authority as canonical to the extent that there is a particular collection of teachings and practices judged to be authoritative and regarded in the Church as a deposit of divine truth.

This last point relates closely to tradition's canonical identity. Unlike the biblical canon, the canonical identity of tradition does not readily lend itself to narrative understanding, although the present study shows that there are ways in which a narrative quality might be ascribed to tradition. The canonical identity of tradition is shaped more directly by the belief that certain teachings and practices have been passed down through the ages since the time of the apostles and that only these teachings and practices—designated as apostolic by virtue of their age, or the circumstances of their definition, or their clarity, or their community-forming power—are rightly included in the authoritative deposit or canon of tradition and, in turn, rightly inform and measure the faithful identities of Catholic believers.[26] Prior to the Protestant Reformation, the canonical identity of tradition was especially closely intertwined with the canonical identity of the biblical writings and conceived as the homogeneous identity of *sacra doctrina*. Since the Protestant Reformation, the canonical identity of tradition has been more differentiated from the canon of biblical writings and to some degree has been defined contrapuntally, and often even polemically, with regard to Protestant belief.

Consideration of the canonical quality of permanence requires that an even more interesting distinction be made between the biblical canon and the analogue of a canon of tradition. As we have seen, the biblical canon reached definitive closure by the early third century C.E., and this fact of closure marks its permanence. Montanism, the belief that God continues to reveal through the prophetic utterances of extraordinary members of the community and in a manner equal in authority to canonical revelation, was deemed a heresy in the early Church. The quality of permanence can also be ascribed to what might be thought of as the canon of tradition. The beliefs, doctrines, and practices that have been judged "apostolic" possess a permanence defined largely by their power to endure in the hearts and actions of the faithful for long periods of time, a permanence believed to mirror the abiding truth of the economy of salvation inscribed and enacted in the canon of tradition. The permanence of the canon of tradition enables one to speak of a "deposit" of the faith that each generation of believers receives from the previous generation—a collection of beliefs, teachings, and practices that remains stable and true throughout the life of the Church. And yet, unlike the biblical canon, the canon of tradition does not possess the permanence of an achieved closure. Tradition as the eventful transmission of the divine Word in history by its very nature resists every notion of permanence as closure, short of the *eschaton*. One may speak of the permanence of what *has* achieved canonical status in the tradition—the Nicene Creed, Chalcedon's christological formula, the liturgical epiclesis, and the practice of venerating the saints all serving as good examples. One finds the literal sense of tradition in the permanence of this achieved canonical status. But the ongoing character of tradition, its very historicity, and the often dynamic development that takes place in so many of its beliefs, doctrines, and practices preclude the possibility of speaking of tradition's canonical permanence as closed.

As was evident in the previous consideration of the biblical canon, these three traits—authority, identity, and permanence—can be understood in a comprehensive way as the coherence of canon: in this case the canon of tradition. The plain sense of tradition is a function of canonical coherence, the power of established Catholic belief and practice, preserved in the truth by the Holy Spirit as the authoritative understanding and enactment of the divine Word, to shape the traditional identity of the believing community. Like the biblical plain sense, the plain sense of tradition achieves its literal meaning within the coherence of its canon, albeit in the case of tradition a canon that continues to grow. Tradition's authority, identity, and permanence are not ascribed to this or that doctrine or practice in isolation from these qualities in other established doctrines or practices. Rather, these qualities of canonical coherence flourish in a holistic network of belief, doctrine, and practice. In this context, the stability of the plain sense is fashioned among the constituents of the canon. Historical critical study of the traditioning process regards chronology, culture, and circumstance as indispensable resources for explaining the authority, identity, and permanence that believers come to ascribe to beliefs, doctrines, and practices. But from a canonical perspective, these qualities may also be understood independently of the particular times, places, and events from which they emerged and with regard to their coherent interrelationship among the beliefs, doctrines, and practices that make up the abiding deposit of faith. The incarnational perspective on the value of human labor evinced in John Paul II's 1981 encyclical *Laborem exercens*, for example, illuminates the authority, identity, and permanence of the Council of Nicea's teaching on the incarnation (325), just as Nicea informs the authority, identity, and likely permanence of the recent encyclical.

The canonical framework for the plain sense of tradition sometimes manifests itself in the propensity to shrink the boundaries of the canon of tradition, to establish a "canon within a canon" that more clearly (or literally) presents the authority, identity, and permanence of tradition. More typically, efforts to formulate a canon within the canon of tradition take place at the level of doctrine, in all likelihood because the conceptualization and practice of canon formation are more closely tied to the literary aspects of tradition. The ancient *regula fidei*, the great professions of faith such as the Nicene Creed, the Apostles' Creed, the Athanasian Creed, Denzinger's *Enchiridion Symbolorum*, the Tridentine *Roman Catechism*, and the recent *Catechism of the Catholic Church* all might be seen as shorter or longer constructions of canons within the canon of tradition. The desire to narrow the canon is itself an intensification of the desire for canon itself and thus, one might say, an intensification of the desire for the authority, identity, and permanence of Christian belief, doctrine, and practice. Indeed, these canonical qualities can be well served by the sharper delineation of narrower canonical expression. The *regula fidei's* articulation of belief in creation, redemption, and the life to come highlights the uncompromising authority of the principal events in the biblical narrative.

The communal recitation of the Nicene Creed in the celebration of the liturgy has powerful consequences for Christian identity. Denzinger's *Enchiridion Symbolorum* neatly presents a catalogue of doctrines that have achieved permanence in the Church. These beneficial effects of narrowing the canon of tradition, however, are ever accompanied by the possibility of deleterious effects in which Catholic authority and identity are falsely limited to the narrower canonical expression and the permanence of the canon of tradition is wrongly regarded as closed.

A canonical perspective on the plain sense of tradition enables us to appreciate how tradition as a whole comes to be judged authentic by the believing and practicing community. Whereas the previously cited examples of canon-narrowing are inclined, to a greater or lesser degree, to portray tradition as a collection of individual propositions whose number is fixed, a more adequate understanding of the canon of tradition is one that recognizes the wider parameters of the coherence of canon and thus the extent to which the canonical qualities of authority, identity, and permanence dwell within the entire network of belief, doctrine, and practice that tradition is. The plain or literal sense of tradition, itself a sensibility for the presence of these canonical qualities, settles in the actual life of the community within this network of Christian belief, doctrine, and practice, and finally as the network itself. The community-forming power of tradition's plain sense functions within this canonical framework not only in particular times, places, and circumstances but also throughout the times, places, and circumstances that the entire and ongoing tradition comprises. Often, this canonical perspective on what I am calling tradition's literal sense has been understood as a universality impervious to time, place, and circumstance, as though the tradition's literal sense accompanies history but only at a distance, hovering as it were above it and serving as an objective measure of Christian faith and action transpiring in history. Such a conceptualization may capture well the abiding quality of tradition's literal sense in a Platonic epistemology that has long held sway in Christian history. One would do better, though, to conceive of tradition's literal sense as a meaning that is transhistorical, not in the sense that tradition's plain meaning transcends time and culture but in the sense that tradition's plain sense is an abiding, time-honored agreement of the community affirmed, lived, and sustained in an utterly historical way, within and throughout the coherence of tradition's canon.[27]

Infallibility

The present consideration of the ways in which the literal sense of tradition arises in the faithful understanding of the community and flourishes in the coherence of the canon has some interesting implications for the doctrine of infallibility, which, of all the senses of tradition, seems to be most closely aligned with the literal. We have seen that the literal sense of tradition stems from a sensibility for the truth of Christian faith and practice, the sense of the faith dwelling in all believers through the presence of the Holy Spirit in the Church. This *sensus fidei* is the capacity of the whole Church to recognize the infallibility of the Spirit's truth, a recognition that reaches ecclesial consensus in dimensions, at least, of tradition's literal sense. This is not to say that the literal sense of tradition can simply be identified with necessary, unerring truth. If the literal sense of tradition is understood as the plain sense, then its authority is an interpretive authority shaped by an abiding consensus among the faithful that yet may change—even to the point that this consensus in belief, doctrine, and practice may be lost to another that over time itself can garner the authority of the tradition's literal sense. The literal sense of tradition as a whole is not infallible, but the Church's belief, doctrine, and practice that *is* infallible is eventually conveyed by the literal sense. How can the Church judge where the infallibility of the tradition lies if tradition's literal sense bears, but does not simply present, an unerring truth?

This question often elicits an answer that frames its response as a definition of infallibility and the conditions of its legitimate exercise and certainty. A likely reason for this orientation is that so much of the Church's discussion of infallibility since the fourteenth century has been devoted to papal infallibility, and this discussion has been largely concerned with defining the power and valid use of the extraordinary papal prerogative. The First Vatican Council's definition of the dogma of papal infallibility makes this point clearly. According to the 1870 conciliar decree *Pastor aeternus*:

> [T]he Roman Pontiff, when he speaks *ex cathedra*, that is, when, acting in the office of shepherd and teacher of all Christians, he defines by virtue of his supreme apostolic authority, doctrine concerning faith or morals to be held by the universal Church, possesses through the divine assistance promised him in the person of St. Peter, the infallibility with which the divine Redeemer willed his Church to be endowed in defining doctrine concerning faith or morals; and . . . such definitions of the Roman Pontiff are therefore irreformable because of their nature, but not because of the agreement of the Church.[28]

This dogma on papal teaching articulates a tradition that had been developing for centuries in the belief of the Church but that, in its formulation at Vatican I, expresses the largely juridical understanding of the Church as a visible structure of authority that was typical of Tridentine ecclesiology.[29] Although the ecclesiology of the Second Vatican Council does not reject this juridical orientation, it does expand its otherwise limited horizon by speaking of the infallibility of the whole Church. From this perspective, infallibility is not conceived primarily as the definition and legitimate use of extraordinary papal power but as the unerring faith of the people of God that the contemporary generation receives and accepts as the truth of Christ from the previous generation. That unerring truth is recognized by the eyes of faith, fathomed by the believing heart, and enacted in the life of love and commitment.

Conceiving of infallibility juridically, in terms of definition and criteria, runs the risk of limiting infallibility to an easily marked commodity that one finds in specific beliefs, doctrines, and practices that are—by virtue of their unerring status—distinguishable from others. But in the act of vital reception, the infallibility of certain dimensions of tradition is a communal judgment about the unerringly true that can be made only in the broader expanse of faith and practice. Like the reception of the faith that it communicates, this judgment takes place within the coherence of the canon of tradition where doctrines and practices garner their authority, identity, and permanence together as authentic representations of the gospel message. Although it is possible to consider a particular belief or practice as though it were an individual proposition and, in this form, to pass judgment on the status of its truthfulness, this judgment can, in actuality, be made only with reference to the canonical setting in which the coherence of tradition flourishes and thus within which judgments on the authority, identity, and permanence of tradition are meaningful.[30]

This holistic understanding of the infallibility of the Church as a dimension of the received and affirmed literal sense highlights a tension in the Church's ability to distinguish its unerring truth. On one hand, the Church's infallible belief, doctrine, and practice cannot be reduced to the literal sense of tradition. Although the literal sense expresses what is an undisputed consensus in the Church for a sustained period of time it yet includes belief, doctrine, and practice that are noninfallible and that in some future moment may lose their status as the literal sense. Thus, one can distinguish between infallible and noninfallible elements of doctrine within the literal sense. On the other hand, the infallibility of belief, doctrine, and practice is woven holistically and even indistinguishably into the coherence of the canon of tradition and thus into dimensions of tradition that possess authority, identity, and permanence, though not infallibly. Within this coherence too, infallible teaching is not limited to what is explicitly defined, as though only the decrees of ecumenical councils and *ex cathedra* papal pronouncements exhausted the number of infallible teachings. Belief, doctrine, and practice within the literal sense that does not reach definition as infallible teaching may yet be unerringly true, even if its infallibility does not stand out in relief from other noninfallible doctrines within the network of tradition.

A juridical approach to infallibility, one concerned with defining the power of infallible definition and the criteria for its use, is inclined to resolve this tension on the side of the distinguishability of infallible teaching, confident that infallibility possesses a propositional clarity that manifests itself in the tradition. This approach disregards the holism of belief, doctrine, and practice. Its inclination to measure the entirety of tradition by the clarity of infallible teaching leads it to overlook the embeddedness of the infallible dimensions of tradition within the noninfallible and vice versa. Resolving the tension can encourage a "creeping infallibility" in which infallibility is utterly distinguishable, though now not from noninfallible teaching but from whatever is other than the tradition itself.[31] Finally, this false resolution wrongly identifies infallibility and a literal sense that has become the only sense of tradition.

It is interesting to consider that a juridical approach to infallibility might be fostered by the very character of the canon of tradition. As noted above, the permanence of the canon of tradition is a permanence of abiding stability. Unlike the canon of scripture, though, the canon of tradition is not closed. Its openness, not only to interpretation but also to substantive development, itself prompts those who live the tradition to reflect on how one might adjudicate the presence of the Spirit in the current historical moment. As this discernment seeks unerring authority, uncompromising identity, and indissoluble permanence, the open-endedness of tradition's canon, the temporality of the discernment, and the anticipation of such future discernments all contribute toward a juridical understanding of infallibility in which the power for making present and future discernments is defined and the conditions and criteria for its right use are delineated. Whereas a common interpretation of the doctrine of papal infallibility associates its development from the late medieval tradition to the 1870 dogmatic definition with a drive toward the authoritative closure of tradition,[32] a better interpretation recognizes the extent to which a juridical understanding of infallibility is just as much future oriented as it is oriented toward the present and the past. In this regard, the modern history of the exercise of the magisterium since the Council of Trent is, as Congar has pointed out, a history of the "living magisterium" and an "active tradition,"[33] which unfolds before an open horizon of time, pluralism, and change. In other words, there is something distinctly and surprisingly modern in the way the nineteenth-century dogma delineated the juridical conditions for the exercise of papal infallibility.

Now this point should not suggest that the juridical sensibility is comfortable with its orientation toward the future and toward the canon's open horizon. Indeed, the very way in which the future beckons the present in a historically conscious world view and calls upon it to come to be in a myriad of ways is often a source of profound unease to those who understand infallibility only in a juridical manner. And it is this anxiety that leads the juridical sensibility to resolve in the ways it does the tension of the distinguishable and the indistinguishable. The prospect of an open canon, and a consciousness of the possibilities of and the conditions for defining the infallible in the face of an uncertain future, makes the distinguishability of the infallible an ever more important and valued trait of tradition in the juridical approach.

Another way of making this same point with regard to the concerns of this chapter is that a juridical understanding of infallibility is impatient with the literal sense of tradition. The infallibility of the Church dwells within the literal sense and yet manifests a *distinguishable* clarity only in relatively few places— such as in the solemn definitions of ecumenical councils; in the professions of the great creeds; and in the only extraordinary exercise of papal infallibility since the 1870 declaration of the dogma, Pius XII's 1951 definition of the Assumption of Mary. The infallibility otherwise conveyed in the literal sense remains ambiguous. Even though the undefined infallibility of the tradition has a plain sense among the faithful that is undisputed and enduringly affirmed as the faith of the Church, it continues to possess an interpretive character within the literal sense.

Any number of factors might explain why the undefined infallible dimensions of the tradition have not been and, one might anticipate, never will be defined. An aspect of the unerring truth of Christ might not be recognized as such even by the Church to which it has been bequeathed. The mystery of belief and practice is sufficiently satisfying to the faithful as the literal sense of tradition. The falsity that stands in opposition to the unerring truth does not threaten the Church in a way that requires the truth's explicit infallible definition. Whatever the reason for the embeddedness of the Church's undefined infallibility in the literal sense, a holistic sensibility toward that infallibility is untroubled by its literal plainness—and untroubled, too, by the abiding and yet changeable permanence of the literal sense as it stands before the openness of the canon and the uncertainties of the future. A juridical understanding of infallibility is impatient with the ambiguity that accompanies the literal sense of tradition, desiring its even sharper clarity through the definition of its infallible dimensions. In contrast, a holistic understanding of infallibility can embrace the uncertainty of the future and, in some respects more consistently than the juridical approach, can appreciate the present responsibility of the literal sense to the past as tradition in which authority is strong enough, identity is clear enough, and permanence is stable enough to preserve the Church in the truth.

Understanding infallibility as a dimension of the literal sense of tradition possesses important implications for the workings of this quality of faith in the life of the Church. Clearly, a holistic understanding of infallibility would judge as problematic any dissociation of the extraordinary papal charism of infallibility from the belief and practice of the whole Church. The teaching of Vatican I that infallible "definitions of the Roman Pontiff are . . . irreformable because of their nature, but not because of the agreement of the Church" is rightly understood as a rejection of any sociological measure of what counts as finally authoritative in the Church, as though the holding of a belief even by an ecclesial majority would constitute that belief's infallible truth. This teaching of the First Vatican Council is wrongly understood as an assertion of the separability of the papal charism from the activity of the Holy Spirit in the whole Church and thus from the uncountable charismatic acts of discerning the presence of the Spirit that take place in the Church from hour to hour and by which the literal sense of tradition is affirmed and upheld. Within this network of belief and practice, the extraordinary papal prerogative occasionally may require exercise to put the literal sense of tradition into even greater relief than it possesses at the present moment. But it would be inappropriate to exercise the extraordinary prerogative of infallibility in matters of dispute in the Church when each side in the disputed matter is able to show, even in the face of disagreement, that its position can be consistent with tradition. Such a disagreement may very well signal a loss of stability in what previous to the ecclesial dispute had been the literal sense of tradition. And where the literal sense is lacking, one cannot even begin to speak of the whole Church's recognition of the infallibility of a traditional belief, doctrine, or practice. Infallible pronouncements should not be a way of securing the ecclesial future by settling dispute in the Church. Infallibility is not a disciplinary power; it is the gift of the Spirit's truth. Its power within the literal sense is the power of confirmation oriented toward the undisputed past and present.

In Congar's description of the modern magisterium as "living," he was certainly referring to the development of the regular practice of the Church's teaching authority in the nineteenth and twentieth centuries. Only in these recent times has the magisterium taught the Church frequently through the explicit means of encyclicals, instructions, declarations, decrees, and apostolic letters. This exercise of the magisterium is one of guidance to the Church, as the magisterium exercises what has come to be known as its ordinary teaching authority. This ordinary teaching office may be distinguished from the extraordinary papal prerogative of infallibility in the sense that its pronouncements, while authoritative, are not necessarily unerring.[34] Since the middle of the nineteenth century, the magisterium has spoken of the ordinary universal magisterium of the Church, by which it has understood an exercise of the teaching office of the bishops throughout the world in communion with the Pope that communicates infallible truth that may not yet have been defined explicitly.[35]

The previous discussion of a holistic understanding of infallibility in the Church applies as well to the authoritative pronouncements of the ordinary magisterium. The magisterium's special role in the Church issues from its teaching charism, a charism that is rightly faithful to the literal sense of tradition as it is believed and practiced by the entire Church. The ordinary magisterium, whether or not its exercise is universal or not, offers its teaching in accordance with the literal sense of tradition as that sense has been established through the past and into the present. This literal sense, however, comprises both infallible and noninfallible dimensions of tradition. When the magisterial charism expresses itself with the authority of the ordinary universal magisterium, its teaching must be unswervingly loyal to the undisputed literal sense of tradition as it has endured over time. And yet, just as the literal sense is subject to revision, so, too, may what has been judged unerring doctrine in the teaching of the ordinary magisterium show itself in some future moment not to be so. In instances in which the heretofore literal sense has been fragmented by a variety of belief in the Church to the point that it no longer possesses stability, the magisterium may still exercise its teaching office—prophetically one might say—by taking account of how the established literal sense might be developing in the present moment and by offering an authoritative vision of the path of development into the future.[36] This prophetic exercise of the teaching office presupposes the authority of the literal sense but refuses to reduce the literal sense to the infallible, as though the faith of the past were an absolute measure of the faith of the present. In any case, it is the literal sense of tradition, in all its authority and in all its productive possibility, that provides an indispensable context for the infallibility of the Church.[37]

Universality

These considerations of the literal sense all point us back to the issue of the universality of the Church. Together with the ancient marks of the Church as one, holy, and apostolic, the catholicity or universality of the Church is an important dimension of the coherence of tradition. Classically, the mark of universality has appeared principally in two forms that might be described as epistemological and ecclesial.[38] Both of these forms of universality might be seen as ingrained in the literal sense of tradition, and both avail themselves of understandings consistent with the analysis of the literal sense of tradition presented thus far.

Epistemological universality reflects the assumption held throughout the Christian tradition (and Western culture largely to our times) that valid knowledge is founded on abstract unities or universals that transcend space and time and in which any particular act of knowing—theological or otherwise—participates. Platonism is the most influential expression of this assumption, although Stoicism also shares its values. Through such noetic participation in what Platonists called the supersensible "form" or *eidos* or what Stoics called the *logos spermatikos*, knowing achieves a universal character that remains impervious to the spatiotemporal character of sensible experience. The Jewish and Christian doctrine of creation complements this epistemological universality by espousing a holistic view of reality in which God is both the source of being and, with the divine ideas now substituting for Platonic or Stoic versions of the noetic ideal, the goal of intellectual striving. To the degree that classical theology claims God as the direct object of its epistemic endeavors, the universal character of its knowledge is all the more presumed.

Ecclesial universality reflects the belief present in the tradition from the early Christian centuries that the truth of the Church is "catholic." This belief, a profession of faith deemed worthy of inclusion in the ancient creeds, advances the epistemological assumptions previously described. The truth of the Church is universal because it lies in the mystery of a God unbounded by space and time. But it is important, as well, to note the spatiotemporal character of this ecclesial mark. The universality of the Church achieves expression principally in ecclesial doctrine—what the members of the Church believe in their hearts and enact through their wills from time to time and place to place. Affirmations of the universality of the Church's teaching set ecclesial faith in a global perspective defined temporally by the continuity of faith that joins each successive generation of believers and spatially by the geographical extension of ecclesial boundaries. The mission of the Church to spread the gospel to all nations is supported by this spatiotemporal conception of universality succinctly expressed in the well-known maxim of the fifth-century monk Vincent of Lerins that the catholicity of the Church lies in what has been believed "everywhere, always, by all." Clearly, epistemological universality and ecclesial universality are complementary claims and values, the universality of the gospel's truth serving as the basis for the Church's universality in space and time and the universality of the Church in history defining its mission and message as the universality of Catholic truth.

Both of these conceptions of universality seem to be at stake in the literal sense of tradition (and scripture, for that matter), albeit in forms that reflect the revision that these conceptions of universality have seen in the modern period. Modern and postmodern critiques of traditional epistemologies may have undercut the credibility of Platonic claims for the foundations of truth in transcendent universals. Yet the claims of faith continue to affirm their objective truthfulness as testimonies to the divine truth and the means of its revelation to the world. Modern and postmodern critiques of traditional ecclesiologies may point up the degree to which traditional ecclesiologies were driven by a colonialist mentality in which the Church understood itself narrowly as an institution bent on success in its missionary efforts to win and retain converts throughout the world.[39] Yet the limitations of this conception do not lead believers to retreat from the Catholic claim that the universality of the Church perdures in the common faith that has flourished and continues to flourish in the rich pluralism of Christian belief, doctrine, and practice throughout times and cultures.

The literal sense of tradition as it has been expounded here expresses both of these notions of universality. As an interpretive value, the literal sense conveys the Church's judgment that God's revelation abides not only in the biblical canon but also in a traditional canon of belief, doctrine, and practice that—in its inseparable relationship to the Bible—is an objective, Spirit-filled norm for truth recognized as such by the community of faith. Within the context of Catholic commitment, truth is affirmed of the literal sense of belief, doctrine, and practice, and, in the scope of that affirmation throughout the whole Church, the universality of the truthful tradition flourishes. Understood in this way, the universal truth of Catholic tradition is not merely a quality of belief, doctrine, and practice but itself a Christian practice motivated by and enacted in the faith, hope, and love of believers. Moreover, the literal sense of tradition is defined by the very fact of ecclesial universality in belief, doctrine, and practice. Where Catholic belief, doctrine, and practice extend throughout the whole Church, there one finds the literal sense of tradition. Where what counts as Catholic tradition is in dispute, there one finds either a schism in which the literal sense is rightly preserved by the orthodox and deviated from wrongly by the heterodox or an instance of belief, doctrine, or practice that has lost its literal meaning and now takes on another, developing sense in the experience of the Church.

This last point might suggest that the literal sense, and thus the universality of the Church's truth and real spatiotemporal presence, is a rather small property. After all, much of the authentic teaching of the Church's magisterium is received among the faithful in a variety of ways. This variety in reception might be judged by some to deviate from the universality of the literal sense, here identified with magisterial teaching unsullied by a variety in reception that could only be a deviation from the one true faith. Furthermore, the fact that some of the magisterium's authentic teaching meets resistance among large numbers of the faithful might be regarded as evidence that the universality of the literal sense of tradition extends only as far as the faith of those who are unquestioningly faithful to every magisterial pronouncement. Making these judgments, of course, reflects a certain expectation of the literal sense and its universality. If one, for example, expects the literal sense of tradition to be presented in every teaching of the magisterium or in every Christian practice that has had currency even for long periods of time in the Christian past, then the conception of universality presented herein will certainly seem rather diminutive, and disappointingly so. Smaller still will seem the universality of tradition, again disappointingly so, if dispute about the literal sense can result not only in the simple alternatives of faithfulness to or deviation from it but also in legitimate challenges to the literal sense or even in its loss in the name of tradition, as the history of Catholicism, I believe, occasionally evinces.

Precisely because proponents of the classical conception of universality have an understanding of truthfulness, orthodoxy, and Spirit-filled tradition that is identified utterly with what I have called tradition's literal sense—to the exclusion of other senses of tradition that might be valued and prized as the authentic faith of the Church—they may very well find themselves disappointed before a universal, literal sense of narrower scope. In such a view, *all* ecclesial truth and *all* ecclesial presence is reduced to the universality of tradition's literal sense, which, in the face of the variety in reception, ambiguity in understanding, and the prevalence of disagreement in the Church, seems remarkably smaller than the universality of times past. My project in the chapters that follow is to show that—even if the nonliteral senses cannot claim, but only perhaps aspire to, the universality of the literal sense—the Church's truthful, orthodox, and Spirit-filled tradition does indeed flourish in both its nonliteral and its literal senses. If the universality of the literal sense as presented here is narrower in scope than imagined in the classical conception of ecclesial universality, as it certainly is, then this need not be a cause for lament. A universality circumscribed by what can really be counted as tradition's literal sense does not at all diminish the Church's truthfulness or the scope of the Church's mission to the world. What it does acknowledge, however, is that the truthfulness of tradition that can be regarded as unerring and the plain sense of the tradition handed on in the Church's mission are smaller than some in the Church might think.

This more modest conception of the universality of the literal sense of tradition is one in which abiding ecclesial meaning is not regarded as an abstract truth envisaged apart from the claims of faith or as a geographical reality simply equatable with visible institutions. If we can say with Vincent of Lerins that the Church's catholicity is to be found in what has been believed "everywhere, always, by all," then we must understand that claim realistically as a description of a tradition whose universality is fathomed as a literal sense grasped by the whole Church through the past and to the present. The literal sense of tradition abides, then—as does the universal affirmation of truth and ecclesial presence it conveys—not as a fixed monument to past belief and practice but as a stable and yet continuing interpretation of divine revelation made and remade in every successive moment by the Christian community.

These reflections on the first sense of tradition all suggest that there is something profoundly paradoxical about the literal sense. It is a norm of Christian belief and practice handed down from generation to generation that is itself normed by that belief and practice. The literal sense possesses canonical properties and yet remains susceptible to change. It possesses a clarity within which the unerringly true often remains ambiguous and hidden. And it presents a claim for epistemological and ecclesial universality that is nevertheless contextualized by the actual, relative conditions of faith and action. These paradoxical qualities derive from the coincidental values of constancy and renewal that inform the literal sense of tradition. In its literal sense, tradition communicates lasting faith and practice in which the Church finds its uncontested meaning, its coherence, the depository of its unerring truth, and its universality. And yet these traits of constancy are ever complemented by the value of renewal—by the simple fact that the literal sense is not merely the literality of a belief, doctrine, or practice but an interpretation that may be judged a sense only in its ongoing affirmation and reaffirmation as the plainly truthful meaning of God's revealed Word in tradition. The next chapter considers how an ecclesial sensibility more attuned to the value of renewal can be conceived as the second sense of tradition.

2

Development-in-Continuity
as a Sense of Tradition

Of the four senses of tradition, the literal sense bears the closest resemblance to an ancient sense of scripture. It is like its ancient scriptural counterpart in a number of ways. The literal sense of tradition assigns the highest value to an ostensible meaning in the interpretive practice of the believing community. It is not inclined to look further than tradition's authoritative meaning in its search for divine truth, for in it the Christian desire for the oneness and steadfastness of Christ's redemptive message has been satisfied. The literal sense of tradition appreciates the literal meaning of faith and practice that permeates the ecclesial community in the present moment as a unity and that binds the tradition from present to past in a settled continuity. And it stays close to the "letter," whose fixed properties are reflected in the interpretive stance that this sensibility offers.

This chapter explores a sense of tradition that does not bear a direct resemblance to any of the ancient scriptural senses. Called the sense of development-in-continuity, this second sense of tradition fully appreciates the historicity of the truth of Christ that is handed down from generation to generation of believers. Tradition's historicity in this regard cannot be reduced to the boundedness of tradition to time, to the temporality of all things ecclesial. Christians in all times and places have recognized this understanding of historicity, even if they have not used the rhetoric of historicity to describe it. Historicity expresses a modern sensibility on what Christians would call, in one way or another, the conditions of created finitude. An ancient sensibility would equate time with corruption or, in theological language, with the sinful consequences of the fall and thus regard time as a vexing threat to the permanence of the literal sense of scripture and, by extension, tradition. A modern sensibility, in contrast, might appreciate the productive capacity of historicity by seeing in time not only a corrupting and sin-laden threat to truth but also opportunities for truth's fuller realization. A premodern understanding of the senses of scripture regards the literal sense as the best resistance to temporal corruption and assumes that meaningful departures from the literal sense must flee time to supernatural referents in the spiritual realm (allegorical sense), the divine will (moral sense), or the eschaton (anagogic sense). The sense of tradition proposed here, on the other hand, values time as a historicity in which God's creativity continues to show itself in new appreciations and configurations of the old faith.

This sense, which recognizes tradition's historicity as a development productive of meaning, also finds continuity to be compatible with that development. The development that this sense of tradition appreciates is not one that anticipates rupture with the past, with what the tradition has represented as indispensably true. And it is not one in which development issues from ecclesial experience de novo, in a manner discontinuous with the past. Rather the sense of development-in-continuity fathoms the truth of tradition as a growth that occurs in a consistent way throughout an ecclesial time and space, a growth that preserves tradition's truth as it develops it. In this regard, there is an especially close connection between the literal sense of tradition and the sense of development-in-continuity. We have seen that the literal sense of tradition, understood as the plain sense, presents an abiding meaning whose constancy is ever renewed in the life of the Church. These same values of constancy and renewal inform the sense of development-in-continuity, though now constancy is appreciated within the flourishing development that brings renewal rather than in the opposite relationship of priorities set by the literal sense.

The development of doctrine has not been explicitly regarded before as a sense of tradition alongside others in the manner proposed in this work. But the notion of the development of doctrine by now does indeed have an established place in the history of modern Christian thought.[1] My goal in this chapter is to construct an understanding of the development-in-continuity of tradition that accords with both the authoritative teaching of the Church[2] and faith's experience of truthfulness in modern and even postmodern times. Such a construction, however, presupposes a background in the various understandings of doctrinal development that have appeared in the modern tradition. Let us proceed, then, by considering the various ways in which nineteenth- and twentieth-century theologians have conceptualized the development of doctrine, configurations that serve both as types and antitypes in my efforts to sketch the second sense of tradition.

Models of Development

The consideration of models of development should begin by noting that doctrinal development is a term that can be applied widely to different kinds of "movements" in the history of faith. In a study entitled "Conceptual Models in the Understanding of the Development of Dogma,"[3] Johannes Stöhr has distinguished eight depictions of doctrinal development[4] labeled the "fixed," the "progress," the "regress," the "syncretist," the "rediscovery of beginnings," the "organic," the "clarification of knowledge," and the "synthesis of dialectical oppositions" models.

The "fixed" model represents the movement of tradition as the constant repetition of a once-given apostolic truth. The "progress" model images each movement in tradition as an advance, as a step beyond an ecclesial present being ever redefined. The "regress" model applies the analogy of cultural decline and death to the doctrinal tradition in order to explain an instance of loss of meaning in the communication of the faith. The "syncretist" model attributes development to the influence of a culture-at-large upon the culture of the gospel message through which the latter is accommodated to the former, though not necessarily in a pejorative manner. The "rediscovery of beginnings" model sees the movement of tradition as a repristination of its primal and insuperably authoritative teachings. The "organic" model appeals to the analogy of life to depict the development of doctrine as a growth from earlier to later, and more mature, expressions of faith. The "clarification of knowledge" model envisages more developed doctrines as the refinement of an idea or consciousness in the course of time. And the "synthesis of dialectical oppositions" model conceives the tradition as the historical encounter of conflicting Christian claims from which a resolved doctrinal truth emerges.

Stöhr has examined each of these models in fine detail, identifying variations on each modular theme as well as proponents and critics of each position. Both his taxonomy and analysis enable his reader to appreciate the many conceptualizations of doctrinal development in the history of Christian thought.

Even from this briefest of summaries, one can surmise that several of the models in Stöhr's classification could not represent the sense of tradition under consideration here. The "fixed" and "rediscovery of beginnings" models so value a constancy defined by an ancient and often hypostatized measure that they regard movement within the doctrinal tradition with suspicion. The "regress" model by definition accounts for not development-in-continuity but only development as discontinuity. And the "progress" model jeopardizes the value of constancy by envisioning a development that ever passes beyond, and perhaps ever leaves behind, a transient and only relatively authoritative present moment in the doctrinal tradition. Of the remaining models, Stöhr has cast his lot with the "organic" model as the best representation of the second sense of tradition, for finally Stöhr's analysis shows him to privilege development-in-continuity as authentic doctrinal development itself.

Stöhr has been careful to qualify the acceptability of the organic model as an appropriate representation of the development of doctrine. He has insisted that the theological use of this model to explain the workings of tradition must avoid understandings of organic growth as the sum of atomistic parts, as a process in which the integrity of what grows is lost in a grand evolutionary setting, or as an occurrence shaped primarily by the environment in which the organic growth of the tradition takes place. Indeed, in Stöhr's view, the organic model achieves its theological intelligibility when placed in the Church's own language of organicism in which the ecclesial community is imaged as the Mystical Body of Christ.[5] So understood, the organic model, now rooted in a tradition of biological imagery as old as the New Testament and affirmed as recently as the documents of the Second Vatican Council, offers a meaningful portrayal of development-in-continuity that conceives growth as the unfolding of a givenness preserved as it matures in time.

One can readily agree with Stöhr that, among the options that he has sketched, the organic model conveys most clearly the compatibility of development and continuity. But Stöhr's classification may be too quick to identify the organic model with authentic development—what I have labeled "development-in-continuity"—to the exclusion of a consideration of elements of authentic development in the "syncretist," the "clarification of knowledge," and the "synthesis of dialectical oppositions" models. Certainly there are differences among these last three models and between each of them and the organic model that Stöhr has prized above all. Yet, in Stöhr's taxonomy, these three models are better understood as various expressions of the organic model's basic assumption that the tradition's development-in-continuity is a growth conceived as the unfolding of a givenness preserved as it matures in time. In addition to this shared assumption, Stöhr's "organic," "synthesis of dialectical oppositions," "clarification of knowledge," and "syncretist" models all describe particular theories of tradition as a development-in-continuity that have appeared in nineteenth- and twentieth-century Catholic theology. In order to avoid confusion with Stöhr's classification and to portray these models within the broader rubric of continuous growth being proposed here, let us rename them, respectively, the organic, the dialectical, the noetic, and the reception models. Here we examine each model, in the order in which it appeared chronologically in the Catholic tradition as an explanation of its historicity.

The Dialectical Model

Johann Sebastian Drey (1777–1853) was the first Catholic theologian to speak of the development of doctrine in a way that attempted to reconcile the historicity of faith and the Christian belief in the once-and-for-all givenness of God's revelation. Like many theologians of his generation, Drey recognized that the intellectual and political currents of the Enlightenment threatened to sweep away the bastions of scripture and tradition that had long provided secure dwellings for Christian truth. Drey and many of his theological contemporaries judged that the Enlightenment flood could not be contained within the narrower riverbed of premodern Christianity; they even entertained the thought that the irresistible waters could have the beneficial effects of widening the ancient river's boundaries and fertilizing the surrounding soil. But if these effects were to be realized, Drey understood, the bastions of Christian truth first had to be shored up with bricks and mortar capable of withstanding the flood of Enlightenment criticism. The concept of doctrinal development provided the new materials to buttress the old, and the work of construction took the form of the new post-Enlightenment theological subdiscipline of apologetics.[6]

Enlightenment critics of religion often argued against the truthfulness of Christian revelation in scripture and tradition by measuring its claims against the standard of a reason liberated, in their view, from faith. Philosophers of the late eighteenth century, such as Hermann Samuel Reimarus, Gotthold

Lessing, and Immanuel Kant, typically conceived Enlightened reasoning as an utterly natural operation that, when faithful to its nature, conducted its analytical business with mathematical precision. But, though mechanical in efficiency and predictability, Enlightened reasoning was finally a constructive power that fashioned the dictates of morality for conscience and, at least according to Kant's 1781 *Critique of Pure Reason*, shaped the very laws of nature framed in the science of physics. Traditional Christian justifications for the truth of the Bible and its authoritative interpretation through the ages—that its moral teaching is divinely revealed and that the integrity of its salvational narrative rests on God's miraculous interventions in the world—could not meet, in the philosophers' judgment, the new canons of intelligibility.

Recently, theologians such as George A. Lindbeck and Ronald Thiemann and philosophers such as Alvin Plantinga and Nicholas Wolterstorff have argued that the Christian narrative, rather than the Enlightenment expectations of proper reasoning, should rightly set the terms by which the intelligibility of Christian truth claims are judged. Though this position has come to be regarded as a respectable—and indeed by some an effective—answer to the Enlightenment heritage of modernity, it was not a viable option in the early nineteenth century. Theologians such as Drey had no extensive experience dealing with a crisis of such proportions. Criticism from an alternative epistemic culture had so challenged the Church's veridical mainstays that its traditional knowledge came to be regarded as questionable in many quarters of society and even as incredible in those quarters most recently empowered amid the ruins of the feudal order. The thought world of early German Romanticism, particularly its understanding of the movement of history through the *Lebensanalogie*, provided an important resource for an apologetics on behalf of Christian tradition—one that could claim intelligibility in the learned circles of the day yet give a faithful account of time-honored Christian doctrine.

Like several of his contemporaries, most notably Friedrich Schleiermacher in his 1799 *Speeches on Religion*, Drey defended Christianity by arguing that its Enlightenment critics had not appreciated its real essence and were thus criticizing only historical manifestations of its truth that were accidental and limited.[7] For Drey, Christian truth unfolds as a development in history, a Romantic conceptualization of God's revelation in scripture and its doctrinal interpretation that enabled the theologian at once to present traditional Christian meaning in contemporary categories; to insist that these categories offered a more adequate account of the workings of the Christian tradition than did earlier theological categories; and to subvert the Enlightenment criticism of Christian belief by contending that Christianity was not the ossified "letter" of scripture and tradition, as the new philosophers maintained, but a development in which the faith of the past was preserved and renewed in the ever-unfolding truthfulness of present-day ecclesial life. The sense of tradition that I call "development-in-continuity," then, emerged as an explicitly modern theological principle from the post-Enlightenment context of Christian apologetics.[8]

Eberhard Tiefensee and Bradford Hinze have shown that Drey employed many images—pedagogic, natural scientific, and mathematical—to depict the development of doctrine. But finally, in their judgment, this variety stands in the service of an organic model of development in which vitalistic metaphors portray Christian tradition as a living organism animated by the divine Spirit.[9] As noted earlier, all the models considered in this section of the chapter illustrate the imagery of growth in which the modern theories of development-in-continuity were set. And the second model illustrated below in the theology of Drey's student and Tübingen colleague Johann Adam Möhler specifically addresses the traits of this broadly organic analogy. Drey, in fact, employed organic imagery so consistently in his writings that it would be easy to draw on his work to illustrate the second model and, through it, the organic underpinnings of all four models presented here.[10] Drey, though, sketched such a distinctive variation on the *Lebensanalogie* that his theology better illustrates the first, "dialectical," model.

In 1819 Drey published a small book on theological method entitled *Brief Introduction to the Study of Theology*. A contribution to the genre of methodological works of the late eigthteenth and early nineteenth centuries known as theological encyclopedia, Drey's *Brief Introduction* was influenced in both organization and content by Schleiermacher's 1811 *Brief Presentation of the Study of Theology*, in which one finds the first explicit theory of doctrinal development in the history of Christian theology.[11] Following Schleiermacher, Drey portrayed Christian tradition as a dialectical process of doctrinal development in which the settled faith of the past encounters and is animated by the living faith of the present ecclesial moment. In *Brief Introduction*, Drey gave this striking explanation of this dialectical encounter: "[A] complete system of [doctrinal] concepts that is thought of not as dead tradition from a time gone by but as the development of a living tradition necessarily bears within it a two-fold element: a *fixed* aspect (*ein* fixes) and a *mobile* aspect (*ein* bewegliches)."[12] For Drey, the fixed element of ecclesial tradition lies in the classical doctrines of the time-honored past that are handed down to present-day believers as established expressions of the Christian mysteries. Drey uses the word "dogma" to name this fixed element and regards the fixity of dogma as the "single objectively . . . valid criterion of Christian *truth*."[13] There is a "closed" or a "completed" (*Abgeschlossene*) quality to dogma, in Drey's judgment, through which it achieves standing in the tradition as an abiding norm and guide for tradition. But in Drey's view this completeness is not something always given but is itself achieved "through extensive development."[14] The "mobile" element in living tradition, in other words, is the heritage of dogma as well as the historical quality of ecclesial faith that has not yet reached dogma's recognized normativeness. The mobile element of tradition is that which "in the development . . . is still conceiving [doctrinal truth]."[15] Theological efforts to represent the mobile element in the present life of the Church yield what Drey has called "scholastic opinion" or "theological opinion" that is characterized by its uncertainty and disputed nature. But in Drey's view, the unsettled disposition of theological opinion can be judged an ecclesial deficiency only when measured against the high standard of explicit dogma. Developing theological opinion, itself a description of developing Christian faith, "can in itself still be Christian truth, which only is not yet developed to the level that it can be universally recognized as such in the Church."[16]

What Drey has called a "living tradition" garners its vitality from the productive meeting of the fixed and mobile elements in the present ecclesial moment. The fixed element offers the continuity of the ecclesial past to the ecclesial present, whereas the mobile element renews that continuity in the present moment, raising an otherwise dead letter to a life-giving spirit that animates the content of Christian truth for tradition's latest times. Moreover, the mobile element offers to tradition new opportunities for the manifestation of Christian truth. It does so not only as the point at which the meaning of dogma comes to life in contemporary faith but also as the resource that its own incompleteness offers to an ecclesial future in which doctrine develops to dogmatic completeness. In Drey's view, tradition is thus the complementarity of the fixed and the mobile in the ongoing life of the Church. Orthodoxy, for Drey the mark of authentic tradition, is the "striving to preserve the completed aspect of the doctrinal concept and to construct the mobile aspect in the sense of the completed aspect and in agreement with it."[17] The balance of orthodox tradition may be lost on one side or the other of its two legitimate constituents. Heterodoxy, Drey maintains, fails to respect the fixed element of tradition either by making "the fixed aspect mobile" or by setting "the mobile in opposition to the fixed." Hyperorthodoxy fails to respect the mobile aspect of tradition as one "denies [the mobility of the doctrinal concept] generally or raises opinion to the level of dogma."[18] Both dimensions of tradition in their proper relationship present the Spirit of God at work in history.

Tradition, understood as at once continuous and developing, is constituted in the creative relationship that Drey has envisaged between the ecclesial past and present, between what has been and is being believed in the Church. But Drey's insistence on the complementarity between the fixed and mobile aspects of a truly "living" tradition should raise caution on the proper use of the label chosen herein for the model of development that his views serve to illustrate. This conception is rightly described as "dialectical" to the degree that the term connotes a process of productive interplay, though not an interplay of opposites that lose their integrity in a higher tertium quid. For Drey, tradition is a movement in which the fixed and the mobile remain indispensable constituents whose relationship accounts for the development of doctrine itself.

It is worth noting that Drey distinguished a particular role for theologians to play in framing the relationship between the fixed and mobile elements in the development of doctrine. Much in the manner of Schleiermacher, Drey held that "the impulse to further developments [in doctrine] and to the clear determination of concepts . . . can only proceed from individuals,"[19] especially individuals who possess theological talent and a mastery of the skills of the discipline. The theologian, acting on behalf of the Christian community, imaginatively fathoms the faith of the past and—through an appreciation for the present state of ecclesial faith—"reconstructs" the contemporary import and meaning of the ancient belief. For Drey, this reconstructive activity of the theologian at once brings life to a "dead and externally given heap of concepts,"[20] extends the ancient continuity of tradition to modern times, and promotes the ongoing development of Christian tradition. Poised extraordinarily in the dialectical interplay of development by virtue of knowlege, insight, and imagination, the theologian is one whose creativity both reflects and energizes the creativity at work in an authentically living tradition. Though in Drey's judgment the theologian's contributions are indispensable to the development of doctrine, they may never rightly be self-serving but must always be faithful to the historical perichoresis of the fixed and mobile elements of tradition. The theologian, like all believers, is finally responsible to the movement of the Spirit of God in the Church, for this movement is the organic life of tradition.

The Organic Model

The early work of Möhler (1796–1838)—particularly his first book, *Unity in the Church* (1825)—offers the richest illustration of the organic model of tradition. As Drey's most accomplished student, Möhler discovered the suggestive possibilities of the Romantic *Lebensanalogie* in the writings of his teacher, though in the work of the student this imagery serves a more comprehensive theological vision.

Möhler's first reflections on the meaning of tradition appear in his lectures on canon law delivered at the University of Tübingen in the years 1823 to 1825. There, Möhler understood tradition as the "ecclesial truths (*Kirchenglauben*) of the first Christian period to the extent that they are regarded as an instruction that has been considered a pronouncement of Christ or of the apostles and as such has been propagated by oral teaching."[21] Echoing and even perhaps overemphasizing Trent's concern for the integrity of an unwritten, oral tradition, these lectures anticipate the anti-Protestant polemics of his later work *Symbolics* (1832) by noting that "even Holy Scripture is only a part of these [oral] traditions which the apostles received from Christ and propagated."[22] The priority Möhler accorded to oral tradition is not only the basis for an effective argument against the Protestant scripture principle but also an expression of the decidedly inorganic understanding of tradition he seems to have held at this early stage in his theological career. All that we know of Möhler's lectures on canon law comes from their reconstruction through student notebooks, and it would be unfair to make any final judgment on his thought on the basis of such sketchy evidence. But it does at least seem that in these early lectures Möhler conceived of tradition in terms of Stöhr's "rediscovery of origins" or even his "fixed" model. In 1823 Möhler seemed to think of tradition as the passing on of a divine truth that lies forever pristine in its primal form, a position incompatible with a notion of tradition as an organic development-in-continuity.[23] By the time of the publication of his first book in 1825, however, Möhler's understanding of tradition had changed considerably.

In *Unity in the Church*, Möhler's thoughts on developing tradition unfold within the work's theocentric, and even more specifically pneumatocentric, ecclesiology. Möhler saw the unity of the Church as visible in its doctrine, its practice, its liturgy, and its hierarchy. But these, and all the visible dimensions of the Church, are manifestations of a deeper and invisible ecclesial unity that dwells in the workings of the Holy Spirit in history. Against deism's rationalistic portrayal of God as mechanistic cause of the natural world, Möhler insisted that the Spirit of God is present to the Church as its very life and that this life imparts to the Church the divine gift of creative power. As we have already seen, Möhler was not the first to recognize the theological value of this organic imagery, which flourished in the intellectual and artistic culture of early nineteenth-century Germany. He was the first among his theological contemporaries, however, to notice how the Romantic rhetoric of organicism could enhance the ancient Pauline metaphor of the Church as the body of Christ.

Paul, Möhler reminded his readers, "calls the totality of believers the body of Christ and thus represents Christ as the animating and shaping principle to which his true followers are related, as the spirit in the human person to the body, as its form, expression, and imprint."[24] But it is important to note that Möhler's reminder is already a novel interpretation, for the somatic analogies in the New Testament passages make no reference to the animated life of the ecclesial community. In 1 Corinthians 12, Paul uses the imagery of the body and its members as a trope for the unity of believers as parts in the whole of the Church. And by introducing the idea of Christ as the head of the body of the Church, the author of Ephesians (4: 15–16) adds to the analogy of whole and parts a powerful symbol of authority that was not explicit in the earlier Pauline letter. Möhler embraced these ancient nuances of the somatic analogy and added to them the explicit assumption that the body is enlivened by the Holy Spirit. "All believers," he claimed, "form . . . the body of Christ and among themselves a spiritual unity, just as the higher principle from which the unity is produced and shaped is only one and the same."[25] The Spirit "cultivates, animates, and preserves" the believing community. It is the "unconquerable, ever-renewing and rejuvenating trove of the principle of new life, the inexhaustible source of nourishment for all."[26]

In Möhler's view, the Holy Spirit is the origin of not only ecclesial unity but also the development of which that unity admits in the tradition of the Church. The Spirit of God enlivens the faith of believers and is the wellspring of their "common, spiritually religious life." This communal life, nothing less than the Church itself, is neither static nor fixed once and for all in some given moment in the ecclesial past. Rather, the communal life of the Church grows and develops in a manner akin to the organic sphere, and tradition is its waxing movement through time. "This spiritual power of life, propagating itself in and bequeathing itself to the Church," Möhler wrote, "is tradition—the inner, mysterious, and inscrutable dimension of this spiritual power."[27] For Möhler, this organic imagery did not entail a simple reversal of the understanding of tradition in his earlier lectures on canon law. Even as the author of *Unity in the Church* portrayed tradition in the most Romantic of ways as the "living Gospel, proceeding from the fullness of the consecrated inner life," he abided by the classical view that the proof of tradition's truth lies in its faithfulness to the teaching of the apostles. And yet the authority of the apostolic age is not conceived in this work simply as a past norm against which the contemporary Church is measured but as itself a living force effulgent in every ecclesial present. "Tradition," Möhler noted in another of the several definitions offered in his 1825 work, "is the expression of the Holy Spirit enlivening the totality of believers, an expression running through all times, living in each moment, and at the same time embodying itself concretely."[28]

Like Drey before him, Möhler believed that the principle of doctrinal development accounts for the organic unity of tradition through the ages, from the normative faith of the apostles to the most recent, consistent, and yet still growing belief of the Christian community. In Möhler's view, traditional development takes place at two levels. At the most particular level, development flourishes in the experience of the individual believer whose religious consciousness matures over a period of time. Therefore, according to Möhler,

> as the divine Spirit did not disappear with the apostles but rather is always present, so too is the apostolic doctrine never something past but, along with the Spirit, present to all times. Yet even in apostolic times this doctrine was not grasped perfectly by each of its hearers, but as something forming itself in each individual at first gradually toward perfect consciousness. Thus, the doctrine in each individual at a given point in time could still appear deficient in various ways and unclear in many relations.[29]

This maturation of the individual believer's living consciousness of Christian truth parallels a grander development that takes place at the level of the entire Christian community, not only as it exists in the present moment but also as it perdures throughout its entire history. Christianity is given to humanity "as a new divine life, and not as a dead concept." Thus, "it is capable of a development and cultivation" that itself will be integrated into tradition's earlier unity.[30]

In Möhler's view, this emphasis on the accommodation of the later to the earlier in the development of tradition does not undermine the newness of Christian tradition but instead authenticates recent development by understanding it in terms of the organic analogy. Just as growth and maturation presuppose the givenness of, and continuity with, an already growing and maturing life, so, too, does doctrinal development already presuppose a living tradition whose vitality is extended and completed in its later development:

> The identity of the consciousness of the Church in the differing moments of its existence in no way, therefore, requires a mechanistic halting of its exis-

tence: *the inner unity of life must be preserved, otherwise it would not be the same Christian Church. The same consciousness develops, the same life unfolds itself ever more; the same consciousness becomes more determinate and ever clearer of itself. The Church achieves the maturity of Christ.*[31]

Within the unity of tradition, then, one can distinguish specific stages in the development of the life of the Church, Möhler citing as examples the teachings of Paul, John, first-century Christianity in general, and the great councils. "Tradition," he insisted, "contains these successive unfoldings of the higher seeds of life through the preservation of the inner unity of life itself."[32]

Were the purpose here a close study of Möhler's understanding of tradition, it would be necessary to consider the many ways he modified the claims of *Unity in the Church* in such later writings as the lectures on church history (1826/1827, 1829/1830) and *Athanasius the Great* (1827).[33] For the present purposes, Möhler's 1825 work is illustrative; it presents a general model of development, a theological theme on which there are many variations that need not be explored here. What, then, were the theological advantages of Möhler's organic model of development and its portrayal of tradition as "living"?

First and foremost, the metaphor's distinction between the inner and outer dimensions of life enabled Möhler to argue, as had Drey, that the Enlightenment critics of Christianity had failed to fathom its inner and essential vitality, the very unity of tradition itself. Second, and along the same lines, the metaphor parried the Enlightenment attack on Christianity by counterattacking what Möhler judged to be the Enlightenment's mechanistic view of God and God's relationship to the world. Third, the metaphor drew on the rhetoric of the intellectual culture of the day and thus provided a currency for theology within that culture. Fourth, its imagery, Möhler believed, could be shown to be consistent with the heritage of the New Testament and, in the words of the book's subtitle, the "spirit of the Church fathers of the first three centuries." Fifth, and of greatest importance for this study's concerns, the organic analogy expressed the growth of tradition in both a direct and a distinctively modern way and did so in a manner that preserved the value of continuity within tradition's growth. The organic model of development enabled the Christian tradition to be represented according to classical sensibilities as a continuous belief and according to modern sensibilities as a developing faith that together constituted the unity of a living tradition.

One further point, which can be made by way of comparison with Drey's dialectical model, is worthy of note here in this brief, illustrative sketch of Möhler's organic model of development. Möhler's approach to development strongly privileges the value of constancy over the value of renewal; unity over plurality; or, in Drey's language, the fixed in tradition over the mobile. And unlike Drey, who insisted on the contributions of individual theological talent to the construction of living tradition, Möhler tended to be suspicious of any individuality that stands out in relief from tradition's organic unity. This is not to say that Möhler failed to appreciate the integrity of individuality in the Church. "If the Catholic principle binds all believers into a unity," he claimed, "then the individuality of the individual (*Individualität des Einzelnen*) may not be negated, for the individual ought to continue as a *living* member in the entire body of the Church." But this enduring individuality of the ecclesial self "only garners the inner Christian principle of life, the inner power of faith, from the totality."[34] Whereas the individual can err by deviating from the tradition, the totality of believers cannot. This freedom from error in the life of the faithful does not lie in a humanly established consensus that sets its own norm for truth but rather in "the totality of the gifts of the Holy Spirit" that dwell "in the totality of believers. . . . Doctrine cannot and may not be considered a human work," Möhler warned, "but rather must be considered a gift of the Holy Spirit."[35]

By implication, the same applies to the development of doctrine. Thus, in *Unity in the Church*, Möhler spoke frequently of "egoistic development" that deviates from tradition, pursuing the selfish and finally heretical impulse that exercises its counterecclesial individuality in a freedom of inquiry that leads to separation from the community of faith and love. Such movement away from the tradition is really no development at all, since it fails to preserve tradition's continuity. Christianity lost to the individualism that characterizes all heresy "would not be conceived as something living but as a dead conceptual array that is neither capable nor in need of development."[36] Quite unlike Drey, whose dialectical model of development valued the productive contributions of ecclesial particularities and even differences to the living truth of tradition, Möhler, it seems, regarded ecclesial particularity as authentic only to the degree that it exudes, expresses, and promotes an already established unity of the Church that is finally the unity of God. In this mystical understanding of tradition, theological insight relinquishes its individuality to a corporate truth, to a "harmony of the individual life with the universal life"[37] in which all proper growth, including doctrinal growth, perpetuates what already has been believed, practiced, and confessed.

The Noetic Model

Even within their respectively dialectical and organic models, Drey and Möhler spoke of the development of doctrine also in analogy to the workings of the mind and thus as an intellectual enterprise. Drey referred to Church doctrine as a "system of concepts" whose development brings an ever greater clarity to Christian belief striving for the completeness of the idea of Christianity itself. Möhler envisaged doctrinal development on a small scale as the gradual refinement of the individual believer's religious consciousness. These are examples of what I call the noetic model of development, which is best illustrated by the influential work of John Henry Newman (1801–1890).

To the best of current scholarly knowledge, *An Essay on the Development of Christian Doctrine* (1845, 2d ed. 1878), by Newman, was not influenced in any direct manner by the earlier work of the German theologians previously considered. In the introduction to his book, Newman made passing mention of his belief—seemingly formed through the report of others—that Continental authors, including Möhler, had written on the subject of the development of doctrine.[38] But there is no cogent evidence that Newman had firsthand knowledge of Möhler's theological reflections on development or even that Möhler or the other Catholic Tübingen theologians were known in any appreciable way at the Oxford of Newman's day.[39] Newman's contribution to the nineteenth-century theology of development, though not the first, deserves appreciation for its insightful recognition of the fact of development itself—a recognition shaped in Newman's historical studies of early Christian tradition—as well as for its unprecedented thoroughness in detailing the traits of genuine development, which he understood as a development-in-continuity.

Although Newman favored noetic imagery in his account of the development of Christian doctrine, it would be wrong to conclude that this approach evinces a subjectivist orientation in his theory. "The idea which represents an object or supposed object," Newman wrote, "is commensurate with the sum total of its possible aspects, however they may vary in the separate consciousness of individuals; and in proportion to the variety of aspects under which it presents itself to various minds is its force and depth, and the argument for its reality."[40] In Newman's estimation, the truthful idea has an objectivity that comes to definition in and through the many ways it may be apprehended. The very multiplicity of subjective perspectives provides content for a more comprehensive explanation that illustrates the idea's "substantiveness and integrity," its "originality and power."[41] An idea of such objectivity possesses "a nature to arrest and possess the mind," and, having taken such hold, "it may be said to have life, that is, to live in the mind which is its recipient."[42] Newman, then, judged the truthful idea to have an organic quality that furnishes the Christian doctrinal tradition with an apt metaphor for its movement in history. Doctrines, like living ideas, take hold of the minds of the masses, causing "a general agitation of thought" and "a time of confusion." This situation produces "conflict" but also productive reflection in which "[n]ew lights will be brought to bear upon the original statements of the doctrine put forward." Doctrines, like living ideas, enter into the court of public opinion where they are weighed, compared, criticized, and revised. And having passed through this evaluative trial, and in proportion to their "native vigour and subtlety," they work themselves into the very assumptions of the community that holds them as true, "strengthening or undermining the foundations of established order."[43] "This process," Newman stated, "whether it be longer or shorter in point of time, by which the aspects of an idea are brought into consistency and form, I call its development, being the germination and maturation of some truth or apparent truth on a large mental field."[44]

The actual doctrines that Newman cited as illustrations of development—Christ, revelation, purgatory, meritorious works, among others—all manifest the traits he ascribed to the development of any idea. Doctrines, like ideas, influence as much as they are influenced, may be stifled as well as promoted in their development, and may be shattered to the complete loss of integrity just as they may come to the richest and most precise refinement in thought and expression. Doctrines that bear the unity of the Christian tradition, though, unlike ideas in general, exhibit a truthful development that can be attributed to the providential design of God. Christianity's natural and true developments "were of course contemplated and taken into account by its Author, who in designing the work designed its legitimate results."[45] Such developments cannot be coerced, for their purposive movement through history is guided by grace and not merely by the thoughts and actions of human persons. Newman assumed that any doctrine communicating the authentic tradition of the Church is yet bound to the workings of historical development within which God's own providential design unfolds. He insisted that "[no] one doctrine can be named which starts complete at first, and gains nothing afterwards from the investigations of faith and the attacks of heresy."[46] History is not a temporal ambit that bears only the possibilities of corruption but is a sphere in which authentic doctrine gathers clarity and strength with the passing of years and through the test of circumstance. And yet, Newman regarded all genuine development as a faithfulness to an earlier tradition, one less clear and less developed perhaps but in any case previous and finally anchored in at least the rudiments of the apostolic tradition itself.

Newman's understanding of doctrinal development, then, locates authenticity primarily in the Christian past—specifically in what Jesus taught the apostles and in what the apostles handed on to subsequent generations of believers—but it yet appreciates the many ways that original teaching comes to further clarification in and as the tradition of the Church. Like an idea that possesses an undefined givenness in mental experience from its first inception and then grows slowly in its definition and clarity with the passing of time, the development of doctrine brings to conceptual and expressive completion what was present, or at least latent, within the original givenness of the earliest faith of the Church.

This orientation to Newman's theory of development locates the very possibility of continuity in the Church's earliest faith, for all development, he assumed, refines that faith's original givenness. Indeed, Newman argued throughout his *Essay on the Development of Christian Doctrine* for what he called the "antecedent probability" of later developments as maturations of the apostolic faith. The "probable" course of argumentation does not offer a final proof or demonstration but instead marshals evidence to claim the reasonableness of historical precedents as causal antecedents of some later event or belief. To judge it antecedently probable, for example, that the doctrine of papal authority is an authentic development of Christianity involves the assemblage of evidence to show that this later doctrinal development at least *could be* a clarification of an early and at least implicit ecclesial belief. As Lash has rightly observed, this style of argumentation is largely negative and apologetic in approach—that is, it makes the case to those who would conclude otherwise that a particular doctrine, papal authority again, for example, is *not* a corruption of the apostolic tradition.[47] This argumentative approach does not require the explicit definition of the earliest Christian faith, as does a premodern understanding of tradition in which later doctrine proves authenticity by faithfully repeating what is perceived to be the distinctive language and conceptualization of the earliest tradition. It only ventures to show that later development has a reasonable antecedent in an early, and perhaps only implicit, Christian faith. As novel as this developmental perspective on the tradition was, however, its most basic assumptions remain classical. The understanding of doctrinal development woven into Newman's antecedently probable style of argumentation regards the very possibility of doctrinal continuity to lie in an orthodox past with which the ecclesial present must accord in order to be a truthful, developed expression of faith.

Newman saw the development of doctrine that antecedently probable argumentation charts and justifies as a process that is "homogeneous, expanding and irreversible."[48] As revelation proceeds, he observed, "it is ever new, yet ever old."[49] Revelation is ever new in its historical development that brings to clarification what came before. But this development remains ever old, since it is an ancient apostolic revelation that comes to fuller expression and in the face of which no new revelation is possible. In this regard, it is correct to say that Newman's theory of development does not allow for progress in revelation if progress suggests a material advance from the earlier to the later in the process of development. Indeed, Newman showed himself to be an unabashed Platonist in his use of the noetic analogy, for he judged the "idea" of Christian truth to be essentially whole from the beginning and thus regarded doctrine's historical development as in some way ancillary to that eidetic wholeness. Unlike a Platonist, though, Newman took the ancillary character of historicity seriously as a real, extended complement to the idea's essential wholeness. And unlike a Platonist, he saw temporality as productive, as a sphere in which God's revelation—given once and for all in the apostolic age—yet achieved a clarity that its earlier wholeness did not necessarily exhibit. The possibility of real development thus lies in the Christian past in a Platonically framed divine revelation, whereas the actuality of development lies in an ever-unfolding Christian present that brings clarification to revelation's once-given truth.

The greater part of Newman's *Essay* outlines and elaborates through historical illustration what he called seven "notes" or traits of genuine development that distinguish its character as the true teaching of the Church from doctrinal corruption. These notes, when taken together, identify the doctrine of "modern Catholicism" that is "simply the legitimate growth and complement—that is, the natural and necessary development—of the doctrine of the early church."[50] All genuine development preserves the "type" of doctrine that develops, much in the manner that biological maturation involves continuity within a species and not a transition in growth from one species to another. All genuine development exhibits "continuity in principles," the generative assumptions from which doctrines themselves proceed. All genuine development manifests a "power of assimilation," the capacity of a Christian teaching to absorb, and to expand within, the cultural facts of the times and places through which it moves while retaining its unity. In the most direct appeal to the noetic analogy among the seven notes, Newman insisted that all genuine development possesses a "logical sequence" in which later doctrines show themselves to be the reasonable issue of their earlier forms. All genuine development bears an "anticipation of its future," a tendency observable throughout a doctrine's past to strive, as it were, toward fuller expression in its history. Concomitantly, all genuine development is "conservative" of its earlier history, supporting and illustrating, rather than obscuring and correcting, its precedents. And finally, all genuine development—as portrayed in the seventh note—is characterized by a "chronic vigour," the lively perseverance of a doctrine throughout the tradition, its truthfulness providing the energy of its endurance.[51]

An exhaustive study of Newman's *Essay* would consider the typology of the seven notes in greater detail and explore Newman's extensive use of historical example to illustrate the workings of each note in Christian tradition. The purpose in this study requires a more distilled approach that weighs the notes together as a single representation of legitimate doctrinal development, and, in this regard, there are several points to be made. First, the seven notes serve Newman's noetic analogy for the development of doctrine. Although the fourth note of "logical sequence" makes the most explicit appeal to the favored metaphor in Newman's *Essay*, all seven notes catalogue characteristics of an idea's organic growth and thus reflect his commitment to the noetic analogy as an especially apt portrayal of developing tradition.[52] Second, no one of the notes is sufficient to diagnose genuine development. Only the appearance of all together constitutes a healthy syndrome of development in which history provides opportunities for the clarification of the truthful Christian idea. Third, the notes' healthy syndrome is one of doctrinal continuity manifested in the traditional value of "fidelity in the development of an idea."[53] And yet fidelity flourishes in the setting of development, a point exhibited well in the rich, verbal qualities Newman ascribed to the notes themselves to highlight the historical course within which continuity moves. The notes, consequently, name the aspects of the orthodox change that Newman believed development to be.

Newman's homogeneous understanding of authentic tradition is shaped by both noetic and historical interests, but it is the noetic that is privileged in his explanation. A noetic analogy in which an earlier eidetic form is always normatively present in a later one shows itself to be some variant of Platonism, and through the use of such an analogy Newman accounted for the stolid continuity he expected to find in doctrinal development as an expression of the unbroken completeness of Christian truth in history. It is also important to note that Newman's Platonic assumptions regarding the unity of the idea that achieves clarity in time support his largely tacit conception of the nature of the mind in which the idea comes to consciousness with increasing clarity. In Newman's view it is not an individual mind that frames the idea of God's revelation but a collective one that itself manifests the unity it purports to grasp. In Newman's *Essay* as in so many of his other writings, this is the collective mind of the Church, which as a whole thinks the thought of developing doctrine. As a consequence, Newman's theory is not inclined to isolate the contributions of individual imagination to the process of development and thus places little premium, if any at all, on the role of personal theological insight in development.[54] The homogeneity of development presupposes the uniformity of a Catholic community in which the unity of the Church is itself the unity of the doctrinal idea.

The Reception Model

The last example of models of development-in-continuity that have appeared in nineteenth- and twentieth-century Catholic theology is what I call the reception model. In the post-Enlightenment period, classical understandings of traditional meaning have been chastised by modernity's keen sense for the historicity of experience and its interpretation, for the thoroughly hermeneutical situation of meaning in the ever-changing conditions of time, culture, and circumstance. Classical sensibilities often judge this historicist approach to pose a dire threat to the very possibility of meaning. The particularity of culture and circumstance, such sensibilities hold, stands in direct opposition to the universality expected of authentic truth claims. And the transience of the passing moment cannot convey meaning that abides, even for a while.

For historicist sensibilities, there is no such disjunction in principle between historicity and meaning, even a meaning that, historically at least, abides. Just as the passing moment may be judged to stand in meaningful relationship to past moments or to anticipate meaningfully those yet to come, so, too, may continuity be attributed to transient historical experience by imagination, will, reason, or an act of faith. Such a humanly affirmed design may appreciate the conditions of historicity while refusing to succumb to their threat of sheer randomness. Although experience ordered in this way might itself be regarded as an interpretation of reality, still grander interpretations organize meaningful experience into semantic systems that postulate an objectifiable pattern in the flow of time or propose ways of understanding relationships between experience's parts and its whole, between its particular and universal dimensions, and between its practical and theoretical orientations. These semantic interpretations, precisely because they are configured in language, are even more manifestly subject to historicity and thus prompt the classicist fear of aimless time more readily than the historicity of experience. Their public face makes their genealogies easier to detail, their assumptions easier to unravel, and their developmental course easier to plot and explain as a capricious history of cause and effect. Nevertheless, the same historicist claims for the meaning of interpreted experience can and have been made for interpreted expression. Interpretation, in any case, ever journeys across this field of historicity, never meeting its timeless boundaries or making permanent abode within its vast landscape.

The reception model of development aligns tradition with historicity by understanding the act of "handing down" within the transience of time, culture, and circumstance and by affirming a continuity that still abides amid the flux. One can understand the "reception" named in this model of development in two distinct and yet related ways. On one hand, reception is, in the words of Congar, an "ecclesiological reality"[55] rooted in the historical dynamics of the act of faith itself. On the other hand, reception is a hermeneutical practice especially distinguished in theology's ongoing contributions to ecclesial tradition.

Regarded as an ecclesiological reality, reception refers to the ongoing acceptance of the teaching of scripture and tradition that takes place in the experience of the Church, as contemporary believers acknowledge in individual and communal acts of faith the truth of divine revelation handed down to them by previous generations of believers. But this acceptance, in which the Church embraces its past as its own meaningful present, cannot receive the past unchanged. Differences in time, culture, and circumstance—the very conditions of historicity—accompany any act of historical reception, especially those in which reception takes place over a great expanse of time, space, and circumstance. The meaningful negotiation of these differences in any particular act of ecclesial reception presupposes that the tradition, in being received, is no longer simply what it once was. The reception of the fourth-century Council of Nicea's profession of faith at the Council of Constantinople some fifty-six years later, for example, not only brought Nicea's teaching on the Father-Son relationship into the more developed Trinitarian confession of Constantinople's Nicene Creed but also sanctioned more powerfully the authority of the earlier council. The recitation of vernacular translations of Constantinople's Nicene Creed in contemporary liturgies may lead communities, in this simple act of reception, to wrestle with or to avoid the problems of exclusive and inclusive gender language and in either case to interpret the Nicene Creed and, through it, the mystery of the Trinitarian God in a way that was unimaginable at the Council of Constantinople. Within this process of reception, the development that takes place as a matter of course is a continuous one in which the age-old faith is communicated to subsequent generations. As continuous, this development is relatively stable, maintaining its unity by a consistency in language and practice that extends through time, culture, and circumstance, if only and certainly most important of all by the claims of faith that the same tradition has been received. And yet the historicity of time, culture, and circumstance poses difference, and thus change, as the inevitable concomitants of this continuity and permeates the ecclesial interpretation that is every act of reception.

Regarded as a hermeneutical practice, reception involves the self-consciously interpretive work of theology and its role in doctrinal development. Even if Möhler's organic and Newman's noetic models covered over the contributions of individual theological insight with the broad strokes of Catholic tradition, the previous three models as *theological* accounts of development-in-continuity all attest to the contributions of theology in this regard. In spite of theology's best efforts to interpret historicity as tradition, its own classical heritage has shaped its response to the challenge of hermeneutical reception in an interesting way. The natural sciences often granted themselves immunity from the interpretive constraints of historicity, and the social sciences and other humanities disciplines respectively originated as explanations of historicity or eventually left behind their classical self-understandings to make their peace with historicist assumptions. Theology, in contrast, has had to acknowledge the historicity of interpretation while at the same time maintaining its loyalty to its traditional subject matter—the abiding, absolute truth of God and the revelation of that truth in scripture and tradition. And as much as the flux and particularities of historicity may be acknowledged within scripture and tradition themselves, and thus within their interpretation, theology that remains within the assumptions of the Church affirms the inspired truth of God's revelation and therefore cannot accept the terms of historicist interpretation entirely as they might be set by the other disciplines. The tension between revealed truth and historicist hermeneutics accounts for a certain ambivalence in modern theology's interpretive practice, and this ambivalence has been heightened as some theological approaches emphasize the traditional doctrine of revelation and others the inescapability of interpretation and the need for revision and relevance.

Theology's modern ambivalence is a manifestation of the same tension between authoritative continuity and the prospect of corrosive change that faith works to reconcile in the act of ecclesiological reception. This reception brings the threat of change into the scope of ecclesial assumptions so that the historicity of faith can be represented as a development-in-continuity. Reception as a hermeneutical practice is capable of the same reconciliation. Just as ecclesiological reception affirms the continuity of faith within and throughout the vicissitudes of historicity, reception as a hermeneutical practice affirms the normativeness of scripture and tradition within theology's ongoing efforts at interpretive reconstruction. And just as ecclesiological reception views the otherwise capricious life of the present moment as an opportunity for tradition, reception as a hermeneutical practice sees in historicity concrete occasions for divine revelation to be brought to life through systematic reflection and to be renewed as theological knowledge.

These interpretive acts promulgate the development of doctrine in three ways. First, theological reflection is a self-conscious act of reception devoted to rendering the Christian past intelligible as the Christian present. In this regard, theology is a hermeneutics of tradition that develops doctrine through acts of understanding, criticism, and appreciation. Second, certain theological interpretations sometimes garner authority with the passing of time and come to be invested by the believing community with the status of tradition. In this case, a theological hermeneutics itself becomes tradition and assumes a place of prominence as what is received in the developing historicity of the Church. Third, theological interpretation, at least in the modern period, promulgates the development of doctrine by explaining the entire tradition as a particular model of doctrinal development. The models of development considered herein are all examples of reception on a grand scale, in which what is received is a particular understanding of the workings of tradition. In this account, tradition itself is presented as a theological hermeneutics. So explained, reception as an ecclesiological reality shows itself to be closely related to reception as a hermeneutical practice, much in the manner that reception as theological interpretation is an important expression of ecclesiological life.

These two distinguishable and yet intimately related conceptions of reception portray doctrinal development as the productive historicity of the present moment, since it is in the present that the meaningful reception of tradition occurs. But if the reception model is appreciated fully, then its account of present reception must be extended to every moment in the tradition's past that in its own day flourished as a present reception of the tradition and a development of doctrine. This insight provides a fuller understanding of the dynamics of reception.

In his classical study of ecclesial reception, Congar coined the term "re-reception" to speak of the Church's continuing encounter with the meaning of tradition's dogmas. He cited as examples the new appreciation of Chalcedon's teaching on the person of Christ in light of contemporary biblical scholarship and Vatican II's contextualized reading of Vatican I in which the minority position of the nineteenth century appeared as the avant-garde in the twentieth century.[56] One would do well to extend Congar's conceptualization of re-reception further than he did, along the lines previously suggested. After all, if contemporary christological reflection on Chalcedon and Vatican II's ecclesiological appropriation of Vatican I's entire conciliar record can be offered as illustrations of *re*-reception, then so can Chalcedon's reception of an earlier conciliar and patristic christological tradition and Vatican I's reception of late Medieval and Tridentine ecclesiological options. Moreover, the same character of tradition as re-received applies to the doctrinal precedents of Chalcedon and Vatican I. This extended understanding of re-reception acknowledges the fine detail of historicity in the etching of tradition.

Historicity in this account no longer appears as a threat to tradition but as a context in which tradition unfolds. To the degree that historicity is placed within the scope of divine providence, it becomes a temporocultural stage on which the Spirit of God enacts the drama of tradition along with a numerous supporting cast of believers that draws its ranks from every generation and from every place the gospel is proclaimed and lived. The reception model of doctrinal development, like the previous three, understands tradition as a growth occasioned by changing times, cultures, and circumstances that attend reception—each act of authentic reception making the tradition more than it previously was in the explicitness, relevance, and appreciation of its teaching.[57] Typically, the growth that characterizes the development of doctrine in the reception model is attributed to the act of reception and not to what is received.

The best-known and certainly most influential expression of this distinction occurs in John XXIII's October 11, 1962 speech convening the Second Vatican Council:

> But from the renewed, serene, and tranquil adherence to all the teaching of the Church in its entirety and preciseness, as it still shines forth in the Acts of the Council of Trent and First Vatican Council, the Christian, Catholic, and apostolic spirit of the whole world expects a step forward toward a doctrinal penetration and a formation of consciousness in faithful and perfect conform-

ity to the authentic doctrine, which, however, should be studied and expounded through the methods of research and through the literary forms of
modern thought. The substance of the ancient doctrine of the deposit of faith
is one thing, and the way in which it is presented is another.[58]

In effect, these words at once recognize the productive value of historicity for
the development of doctrine and guard against historicity's corrosive power
by distinguishing between a content of tradition untouched by historicity and
a form into which tradition is received and in which historicity is ecclesially
domesticated by tradition's truthful substance. Magisterial teaching since the
Second Vatican Council—particularly in the declaration of the Congregation
for the Doctrine of the Faith, *Mysterium ecclesiae* (June 24, 1973)[59]—has reiterated this distinction between form and content as the surest way of acknowledging the legitimate development of tradition that occurs in ecclesiological and hermeneutical reception while protecting the unchanging
truthfulness of the deposit of faith.[60]

Finally, it is important to note that these two distinguishable but related
concepts of reception can suggest different emphases on the role of individual
contributions to the development of doctrine. On one hand, because theology
is a self-consciously interpretive enterprise and thus—at least at its best—
aware of the power, limits, and responsibilities of human creativity at work
in all interpretation, reception as a hermeneutical practice is inclined to value
individual initiative in interpretive reception. The theological interpreter holds
an important and influential place in a reception model of development, for
it is the theologian's imagination that offers possible explanations of historicity
as tradition for the Church. Yet, by sublating creative imagination in a theological interpretation that highlights the authority of the received tradition
to such a degree that the act of reception—which always does in fact involve
change—is portrayed as negligible, even the hermeneutical version of reception can reflect the sensibilities of the organic and noetic models. Reception
as an ecclesiological reality, on the other hand, is inclined to diminish the
role of individual initative in reception, since it typically understands reception
to unfold finally in a corporate act of faith, the *sensus fidei*, in which individuality does not stand out in relief from the community. And yet here, too, in
a parallel fashion, a minority trait is discernible within the emphasis. To the
degree that the communal act of faith that makes for ecclesiological reception
is itself drawn from individual acts of faith in which past tradition meets
present historicity, the contributions of individual believers to the development of doctrine at least need not be judged entirely negligible and at most
might be seen as exemplary and influential instances of corporate reception.

The Modern Models and the
Problem of Prospectivity

These four basic accounts of development-in-continuity have exerted a powerful influence on understandings of tradition and the theological enterprise

in the nineteenth and twentieth centuries. One might go so far as to say that their effect on the modern Christian self-understanding has been revolutionary. The models together represent the efforts of theological reflection to salvage the orthodoxy of premodern Christian belief for an era in which the assumptions of historical consciousness have been undeniable for all but the fundamentalist and irresistible for those who have embraced modernity's critical perspective. Even for those who stand uncomfortably between the positions of fundamentalism and historical consciousness, the principle of doctrinal development remains a formidable explanation whose cogency is the very source of traditionalist discomfort. In addition to their apologetical value, the models of development are a creative response to the facts of actual doctrinal change as they have been uncovered by a scholarly approach to the discipline of church history. Nineteenth- and twentieth-century historians have shown that ancient and medieval Christians have not believed the same things in every respect and in the same ways, even when the belief in question lay at the heart of the tradition itself. The models of development have been effective explanations of how this irrefutable variance in belief that only appears as change in the historian's cold eye can be understood as a development-in-continuity, and thus as tradition, through the eyes of faith.

As much as the nineteenth- and twentieth-century models of development-in-continuity have contributed to a modern understanding of tradition, no one of them or all of them together could serve the presentation of the senses of tradition offered here. Although each possesses certain virtues that the constructive efforts of this study seek to promote, all share a vice that its reconstruction of development-in-continuity must avoid if it is to explain the workings of tradition well. An adequate account of development-in-continuity will be one that is faithful to classical Catholic beliefs regarding the authority and normativeness of tradition, that reconciles theological explanation with the scholarly evidence of change in the history of doctrine and practice, and that can stand in meaningful relationship to the other senses of tradition that speak of developments discontinuous with the past. In order to meet these criteria of adequacy, this account of development-in-continuity must affirm the traditional value of constancy while refraining from explaining this value in terms of what I call the "prospectivity" of the modern models—a trait that the modern models share with the classical conception of tradition. If this study acknowledges a measure of compatibility between the dialectical and reception models in their particular regard for the authority of the present, and a measure of compatibility between the organic and noetic models in their particular regard for the authority of the past, then the dialectical and organic models can be invoked here to illustrate the virtues of the modern models that the theory of tradition presented herein should incorporate and the prospectivity that it should avoid.

The dialectical model has much to offer this study's reconstruction of development-in-continuity. Like all four models, the dialectical model recognizes the historicity of tradition, though only it and a certain understanding of the reception model embrace historicity with open arms. Much in the manner of a reception model appreciative of tradition's contemporary relevance, the dialectical model understands tradition as a rich and ongoing conversation between the established and the emerging faith of the Church. The model's understanding of the present moment as the renewable context for meaningful encounter with the Christian past is an imaginative way of portraying the growth of doctrinal development. The model assumes that nothing of the orthodox past is left behind in this development. And yet the premium it places upon theological creativity and its responsibility to the contemporary experience of the Christian community in framing the movement of a living tradition assumes that growth is not simply the repetition of an original givenness but its real and ongoing maturation. Even though the intellectual interests of philosophy—Friedrich Schelling's in particular[61]—and not history, provide a template for Drey's explanation, his model explains well the pluralistic and at times conflictual give-and-take of discourse and events in church history that neither historical-critical reasoning nor an adequate theory of tradition may ignore.

As much as the dialectical model contributes to the model of development herein, it does have drawbacks that are better avoided in our reconstruction. First, the dialectical model's willingness to take the pluralistic exchange of historical positions and events seriously might suggest that opposition, and perhaps even heresy, is a necessary context for the flowering of orthodox truth. Hans Urs von Balthasar, following Karl Barth, is correct in condemning this view that makes falsity somehow an aid to the promotion of Christian truth, as though falsity were the surreptitious work of grace and not the consequence of sin.[62] Second, the appreciation of theological imagination in this model might suggest that individuals, even theologically talented individuals, speak for the tradition. Drey insisted that theological creativity is rightly understood only as faithful insight into the workings of the Spirit of God in tradition and in the Church. And yet there is no denying that the value placed on theological creativity particularly in this model and in some versions of the reception model has been regarded with much suspicion on the part of the magisterium in the nineteenth and twentieth centuries—and occasionally for good reason.[63] An adequate model of development-in-continuity must affirm the creativity of theologians, and all believers for that matter, as a faithful rendition of Catholic anthropology in which personal cooperation always accompanies the prevalence of grace, without either exaggerating that creative power or severing its responsibilities to the tradition it serves.

Third among this study's reservations about the dialectical model is its rather unnuanced understanding of the dogmatic past as finished. For Drey, all doctrinal development seems to have a telos in what he called its "completed" state as a recognized dogma of the Church. Drey judged tradition in such a state to be "fixed" and in itself felicitously incapable of further development. This most authoritative doctrine possesses an utterly settled character as the traditional past. But this conception of the traditional past runs the risk of obscuring how ongoing doctrinal development can modify the Church's understanding of its hitherto accepted tradition. The achievement of Drey's model that brings it distinction as the first modern Catholic theory of doctrinal development is the importance it accords to the "mobile" aspect of tradition and thus to the ways the tradition continues to unfold here and now. But the fixed aspect of tradition remains as immobile as any past facticity, and Drey's model expects orthodox continuity to be constituted in the extension of tradition's fixed aspect to mobile doctrine truthful enough to be ranked as the dogmatic past in some future time. As committed as Drey's dialectical model is to the reciprocal relationship of past and present faith as the sustenance of living tradition, it attributes authority and continuity to a traditional past that is finished and complete and therefore in itself impervious to the development that only a certain, separable dimension of tradition undergoes.

This same regard for the unchanging authority of the past is expressed even more forcefully in Möhler's organic model of development. The organic model's principal strengths are its clear representation of the traditional value of constancy; its recognition of the historicity of a developing tradition expressed in compelling imagery of growth; and the power of that imagery to convey a sense for the unity of the Spirit of God at work in the Church, guiding its traditional journey through the ages. These are qualities that any model of doctrinal development would aspire to make its own, even if not in ways that exactly follow Möhler's.[64] Less worthy of imitation is Möhler's suspicion of individual creativity in the workings of development, a suspicion that finally can be attributed to the theocentric perspective he has adopted in his theology of tradition. Möhler's organic model finds such exclusive cause for the growth of tradition in the animating force of the Spirit that there is little room alongside pneumatic power for human cooperation that is anything more than sheer receptivity for the divine activity. Doctrinal development depicted in this fashion runs the risk of attributing so much to divine grace that human responsibility is unduly diminished.

The organic analogy well serves a theory of doctrinal development precisely because it presents the growth of tradition as a maturation in which an earlier form of ecclesial life is completed in a later one. The analogy thus aptly accounts for the historical continuity of a tradition grounded in an original and once-given revelation. But to the degree that a theocentric perspective informs the organic analogy, development becomes the manifestation of an inexorable continuity in which the unity of an unchanging past—itself the reflection of God's oneness—appears in new times and places that are susceptible to the same unity. In Möhler's theocentric-organic model, tradition is a harmonious chord struck long ago that brooks no dissonance within its single tone. Tradition's harmony resonates in history, and hearing its resonance may admit of some of the variation inherent in the acoustics of historical life. But no particular hearing, or all of them together, may change the original register, and every hearing, to be true, must finally be attuned to the once-struck harmonious chord.

This way of privileging the past to account for the continuity and thus normativeness of belief, doctrine, and practice results in what I call a "prospective" conception of tradition. A prospective conception regards tradition as finished or completed and locates its finished or completed character in what has already transpired in its past. Premodern or classical prospectivity views tradition as a truthful deposit of faith handed down unchanged to later generations. Modern or Romantic prospectivity sees tradition as a development that manifests but the historical nuances of an original apostolic truth. Aside from Newman's allusion to clarification, neither premodern nor modern forms of prospectivity specifically use optical imagery in conveying their shared assumption about tradition's finished or completed character. And yet an optical metaphor is especially helpful in appreciating the prevalence of this conception in Christian history, perhaps because the very notion of Christian tradition suggests the purposive "seeing" of divine providence. A prospective conception of tradition is "forward looking." Its perspective is situated in an authoritative past—in classical terminology, the apostolic age—and, from that point, the integrity of tradition emerges from a historical prospecting for the continuity of God's revelation in later times and places. The classical or premodern version of this prospectivity thinks of these instantiations as hand-to-hand transmissions of the original revelation that carefully preserve God's truth from corruption in a fallen history, whereas the Romantic or modern version thinks of these instantiations as malleable appearances of God's truth in a more benign history whose change is now understood as development. But in both cases, tradition is conceived prospectively as a "looking forward." The apostolic truth that tradition promulgates, one might say, is imagined as an observer looking across history for self-reflections in texts, rituals, persons, and events. And whether these self-reflections are regarded as static receptions (premodern) or developmental disclosures (modern), they are judged to be tradition from the ancient stance and perspective of apostolic truth as the imagined observer.

The optic at work in this prospective conceptualization skews the ordinary conditions of time and space. As apostolic truth is personified as observer and judge, its glance across the span of tradition proceeds not from the present but from the authoritative past or, better, from a past that functions as an ever-recurring present. Like any human gaze, this observer's temporal line of sight across tradition ends at the horizon of the future. Yet, unlike that of human vision, the intervening landscape in this observer's visual field is the actual present moment that now is surveyed from a hypostatized, unchanging past in which the observer—a personified traditional authority—always stands, surveying the entirety of tradition from its own definitive perspective. Traditional continuity derives from the unity of this all-embracing perspective, which takes its point of departure from the apostolic age. What a personified apostolic truth might "see" across this landscape may change, but its perspective—a past that functions as an ever-recurring present—cannot. In this regard, authority in a prospective conception of tradition would be as resistant to change as would the stance—and thus the perspective—of an observer who surveys distant objects, whether they are fixed or moving.

If this analogy is at all apt, then it should also be clear that the personified truth imagined as the observer in a prospective conception of tradition is the Spirit of God itself. Prospective conceptions of tradition, then, take a divine perspective in their regard for the tradition.[65] They imagine the historical sweep of tradition from the standpoint of its earliest period and the authority attributed to it. The result is that tradition is conceived in terms quite unlike the ways in which tradition is actually experienced within the conditions of human historicity by the same conceivers. Although one can imagine a tradition seen through God's eyes, it would be much more appropriate to regard tradition through the eyes of faith—from a standpoint that is always the actual present from which the divine Spirit at work in history can be perceived only "in a mirror, dimly" (1 Cor. 13:12). This is the approach that this study commends.

It is not difficult to understand why prospectivity has been the preferred, and indeed exclusive, conceptualization of tradition. Prospective conceptions of tradition offer the most lucid way of expressing the Christian belief in the absolute and universal truth of the Word of God. As a theocentric perspective, prospectivity assumes a privileged vantage point in order to judge, seemingly with the least ambiguity, whether or not particular instances of handing down or development are indeed continuous with revealed truth. The prospective conceptualization is a way of asserting the continuous clarity of tradition as a faithful rendering of the truth of Jesus Christ taught to the apostles and by them to the whole Church. A prospective tradition does much to protect the absolute and universal truth of divine revelation from either the slippage that could ensue in hand-to-hand transmission or the relativization that could more easily accompany historical development. Its stance in configuring tradition remains a pristine past in which truth is not yet subject to corruption. Whereas the Catholic belief in the absolute and universal truth of God's once-given revelation is basic and indispensable, the prospective conception of tradition that has sheltered that belief is not. The Catholic belief in a closed revelation need not, and should not, extend to belief in a finished or completed tradition, if only because tradition continues in history.

The prospectivity of premodern and modern understandings of tradition stems from the perceived value of this conceptualization in explaining tradition's authoritative continuity. Because historical studies and hermeneutical theories respectively show that what the Church now regards as tradition in fact did not and in principle could not have been so regarded in earlier times, the modern appreciation for the historicity of belief, doctrine, and practice has made the classical version of prospective continuity difficult—if not impossible—to maintain. The Romantic version of prospectivity, which makes continuity an abiding constant within development, is the modern theological response to the untenability of the classical version. Möhler's organic and theocentric model of developing tradition highlights this modern prospectivity to the greatest degree. But to some extent it is a feature of all four models of development. The prospectivity of the dialectical model lies in the authority that Drey extended to the fixed aspect of doctrine and to the priority accorded to fixed dogma in the definition of traditional orthodoxy.[66] The prospectivity of Newman's noetic model appears in the Platonic cast of his eidetic analogy. The explicit or implicit unity of the Christian idea occupies the prospective standpoint in the apostolic age, and development through clarification—an ocular metaphor—is measured against the objectivity of this idea that finally is God's. The prospectivity of the reception model surfaces in its distinction between form and content, the latter conceived as the unchangeable truth of tradition and the former as the changing conditions of receptivity. In this modern hylomorphism in which content functions as a stalwart actuality and form as an adaptable potentiality, traditional content becomes the primeval observer surveying history for opportune receptions that faithfully preserve content's integrity, the steadfastness of its gaze unchanged by what it sees and even by what in reception it becomes.

The prospective orientation of both classical and Romantic understandings of tradition reflects the Catholic commitment to the importance of continuity in the claims of tradition. And yet, as this study's analysis has suggested, prospectivity is a problematic conceptualization of tradition on at least two counts. First, premodern and modern prospectivity require that tradition be imagined from a divine point of view and not in the ways it is actually experienced by believers in history. If the Catholic belief in traditional continuity could be conceived in terms consistent with the actual experience of believers and yet still in a manner that did not compromise the continuity of divine truth, then this conceptualization would have an advantage over prospective explanations. Second, premodern prospective continuity cannot be reconciled with the facts of history or hermeneutical insights on the workings of human understanding. Modern prospective continuity can achieve such reconciliation only by resorting to metaphysical explanation that makes traditional content latent in the history of changing forms. If the Catholic belief in traditional continuity could be conceived in terms consistent with both the facts of history and an adequate hermeneutics and yet still in a manner that did not compromise the continuity of divine truth, then this conceptualization would have an advantage over prospective explanations. The section that follows sketches an understanding of development-in-continuity that I call a "retrospective" conception of tradition.[67] This understanding of development possesses both of the advantages just noted and serves the larger interpretive scheme of this study as the second sense of tradition.

A retrospective conception of tradition measures continuity not by taking a divine stance in the original event of Christian revelation and imagining traditional time from a privileged, timeless point of view; rather, it does so by envisaging tradition from the actual limitations of the present moment and "looking back" to the Christian past to configure traditional continuity. A retrospective conception of tradition, like any modern model, represents tradition as a development or growth. Here, though, development is always acknowledged, believed, and, in faith, understood within the conditions of the present moment. This present moment, then, and not an idealized past *in illo tempore* imagined as a divine present, becomes the retrospective point of orientation in tradition's visual field. And as the present-day observer surveys the past of a developing tradition, continuity shows itself in retrospect, initially in the judgments of individual believers and eventually in the shared judgment of all together.

Although all the modern models of developing tradition are prospective to a greater or lesser degree, some are also retrospective in the same varying measure. The dialectical model is retrospective in the relative authority it accords to present doctrinal mobility that looks back to the fixed, dogmatic past in order to assess the relationship between traditional continuity and development. Newman's noetic model exhibits a retrospective orientation in the distinctiveness of its antecedently probable argumentation that looks back into the Christian past from a present standpoint in the development of doctrine to find in the past at least implicit precedents to current development that might justify claims for the continuity of tradition. Of all the modern theories, the reception model bears the closest resemblance to the retrospective conception of tradition. In its regard for development as an interpretive consequence of historicity, the reception model is inclined to link continuity closely to the conditions of development. And since the act of reception occurs only in the present moment, receptive believers must look back to the past from the standpoint of the present in order to ponder the ongoing continuity of the tradition.

One might be inclined to object at this point that, because the classical conception of tradition and Möhler's organic model of development concede the highest degree of authority to the Christian past and must thus highlight past authority in any judgment about the authentically traditional present, these explanations are most truly retrospective. Certainly the classical and organic conceptions "look back" to the past for normative direction, as any conception of tradition does. But if the current understanding of tradition can be enhanced at all by the use of these visual metaphors, then it is important to appreciate the way each metaphor highlights perspective and its role in defining traditional continuity. The classical and organic conceptions of tradition look back to the past, though specifically to the apostolic age that immediately becomes the point of orientation in tradition's visual field and from which traditional continuity can now be surveyed prospectively. This is a naïve or uncritical retrospection in which the observer flees the conditions of historicity for the sake of a divine, though only imagined, perspective. A retrospective conception of tradition always makes the actual present moment its standpoint and from this human perspective looks back to the Christian past for a continuity that cannot be surveyed across a finished past but is instead glimpsed continually in and as tradition's development. This critical retrospection blocks prospectivity by situating its regard for the past realistically and by remembering that tradition is no more finished than the history in which it unfolds.

A Retrospective Conception of Tradition

A retrospective conception of tradition approaches the task of accounting for a graceful history by distinguishing between the workings of the Spirit of God in tradition and the *recognition* of the Spirit's workings in a particular understanding of developing tradition. Prospective conceptions tend to blur this appropriate distinction by assuming too quickly a supernatural perspective and by representing tradition from this divine standpoint. Portraying the tradition retrospectively involves a more modest approach to a theology of tradition, one properly aware that the activity of the Holy Spirit in tradition remains mysterious, even when that activity can be represented as tradition's literal sense. The divine activity is even more mysterious, and as a result ambiguous, when it is represented as the sense of development-in-continuity and as the other senses of tradition considered in subsequent chapters. In its efforts to convey a sense for the activity of the Spirit in history, a retrospective approach to tradition, then, is aware of its own hermeneutical character. Recognitions of the Spirit's activity as at once continuous and developing are functions of the experience of faith and are thus as interpretive as any human experience. Representations of the Church's experience of development-in-continuity in a particular schematism of tradition must reflect the interpretive character of subjectivity and must manifest as well the even more markedly interpretive traits of objective, symbolic expression.

This interpretive awareness, which refuses to conflate a claim for the divine activity as tradition with the divine activity itself, stems from the retrospective model's commitment to representing the tradition as a development-in-continuity always from the standpoint of the passing present moment. If we take the present seriously as the inescapable point of departure for any configuring of tradition, then we must say that any grander description of the development-in-continuity of God's revelation in history begins in an act of faith in *this* time, in *this* place, and in *these* circumstances. The act of faith as it unfolds in this or that faithful life is a regional experience, one bound by the general conditions of historicity but also by the fine detail in which these conditions make their way into a human life through the particularities of demeanor, memory, relationships, tragedy, success, love, loss of hope, anger, forgiveness, and a host of others—all occasions of sin and grace in which faith is formed in this way or that as it shapes its orientation toward God in life. Faith is not an individualistic experience. As an orientation toward God, faith is the experience of a relationship and, as Martin Buber has reminded us, it is the experience of the primary relationship in the realm of personal existence.[68] Moreover, faith has communal dimensions that are not only the consequence of faith's desire to share its encounter with God but also the context in which the act of faith emerges and in which it continues to be sustained. Indeed, one might describe the desire to represent tradition as faith's yearning for its communal heritage. And yet, even if faith is not individualistic, there is no denying that faith occurs in life as an individual's experience and as such possesses a regionality, a limitedness, and a particularity that is characteristic of the act of faith itself—traits of the subjective encounter with God that need to be valued and appreciated for the many ways they manifest the religious life.

So distinctive is this regional character of faith that its traits might be ascribed as well to the community's apprehension of faith, which is bound just as much by the fine details of historicity that ever unfold in the present moment. Although there is rightly an inclination in the Catholic tradition to portray the faith of the Church as a unity throughout times and places, one should not overlook the extent to which that unity actually appears in regional ways in individuals, in communities, and even in *the* community of the whole Church. Even the faith of the whole Church is always experienced in a determinate way with the passing of each moment, an appreciation for the particularity of faith in history that increases as one envisages the sedimentation that this universal faith possesses in local communities and in the smallest reaches of the individual's encounter with God. Here is where a retrospective conception of tradition takes its stand—in the regional character of tradition's present moment that is reflected in not only the individual believer's experience but also every possible dimension of the life of faith.

Tradition is recognized, and in the community of recognition affirmed, from the perspective of regional acts of faith as these acts of faith look back to the past to find occasions for continuity in the beliefs and practices of the previous generation, a fourteenth-century generation, a fourth-century generation, or—and above all—a first-century generation of Christians. Since continuity is a relationship that can be postulated only through a judgment made in the present moment, the continuity in which tradition is established can be affirmed only retrospectively from a present standpoint.[69] The tradition *can* be, and we have seen that it typically is, imagined prospectively. At its best, this prospective conceptualization is a way of picturing clearly the unity of tradition in which Catholic belief places much stock. At its worst, though, the prospective conceptualization disguises the retrospective way in which tradition is actually encountered within the limitations of present faith. Moreover, as the current analysis proceeds, it will become clear that the prospective conception obscures the interpretive pluralism suggested by multiple senses of tradition and thus diminishes the richness of meaning that tradition might otherwise convey.

Recognizing continuity with past belief and practice involves the retrospective gaze of a regional act of faith. But it is important to note that what this gaze falls upon and what it sees relation to were themselves, in their own present moment, regional acts of faith bound to their own time, place, and circumstances and experienced as the faith of the whole Church—yet in a particular time, a local community, or, initially at least, as the experience of an individual believer. The gospel of John, for example, originally expressed the faith of a Christian community whose belief was to some degree at odds with that of other Christian communities.[70] However imperial its atmosphere, Nicea was but a local council to the bishops in attendance. The thirteenth-century theologian Peter Olivi made questionable arguments in support of a doctrine of papal infallibility that came to dogmatic definition in the nine-teenth century. The judgments that the gospel of John was divine revelation, that Nicea taught orthodoxly on the eternal divinity of the Son of God, and that Olivi's position—questionable in the thirteenth century—was infallible ecclesial faith were made by later Christian communities and eventually by the whole Church searching for and postulating continuity with the past. Tradition emerges in judgments of continuity such as these, which stretch beyond the recognition of the individual or a local community and become the communal recognition of the whole Church—though one that still occurs in the regionality of a particular temporal moment. At this point, the judg-ment of continuity has itself become an act of faith—a belief in the truth, authority, and integrity of tradition. And if that judgment that has now be-come an act of faith recognizes continuity across generations of believers, universality is ascribed to it. And as that universality is believed and practiced in the present moment, it garners meaning in the Church as what I have called the literal sense of tradition.

Here at the heart of a retrospective understanding of development-in-continuity, we meet the literal sense of tradition. As shown in the previous chapter, the literal sense should not be regarded as a static, meaningless letter but as a sensibility whose continuity must continually be renewed in the actual belief and practice of each generation of believers. In light of this study's analysis of the sense of development-in-continuity thus far, it should be clear that a close relationship exists between the first and second senses of tradition. Both are sensibilities that have their telos in the historical work-ings of the Spirit of God, though the literal sense rests more easily in its claims, more confidently in its emphasis on what abides. The literal sense especially appreciates the value of constancy in its regard for tradition but not to the exclusion of the value of renewal. The sense of development-in-continuity especially appreciates the value of renewal but not to the exclusion of the value of constancy. The second sense of tradition is more inclined than the first to attend to the ways in which traditional continuity moves from century to century, generation to generation, and even from moment to moment.

As has been shown, a retrospective conception of development-in-conti-nuity represents traditional continuity not as a relationship that extends pro-spectively from past to present but as a relationship defined by the perspective of the present moment looking back to the past. Considered most simply, continuity is a regional act of faith's recognition of its consistent relationship to a regional act of faith in the past. If this recognition becomes grandly communal, embraced by the whole Church, the continuity is judged in faith to be tradition and is appreciated as the literal sense. The second sense of tradition is more attuned than the first sense to the repetition involved in this recognizing, embracing, and judging in faith—a repetition that can be imag-ined to occur at various intervals of time but that, precisely because it is a function of time, actually occurs without rest. In the context of this repetition, retrospection cannot be halted and hypostatized as a single act of looking backward and recognizing, embracing, and judging in faith. Rather, within the Christian tradition, every retrospection is the gaze of a present regional act of faith that looks back to a previous regional act of faith that in turn looked for continuity in its own past. By the same token, the present act of continuity-recognizing retrospection may, and in all likelihood will, be retrospected for continuity by any number of future acts of tradition-seeking faith whose present points of departure cannot now be anticipated.

Such a thoroughly temporal depiction of development-in-continuity might suggest a proliferation in faith's present searches for traditional meaning too unwieldy to produce more than the weakest, most individualistic, and capricious of continuities. It is important to recall, however, that the act of faith—though most regionally individual—is never properly individualistic and always normatively measured by the faith of the Church. This recollection applies as much to continuity-seeking acts of faithful retrospection in the past as it does to such acts in the present. Thus, an individual act of faith by any present believer may recognize a relational continuity to a past act of faith. That judgment, however, will not take shape as the judgment of tradition unless it is embraced by local communities and eventually by the entire ecclesial community. These same dynamics apply to the past faith that constitutes the object of a present recognition of continuity. It is possible that individual past acts of faith that were never embraced by the community in their own time could be identified as continuous by and with a present act of faith. The more likely eventuality, however, is one in which the retrospected past faith is embraced by tradition-seeking judgment in the present for its authority as a proven communal act of faith that has, in turn, already claimed continuity with its own past. In other words, envisaging the tradition as retrospection means that continuity widens across the ages as present faith looks back to the past and believes in its continuous relationship with previous communities of faith. Tradition is the layering of present affirmations of backward-looking continuity, one on top of the other, to form an overarching continuity defined from the perspective of the current experience of the Church as it takes account of all the belief, practice, insights, and eventualities that lead it to see continuity in one way rather than in another—a perspective that will be redefined in however slight or surprising a way in future repetitions of this process.

Development in tradition occurs as this *same* act of continuity-establishing retrospection. By adopting a prospective approach to tradition, the four modern models of development tend to distinguish between continuity and development as separate realities within the traditioning process. The retrospective model, though, would have no cause to distinguish between continuity and development. What we call the development of doctrine ensues in the repetition of believing in the heritage of faith in which a belief in continuity aligns itself in a particular way to a previous belief in continuity that in its own day did the same. Each present belief in continuity adds its own layer of retrospective continuity to tradition, causing it to "grow" as all four modern models of development recognize, albeit from an idealized prospective stance. It is important to understand this growth interpretively, as the reception model of development does. The premodern understanding of tradition as hand-to-hand transmission lucidly expresses the communication of belief and practice from generation to generation. But the prospectivity of this understanding regards this "handing down" as the tradition-constituting act. "Handing down," an undeniable fact in all aspects of cultural life, is better conceived as the possibility of tradition that becomes an actuality—an opportunity for tradition that may be seized—only in the present communal judgment of continuity. This communal judgment receives the past in a certain, determinate way that in its particularity establishes a new sense of continuity even when to all intents and purposes the present judgment of continuity does not seem to be different at all from the continuity handed down. Traditional continuity is a development, and, through this identity of continuity and development, the development affirmed as tradition is regarded as continuous.

In this holistic understanding, the distinction between the form and content of tradition affirmed by the magisterium and many theologians after Vatican II as a way of recognizing doctrinal development while preserving the authority of the past no longer explains the workings of tradition well. If traditional continuity is itself development and traditional development the ever-repeated judgment of continuity, then there is no way to distinguish between an isolatable continuous content that serves as the essence of tradition and a historical, contingent form in which content is manifested. Although this distinction intends to maintain the authority of the Christian past, here identified by the rubric of content, it does so in a manner that is hermeneutically indefensible. There is no experience of a hypostatized "content" of tradition transcending its historical expression or of a distinguishable form that in principle could be "filled in" in this way or that. A hermeneutics based on those assumptions may be interested in promulgating a theory of interpretation intelligible in the thought world of Aristotelianism or Romanticism or in laying the groundwork for authorial responsibility to an "objective" subject matter.[71] But doing so requires an abstract distinction that prescinds from the way in which tradition, or any subject matter, is actually encountered as an interpretive concern. Tradition is a historical reality. It unfolds in an incarnational world in which the Word has already become flesh and now eternally possesses an inseparable, unsubstitutable concrescence of humanity that stands as a condition of Christian knowledge of the divine. Tradition's truth cannot stand apart abstractly from the conditions of historicity. Rather, the claims of tradition are a posteriori and can be made and interpreted only as they are really experienced—that is, in particular determinations of faith seeking their communal heritage and in which "form" and "content" name the same, present, retrospective configuration of developing continuity. In this regard, distinguishing instead between the values of constancy and renewal, qualities of the first two senses of tradition, captures the impetus of the content-form distinction without falling into its error. Constancy and renewal are aspects of the same, single reality of tradition that stand in mutual relation and that, respectively, name the traditioned values ascribed to continuity and development. Whereas the content-form distinction identifies the substance of tradition with content and historicity with form, the values of constancy and renewal are both dimensions of tradition that, respectively, might achieve emphasis as the literal sense or the sense of development-in-continuity, though always as senses of tradition's single, continuous movement.[72]

The reflections of the contemporary philosopher Donald Davidson on the workings of metaphor can be helpful in appreciating this singularity of continuity and development in tradition. In classical and Romantic theories of language, Davidson has noted, the metaphor is seen "as primarily a vehicle for conveying ideas."[73] The metaphor depends on a first meaning that it extends into novel circumstances where, now as metaphor, it achieves a second meaning. One might say that the metaphor works as a linguistic pivot that turns on the original meaning, swiveling to appear as any possible second, metaphorical meaning. The distinction between form and content in modern theories of doctrinal development depend on this customary understanding of metaphor. The content of tradition is regarded as a fixed commodity, an unchanging literal meaning that supplies continuity. And the form of tradition then becomes a metaphorical extension of content's literal meaning to the novel circumstances of historical development. Just as the metaphor depends on an original meaning for its own second meaning, tradition's developing form depends on an ancient fixed content for its historical, "metaphorical" significance. Understanding the metaphor, whether it occurs as a poetic image or as a Christian doctrine, involves understanding both the second *and* first meanings separately, since the former depends on the latter. Davidson has proposed instead that the metaphor derives its intelligibility not from a first meaning implicit in the metaphor but from its use in particular circumstances.

For Davidson, the metaphor does not do its work "by having a special meaning, a specific cognitive content"[74] that is encoded within the metaphor's expression. The metaphor does have a meaning or a truth to tell. However it is described, though, the metaphor's point lies in its linguistic use to say something about something. The metaphor's meaning, in Davidson's judgment, is a literal meaning, and the metaphor says nothing beyond this literal meaning. By calling the metaphor's meaning "literal," Davidson has made it clear that he is not thinking of an abstract meaning anchored in a metaphysical order and manifested in language. Indeed, the literal meaning of metaphors for which his work speaks stands opposed to precisely such an "original" sense. Literal meaning for Davidson is functional and akin to the literal meaning sketched in these pages as the first sense of tradition. Literal meaning depends on no other and is completely responsive to the occasion of its use. It takes shape through the particular circumstances that provide sufficient context for its meaning. What the metaphor's literal meaning signifies is what it is employed to say in these or those circumstances. Metaphors, Davidson has observed, "cannot be paraphrased, . . . not because metaphors say something too novel for literal expression but because there is nothing there to paraphrase."[75]

Were Davidson's understanding of metaphor applied to the second sense of tradition, the typical distinction between form and content as a way of construing development and continuity in tradition would prove to be untenable. The form-content distinction fuels ancient and Romantic understandings of metaphor, content providing the pivot in original meaning and form providing the linguistic extension of meaning through metaphor. But if metaphor possesses only a literal meaning governed by use, then the form-content distinction has nothing to name on either side of the form-content hyphen. The same applies to the separability of development and continuity, which form and content, respectively, signify. To say that tradition is a development in the manner of the retrospective model is to offer a metaphor in which an original continuity from which "development" garners its meaning is *not* encoded. In the retrospective model, every ecclesial postulation of continuity with the past that itself develops tradition functions in the same way as Davidsonian metaphorical signification, for each configuration of tradition presents a literal meaning governed by the circumstances in which and for which it is configured.

Continuity and development are both affirmed in this regional act of faith literally conveyed in the use to which belief and practice are put now by the faithful community. And this very continuity and development, the present representation of tradition, will soon be the object of an imminently future act of retrospection that in its own affirmation of development-in-continuity will formulate the present's relationship to the past's accumulated retrospections in yet another particular, literal way. Each literal affirmation of continuity will construe the past anew and in such a way that literal construals of the past from the past will be taken up and re-represented literally in the most recent affirmation. Tradition, in other words, understood along the lines of the Davidsonian metaphor, cannot be paraphrased because—to repeat the philosopher's words—"there is nothing there to paraphrase." Tradition is a communally held portrayal of the present's relationship to the past, in which development and continuity name the same act of ecclesial faith that constitutes the portrayal. Development is not the latest way of putting an ever-existing continuity. Rather, tradition is the constancy and renewal—and in this sense the continuity and development—that characterize the entire life of the Church in time and culture and that are represented as a particular understanding of that whole ecclesial life.

At this point, some might be inclined to question the integrity of the continuity proposed in this retrospective conception of tradition. Can a continuity defined by present acts of retrospection bear the weight of tradition's true unity? Is retrospective continuity anything more than an evanescent perception ready to yield to its successor, which then prepares to yield to *its* successor, so that tradition is no more than an array of finally unrelated continuities? Can a continuity that is itself a development transcend relativism? How can retrospective continuity be reckoned with the classical Catholic belief in the apostolic tradition, the teachings that Jesus taught to the apostles—who, through the inspiration of the Holy Spirit, then handed them down to the Church—and that are themselves the measure and norm of all later tradition? These important issues are addressed in turn.

Concerns about relativism are real and unavoidable whenever the fact of historicity is acknowledged, and, since the retrospective model explains tradition in full view of historicity, these concerns must be faced. The advantage of the retrospective model is that it accounts for tradition from the standpoint of its actual experience, which can take place only in the present and within the historicity of creaturely existence. Ironically, it may be the modesty of this creaturely perspective that prompts the charge of relativism. The long-standing history of prospective conceptions of tradition, both premodern and modern, defines a normative backdrop against which the retrospective model must stand in exhibiting its virtues for theological consideration. In light of the comparison, the retrospective model finds itself at a disadvantage. To the degree that the unity and universality of tradition are conceived in the manner of the prospective conception, the retrospective model can seem to be relativistic simply in its refusal both to view tradition from an imagined, divine standpoint and to portray unity and universality from that idealized perspective.

Judged apart from this prejudicial comparison, the retrospective model is indeed able to portray the unity and universality of tradition in a nonrelativistic way. A particular retrospection, after all, achieves the authority of tradition only when it is claimed as tradition by the whole Church in a communal act of faith. The universality of tradition lies in this act of ecclesial commitment, the Church's response to the graceful activity of the Holy Spirit in history and an act that is itself possible only through that same grace. As shown in the last chapter, this universality is not properly understood epistemologically or geographically but as a Christian practice that in this case flourishes in the very act of the whole Church's affirmation of continuity with the past. The claim for traditional continuity is a claim for temporal universality, the belief of the present-day community that its faith is the faith of the ages. And yet this communally universal affirmation of temporal universality inescapably takes place regionally in a present ecclesial moment in which development ensues in the very act of affirming continuity. For those who view tradition in its entirety or "essence" or "content" as impervious to time, this ascription of universality to tradition's retrospective claims will seem insufficient or, worse, the passing mark of relativism itself. Tradition, however, is not an uncreated reality but rather a reality fully enmeshed in time and culture, the relative substance of historicity. The unity and universality of tradition across times and places, like the faithful practice that affirms it, is a claim made here and now, in this time and place, about the constancy of this faith through times and places—a claim that renews the tradition and through which the tradition grows. This communal claim for the unity and universality of tradition, like all acts of creaturely existence, is thoroughly relative—especially to the present, to the past, to all sorts of places, to scripture, and, above all, to God. And yet the scope of the claim, the unity and universality of tradition retrospectively affirmed, staunchly denies relativism wherever the claim poses the constancy of tradition.[76] Its repetition in each passing generation and in every Christian life should not be, for the community of faith, a sign of corruption but of the renewal that every claim for constancy is.

A retrospective understanding of continuity can be reconciled with the classical Catholic belief in the apostolic tradition, though in a way that avoids its prospective orientation. The belief in the authority of the apostolic tradition is at least as old as Paul (1 Cor. 15:3–5). The truth of the apostolic tradition is "the good treasure" (2 Tim. 1: 14) entrusted to the Church, a kerygmatic "deposit" of faith that the Church has heard from the apostles.[77] This belief is found in the writings of many of the early fathers.[78] The Council of Trent's definitive teaching did not fail to portray tradition as the truth of the gospel "that the apostles received from Christ himself . . . [and] from the apostles under the inspiration of the Holy Spirit."[79] In a premodern conception of tradition, this deposit is understood as a truth completely given as revelation in apostolic times and communicated hand to hand, orthodoxly intact, from generation to generation. In modern theories of development, and especially in the organic and noetic models, the deposit is the source of later growth and clarification, a truthful givenness finished as a content-laden resource for tradition in which all subsequent development is at least implicit.[80] Both understandings of the apostolic deposit of faith, premodern and modern, envision its continuity prospectively, as though the apostolic age were a timeless present from which traditional continuity could be surveyed in a field of vision stretching from an idealized present-past through the real past and to the actual present. There is some modification in prospectivity and its relationship to the apostolic deposit from the premodern to the modern view. The premodern understanding of prospectivity regards the deposit as utterly complete, manifest, and clear throughout tradition from, and especially in, the times of the earliest Church. History is the sphere of not only the deposit's communication through faithful transmission but also its possible corruption. Modern versions of prospectivity affirm the completeness of the deposit, at least as a resource, from the times of the earliest Church. Here, though, the prospective gaze cannot see the deposit clearly in the apostolic age but only in the gradually enhanced clarity of later times through which development has occurred. From the stance of modern prospectivity, this clarity remains obscure relative to a future beyond the present in which further development can be anticipated. History is the occasion for productive doctrinal growth. Since modern versions of prospectivity look forward across a historical field in which the landscape continues to shift, the deposit remains less or more but never perfectly in focus, though it is visible in every age.

As a model of development-in-continuity, the retrospective conception of tradition, like its modern predecessors, is reluctant to identify the apostolic tradition with the strong sense of closure and the expectation of the deposit's finished clarity so typical of premodern prospectivity. All models of development are inclined to acknowledge the mysteriousness of the deposit within time, that what comes to be affirmed as the deposit of faith in later times was not necessarily recognized as such in earlier times. But unlike its modern predecessors, the retrospective conception of development-in-continuity eschews any prospective standpoint in its account of the apostolic tradition, choosing instead the regionality of historical faith as its point of departure for regarding the deposit of faith. It is from the regional present that the Church, in a communal act of faith, configures the continuity of its heritage by arranging the continuities of the past in a certain way and attributing the authority of the apostolic tradition to this arrangement. However this arrangement configures the past, the arc of its affirmed continuity stretches from the present affirmation to the belief, doctrine, and practice of the earliest Church and thus to the authority of the teachings of Jesus and the apostles.

This retrospective continuity need not be one that in every respect extends from the present to the apostolic age in a line that, if traversed in the opposite direction—from past to present—would remain unbroken. Certainly there are traditional beliefs, such as the belief in the divinity of Jesus as the Son of God, that are ranked in the apostolic deposit because they have been affirmed in every act of retrospection throughout the ages, such that the present act of retrospective continuity affirming these beliefs embraces every previous act of their retrospective affirmation across every previous generation. There are other beliefs, however, that the Church at some moment affirms as the apostolic deposit but that historical study shows cannot be traced in an unbroken line from the apostolic age to the later moment of affirmation.[81] The Catholic belief in the Immaculate Conception of Mary is a good example.

In 1854, Pius IX defined the dogma that Mary in her conception was preserved from original sin, a claim for the dignity of Mary in the economy of salvation and the expression of a long-held Catholic belief. The language of the definition portrays the dogma as "a doctrine revealed by God . . . [which] therefore must be firmly and constantly held by all the faithful"[82] and thus ranks the belief within the deposit of faith. Study of the history of doctrine, however, shows that this belief did not begin to gather strength in the Church until the fourteenth century, that no less an authority than Aquinas did not hold it,[83] and that the belief was beyond intellectual conception prior to the fifth century when Augustine's theological battle with the Pelagians did much to develop the doctrine of original sin.[84] Faced with such results of historical research, those still sympathetic to premodern prospectivity may defend the unbroken continuity of the deposit by appealing to Trent's teaching on "unwritten" apostolic traditions and attributing the textual silence of the early centuries to a steadfast verbal communication that became literary only in later times. Faced with the same historical evidence, those sympathetic to modern prospectivity typically defend the unbroken continuity of the deposit by invoking the distinction between latent and manifest belief, through which the unbroken continuity can be understood along the lines of the organic *Lebensanalogie*.

The retrospective model of development-in-continuity offers a better explanation of the apostolic deposit in the face of such historical evidence, because it does not base its view of continuity on prospective assumptions and because it understands continuity *as* development. To the degree that a retrospective approach regards the apostolic tradition in faith and from the present moment, it can see and affirm continuity across the apparent brokenness of history. Both the premodern and the modern conceptions of tradition are embarrassed by the gaps in history that historical-critical investigation constantly turns up in their prospective accounts of continuity. Their defenses are, respectively, a mild gnosticism and a Romantic metaphysics. A retrospective approach offers ways of understanding the chronological gaps from a theological perspective in which continuity is affirmed across wider spans of time now construed by the believing Church in the pattern of tradition. The retrospective affirmation of continuity in any moment affirms anew previous affirmations in which the tradition is sedimented from generation to generation. This layering of affirmations presently affirmed does not represent chronological time; instead, it postulates faithful bonds of unity and universality across times, places, events, and persons back to the apostolic age in which faith locates the tradition's most basic beliefs.

If the unity and universality of tradition are ascribed to the communal and always regional act of configuring tradition, then that retrospective affirmation can find relational continuities through the sedimentation of past beliefs that need not be troubled by chronological gaps. My previous example of the traditional belief in the Immaculate Conception can again provide illustration. Considered from the retrospective standpoint, the Church's current infallible belief in the defined dogma of the Immaculate Conception can regard the tradition as one in which fourteenth-century Christian communities—and Catholic ecclesial communities thereafter—began to see a continuity in belief that embraced previous retrospective affirmations of the sinlessness of the Savior, the dignity of Mary as the Mother of God, and Augustine's intensification of Paul's strong doctrine of human fallenness in a new configuration now affirmed as tradition. Since the sedimentation in previous beliefs now confirmed as the Church's belief in the Immaculate Conception extends to the apostolic age, the unity and universality of Catholic tradition can legitimately be ascribed to the dogma now regarded—as it was not by Aquinas and so many earlier Christians—as a belief rightly included in the apostolic deposit of faith. Regarding affirmations of continuity as themselves developments means that the Church's perspective on the deposit of faith moves in and as tradition. But that continuous development is always construed from the present moment, and from this standpoint the pattern of tradition is defined by a stance on its literal sense and not by what is often the rival continuity of chronological time. Through ecclesial eyes that look for traditioned meaning from the present to the past, ordinary time is always extraordinary.

I cannot conclude this account of the retrospective conception of tradition without attending specifically to the role of believers in the making of tradition. The many ways in which the retrospective approach detailed here proceeds from and respects the regionality of faith in traditional portrayals means that it, like the dialectical and reception models, values the contributions of individual believers to the historical unfolding of tradition. Acts of retrospective continuity that develop the tradition must be made, of course, by the entire ecclesial community in order to possess authority. Tradition is the business of the whole Church. The faith that believes in tradition is corporate. Yet the communal act of faith that posits the unity and universality of tradition is sedimented in local communities and finally in the faith of individual believers, in the past as in the present. The Spirit of God is present to and at work in all these dimensions of the Church's graced life. Usually, this presence is fathomed as the steadfast comfort that the Spirit's sanctifying power offers in the face of creaturely fallenness. Occasionally, individual insight discerns the Spirit's eventful presence to the Church and the world as the surprise of *aggiornamento*, as challenge and call to prophetic response, or in a theological interpretation that renews the familiar, making it more familiar still. Insights of this order have an *élan* that transforms lives—and even sometimes the life of the entire Church—for they see the Spirit's steadfast movement with unusual clarity or, in what may amount to the same, appreciate how thoroughly mysterious the Spirit's presence to history is. Such insights, rightly understood, view the traditional past from the standpoint of the ecclesial present and, again only from the present and in light of the retrospective gaze, are capable of imagining the imminent direction of the Spirit's steadfast movement. These insights may prove to be true or false, in the judgment of an individual believer or in the judgment of a local community. They prove to be tradition when all in the Church look in the direction of an insightful individual, or locally communal retrospection; see and imagine what the insightful believer or local community sees and imagines; make that insight a universally communal act of faith; and, through it, affirm a continuity with the continuities of the past that develops tradition. Without the finally efficacious insights of individual believers, tradition would cease to be, for, if continuity and development are truly the same, the constancy of tradition would disappear in the absence of tradition's insightful renewal.

Postmodern Allegory

This chapter began by noting that the second sense of tradition does not bear direct resemblance to any counterpart in the ancient senses of scripture. But perhaps, in consideration of the model of development-in-continuity proposed here, I can qualify that judgment and speak of at least an indirect resemblance between the second sense of tradition and the ancient allegorical sense of scripture. This resemblance can be only indirect, since the ancient allegorical sense of scripture and the second sense of tradition are products of strikingly different assumptions and thought worlds. Ancient allegory brings the metaphysical assumptions of a Hellenistic world view to its reading of scripture. It extends its anxiety about the temporality and corruptibility of the body to scripture's literal sense, its reading seeking the freedom of a hidden, timeless truth gained by escape from the literal. The second sense of tradition offered in the previous pages is best described as postmodern, though it is important to say precisely how it is rightly brought under the rubric of that confusing nomenclature.[85] First, it is important to note that the second sense of tradition shares with premodern and modern conceptions a firm belief in tradition as the Word of God authoritatively interpreted in and through the Church in its journey through history. The sense of development-in-continuity affirms tradition as the reception of the apostolic deposit of faith and thus as the reception of God's revelation that brings the gospel's salvational tidings to Church and world. Unlike the premodern conception of tradition, the second sense appreciates the historicity of all things ecclesial and with the modern conception portrays tradition as a development. The second sense is postmodern in its allegiance to the present ecclesial moment as the recurring standpoint from which tradition's constancy and renewal are configured. Though it values creativity in the traditioning process as do some of the modern models, it eschews modern prospectivity and the chronological teleology that governs its understanding of continuity. Within this very specific sense of the postmodern, it may be possible to notice an indirect resemblance between the second sense of tradition and ancient scriptural allegory that would allow a consideration of the second sense as postmodern allegory.

At once, of course, all the reasons for not pursuing such an oxymoronic rubric present themselves. The ancient allegorical sense is mystical, whereas the second sense of tradition is ecclesially pragmatic. Ancient allegory judges time to obfuscate, whereas the sense of development-in-continuity judges history to be productive of meaning. Ancient allegorical readings venture escape from the literal sense, whereas the second sense of tradition embraces it. Ancient allegory is dyadic in sensibility, treating the scriptural text as metaphor bearing a hierarchical double meaning. Retrospective development-in-continuity is holistic in sensibility, treating tradition as an unparaphrasable metaphor, single in meaning, in which form and content cannot be distinguished. These differences seem to suggest an unbridgeable gulf between the ancient allegorical sense of scripture and the second sense of tradition. Yet there is some small sense in which the premodern can inform the postmodern at the level of practice.

In a recent work, David Dawson explored ancient Jewish, Gnostic, and Christian allegory in the work of Philo, Valentinus, and Clement of Alexandria, respectively.[86] Although Dawson detailed the ways in which each allegorist went about his interpretive business, he was more comprehensively interested in the strategy of allegory as a reading practice. In a traditionalist understanding, allegory is "a way of plumbing and expressing the spiritual depths of religious texts, especially the Bible." It assumes that there is a " 'more spiritual' meaning hidden beneath the 'letter' of scripture."[87] By attending to "the historically specific ways allegory's essential conflict of meanings actually engaged social and cultural practice in the ancient world,"[88] Dawson sought to show how this understanding of allegory actually worked. In Dawson's view, interpretations or readings are ways of negotiating the literal sense, the text's commonly accepted meaning, which actually instantiates the wider meaningfulness of sociocultural life.

This negotiation can take place in several ways. First, an allegorical reading might domesticate a past literal sense that has become strange in recent sociocultural circumstances by showing how the strange literal sense actually possesses the meaning of a current, familiar literal sense that governs the allegorical reading. Second, by challenging the familiar, present literal sense, an allegorical reading might call into question the sociocultural assumptions, values, and behaviors it textually embodies. Third, an allegorical reading might revise culture not by criticizing it, as in the previous form of negotiation, but by using allegory "to enable scripture itself to absorb and reinterpret culture"[89] This strategy is practiced by allegorists who are so committed to the literal sense of a religious scriptural text that they make their interpretive task the extension of scripture's literal meaning to extrascriptural, sociocultural meanings at large. Allegorical reading in this negotiation is intratextual. Allegory becomes the extended literal sense that results from reading culture through the eyes of the page's literal sense and, from reading it in this way, transforming it into another concrescence of scriptural meaning. However ancient allegorists negotiated the literal sense, the result in Dawson's judgment was "a particular strategy by which [they] claimed authoritative originality for their interpretations."[90]

If it is possible to posit an indirect resemblance between the ancient allegorical sense of scripture and the second sense of tradition, then it would be along the lines of Dawson's functional approach, which is consistent with this study's postmodern understanding of development-in-continuity. Dawson's first example of allegorical negotiation of the literal sense might be described as "hermeneutical," since allegory emerges in a correlation of the literal sense's customary meaning with new cultural circumstances that are themselves also accorded authority in the balance of understanding. To the degree that the second sense of tradition ever draws on the temporocultural regionality of the act of faith in configuring development-in-continuity, it can and should appreciate the contributions of hermeneutical correlation to traditional renewal.

Dawson's second approach to the allegorical negotiation of the literal sense might be described as "critical," since allegory emerges in dissatisfaction with and criticism of the received literal sense. To the degree that the second sense of tradition is always put to work in the retrospective reconfiguration of what is "handed down," its reading of the received literal sense is never properly complacent and ever eager for the renewal of tradition's constancy. This critical dimension of the second sense of tradition need not manifest itself as outright dissatisfaction, though on occasion particular configurations of tradition may bear the mark of a prophetical spirit thoroughly dissatisfied with the Church's habitual regard for the literal. More typically, the critical negotiation of the literal sense stems at least from an unease with a traditional constancy not informed sufficiently or at all by the value of renewal. This sensibility of unease on the part of an individual believer, a local community, or the entire Church is the impetus for the restoration of balance in these values.

Dawson's third approach to the negotiation of the literal sense might be described as "narrative" or "postliberal," since allegory here is conceived along the lines labeled as such and commended by Lindbeck in his influential book *The Nature of Doctrine*.[91] Allegory now assumes the style of an extended scriptural narrative in which all real meaning is the theologically normative meaning of the Bible. To the degree that the second sense of tradition frames development as continuity, it can and should appreciate an interpretive orientation that proceeds with the priority of the literal sense in mind and that stresses the value of constancy in the tasks of imagining and configuring renewal.

Understanding the second sense of tradition as allegory defined by its ancient assumptions would be anomalous. But understanding the second sense of tradition through Dawson's account calls attention to its interesting, though only formal, kinship to the practice of ancient allegory. Configurations of tradition as development-in-continuity are allegorical to the extent that they are negotiations of the literal sense that remake it in the face of possible conflicts of meaning. The allegory of the most recent reconfiguration of continuity, itself a development, settles the conflict in a new configuration of the old. This kind of allegory does not cull "deeper" meanings from tradition in the manner of an ancient allegorical reading of scripture, for there is no metaphysical "content" to tradition's truth distinguishable from its literal "form." The imagery of "deep" and concomitantly "shallow" meanings is but a variant of the content-form distinction and, like it, dependent on the assumption of a higher standpoint from which degrees of depth can be gauged. In this postmodern allegory, the metaphysical assumptions of prospectivity, whether premodern or modern, are left behind as the allegorical reading that tradition is proceeds from the limitations of a present moment claiming its holistic bonds to its past. The language of "depth" is supplanted by the language of historicity, though this rhetoric is unwilling to speak of historicity in a way that relinquishes depth's spiritual density.

Second-sense configurations of tradition are allegorical to the extent that they may negotiate and remake the literal sense through any and all of the interpretive strategies that ancient allegorists could and did employ. These negotiative strategies are postmodern both in their historical-critical awareness and in the pragmatism of their use. The proposed representation of development-in-continuity does not exclude any one of the negotiative strategies in configuring tradition. The strategies can and should be employed ad hoc as circumstances require. And since each alone depicts the mutuality of constancy and renewal in a particular way, the representations of the second sense of tradition do well to avail themselves of all three of the allegorical options. As demonstrated in the final chapter of this study, however, there is a special kinship between the sense of development-in-continuity and what Dawson has described as the hermeneutical negotiation of the literal sense. The second sense of tradition is also allegorical in its appreciation of interpretive originality engrained in its assumption that the literal sense is not an ossified given and that development is not the betrayal of tradition but a condition of its creaturely existence. The second sense is postmodern allegory in its expectation that development is not an alternative to, but rather another perspective on, tradition's literal sense.

This indirect homology between ancient allegory and the second sense of tradition manifests itself in one final respect. In its own self-understanding, ancient allegory served a vision of the biblical text as the encodement of divine mystery. Allegorical interpretation looked past the veil of the literal sense, which offered only the veneer of mystery, toward the words' inner sanctuary in which the mystery was more manifestly on display. In the light of this hidden mystery now insightfully exposed, the allegorical sensibility could read the narrative of scripture differently from, and more fully than, those whose interpretive regard settled only on the dim, literal sense. In its very movement beyond the literal sense to its proper spiritual object, allegory opened a space in which other interpretive senses could proliferate as ways of encountering the inexhaustible meaning of the divine life as will (moral sense) or as beatific vision (anagogical sense).

Understood as postmodern allegory, the second sense of tradition affirms, appreciates, and yearns for the mystery of the divine life no less than its ancient counterpart, though it is wary of ancient allegory's binary assumption that mystery is encoded in the text. If, by analogy, tradition can be understood as text, then postmodern allegory is too respectful of the text's literal sense to regard the divine mystery as encrypted in it, or hidden behind it, or carried along with it. The second sense of tradition understood as postmodern allegory finds the mystery of the divine life in the historical presence of the Spirit of God to the Church. Configuring and reconfiguring tradition retrospectively in representations of continuity with the past that are themselves developments is a matter of naming that presence in every passing present moment. This naming is a task without historical closure, for the mystery of the Spirit lies in its utter presence to a historicity that still and complexly unfolds and to which the attributions of Spirit-filled continuity and Spirit-filled renewal can be made only as acts of faith. The sense of development-in-continuity offers another perspective on tradition's literal sense. But in its very distinction from the literal sense, this postmodern allegory—like ancient allegory—opens a space in which other interpretive senses may proliferate to account for the wider possibilities of tradition's development. The senses of tradition presented in the next two chapters divide the second-sense identity of continuity and development and set renewal in testy relation to constancy.

3

Dramatic Development as a
Sense of Tradition

The close relationship shared by the first two senses of tradition derives from their common concern for tradition's abiding movement. The literal sense finds tradition's meaning in its durable beliefs, doctrines, and practices, those that have shown themselves to last. By lasting, these beliefs, doctrines, and practices attest to their truthfulness as the Word of God believed and enacted in the Church. This study's functional approach to the literal sense has called attention to its historical character by noting that the literal sense is not a "letter" preserved to the point of ossification and impervious to history and culture but a sense that flourishes in and through its continual affirmation from time to time and place to place. The sense of development-in-continuity appreciates this developing aspect of the literal sense more than the literal sense does, and in this respect might be conceived as a gloss in sensibility on the more stolid literal sense. The second sense surpasses the literal sense in its esteem for the renewal that any affirmation of constancy entails. The discussion in the previous two chapters readily distinguishes between constancy and renewal as values of the literal sense and the sense of development-in-continuity, though the retrospective understanding of the second sense regards continuity and development as names for the same unfolding of tradition. "Continuity," we have seen, does not name a separable dimension of tradition, a "content" that is self-identically the same in all times and places any more than "development" names a separable dimension of tradition, a "form" that changingly conveys material continuity. Rather, retrospective claims for tradition affirm a particular configuration of continuity with the past that is itself—sometimes minimally, sometimes maximally, but yet inevitably—a development of tradition. And this development, in turn, is nothing more than a present-day affirmation of continuity with the past.

Consideration of the first two senses together, as just suggested, might lead to an image of the second sense as a relief issuing from the plain surface of the literal sense and the traditional values of constancy and renewal as the material common to both background and foreground. This image of the relief suggests both the distinguishability and yet inseparability of the first two senses of tradition. They are inseparable in their common sensibility for and representation of the traditional values of constancy and renewal; they are distinguishable by the degree to which they highlight renewal alongside constancy. Yet if the second sense of tradition can only stand out in relief against the background provided by the first, it is because the value of constancy

100

retains a primacy among the concerns of both—even for the second sense, which distinguishes itself from the first through its relatively greater attention to the traditional value of renewal. Constancy acts as a gravity by virtue of which the sense of development-in-continuity is held in close orbit around the literal sense, though the course of its own sensibility and representation has an integrity that stems from its greater regard for renewal. Through its single-minded attention to constancy, the literal sense measures the sense of development-in-continuity more thoroughly than the latter ever measures the former, for both senses, considered together in their mutual relationship, are committed more ardently to constancy.

This chapter turns to a sense of tradition that is attuned to the loss of the constancy prized highly by the first two senses. This third sense of tradition in the schema is called the sense of dramatic development. This sense judges that a particular belief, doctrine, or practice is developing in such a way that its current authority as the authentic teaching of the magisterium,[1] and thus its status as either the literal sense or the sense of development-in-continuity, will be lost at some later moment in the life of the Church and that such a teaching or practice exhibits signs in the present moment that this final loss of authority has begun to take place.

Clearly, this study's name for the third sense of tradition is something of a euphemism. If this sense discerns the signs of a break in traditional constancy, then it claims to fathom a movement in which a previously sustained belief, doctrine, or practice ceases to be renewed. If the third sense recognizes a development that is discontinuous with the past, then it, unlike the second sense, is able to distinguish finally between continuity and development and thus between tradition and its loss. To portray the loss of tradition as "dramatic" may seem to be too mild for the phenomenon sketched in the previous definition or, worse, an outright obfuscation of it. Perhaps, though, this somewhat euphemistic way of speaking of the third sense is necessary to describe a regard for tradition that, prior to our own time, was not only indescribable but also unthinkable. The prospective orientations of premodern and modern conceptions of tradition precluded the loss of established tradition other than by its faithless betrayal. Whereas the apostate was capable of "dramatic development," the tradition was not. The current use of the word "dramatic" in naming the third sense intends to convey the striking character of a development perceived by many in the Church as discontinuous with the past. "Dramatic" suggests that an earlier understanding of tradition has become "conspicuous" in Martin Heidegger's sense,[2] that it comes to the notice of the community of faith by virtue of its present inability to offer the meaning it once did.

If the term "dramatic development" is euphemistic, then perhaps it is because it seems to be a traditional designation for what is *not* tradition at all. From this perspective, the term "dramatic development" seems at best a polite and at worst a self-deceptive designation for what is, in fact, a reversal in Christian belief, doctrine, or practice and, as such, a critical challenge to the very possibility of tradition. In the pages that follow, I argue that dramatic development is indeed a sense of tradition and thus not only a legitimate entry in our theory of tradition but also, and more important, a Christian sensibility responsive to the workings of the Spirit in history that any configuration of tradition purports to represent. Prospective conceptions of tradition, both premodern and modern, would judge the dramatic development of long-established beliefs, doctrines, and practices to be incommensurate with their understandings of the continuity of the apostolic deposit. In contrast, a retrospective conception of tradition can find a place for dramatic development within its particular understanding of continuity and apostolic authority.

I begin by considering clear examples of the dramatic development of tradition in the Christian past and proceed by identifying criteria for determining possible, more obscure, candidates for dramatic development in the present experience of the Church. My discussion of criteria for the practice of this sensibility highlights the close relationship between faith and reason that the Catholic tradition has typically affirmed, though it explores that relationship by enlisting the aid of contemporary philosophers whose work is only beginning to garner recognition as a resource for theological reflection. And to the degree that the following analysis of dramatic development stresses the importance of faith-informed argumentation in configuring tradition and, concomitantly, in perceiving when and how its constancy has been lost, it pays particular attention to the theologian's contributions to the discernment of the third sense.

Dramatic Development: Illustrations and Criteria

Because this study's definition of dramatically-developing tradition takes its point of departure from the contemporary experience of the Church, it portrays the dramatic development of tradition as an event that seems to be taking place presently, as some believers judge a belief, doctrine, or practice to show signs of the loss of its traditional authority. Were it possible to speak of dramatically developing tradition from only this perspective, its very existence would be debatable, since this study's definitional point of departure in contemporary experience takes its stance amid questionable claims about the character of traditional development. Only time will tell whether or not a judgment of the third sense is founded. But the fact that tradition *has* developed dramatically is not in doubt, since historical-critical study has shown that long-standing doctrine and practice have developed in such a way that the authentic teaching of the magisterium in an earlier historical moment later lost authority.

John T. Noonan has identified four examples of long-standing moral teaching that has changed significantly. Three of these four qualify as examples of dramatic development. From at least 1150 to 1550, Noonan observes, the Church taught that "seeking, receiving, or hoping for anything beyond one's [monetary] principal—in other words, looking for profit—on a loan constituted the mortal sin of usury."[3] This teaching—which forbade usury as contrary to the gospel, Church law, and the law of nature; was promulgated by three ecumenical councils, popes, and bishops; and was unanimously taught by theologians—gradually became obsolete with the development of capitalist economies in the modern period and the moral approbation of lending at interest on the part of believers, hierarchy and laity alike. Another example can be found in the Church's regard for slavery. As late as 1860, Noonan has pointed out, "the Church taught that it was no sin for a Catholic to own another human being; to command the labor of that other human being without paying compensation; . . . [to] sell him or her for cash; [or] to do the same as to his or her offspring."[4] The institution of chattel slavery described in these its features was not only tacitly approved by popes, bishops, and theologians throughout the Christian centuries but also explicitly praised by Church authorities as in accord with the natural law and even as the teaching of divine revelation. One begins to see the reversal of this teaching in Gregory XVI's condemnation of the slave trade, though his 1839 magisterial salvo against the comprehensive institution continued to allow for some of its existing particulars, such as "occasional sales by owners of surplus stock."[5] From Leo XIII, through the popes of the twentieth century, to the teachings of the Second Vatican Council, the institution of slavery has been so vigorously condemned that the Church's earlier accommodation stands only as a scandal to be deplored and not at all as an instance of less-developed teaching that has now developed fully.

A third among Noonan's examples that can be invoked as an illustration of dramatically developed tradition is the 1,600-year-old teaching and practice that runs counter to the recent "moral doctrine on the freedom that should attend religious belief."[6] From the year 350 to the middle of the twentieth century, the Church taught and acted on the belief that faith at odds with the Church did not possess a right to the freedom of its diversity and expression and, more, that persons at odds in belief with the Catholic communion could be punished—corporally and even to the point of death—for what the Church judged to be their false belief. In spite of the complaint of a vocal minority at the Second Vatican Council who argued that an ancient teaching of the magisterium was being abandoned, the council fathers affirmed the freedom to believe as a sacred right in accordance with an understanding of human dignity revealed by God and thus, as a teaching—albeit long neglected—rightly included in the apostolic deposit of faith.[7] The council's 1965 *Dignitatis humanae* ("Declaration on Religious Liberty") rendered obsolete the traditional teaching on the disciplinary rights of the Church in the face of religious difference.

Noonan's examples are all drawn from the moral teachings of Catholic tradition. A clear example of a doctrine of faith that has developed dramatically is the traditional teaching on the exclusion of the separated churches from membership in the one, true Church. The condemnations of the Council of Trent (1545–1563) and the First Vatican Council (1869–1870), read in their own historical context and not with the sensibilities of recent ecumenical times, leave little doubt that the Protestant confessions are in schism and that members of the Protestant churches are outside the one, true Church of Christ. Pius XII's 1943 encyclical *Mystici corporis Christi* ("On the Mystical Body of Christ") reiterates this centuries-old tradition by appealing to the imagery of the Church as the mystical body of Christ. According to the encyclical, the Spirit of Christ animates Christ's body, a metaphor for the visible structures of the Roman Catholic Church. Membership in the one, true Church presupposes identification with this body, and, consequently, the Protestant communions are judged to be outside the Church. This judgment of schism on the Protestant churches, a Catholic dogmatic truism from Reformation times to the eve of the Second Vatican Council, is accentuated in the encyclical's claim that, though the Spirit of Christ "provides for the continual growth of the Church, He yet refuses to dwell through sanctifying grace in those members who are wholly separated from the body."[8] Although contemporary theologians might be quick to seize on the interpretive latitude of the word "wholly," there is little doubt that the tone and substance of the encyclical express the traditional teaching that outside the Church, understood as the visible Church of Rome, there is no salvation and that, since schismatics stand outside the Church, they stand outside the saving grace that animates the ecclesial body.[9]

The teachings of the Second Vatican Council so changed these traditional teachings that their development can be judged dramatic only in the sense just defined.[10] According to Vatican II's *Unitatis redintegratio* ("Decree on Ecumenism," 1964), those "who believe in Christ and have been properly baptized are put in some, though imperfect, communion with the Catholic Church."[11] To the degree that the teaching of *Mystici corporis Christi* on membership in the Church reflects the traditional teaching on the necessary means of the visible Church for salvation, it is worthy of note that the reversal of its teaching in *Unitatis redintegratio* depends on the important distinction drawn between the "Church of Christ" and the "Catholic Church" in *Lumen gentium* ("Dogmatic Constitution on the Church," 1964). The Church of Christ, according to this most central of the conciliar documents, "subsists in" the Catholic Church,[12] a distinction and a relationship that allowed the reality of the Church and the salvation promised to it by Christ to be envisaged beyond the physical institution of the Roman Church. One could argue as well that this crucial ecclesiological distinction had something of a theological precedent in a distinction between the invisible "Church of charity" and the visible "juridical Church" condemned by Pius XII in *Mystici corporis Christi*.[13] But even if interpretive qualifications can rescue Pius's condemnation from the status of dramatically developed tradition, there can be no doubt that Vatican II's ecclesiological distinction rendered obsolete the traditional teaching on membership in the institutional Roman Catholic Church as a condition for salvation. According to *Lumen gentium*, after all, "those too may achieve eternal salvation . . . who, through no fault of their own, do not know the Gospel of Christ or his Church, but who nevertheless seek God with a sincere heart, and, moved by grace, try in their actions to do his will as they know it through the dictates of their conscience."[14]

It is possible to hold the view, as have the fathers at Vatican II with regard to their teaching on religious liberty, that seemingly later teachings have actually been taught from the very earliest tradition and that, consequently, dramatic development has not occurred in the tradition because beliefs, doctrines, and practices long thought to be authoritative actually were not. This position, however, as an expression of prospective assumptions about the nature of tradition, is difficult to reconcile with the factual record of Christian history. Its prospective orientation requires what the vast majority of Christian believers through the ages confessed and practiced as tradition to be ignored, explained away, or even regarded as sinful belief, doctrine, or practice masquerading as tradition. One could also argue that some of the examples cited were not explicitly taught by the magisterium at the highest level of its authority. There are no papal encyclicals, conciliar teachings, or infallible pronouncements to the effect that slavery is a virtuous institution or that Protestants are inevitably damned. Yet, as we have seen, a consistent reading of the authoritative teachings of earlier times leads to the conclusion that the magisterium eventually stopped teaching and even reversed some of its long-held traditional teachings about slavery and the membership of Protestants in Christ's saving Church. One should be wary of this argument's tendency to reduce tradition to only what is written, as though the absence of Christian belief and practice from explicit definition in the pages of Denzinger disqualifies its status as authoritative tradition. In the consideration of what does and does not abide in Catholic tradition, it is important not to overlook that Trent, after all, spoke of the authority of unwritten traditions. Moreover, these long-held and eventually reversed beliefs, doctrines, and practices were sustained as the literal sense of tradition by a multitude of believers. Against these objections to tradition's loss, one can conclude that tradition *has* developed dramatically and that, on the basis of the historical evidence pointing to this conclusion, it is reasonable to assume that there may be particular beliefs, doctrines, and practices undergoing dramatic development now.

The authority of such doctrine in the Church's present life presents a knotty problem for all in the Church, but here the concern focuses on Catholic theologians and their work. On one hand, Catholic theologians affirm their interpretive responsibility to the "Word of God, whether in its written form or in the form of Tradition"—that is, the "doctrine, life, and worship" of the Church handed down "to every generation." Moreover, Catholic theologians recognize the authority of the teaching office or magisterium of the Church, which has been entrusted with "the task of giving an authentic interpretation of the Word of God."[15] On the other hand, as moderns, Catholic theologians recognize the fact of the development of doctrine and the role played by creative theological reflection in promulgating that development through the years. As they encounter doctrine presently and authentically taught by the magisterium, Catholic theologians sometimes find themselves judging that a doctrine will undergo development in dramatic fashion, so that the authoritative teaching of today will not be the authoritative teaching of some tomorrow. Hence our knotty problem: How is tradition in the midst of such development authoritative for theology and, of course, for the Church?

This knotty problem suggests yet another: By what criteria does the theologian, or any believer for that matter, judge authentic teaching to be currently in a state of dramatic development? There are several ways of answering this question. An answer of wide interpretive latitude might suggest that all tradition is developing because even the literal sense is always being appropriated anew in the present moment of faith. If all doctrine develops at least in this minimal way, then one might think that *dramatic* development is at least a possibility for all doctrine. Such, however, cannot be the case. Were this possibility to be realized for elements of the literal sense that carry the infallible authority of tradition—doctrine as basic to Catholic belief, for example, as the Chalcedonian dogma on the person of Christ or the Tridentine dogma on the necessity of grace for salvation—the result would be the development of *another* tradition rather than the development of doctrine *within* the Catholic tradition. Clearly, then, all doctrine cannot develop dramatically, at least not without rendering the matters under consideration moot for want of the very tradition in which they are meaningful.

The search for criteria for judging when doctrine is currently in a state of dramatic development might appeal to Catholic dogmatic presuppositions themselves. At the very least, one might think, doctrine that is not infallible may be capable of dramatic development. Yet this negative and minimal criterion proves to be useless for making the judgment concretely, because it begs the question in two respects. First, since the infallibility of doctrine expresses the infallibility of the whole Church's faith, that infallibility often does not reach the level of explicit definition, say, in the decrees of ecumenical councils and the occasional pronouncements of the extraordinary magisterium. Thus, although the assumptions of Catholic dogma seem to imply that dramatic development could occur only among noninfallible doctrines, the lack of explicit definition of infallible teaching makes it difficult to know with precision which doctrines are infallible and which are not. This, of course, is just a more fundamental way of stating the initial problem of determining criteria for doctrine currently in a state of dramatic development. Second, reference to a doctrine's noninfallible character as a minimal criterion for judging an instance of dramatic development means little if that doctrine is taught authentically by the magisterium, presumably as the unerring faith of the whole Church or, in this study's terminology, as the literal sense of tradition. Catholic theologians, like all believers, are responsible to that authentic teaching and yet know that on several occasions magisterial teaching has developed dramatically. This dilemma leads again to the same problem. No facile distinction between infallible and noninfallible doctrines, then, will enable the identification of dramatically developing doctrine with any reliability.

Catholic belief in the infallibility of the Church, though, suggests another possible criterion that proves more reliable. According to the Second Vatican Council, the "whole body of the faithful who have an anointing that comes from the holy one . . . cannot err in matters of belief." This unerring belief appears in "the supernatural appreciation of the faith (*sensus fidei*) of the whole people, when . . . they manifest a universal consent in matters of faith or morals."[16] The *sensus fidei* is not a self-subsistent belief isolated from other dimensions of ecclesial life and practice, including the hierarchical teaching office. Indeed, the unerring sense of the faith is guided by the magisterium, relying on its teaching for the preservation of its truth. Yet, at the same time, the sense of the faith is the faith of the "People of God, . . . from the bishops to the last of the faithful"[17] and thus cannot be reduced simply to the teaching of the magisterium. Magisterial teaching that has not been received in belief and practice by a wide segment of the faithful, then, offers a more reliable, but still incomplete, criterion for sensing the dramatic development of tradition in the present life of the Church.

This criterion is not without its ambiguities. Sociological findings may be helpful in locating teaching not received by the faithful, but polling results finally cannot establish the extent of doctrinal reception. In addition, there remains the theological issue of how one understands *Lumen gentium*'s reference to "the whole body of the faithful" in which infallibility resides. Does this phrase refer to the baptized; to practitioners of the faith; or more self-referentially to those who do indeed possess the unerring sense of the faith, however difficult it may be to determine its character or their number? This question points to the inherent difficulties attending judgments about doctrinal reception, particularly at the level of distinguishing that dimension of the literal sense that is truly the infallible belief of the Church. Although appeal may be made to social-scientific data in testing the reception of doctrine in the Church, one must rely finally on the sense of the faith itself—as it is continually and retrospectively configured—in judging whether doctrine has been received by the faithful, who, in turn, may evaluate the legitimacy of the judgment. In any case, defining the unerring faithful as those who receive all magisterial teaching in faith and practice wrongly equates the infallibility of the Church with obedience to the magisterium in any particular historical moment and ignores both the workings of the first two senses of tradition and the fact of dramatic development in the traditional past.[18] The criterion of reception, then, remains ambiguous, though by nature and not by fault. This ambiguity can be mitigated somewhat by two supplementary criteria.

A second criterion for judging current dramatic development is that the magisterium also invokes theological argument in the presentation of its teaching. The magisterial practice of supporting teaching with or actually offering teaching through theological argument can be found as early in the tradition as Leo I's fifth-century *Tome* on the person of Christ[19] or as recently as an encyclical of Paul VI and an instruction of the Congregation for the Doctrine of the Faith to which I turn shortly for examples.[20] The magisterial use of argument to convey authentic teaching is not necessarily a symptom of its noninfallible character, as the illustration of Leo's *Tome*—a strong textual influence on the Chalcedonian decree—testifies. But the use of theological argument in magisterial teaching is a reliable symptom that the doctrine taught is in a state of development, which itself prompts the need for argument. There are three reasons for this argumentative need, to which I refer, respectively, as the circumstantial, the logical, and the rhetorical. First, argument is deemed necessary because the teaching addresses changing cultural circumstances in which a simple reiteration of traditional doctrine would not suffice. Argument serves as a way of mediating traditional meaning to novel issues, problems, or situations. Second, argument is deemed necessary because this mediated teaching requires a specific and convincing application of the tradition's more basic beliefs, an application that represents a movement to doctrine more derivative, though not necessarily less authoritative. Logic (here following its traditional rules!) serves the magisterium by demonstrating the reasonableness of the application, by showing how the teaching's conclusion derives its authority from a major premise (more basic beliefs) rightly modified by its minor (changing cultural circumstances).[21] Third, argument is deemed necessary because unanimity in the Church is lacking for the doctrine in question. Argument thus has the rhetorical goal of persuasion.

These first two criteria for dramatic development, when taken together—magisterial teaching that one judges not to have been widely received by the faithful and that presents its teaching through theological argument—provide good direction for determining doctrine clearly in a state of development, doctrine, in other words, that receives the tradition by configuring it somewhat differently from its past. A third criterion must be added, however, for distinguishing development that is more likely to be dramatic. That criterion, itself a supplement to the previous two, is that the theological argument by which magisterial teaching is supported or conveyed does not prove convincing to a wide segment of Catholic theologians. If the magisterium supports or conveys its teaching by the logical application of more basic beliefs to changing circumstances in order to persuade the faithful who are disinclined toward its reception, *and* that argumentation does not convince a wide segment of those in the Church knowledgeable about the tradition to which it appeals and able to assess the viability of the argumentative application to present circumstances, then the likelihood increases that such teaching is developing dramatically. Dramatic development could be encouraged in such an eventuality as theologians offered criticism of the current teaching, showing how and why the doctrinal argument advanced did not justify the teaching or offering alternative arguments that advanced another version of consistency with traditional beliefs and with the current beliefs of many in the Church.

The addition of this criterion to the first two might suggest some misunderstandings that need to be addressed quickly. First, this criterion's attention to the cogency of magisterial argument among theologians should not suggest that theologians speak for all the faithful. All the faithful, however, are not concerned with arguments for the justification of belief or argument as the expression of belief, whereas theologians as a matter of professional knowledge and responsibility are. With respect to the matter of cogency in magisterial argument, they thus offer a gauge that one would not expect to find among large numbers of the faithful. Second, this criterion could seem to regard theologians as a final court of appeal in the assessment of the Church's teaching, as though the authority of theologians trumped the authority of the magisterium. As already noted, this view, which is contrary to Catholic belief, is not defended here. With regard to both of these concerns, this last criterion has no standing in its own right, as though magisterial teaching would need to be cogent to theologians before its enduring value for the Church could be established. Rather, this criterion is meaningful only in its relationship to the first two, all three together forming a unified complex of criteria for distinguishing likely instances of dramatic development—magisterial teaching that one judges not to have been widely received by the faithful and that presents its teaching through theological argument that does not prove convincing to a wide segment of theologians.

This single evaluative principle of this study attempts to identify dramatically developing belief, doctrine, and practice by way of counterpoint to the Catholic belief that the infallibility of the Church dwells among all the faithful. It offers, then, a criteriological *via negativa* whose powers of identification can never constitute a proof, and no more than an indication, of doctrine in a state of dramatic development. One would do well to think of it as a heuristic that enables one to consider the problem of the authority of such doctrine further. This can be done by examining three examples of recent magisterial teaching.

Possible Examples of Dramatically Developing Doctrine

Paul VI's encyclical *Humanae vitae* ("On the Regulation of Birth," 1968) and the Congregation for the Doctrine of the Faith (CDF) teaching *Inter insigniores* ("On the Question of the Admission of Women to the Ministerial Priesthood," 1976) seem to offer examples of Church teaching that fit the now single criterion of dramatic development of this study. I examine each in turn with regard to the three aspects of the criterion: reception, argument, and cogency.

Humanae Vitae

Humanae vitae develops by argumentation the teaching of Pius XI's encyclical *Casti connubii* (1930) that it is sinful to "deliberately frustrate [the] natural power and purpose" of the "conjugal act [which] is destined primarily by nature for the begetting of children."[22] Paul VI's 1968 encyclical more specifically forbids as contrary to the natural law and thus to the will of God the artificial regulation of birth by direct abortion, direct sterilization, or by "any action, which either before, at the moment of, or after sexual intercourse, is specifically intended to prevent procreation."[23] Any consideration of this teaching's reception among the faithful would need to acknowledge differences among the three forms of regulation that the teaching judges equally illicit. Abortion, for example, differs from sterilization and any other artificial means of regulating birth because it involves "the direct interruption of the generative process already begun."[24] And even though many in the Church would qualify by context and circumstance the encyclical's absolute strictures against abortion, "even for therapeutic reasons,"[25] few in the Church would not regard abortion as a tragic act. On the other hand, many social-scientific studies conducted in the past twenty-five years have found that a large percentage of Catholics do not accept the encyclical's proscription of artificial, preventive means of regulating births.[26] Although I know of no sociological study that has made such a comparison, I think it fair to say that—among those who do not accept this aspect of the encyclical's teaching—few would regard the use of artificial, preventive means of birth control as constituting a tragedy of the same proportions as abortion. Indeed, few among those who do not accept the encyclical's narrower prohibition would regard the practice of such forms of birth control as tragic at all. If this judgment is sound, then it is *Humanae vitae*'s prohibition of artificial, preventive means of birth control in particular that has not found reception among a wide constituency of the faithful. I focus on this aspect of the encyclical's teaching as a possible example of dramatically developing doctrine.

Humanae vitae presents its teaching through argument for all three reasons already noted. The encyclical begins by noting the changing historical circumstances that have prompted its teaching, among them the rapid increase in the world's population; a new social understanding of the dignity of women; and technological advances that permit the rational control of nature, including the natural laws of reproduction.[27] Paul VI's unprecedented formation of an advisory commission that included lay members, for the purpose of studying and reporting to him on the issues of the encyclical, might be seen by some as an expression of his keen sense that the Church faced circumstances novel enough to preclude a simple reiteration of the teaching of *Casti connubii*. To the encyclical's own list of such circumstances one might add the growing lack of the traditional teaching's reception among the faithful.

The logical argument developed in *Humanae vitae* to defend the prohibition of artificial, preventive forms of birth control is relatively simple. Its major premise is the basic Christian belief that all lives should be open, and faithful in action, to God's will. This major premise is qualified by two minor premises: (1) that God's will is inscribed in the natural law that governs procreative acts in marriage and that the consummate meaning of sexual union in marriage lies in its fecundity[28] and (2) that in the inseparable connection between its "unitive" and "procreative significance," sexual union "fully retains its sense of true mutual love and its ordination to the supreme responsibility of parenthood."[29] Logical mediation from the major premise to the first of these two minor premises results in the encyclical's particular conclusion bearing on the intentional moral range of the married couple's reproductive decision: "From this it follows that they are not free to act as they choose in the service of transmitting life, as if it were wholly up to them to decide what is the right course to follow."[30] Both minor premises are invoked to arrive at the conclusion of the Church's traditional teaching: "The Church, nevertheless, in urging men to the observance of the precepts of the natural law, which it interprets by its constant doctrine, teaches that each and every marital act must of necessity retain its intrinsic relationship to the procreation of human life."[31] Artificial, preventive forms of birth control are forbidden because they destroy this intrinsic relationship between the unitive and procreative dimensions of sexual union and thereby elevate the will of the married couple above the will of God both for the general institution of marriage and for their particular lives. Since the encyclical begins by acknowledging the "questions"[32] these matters have provoked in the Church, and moves to its final section by anticipating that "not everyone will easily accept this particular teaching,"[33] it offers its argument in recognition of a lack of unanimity among the faithful on this issue, undoubtedly with persuasion as one of its goals.

Demonstrating that the argument of *Humanae vitae* has not proved cogent to a wide segment of theologians would be a rather superfluous task. Indeed, the many criticisms leveled by theologians at the encyclical's reasoning stand side by side with its teaching's lack of reception as the clearest illustrations of the problem of authority in the contemporary Church. One would be hard-pressed to find a critic who challenged the encyclical's major premise—that all lives should be open, and faithful in action, to God's will. *Humanae vitae*'s theological critics have addressed instead the validity of both minor premises and the manner of their logical relation to the major premise to yield the teaching's conclusion. Charles E. Curran, for example, has criticized the encyclical's "physicalism," its inscription of the divine will upon every conjugal act as though providence works exclusively in the teleology of biological structures.[34] And when reasoning is put at issue, the encyclical's physicalist assumptions prevent its logic from distinguishing between the major and minor premises in its argument. One might even say that the argument's minor premises so eclipse its major premise that it becomes impossible to logically reach the reasonable conclusion, say, that a married couple could be open to the will of God by having a fecund marriage while yet, at times, practicing artificial contraception. Joseph A. Komonchak has noted that because the encyclical makes no attempt to justify what I have called its minor premises, it is no argument at all.[35] Rahner has observed that arguments from the natural law, such as *Humanae vitae*'s, cannot prescind from the expectation of logical cogency, since reasonableness is at least one of the expectations of appeal to the natural law. And yet, in his view, this cogency is lacking in the encyclical's line of argument, which does little more than state its premises.[36]

If space permitted, we could treat a number of other consequential criticisms of the encyclical's argument, especially those that find a conflict in moral intentionality posed by its approval of the rhythm method of birth control. Let it suffice to say that the many theologians who have criticized the teaching of *Humanae vitae* have done so by attending to the inconsistencies they have found in the reasoning with which its teaching was promulgated.

Inter Insigniores

Inter insigniores—a CDF teaching published on October 15, 1976, with the approval of Paul VI—presents a rationale for the Church's long-established practice of restricting priestly ordination to men. Like *Humanae vitae*, *Inter insigniores*, it seems, has not encountered wide reception among the faithful. In fact, sociological evidence suggests that the acceptability of the ordination of women among Catholics in the years since the document's publication has increased substantially. One example (typical of North American and Western European countries) is a 1977 Gallup poll that found 41% of American Catholics to favor the ordination of women, a statistic that had increased to 63% by 1993.[37] As noted earlier, one must be wary of reducing the *sensus fidei* to the findings of sociologists and doubly wary of generalizing the Catholic beliefs of some nations as the belief of the whole Church. Yet this increase in the acceptability of the ordination of women among believers is telling, enough so to judge that the teaching of the Church in question has not been widely received by the faithful. The most likely explanations for this increase are a growing awareness of injustices toward women in traditional societies, the strength of movements for the equal rights of women, and a resulting expansion of the role of women in social structures and responsibilities customarily reserved for men. One cannot completely discount, however, the influence of the document's argument itself on the increasingly wider lack of reception of the teaching among the faithful over this period of time.[38]

All three reasons—circumstantial, logical, and rhetorical—for the appeal to argument in the promulgation of magisterial teaching can be found in *Inter insigniores*. The exclusive ordination of men to the priesthood is, after all, a practice that dates in some form to the first-century Church. The need to justify such an ancient practice stems from changing circumstances in which argument is called upon to defeat perceived challenges to the tradition. The document's opening paragraphs identify those changing circumstances as the modern recognition of the full equality of women, the wider participation of women in the apostolate of the Church, the unqualified admission of women to pastoral office in some Protestant churches, and arguments by Catholic theologians for the ordination of women to the priesthood.[39]

Logical mediation is deemed necessary in *Inter insigniores* to bring the tradition's most basic beliefs to bear upon these changing circumstances. Several ancillary arguments in the document serve to refute scripturally and historically based defenses of the ordination of women. The teaching notes in passing, for example, that the "undeniable influence of prejudices unfavorable to women" in the writings of the Church fathers had negligible effect on their pastoral practice and spiritual direction.[40] The argument "from origins" continues by observing that "Jesus did not call any woman to become part of the twelve" even though his attitude toward women did not conform to, and indeed even "deliberately and courageously broke with," the customs of his time.[41] Moreover, the apostles did not consider women candidates to complete the Twelve in the Pentecost Church, even though Mary herself occupied a privileged place in their circle. Neither did Paul extend full ministerial powers to women.[42] As important as these arguments "from origins" in the document are for defending the continuity of ecclesial practice against counterarguments for change, they are secondary to what I call its argument "from representation."

Although *Inter insigniores* portrays its reasoning "from representation" as a matter "of clarifying [its] teaching by the analogy of faith" and not as a matter "of bringing forward a demonstrative argument,"[43] the manner in which its premises lead to its conclusion seems to involve elementary deduction. The argument's major premise is the "Church's constant teaching" that "the bishop or the priest, in the exercise of his ministry, does not act in his own name, *in persona propria*: he represents Christ, who acts through him." In the ministry, then, the priest "acts not only through the effective power conferred on him by Christ, but *in persona Christi*."[44] This major premise is qualified by the minor premise that the incarnation of the Word "took place according to the male sex," a fact that does not imply a superiority of men over women but that nonetheless conveys a harmony in the plan of salvation revealed by God that is symbolically important for the economy of revelation.[45] Logical mediation yields the conclusion of the teaching that women cannot be priests because—since the savior was a male—as females, they could not act ministerially *in persona Christi*. This argument's minor premise addresses contemporary cultural shifts in which feminist sensibilities would no longer assume that metaphysical conceptions such as *persona* are intrinsically male or would insist that such conceptions transcend social (and ecclesial) bias only when they are understood in a gender-inclusive manner. The rhetoric of the argument exhibits an awareness of the claims of these sensibilities and of the need to convince those who find the traditional belief incredible—even to the point that the document anticipates and rebuffs counter-arguments to the centrality it accords the maleness of Christ.

As in the case of *Humanae vitae*, so many theologians have found the argumentation of *Inter insigniores* to be problematic that demonstrating its lack of cogency to a wide segment of their number becomes a trivial task. Although several theological responses have criticized the appeal of *Inter insigniores* to scripture and the history of the early Church as legitimate warrant for its exclusion of women from priestly ordination,[46] the most consequential criticism has addressed the argument "from representation." Elizabeth A. Johnson, among others, has criticized the crucial role of Jesus' maleness in the argument by setting its notion of representation in the orthodox christological tradition. The Cappadocian rule of faith "What is not assumed is not saved," she has noted, defined the proper understanding of human *persona* in the fourth-century controversy on the humanity of Christ. The rule judged wanting any notion of the humanity of Christ that excluded anything essentially human from his existence, since the excluded human dimension would not share in the hypostatic union and thus would not enjoy the union's saving effects. "If maleness is constitutive for the incarnation and redemption," Johnson has observed, "female humanity is not assumed and therefore not saved."[47] Privileging Jesus' maleness, as *Inter insigniores* does, particularizes the human notion of *persona* in a way that puts it at odds with the ancient rule of faith, thus destroying both the Christian notion of human person implicit in the rule and any possibility of its legitimate representation, even and perhaps especially if the object of representation is the person of Christ. Johnson has concluded that an "egalitarian anthropology that holds that women and men are equally created in the image of God and are equally one in Christ through the waters of baptism" offers a more adequate resource for considering the issue of priestly ordination.[48] From the perspective of the argument's logical structure, one might understand her point to be that such an egalitarian anthropology would better shape a minor premise and thus properly qualify the major premise's largely uncontested expectation of how the priest in ministerial duties represents the person of Christ.

Both teachings, then, appear to fit the criterion of dramatically developing doctrine, primarily because they do not seem to have been widely received by the faithful and secondarily, yet importantly, because they also advance their teaching by arguments that have not proved convincing to a large number of those in the Church professionally committed to the task of bringing understanding to faith.

Arguments That Matter Not

The reader may benefit here from a reminder that the efforts thus far to identify candidates for dramatically developing doctrine serve the broader purpose of considering the theological problem of such doctrine's authority within tradition. One could address this issue in a general fashion simply by reference to the large body of literature on authority in the Church, the teaching prerogatives of the magisterium, and theological responsibility that has appeared since the Second Vatican Council. Here, though, this question is pursued more specifically by focusing on two of the features previously proposed for candidates for such doctrine: the arguments offered to advance a teaching and their cogency.

If both doctrines fit this study's criterion on the counts of reception, argument, and cogency, they share an additional commonality with regard to the last two aspects. *Humanae vitae* directly and the broader magisterial tradition of *Inter insigniores* indirectly subscribe to the view that finally neither their arguments nor the cogency of their arguments is consequential to the authority of their teaching. *Humanae vitae* expresses this position in its pastoral directives to priests:

> For it is your principal duty—We are speaking especially to you who teach moral theology—to spell out clearly and completely the Church's teaching on marriage. In the performance of your ministry you must be the first to give an example of that sincere obedience, inward as well as outward, which

is due to the magisterium of the Church. For, as you know, the pastors of the Church enjoy a special light of the Holy Spirit in teaching the truth. And this, rather than the arguments they put forward, is why you are bound to such obedience.[49]

This same point is made indirectly in the magisterium's recent teaching on the exclusion of women from priestly ordination, not in *Inter insigniores* but in John Paul II's promulgation of its doctrine in *Ordinatio sacerdotalis* ("Apostolic Letter on Ordination and Women," May 22, 1994). This text notes the conclusions of the arguments of *Inter insigniores* "from origins," fails to mention what many would consider to be its principal argument "from representation," reiterates the constancy of the Church's universal tradition in excluding women from priestly ordination, and concludes with the Pope's particular contribution to the issue: "Wherefore, in order that all doubt may be removed regarding a matter of great importance, a matter which pertains to the church's divine constitution itself, in virtue of my ministry of confirming the brethren . . . I declare that the church has no authority whatsoever to confer priestly ordination on women and that this judgment is to be definitively held by all the church's faithful."[50] The status and purport of this teaching continue to be discussed in the Church.[51] For the purposes of this study, it is important to note that the Pope has provided the context for his teaching in the remarks that precede the declaration just quoted. In spite of the Church's consistent teaching even to the present day, the reservation of priestly ordination to men alone, he stated, "in some places . . . is nonetheless considered still open to debate, or the church's judgment that women are not to be admitted to ordination is considered to have a merely disciplinary force."[52] If the Apostolic Letter responds to these circumstances and offers its teaching with the intention of removing doubt in the Church, then at least one of its purposes is to close debate on this issue. This purpose, coupled with the letter's omission of reference to the central and most debated argument of *Inter insigniores*, amounts to an admission that neither magisterial arguments for the exclusion of women from priestly ordination nor their cogency finally matters, since the charism of the Church's teaching office alone is the basis of its authority.

The final dispensability of argument in magisterial teachings conveyed by argument is affirmed as a general principle in the CDF's *Donum veritatis* ("Instruction on the Ecclesial Vocation of the Theologian," May 24, 1990). *Donum veritatis* addresses several matters concerning the responsibility of theologians to the magisterium, focusing particularly on the legitimacy and means of theological dissent from authentic teaching. One way in which theologians defend the legitimacy of dissent from "non-irreformable magisterial teaching,"[53] it claims, is by adopting a hermeneutical posture that regards such teaching as only one voice among many in an ongoing theological debate. "Certainly," the text states, "it is one of the theologian's tasks to give a correct interpretation to the texts of the magisterium, and to this end he employs various hermeneutical rules. Among these is the principle which affirms that magisterial teaching, by virtue of divine assistance, has a validity beyond its argumentation, which may derive at times from a particular theology."[54] Right theological interpretation, then, should regard the argumentation of magisterial teaching as supplementary to its conclusion, as, on one hand, a dimension of its presentation that theologians must strive to understand with an "intense and patient reflection"[55] and yet, on the other hand, a dispensable contingency should such reflection fail to yield the understanding sought.

When all sincere effort to appreciate the truth of magisterial teaching has proved fruitless, the theologian may express personal dissent only by means of confiding privately in the magisterial authorities. One concern that might be communicated in this one valid practice of dissent is how "the arguments proposed to justify [the teaching]" are problematic. And when voiced privately, such objections can have the happy consequence of contributing "to real progress and [providing] a stimulus to the magisterium to propose the teaching of the church in greater depth and with a clearer presentation of the arguments."[56] Although one rejoices in any manifestation of collegiality, reconciliation, and progress in the doctrine of the faith, one cannot help but notice that the results of this private consultation extend only to magisterial argumentation and not to magisterial conclusion. As a result, argumentation becomes a gloss to conclusion—a supplement capable of clarification, modification, or even as much as separation without fear of effect upon the teaching it purports to convey. Perhaps the text's expectation that an unsatisfactory resolution to private consultation is a call to the theologian "to suffer for the truth, in *silence* and prayer"[57] is yet another expression of its view that the weighing of ecclesial argument in public would be as useless as it is scandalous, since the argumentative dimension of magisterial teaching finally matters not.

Clearly the tone of this study's analysis suggests that something is amiss in the presumed separability of argument and conclusion in the authentic teaching of the magisterium. The following section considers how the assumed contingency of magisterial argumentation bears on the theological problem of the authority of dramatically developing doctrine. At this point, however, it is important to state unequivocally that this problem cannot be addressed by undermining in any way the charismatic authority of the Church's teaching office, itself one of the tradition's basic beliefs. A more fruitful approach to this problem should consider how reasoning properly justifies a tradition of basic beliefs and, through such justification, gains cogency among faithful believers. The account of epistemic justification offered by nonfoundationalist philosophers can help to shed light on these issues.

Arguments without "Foundations"

Although there is no definable school that represents the epistemological sensibilities of nonfoundationalism, there is at least a family resemblance of such philosophical commitments in the tradition of American pragmatism. Building on the work of an older generation that includes Charles Sanders Peirce, William James, and John Dewey, such contemporary pragmatists as Wilfrid Sellars, Willard Van Orman Quine, Richard Rorty, and Richard J. Bernstein share several common assumptions that might be described as nonfoundationalist.[58] All are keenly suspicious of the Cartesian understanding of the philosophical task in which thinking is called upon to establish a "first philosophy," an architectonic of all knowledge grounded on some immediately experienced, self-certain principle that serves as "foundations" for the entire edifice of knowledge. All oppose traditional understandings of the philosophical justification of belief in which reasoning is expected to show the validity of claims to knowledge finally by appeal to indubitable "foundations" on which such claims rest. All regard the business of philosophy, at least at this moment in its history, as the criticism of Cartesianism and the formulation of more adequate accounts of knowing in which claims to knowledge are justified without appeal to foundationalist principles.

Although the nonfoundationalists frequently personify the foundationalist error by reference to René Descartes, foundationalism is as old as the Platonic tradition in Western philosophy. Whether the "foundations" of knowing appear in such philosophical accounts as Plato's eternal forms, Descartes's clear and distinct ideas, John Locke's givenness of sense experience, or Kant's transcendental categories of the understanding, they are esteemed by their proponents as immediately justified beliefs whose certainty justifies more derivative claims in the larger body of knowledge. Since the very purpose of "foundations" is to ensure the indubitability of knowledge, or at the very least the possibility of such unquestioned certainty, foundationalists ascribe universality to whatever principle they advance as the authenticator of truth claims. As Rorty has observed, foundationalists seem to assume that epistemic "foundations" possess an immediate veridical élan that permeates the entire system of knowledge and "causes" whatever truth dwells among its mediate claims.[59] Noninferential and indisputable, the "foundations" provide a point of departure for logical deduction or a foothold for thinking's inductive climb toward valid knowledge.

Generally speaking, one could say that nonfoundationalist criticism makes its target any variety of rationalism or empiricism that expects "foundations" for knowledge, whether in ideas or sense data, to establish the certainty of epistemic claims. Traditionally, foundationalists have been anxious at the prospect of justifying claims to knowledge if such foundations do not exist. Claims to knowledge, after all, can be justified only by appealing to other claims to knowledge. And if there is not an utterly basic claim, a knowledge whose immediate certainty is indubitable, then, the foundationalist fears, the justification of knowledge becomes a dizzying, infinite spiral of skepticism in which even the possibility of certainty in any instance is jeopardized. Nonfoundationalist philosophers have argued that this, in Bernstein's well-known diagnosis, "Cartesian anxiety" is a needless worry, though one prompted by strong, epistemic prejudices.[60]

The philosopher of science Wilfrid Sellars has argued that the foundationalist conceptualization of knowledge is energized by what he has called the "Myth of the Given," the "idea that there are inner episodes, whether thoughts or so-called 'immediate experiences,' to which each of us has privileged access," inner episodes furnishing "*premises* on which empirical knowledge rests as on a foundation."[61] Although the givenness of experience is an ordinary fact of epistemic life, the imbuing of a particular dimension of experience with an authoritative givenness leads to the foundationalist schema of knowledge, in which a supposedly certain experience is called upon to provide assurances that it really cannot. There is no evidence, Sellars contends, that such a foundational, unmoved mover of knowledge exists. Indeed, as any number of the critics of foundationalism have been quick to point out, the many, and quite different, candidates for "foundations" in the history of philosophy mutually deconstruct their respective claims to immediate and obvious certainty.

Typically, nonfoundationalists argue against foundationalism by offering a view of knowledge in which its claims are relatively and mutually defined and in which the justification of knowledge is an ongoing, revisable enterprise. Sellars, for example, points out that even the most basic report of a supposedly foundational sense experience—as in the claim "This looks red"—presupposes such a proliferating host of concepts, conditions, and circumstances that our wider network of claims to knowledge is inescapably implicated. And in this wider network, epistemic claims are mutually constituted without appeal to any truth that is immediately given. Knowledge cannot be but inferential, even if one can distinguish between more basic or more complex dimensions of its inferential character. In Sellars's judgment, this reciprocity between more basic and more complex modes of inferential knowledge compromises not the authority of knowledge itself but only the foundationalist authority of the myth of the given. "For empirical knowledge," he has stated, "like its sophisticated extension, science, is rational, not because it has a *foundation* but because it is a self-correcting enterprise which can put *any* claim in jeopardy, though not *all* at once."[62]

Like Sellars, Quine rejects any rationalist or traditionally empiricist manner of accounting for human knowledge. Philosophy, for Quine, provides no "*a priori* propaedeutic or groundwork for science." Neither does it offer some "external vantage point" from which knowledge can be constructed. Rather, philosophy is "continuous with science."[63] Its task involves the critical examination of the formation of concepts from sensory evidence, the work of scientific construction itself. For Quine, though, the process of concept formation is inseparable from the formation of meaning in words, sentences, and the entire system of language itself. "Meaning is," according to Quine, "what it does," and what it does is place value on sensory stimulations in particular circumstances. Meaning is not a transcendental quality, a foundation on which sentences must rest in order to possess meaning; it is a function of how sentences are used and through such use acquire significance.[64] Meaning, then, is behaviorally layered within the complex strands of sentences that configure the "web" of belief, Quine's compelling metaphor for knowledge itself. Although a foundationalist, to pursue the metaphor, might expect the web's fixed integrity to rest upon a single strand, Quine has situated the web's meaningfulness in the constant revisions to its weaving called for by the circumstances of its use. Our "statements about the external world," he has maintained, "face the tribunal of sense experience not individually but only as a corporate body."[65] And the corporate body of knowledge is not only foundationless but also utterly flexible.

Sellars and Quine's nonfoundationalist perspective on the constitution of knowledge also has implications for their understanding of epistemic justification—that is, the task of providing arguments of sufficient warrant for claims to knowledge or beliefs. Clearly, if knowledge does not possess foundations, then neither do the arguments one offers to justify beliefs. This study has already noted that the prospect of foundationless belief stirs the foundationalist's fear of an infinite justificatory regress in which even the possibility of warranted claims would be undercut. Sellars and Quine, however, have not found this prospect threatening. The arguments by which belief is justified, they have held, need not lead logically to a final grounding principle that brings the business of making justificatory arguments to closure. For both, justificatory argumentation in support of claims to knowledge is an activity internal to the claims for which one argues.

For Sellars, justifications of belief fall within the scope of theorizing, the activity of explaining the beliefs one holds. Their arguments, he has proposed, are best understood as self-correcting, inductive generalizations, as accounts of a rational system's reasonable coherence offered from within its own network of belief. Similarly, Quine has affirmed this contextual, self-referential view of justification in what has come to be known as his doctrine of holism. According to this thesis, parts of theories, including for present purposes justificatory arguments, are "not separately vulnerable to adverse observations, because it is only jointly as a theory that they imply their observable consequences."[66] Parts of theories, in other words, including the reasoned arguments on behalf of more basic background beliefs, do not simply collapse in the face of conflicting data. Justificatory arguments so foster the basic beliefs they serve—the two utterly intertwined in the proliferating network of claims to knowledge—that contrary evidence more typically will lead to their revision than to their abandonment. Both Sellars and Quine have rejected what Michael Williams has called a "genetic" conception of justification, in which the cogency of arguments on behalf of beliefs is assumed to be caused by the immediately certain, foundationalist principle to which they are logically joined.[67] For both, justificatory argumentation is as foundationless, continuous, and resistant to closure as efforts to accommodate language to experience.

The purport of Sellars and Quine's nonfoundationalist view on the task of justification is that what is called knowledge *is* its justification, itself an open-ended process of explaining—one might say arguing for—the beliefs valued in particular meaningful contexts. In the absence of "foundations," arguments are the principal means by which basic beliefs are themselves shaped and by which their values gain cogency and thus authority. Arguments, then, are indispensable to claims to knowledge in this nonfoundationalist perspective, for the reasons they provide for beliefs not only support, relate, criticize and revise those claims but also *are* those claims themselves. By the same token, this nonfoundationalist understanding highlights the degree to which the contributions of argument to justification are diminished in a foundationalist understanding of knowledge. Deductive and inductive arguments in such a foundationalist schema justify a truth claim that itself requires no justification, since its epistemic authority is regarded as immediate and obvious. Whatever logical authority justificatory arguments possess in a foundationalist conceptualization of knowledge derives finally from the "foundations" from which such arguments proceed or to which they lead in an epistemic return to origins.

In this "genetic" conception of justification, such arguments are separable from, and thus in some measure supplements to, their "foundations." Whereas the separability of "foundations" and argumentation is a constant in foundationalist argumentation, the extent of separability may vary. "Weak" versions of foundationalist argumentation may account for the logical connections between and among derivative, mediate claims to knowledge, thereby showing the integrity of the body of knowledge they present. Or such argumentation may confirm the purported certainty of foundationalist claims or experiences to which it has pledged logical allegiance. In comparison to a nonfoundationalist conception of justification, weak versions of foundationalist argumentation diminish the value of argumentation, though argumentation is not so separable from its "foundations" that it can be deemed indispensable. "Strong" versions of foundationalist argumentation diminish the value of argumentation even further. Resting assured that their justificatory explanations mirror the indubitability of their first principles, strong versions of foundationalism would regard their argumentation to be completely separable from, because they are utterly supplementary to, the "foundations" they serve. Here arguments, but glosses to an immediately given truth, are finally dispensable and thus matter little if at all.[68]

Reasoning with Authority

In recent years a number of theologians have touted the value of a nonfoundationalist approach to knowledge for theological reflection. The advocates of this approach—most notably Lindbeck, Thiemann, Stanley Hauerwas, and Charles Wood—largely have been Protestant theologians who have found the nonfoundationalist perspective helpful in refuting the apologetical use of universal theories in many modern theologies and in fostering a descriptive approach to theological interpretation consistent with a Reformation understanding of theology as scriptural exegesis. Although several Catholic theologians have produced works compatible with a nonfoundationalist perspective,[69] this approach has often stirred Catholic suspicion, perhaps because variations on the transcendental method advocated by such influential Catholic theologians as Rahner, Bernard J. Lonergan, and Tracy are often cited by Protestant nonfoundationalists as examples of the foundationalist error.[70] There are any number of reasons for Catholic sensibilities to be wary of the nonfoundationalist approach to knowledge. There is no reason in principle, however, to think that nonfoundationalist philosophy could not prove helpful in illuminating Catholic commitments on any number of issues, especially the proper relationship between faith and reason.

Like any philosophical stance, nonfoundationalist criticism can be put to use legitimately in a Catholic setting only if measured choices are made about which of its insights are valuable and how those insights are used to clarify beliefs that are basically Catholic. Catholic assumptions about the nature of religious reasoning, for example, could not possibly make room for the typically nonfoundationalist view that all knowledge is relative or that universality cannot be ascribed to truth claims. But to the degree that nonfoundationalist sensibilities work to expose exaggerated and finally unsustainable claims for the justification of belief, and foster an understanding of the workings of reason true to our actual beliefs and practices, they are indispensable for appreciating the conduct of right reasoning—including the reasoning invoked as authoritative in the Catholic tradition by the magisterium, theologians, and the faithful.

A nonfoundationalist perspective on the justification of belief suggests that the magisterial understanding of argumentation in its teaching is foundationalist, and even strongly so. Extra-ecclesial sensibilities would reach this conclusion, no doubt, because the magisterium's authoritative appeal to the charism of its office would appear to be an immediately justified belief supporting the claims issuing from the exercise of office. In this view, the charge of foundationalism amounts to the judgment that magisterial arguments cannot possess authority, since the teaching office does not possess the charism that supposedly grounds its authoritative claims. But one of the advantages of a nonfoundationalist perspective is its appreciation for how claims to knowledge are contextualized, standing always in a particular framework of meaning in which commitment, practice, and belief interrelate as they serve more basic, if not foundationalist, beliefs. To the degree that the charism of the teaching office is a part of the common stock of basic Catholic beliefs, Catholic sensibilities would not find it to be comparable to the "foundations" that reason alone would criticize in traditional epistemologies. Yet even within the circle of Catholic faith, nonfoundationalist criticism suggests another respect in which magisterial argumentation is foundationalist and thus—measured by the very values of the Catholic tradition—in need of revision.

On the face of it, the magisterium seems to exhibit a foundationalist regard for reasoning by skewing the proper argumentative relationship between the Catholic tradition's basic beliefs and the reasoned extension of those basic beliefs to new circumstances. In *Humanae vitae*, for example, natural law reasoning is so conflated with the tradition's more basic belief in divine providence and human openness to God's workings in the world that the encyclical's natural law arguments eclipse their major premise, as though the family lives of believers could be open to God's will only if the practice of artificial contraception were excluded. Here, magisterial reasoning, now virtually overwhelming the basic belief, takes on the character of "foundations" that immediately justify the encyclical's teaching. By making maleness an indispensable trait of the savior's humanity, *Inter insigniores* also conflates argument with its premise that the priestly office represents the person of Christ, thereby creating "foundations" for belief that not only immediately justify its conclusion but also do so by contradicting the tradition's basic, albeit indirect, teaching on the nature of humanity as embraced and saved by Jesus Christ. In both cases, an arguable claim is imbued with the certainty of a first principle, even though traditional beliefs more basic than those cited in a foundationalist manner stand ready in the context of faith as viable resources for authoritative, alternate arguments.

The magisterium's judgment regarding the dispensability of argumentation in its teaching further evinces a foundationalist regard for reasoning even within the setting of Catholic values, for this judgment so assumes the obvious certainty of the first principles seen to be reflected in the teaching's conclusion that the arguments by which it is reached do not share in its authority—an especially surprising stance in light of the fact that the teaching in question is presented as argument. This disjunction of conclusion and argumentation—itself raised to a general principle of magisterial teaching in *Donum veritatis*—exhibits the foundationalist assumption that immediately justified beliefs "cause" the truth of mediately justified beliefs, an epistemic etiology that, in strong versions at least, makes both argumentation and its cogency superfluous.

Whereas the magisterium is inclined to explain its regard for the dispensability of argumentation by appeal to the charismatic authority of its office, a nonfoundationalist approach to the traditional knowledge it safeguards would expect that same charism to be exercised within the ongoing justification of belief in the history of faith. Within this ecclesial context, the magisterium occasionally practices the charism of authentic teaching by reiterating ancient beliefs so basic to the tradition's knowledge that they pass unquestioned from age to age as the literal sense. Frequently, though, the magisterial charism is exercised in the extension of Catholicism's basic beliefs to present circumstances that call for their guidance or that challenge customary forms of their application. Argumentation is rightly regarded not as a merely accidental dimension of this extension but as the very way in which the magisterium, in the terminology of nonfoundationalist philosophers, justifies its present teaching with regard to the tradition's ancient and basic beliefs—that is, to the literal sense. This, of course, does not mean that the charism of the teaching office is in thrall to reasoning whose soundness is gauged by philosophical criteria of one sort or another. The justification of the Church's belief takes place in the Catholic tradition's own authoritative network of commitments, doctrines, and practices. But the explanation of the faith that justification involves must be measured by standards of coherence and cogency that *in their own terms* are no less rigorous than any epistemic ideal. With regard to reasoning in magisterial teaching, this means that the charism of the teaching office is meaningfully exercised within, and not apart from, the faithful argumentation for uses to which basic beliefs might be put. When employed by the magisterium to convey its teaching, such argumentation is properly regarded as being authentic and thus as mattering as much as a teaching's conclusion, since both are normatively bound to the tradition they promulgate.

This discussion leads to the modest conclusion that arguments should be understood as authoritative in the Church's authentic teaching and as inseparable from the conclusions they advance. In light of this analysis, I can now consider the problem of the authority of dramatically developing tradition for the Church, and for Catholic theology in particular.

Efforts to consider this question, however tentative, must begin by noting the hermeneutical modesty with which this issue is rightly approached. The criterion for guiding the sense of dramatic development presented earlier in these pages offered not a sure method for identifying such belief, doctrine, or practice but rather a heuristic for noticing possible, more likely candidates for currently authoritative tradition that may one day lose its authority. Although reception was the most important aspect of this criterion, the supplementary aspects of argumentative presentation and cogency together mark doctrine that is developing (because argument is deemed necessary to mediate basic beliefs to current circumstances) and perhaps developing dramatically (because the very arguments conveying doctrine that has not been received by the faithful fail to prove cogent even to a wide segment of those in the Church qualified to judge the validity of argument). As noted earlier, the authority of dramatically developing doctrine is an important issue for all in the Church, though the concern here is more specifically with the authority of such doctrine for theological reflection, itself often a considerable influence on the dynamics of development of any sort. And any theological judgment regarding even the possible identification of dramatically developing doctrine does well to acknowledge its own potential for error. After all, this study's two possible examples of dramatically developing doctrine have long had a place in the belief, teaching, and practice of the Church, even if not in the particular argumentative forms in which they more recently have been presented.

Only the most cavalier disregard for that tradition would judge with certainty and without ambivalence that these or any beliefs, doctrines, or practices of the Church are indeed examples of dramatically developing doctrine. Nevertheless, theologians occasionally judge—properly with ambivalence and without certainty—that a particular belief, doctrine, or practice is developing dramatically. No such judgment, though, could undermine the current status of the doctrine or practice in question as the authentic teaching of the magisterium, for such a consequence would elevate theological assessment above the charism of the Church's teaching authority. Even as these doctrines or practices stand in the argumentative forms in which the dramatic character of their development might be recognized, they still possess the authority that issues from any pronouncement of the ordinary magisterium as the authentic interpreter of God's revelation in scripture and tradition. The authority of doctrine in the Catholic tradition is not measured solely by what has been or at some future time will be taught by the magisterium and received by the faithful. This expectation would gauge authority statically by reference to unanimity alone, ignoring the much more contested development that many authoritative teachings have had and continue to have in the Catholic tradition. Dramatically developing tradition, then, possesses authority for Catholic theology—to say nothing of the life of the Church—as long as it continues to be taught authentically by the magisterium.

The analysis herein, however, has led to the valuation of the authority of magisterial arguments as charismatic means of promulgating the tradition's basic beliefs in current circumstances. Although it is important to acknowledge the magisterial authority of these arguments, failures in their cogency and reception can mean only that their authority remains ambiguous, and thus questionable, for the Church. Although the juxtaposition of authority and ambiguity is apparently oxymoronic from the perspective of a foundationalist regard for the justification of ecclesial belief in which argument and conclusion are separable, it is meaningful in a nonfoundationalist regard for the justification of ecclesial belief. In this epistemic perspective informed by Catholic commitment, argument, conclusion, and basic beliefs are inextricably bound together in the historical context of tradition in which the discernment of God's Spirit at work in the Church is rarely, if ever, exhaustive. Should magisterial arguments fail to convince, then better, more coherent, traditionally faithful arguments need to be offered by those in the Church who have the ability to justify ecclesial belief. *Donum veritatis* supports this directive by encouraging theologians to contribute to the improvement of magisterial argument, though it expects theological insights to be communicated in private and assumes that such improvement will be indifferent to whatever magisterial conclusion has already been reached. A more dialogical understanding of *ecclesia*, and one more committed to Vatican I's teaching on the complementarity of faith and reason,[71] would not fear public discussion in the Church about how its basic beliefs are logically extended to current circumstances and would be open to the possibility for such dialogue to be the very means of retrospective development-in-continuity.[72] The same sensibilities would hold fast to the necessary consistency between argument and conclusion in the Church's authoritative teaching, regard the cogency of such teaching as a value of tradition-bound faith, and remain open to revision in both authoritative conclusion and authoritative argumentation.[73]

Reasoned argument truly informed by and demonstrating the consistency of traditional faith can never be extraneous to the authority of the Church's teaching, any more than reasoning truly in the service of faith can be foreign to the purposes of the Church. The expectation that faithful reasoning will lead to utter unanimity among the faithful would seem to be a symptom of a foundationalist understanding of its workings, as erroneous in the sphere of ecclesial knowledge as it is in any other. When conducted authoritatively, ecclesial reasoning respects the pluralism of argumentative possibilities within the tradition it holds sacred, seeks to align its expectations with what the Church has believed and continues to believe, and recognizes its own responsibility to the development of Catholic tradition, even in the rare cases when that tradition develops dramatically.

Reconfiguring Continuity

If the sense of development-in-continuity issues in a representation of tradition that can be likened to postmodern allegory in its functional negotiation of the literal sense, then as allegory its configuration of tradition—whether through hermeneutical, critical, or postliberal approaches—appears as a narrative that is as ongoing and open-ended as the history it portrays as Spirit-filled and providential. The representation of the second sense inevitably entails a regard for tradition as the story of the Holy Spirit at work in the Church through the ages. To the degree that the tradition represented in the story is understood prospectively, the narrative plot—however open-ended—is conceived as unfolding from beginning to end, with every event forever secured in the narrative structure. The notion of a sense of tradition like the third sense presented here seems incongruous with such a prospective understanding of the development of tradition, to say nothing of a classical understanding of prospectivity. The sense of dramatic development apprehends a movement of tradition in which the story of the Holy Spirit at work in the Church moves in a direction utterly unanticipated in light of accustomed narrative expectations. The prospective orientations of both classical and Romantic understandings of tradition make the idea of unanticipated narrative direction strange enough, even if this strangeness is mitigated somewhat in the Romantic conception of development.

Yet the sense of dramatic development asks these traditional sensibilities to depart even further from their customary expectations. The third sense calls on traditional sensibilities to imagine a story of the Holy Spirit at work in the Church in which even significant eventualities in the ongoing plot, those long thought to be central to the integrity of the narrative structure, are now regarded as dispensable. To the degree that tradition is prospectively conceived as abiding representation—either as canon or as development—dramatic development seems not to be a sense of tradition at all but rather tradition's loss, an unwinding of traditional coherence that concomitantly vitiates the nature of tradition itself. If tradition understood as postmodern allegory does have a storied shape, then how can dramatic development, with its alleged disregard for narrative coherence, have a place among tradition's legitimate senses?

The answer to this question lies in the discussion of the sense of development-in-continuity, for the third sense of tradition emerges in the workings of the second. The second sense's negotiation of the literal sense gives rise to a postmodern allegory whose narrative construal of tradition is not prospective but retrospective in orientation. Taking its point of departure always in the present moment of faith's historicity, the sense of development-in-continuity continues the telling of tradition's story by fathoming and representing a particular configuration of continuity with the past. This configuration, or narrative as it might now be called, is not one governed by chronological time or its attendant causality of unbroken linear sequence. Rather, its plot develops, as continuity with the past is retrospectively affirmed in an ecclesial time in which the heritage of Catholic belief and practice stretches from the present to the apostolic age, and the tradition's narrative coherence is set across times, places, and events by the Church's current understanding of its story. Any particular configuration of continuity, itself a development, regards history through the eyes of faith as a tradition whose meaningful narrative must be plotted differently from previous configurations of continuity with the past, if only because the most recent affirmation of traditional continuity articulates the standpoint of—and includes in its plot—the tradition's most recent moment that a moment before was not. On rare occasions, such narrative construals represent continuity with the past in such a way that long-held, repeatedly affirmed claims for continuity are no longer included in the most recent configuration of continuity claimed as authoritative by the Church.[74] This is what occurred at particular points in the Church's tradition with regard to the examples of dramatically developed doctrine and practice with which this chapter began.

This is not to say that the retrospective configuration of tradition in any present moment may depart capriciously from the sedimentation of claims for continuity throughout the Christian past that are largely if not entirely affirmed in the most recent representation of development-in-continuity. We have seen that the first two senses, considered together, are invested more in the constancy of tradition than in its renewal. The movement of tradition that characterizes both, however, is typically the movement of renewal that—again I should emphasize—on rare occasions can drift from its customary relationship to constancy and become a movement of change that breaks with tradition as dramatic development. This movement, though, while breaking with tradition, need not be seen as tradition breaking, as it nearly always is through prospective eyes. The sense of dramatic development is a legitimate sense of tradition when its judgment on the dramatically developing character of certain doctrines and practices issues from the *sensus fidei* and because its claims regarding the loss of tradition's authority on the part of certain doctrines and practices inevitably involve the unprecedented affirmation of others and their coherence in tradition's narrative construal, now plotted in a different fashion through the judgment of the third sense.

It is clear that the dramatic development of such traditional practices and teachings that involve the morality of usury and slavery; the rights of the Church over the unbeliever; and membership in, and the availability of salvation outside, the Catholic Church did not result in the loss of tradition's narrative coherence. Indeed, one might say that, as the lines of narrative coherence were drawn retrospectively without reference to these long-held beliefs and practices, the narrative of tradition became more coherent, more truthful, and more universal. And if the narrative of tradition can possess these desirable traits as a consequence of doctrines and practices having developed dramatically in the past, then it would be reasonable to expect that these same traits could be the consequence of the judgment that certain traditional doctrines and practices are now developing dramatically. The judgments the third sense makes in the present moment, though, undeniably cause consternation among many of the faithful, for they challenge the most basic Catholic assumptions about what faithfulness means. The exercise of the sense of dramatic development stirs the anxieties of the ecclesial community by reminding its members of points they are inclined to forget—that the literal sense is but a sense and not a letter; that established tradition can lose authority and even show itself to be false with the passing of time; and that the apostolic deposit of faith possesses an obscurity capable of greater clarification in any present moment, not only through the fuller manifestation of an already defined continuity but also through the retrospective reconfiguration of the apostolic heritage in ways that leave behind earlier, authoritative versions of its continuity.

The role of faith-filled reasoning is important in the workings of all four senses of tradition explored in these pages, though its importance is especially keen in the workings of dramatic development. When many in the Church sense that tradition is developing dramatically, that what has been and continues to be regarded by many believers as the literal sense of tradition no longer is rightly fathomed and represented as such, the legitimacy of this sensibility cannot be established by feeling or simple assertion. The third sense will always remain ambiguous in any present moment, since it can anticipate only a future result that has not yet occurred and finally may not occur. The third sense, too, is but a sense. Its exercise by no means guarantees the truthfulness of its judgments. If the sense of dramatic development is to justify the legitimacy of its claims, then it must do so with reference to the background beliefs of tradition itself. Reasoning and argumentation from the presuppositions of faith are the means by which this justification occurs. Arguments matter in authoritative teaching precisely because they show, or fail to show, how a traditional claim—even one long held—is or is not justified within a particular configuration of the second sense, which shares the value of constancy with the literal sense. The magisterium, theologians, or believers at large may judge the authority of a particular understanding of the literal sense to be compromised by virtue of an alternative understanding of tradition. Or the magisterium, theologians, or believers at large may defend the established literal sense in the face of judgments claiming the dramatic development of certain elements of its belief, doctrine, or practice. In either case, faithful reasoning cannot shirk the task of offering arguments measured by the developing continuity of tradition that justify the claims by which the Church professes its belief. Justifying the claims of the third sense, even when, with the passing of time, a belief, doctrine, or practice shows itself to have developed dramatically, finally leads not to tradition's loss but to its gain, for the eventual fact of dramatic development can mean only that the loss of authority on the part of a particular belief, doctrine, or practice has made the old new and the new old in the most recent affirmation of tradition's developing continuity.

4

Incipient Development as a Sense of Tradition

Dramatic development is a sense of tradition that anticipates a possible future in which tradition's faithful configuration no longer includes a belief or practice previously moored, even for long periods of time, in the authoritative tradition. The criterion for discerning possible instances of dramatically developing tradition has ascribed great importance to the receptive power of the Church's communal sense of the faith. More than the argumentative style of magisterial teaching and the lack of cogency of such teaching for theologians, the sense of the faith provides the most reliable evidence for beginning to judge the sense of dramatic development. The sense of dramatic development, like all four senses considered here, must be understood as an exercise of the *sensus fidei*, even if indirectly as an exercise of striking non-reception. It proves itself to be the *sensus fidei* when its judgments are confirmed by the belief of the whole Church.

This study's discussion of the literal sense and the sense of development-in-continuity has presumed that their representation was indeed already an expression of the *sensus fidei*, since only the belief of the whole Church and its representation as tradition could qualify as the first or second sense. The sense of dramatic development differs in this regard from the first two senses in that in the present moment it is not affirmed by the universal Church as its faith. The claim that a belief, doctrine, or practice is now developing dramatically is necessarily far more contingent than the claims of the first two senses. A claim now on behalf of the third sense will not garner the same degree of ecclesial consensus on the character of the *sensus fidei* as the first two senses have garnered. Yet the consensus of the faithful in varying degrees of affirmation measures the claims of all three senses of tradition considered thus far. This priority of ecclesial consensus is not found in the case of the fourth, and last, sense of tradition—the sense of incipient development—which is the focus of this chapter.

Claims for incipient development commend the traditional value of beliefs and practices that have not held currency in the Christian past but that have appeared recently among a relatively small number of the faithful. This minority in the Church may be as small as a single believer or as large as a truly significant minority, however its number is set. The sense of incipient development is the experience among this smaller number of the faithful that an uncustomary belief or practice possesses authority that now deserves recognition in the Church as its tradition. Incipient development, then, is an ecclesial sense for the novel. The novel may present itself, on one hand, as an innovation, as a belief or practice that has never been previously believed or practiced in the tradition and thus as a belief or practice localized by contemporary time and, often further still, by contemporary place. Incipiently developing belief and practice, on the other hand, may emerge as an understanding of established tradition that is so uncustomary within the tradition's history of retrospective affirmations that its novel interpretation of the Christian past calls for nothing less than a reconfiguration of previous configurations of continuous development. The sense of incipient development calls to the sense of development-in-continuity from their shared present, though one that, for the fourth sense, is oriented more toward the future than toward the past. In this regard, the fourth sense is like a herald beckoning the second sense to further, truthful development. The words bespeak the renewal of tradition that the sense of incipient development fathoms in the historical experience of the Church with a far greater sense of urgency than do the first two senses.

The sense of incipient development is tradition's imagination. It incites the second sense, and through it the first, to (1) envision a longer or wider and in any case richer continuity than the one framed in tradition's most recently configured pattern and (2) consider the value of new ideas, possibilities, and opportunities that might be occasions for tradition's truthful development. In its appreciation for the novel, the sense of incipient development can regard tradition anew—the novelty of a present insight, event, or problem serving as a lens through which all of established tradition looks different in astonishingly new clarity or through which beliefs and practices long lost in the distant past can now be seen by and magnified for tradition's present eye. If the fourth sense is tradition's imagination, then its creative power is often prophetic. The sense of incipient development apprehends what might be or what should be in the renewed development of tradition. In its openness to a future that bodes the transforming fulfillment of the ecclesial body, the fourth sense resembles the ancient fourth sense of scripture. Like the anagogic sense, the sense of incipient development yearns for an eschatological meaning, though, unlike the ancient scriptural sense, the fourth sense of tradition ponders the eschaton historically and not metaphysically. But its postmodern avoidance of the metaphysical does not stem at all from a denial, on its part, of belief in "the resurrection of the body and life everlasting," the Nicene Creed's closing testimony of faith that voices anagogic expectation; it stems from a deference to the conditions of historicity in which the faith of the present anticipates its future renewal. In a manner consistent with the first three senses, the fourth sense of tradition discerns what it claims to be tradition from the limitations of the present moment, however much it seeks to remold the present and its past heritage in the cast of an imagined future.

As a sense shared by the relatively few and not by the whole Church, incipient development often finds its position amid the claims of the first two senses to be as precarious as that of the third sense. Tradition, after all, can emerge definitively only in the claims of the first and second senses. And in their kinship as the represented claims of the entire people of God, the literal sense and the sense of development-in-continuity together prize the traditional value of constancy over the traditional value of renewal. Claims on behalf of the new—whether the new appears indirectly as a judgment on the obsolescence of an established belief or practice or directly as a judgment on the authority of a belief or practice unsecured in the Christian past—are usually met with a certain reserve on the part of the first two senses, if only because such claims call for constancy's redefinition. Sometimes the first two senses show outright disdain toward claims on behalf of the new, even when made in the name of renewal, since such claims can be judged threats to the constancy they treasure. The literal sense is particularly resistant to the fourth sense. Except on those rare occasions in which a claim on behalf of the new utterly supports the stolid constancy of the first sense, the preponderant concern of the first sense for what abides in tradition leads it to regard the fourth sense with deep suspicion. The commitment of the second sense to the renewal of continuity leads it to regard the fourth sense if not with suspicion then at least with the concern that its apprehension of and claims for the authority of the new will contribute to tradition's errant deviation from its authoritative past rather than to its meaningful continuance.

The fourth sense resembles the third sense in its openness to the illuminating possibilities of contrast alongside tradition's continuity. Like the sense of dramatic development, the fourth sense gravitates toward a striking alternative to tradition that demands a reformulation of traditional understanding. Whereas the third sense discerns traditional contrast in the development of an old doctrine or practice toward obsolescence, the sense of incipient development finds contrast in a new belief or practice that clamors for recognition amid the old or even—should its rhetoric take such shape—*as* the truly old. Both dramatic and incipient development are corrective senses dissatisfied with tradition's current definition, ready and eager to point a better way back to the apostolic age or forward into the ecclesial future. And both offer their vision of what tradition might be as an expression of minority sensibilities that remain unproven in the present moment. At this point, the third and fourth senses diverge, only to converge again in their common orientation. The proving of the third sense with the passing of time results in the absence of a previous presence, whereas the proving of the fourth sense results in a presence that fills a previous absence. Yet the proving of either the third or fourth senses in the life of the Church leads to a configuration of tradition that differs from previous configurations and thus to the development of tradition.

The third and fourth senses, then, are the impetus to the development of Christian doctrine and practice within the scope of creaturely power. Each in its own way appreciates the striking movement of which faith in history is capable. And by posing such striking movement to the traditional value of constancy, the third and fourth senses influence the sense of development-in-continuity, and through it the literal sense, in significant ways. Whether negatively or positively, the third and fourth senses present occasions for the renewal of tradition to the second sense that at first can be seen only on the periphery of its typically retrospective field of vision. Third- or fourth-sense claims begin as the belief or practice of the few that stand in contrast to the doctrine and practice of the many. But any one of these occasions for renewal, as a third- or fourth-sense claim on behalf of the *sensus fidei*, can become so veridically compelling in the experience of the Church that its increasing authority pushes it closer and closer to the center stage of traditional constancy and before the direct gaze and attention of the second sense. And there, in full view of the second sense, a third- or fourth-sense claim may gather such truthful strength in the community of faith that the second sense becomes obliged to do more than take notice and must now integrate what was disorienting contrast into the continuity of authoritative tradition. At the point of their apprehension and representation by the second sense, the senses of dramatic and incipient development lose their integrity, which returns as these sensibilities fathom other occasions for renewal. The incorporation of third- and fourth-sense claims in a second-sense configuration of tradition can be understood as their most heightened influence on the second sense, though at this juncture these striking senses of development become indistinguishable from the second sense and its apprehension of developing continuity. If this influence is profound enough, it can extend with the passing of time to the literal sense itself, which is always, though less perceptibly, subject to the power of renewal.

Of these two senses of striking development, it is more the sense of incipient development that bears the responsibility of renewal. The third sense appears in tradition with far less frequency than does the sense of incipient development, which is a practiced habit of faith. The fourth sense is both naturally and gracefully oriented toward an unfolding history that is new in every moment and within which the eventful passage of time offers a host of opportunities for tradition's vital promulgation. The third sense is exercised not as a matter of course in the life of faith but as an extraordinary judgment in a time of crisis. Its novelty lies in an exception to a previous understanding of the rule of faith. Moreover, the sensibility of dramatic development itself is stirred by the discernments of the fourth sense, as novel, fourth-sense understandings of the past suggest unprecedented configurations of tradition in which long-established beliefs, doctrines, or practices no longer seem to possess the authority they once did. In this regard, even the development fathomed by the third sense has its cause in the fourth as the discernment of the new prompts a judgment about the old that questions its traditional future.

The fourth sense of tradition may be the last, but it certainly is not the least, in our fourfold schema. Indeed, the reflections here on the relationship between and among the four senses suggest that none can be least. And although one would do well to recognize the priority of the first and second senses for their clearer representations of the *sensus fidei*, these cannot be accorded the status of "most" among the senses. Neither may either one of the other two. None of the senses can be least or most, precisely because all are holistically related expressions of the one sensibility of the faith that is preserved in the Church by the Spirit of God. The differentiation that this fourfold schema brings to this finally singular sense of the faith enables the appreciation of its clarity and ambiguity, which is to say its mystery, in the tradition that believers profess and practice. An appreciation of that differentiation continues as this chapter attends to the particular activity of the sense of incipient development, considering examples of the fourth sense at work in the past and the present, examining the discernment of the fourth sense as a regional act of faith empowered by the Spirit and as ecclesial reception oriented toward the future, and exploring the construal of incipience in the narrative of tradition.

Examples of Incipient Development

The idea of incipiently developing belief and practice may be strange in a premodern conceptualization of tradition in which the novel and the traditionally authoritative can stand only in oxymoronic juxtaposition.[1] But the modern understanding of developing tradition has domesticated this idea that is so foreign to classical sensibilities. Unlike the idea of dramatic development, the idea of incipient development, at least of a particular kind, is at home in a modern understanding of tradition. Although the assumption of prospectivity that it shares with the premodern conception of tradition causes it to balk at an unprecedented novelty, a modern conception of developing tradition can embrace a consistent novelty in ecclesial experience and representation by invoking the Romantic distinction between the latent and manifest or the post–Vatican II distinction between content and form. In these similar explanatory strategies, what I have called "incipient development" is relegated to manifestation and form and thus to a contingent dimension of tradition that can accommodate change on the recent margins of apostolic latency and content, themselves the tradition in its unchangeable necessity. Yet all four modern models of development offer an alternative to the classical understanding of tradition as uncorrupted hand-to-hand transmission in their appreciation for the productive power of the novel, if not *as* then *within* the tradition of the Church.

The sense of incipient development considered here enjoys the pathbreaking achievements of such nineteenth- and twentieth-century theologians as Drey, Möhler, Newman, and Rahner, as well as the benefits of such magisterial teaching as *Dei verbum* and *Mysterium ecclesiae*—all of which recognize the value of doctrinal development, and thus of the novel, in the life of the Church. We have seen, however, that to the extent that this modern understanding of tradition remains prospective in orientation, it represents tradition from an idealized, past standpoint divorced from the real circumstances of present faith and from which tradition's gaps in historical chronology can be given only dubious account. Moreover, to the extent that the modern conception relies on the form-content distinction to safeguard its prospective assumptions, it accounts for the relationship between the old and the new in traditional development by recourse to a faulty epistemology. The current treatment of incipient development, then, must build on the modern conception's appreciation for the novel in the traditioning process but must do so by considering the novel through a sense of tradition consistent with the other senses examined in the previous chapters. And this means, above all, that the orientation of the fourth sense toward the future and its sympathetic regard for the novel must be consistent with the workings of the literal sense and the sense of development-in-continuity portrayed herein.

Incipiently developing belief and practice can be illustrated by first showing, as in this study's propaedeutic to possible examples of dramatic development, that this sort of striking development has clearly occurred in the past. The current delineation of candidates for belief and practice now developing incipiently will be all the more credible in principle if it can identify examples of beliefs or practices that *have* developed from incipience to the traditional continuity of the first or second sense. Doing so is not difficult. Examples are legion and are limited only by the actual number of discrete beliefs and practices that make up Christian tradition. All Christian belief and practice, even belief and practice that is most basic to the tradition, began in a particular historical moment. To the degree that it began, any belief or practice possessed an incipience. And to the degree that its beginning perdured and through perdurance gained authority in the course of time, any doctrine or practice recognized within the authoritative continuity of tradition possessed an incipient development. Moreover, belief or practice that has developed incipiently to the point of its configuration in the Church as first- or second-sense tradition sometimes encounters present-day apprehensions of the novel that claim authority and influence its established understanding. Such doctrine or practice might be said to be developing incipiently to the degree that it is brought into the ambit of current incipient development that offers an unprecedented perspective on its traditional meaning and subjects it to the power of the novel in a striking fashion.

Beliefs such as the resurrection of Jesus from the dead and Christ's Second Coming to judge the living and the dead, doctrines such as original sin and transubstantiation, and practices such as the veneration of the relics of the saints and Lenten fasting were all incipiently developing at least from the time of their first historical appearances and throughout the time that led to their inclusion in tradition as first- or second-sense claims. At first a few believers, and perhaps initially but one, claimed the authority of a belief or practice as authentic Christian tradition. And even though few at first made this claim, and far more in the Church at the same time were ignorant of it or even repudiated it as inconsistent with tradition's present contours, the claimants on behalf of the incipiently developing belief or practice proved to be correct in their judgment with the passing of time, however short or long the period of incipient development. Having found examples of incipient development that has already occurred in every established doctrine or practice of tradition, let us examine one in closer detail before proceeding to present-day candidates for incipient development. The christological doctrine of the Father-Son relationship serves well.

At the Anatolian Council of Nicea in the spring of 325, the Alexandrian presbyter Arius and his followers were condemned for holding the view that Jesus Christ, the Son of God and savior, "was not before he was begotten."[2] The Arians denied neither the extraordinary filial relationship between God and Jesus, whom they regarded as the incarnate divine *logos*, nor his effective status as the savior of the world, as modern Arian scholarship has come to appreciate.[3] The Arians, though, clearly held that the being of the *logos* was created by God and, more, that the Son of God was not created out of any substratum of the Father's uncreated being but out of nothing, like all the things of the universe that were brought into existence by the Father through the mediating agency of the Son. Broadly speaking, the Arians were excommunicated at Nicea for their christological subordinationism, their belief that the Son of God is inferior to God the Father. The teaching of the council—that the Son of God is "begotten, not made, *homoousios* [one in being] with the Father"—condemned the Arian subordinationism, and through it all forms of subordinationism, thus affirming that the Son of God, with the Father, is without beginning.

Study of pre-Nicene Christianity with regard to this most important item on the conciliar agenda shows that subordinationism not only was prevalent in the early Christian centuries but also possessed, by virtue of its prevalence, a normativeness that only gradually—first in the third century and definitively in the fourth—came to be challenged by many as heterodox belief. One can turn for examples to the early apologist Justin Martyr, whose reliance on the Middle Platonism of his day led him to portray Christ as "second God"; or Theophilus of Antioch, whose strongly Jewish Christianity avowed the creation of the *logos* by God; or Tertullian, who still spoke of the created generation of the Son from the Father even as he struggled to maintain the unity of Father and Son and the creaturely difference between the Son and the universe; or Origen of Alexandria, who maintained the uniqueness of the Father by affirming the creaturely status of all other existence, including the Son and the Spirit, albeit a creaturely existence eternally created by the Father.[4] In each case, christological subordinationism of one form or another seemed to be a tacit rule of faith, undoubtedly because such subordinationism preserved the transcendence of the Father and thus the crucial distinguishability of Father and Son for any faith that did not err on the side of modalism or Sabellianism.

Certainly the particular traits of Arian subordinationism explain most of all why it, of all the early Christian variants on subordinationism, came to be judged as heretical by the now orthodox majority. But to the degree that the condemnation of Arianism at Nicea represented the rejection of *any* christological subordinationism, the conciliar teaching can be understood as a powerful expression of a development of doctrine in which believers increasingly made claims for the uncreated being of the divine *logos*. One can understand this development in historically generous terms, extending its trajectory back to the belief of Athenagoras in the ingenerate rationality of the divine Word in the mind of God and the suspicion of Irenaeus of Lyons concerning the language of generation to express the Father-Son relationship.[5] The *Expositio Fidei* attributed to Gregory Thaumaturgus (written c. 260–270) offers more explicit textual evidence for this development in its profession of belief in a Son of God who is "eternal of the eternal" and in a Trinity in which there is "nothing of the created, nothing of the slave."[6] The teaching of Nicea capitulates this development in a definitive way, if not in its own time then certainly in the retrospective judgment of later Christian communities to the present.

Somewhere in the course of this shift from the normativeness of christological subordinationism to the authoritative teaching of Nicea on the Father-Son relationship, incipiently developing tradition first made its appearance, as a few Christians, or perhaps initially but one, made an explicit claim for the authority of a nonsubordinationist christology. Gregory's *Expositio Fidei* offers a lucid textual illustration of such an explicit claim. But there is no reason to think either that his was the first expression of this explicit belief or that the first claim along these lines was made in writing. As incipiently developing belief, the explicit claim for a nonsubordinationist christology entered the tradition as something striking, without precedence in the circulating scriptures that came to be regarded as the New Testament or in the earlier Christian writers accorded authority in the nascent Church. Though striking, this incipient development even in its earliest appearance may have been met with eager nods of agreement in some Christian communities. But the strength of Arian belief throughout the Christian world after Nicea makes it reasonable to conclude that the striking character of this incipient development would have been regarded as a scandalous betrayal of the true faith in other Christian communities decades, and perhaps even centuries, before the council was convened.

The high christology professed by the fathers at Nicea in 325 is a good example of an incipiently developing belief moving closer toward its incorporation in tradition as a second-sense claim that retrospectively configures previous claims for continuity in such a fashion that these are now defined in terms of the present-day claim, in this case the Nicene condemnation of subordinationism. The division in the Church on Nicea's teaching in the aftermath of the council is telling evidence that its exclusion of subordinationism from authentic Christian belief was not yet a second-sense claim for tradition (to say nothing of a claim that had achieved the authority of the literal sense), if one expects first- and second-sense claims to be the professed belief, doctrine, and practice of the whole Church. Were one to look for the time at which this incipiently developing belief became second-sense and eventually first-sense tradition, a broad span of time could be posed from the Council of Constantinople's sanctioning of Nicea's christology in its profession of faith, known to later tradition as the Nicene Creed, to the defeat of Spanish adoptionism by the eighth-century Carolingian theologian Alcuin.[7]

Within this history of incipient development is revealed another instance of incipient development in the conciliar proposal of the *homoousion* formula, as Nicea's particular way of framing the Father-Son relationship while forbidding christological subordinationism. According to Eusebius of Caesarea—an Arian bishop at the council and the Emperor Constantine's court theologian—it was the emperor himself who suggested the word *homoousios* as a gloss on Eusebius's own credal proposal for the expression of a common faith, an account that contemporary historians find little cause to doubt.[8] Although there is every reason to think that Constantine's intention was compromise, the result was quite the opposite. A majority of those who opposed subordinationism found the word to be a clear expression of their faith in the peculiar dignity of the Son, whereas the Arians nearly all saw an expression of a faith at odds with the ancient christological tradition. Even defenders of the council recognized that the word was a novelty if measured against the linguistic common stock of scripture and tradition.

The efforts of the Alexandrian bishop Athanasius to defend the teaching of Nicea in the generation after the council is a well-known chapter in church history, one that can be revisited briefly to illustrate the incipient development of the *homoousion* formula. Precisely because the atmosphere of the Church was so charged by the most fundamental disagreement between Arian and Nicene communities on the issue of the proper configuration of traditional continuity, incipient development within an incipiently developing tradition proved especially problematic to such an ardent defender of Nicea as Athanasius. On one hand, Athanasius judged the *homoousion* formula to be a faithful rendition of the orthodox faith, in spite of its absence from the traditional language of the faith. On the other hand, he recognized that the formula caused offense not only to the Arians, for whom the novelty of the formula confirmed the falsity of the belief it expressed, but also to supporters of the nonsubordinationist stance of Nicea, for whom the novelty of the formula was a scandal of innovation. Athanasius negotiated his defense of Nicea and his aim to make his vision of the Great Church as accessible as possible by ever claiming the truth of the *homoousion* formula as authentic tradition while suggesting, at least for certain audiences, that the formula alone need not be the final arbiter of Nicea's christological faith.

In the first three books of Athanasius's four-book *Orations against the Arians*—probably written over a period of time between 340 and 360[9]—he made reference to the *homoousion* formula only once, choosing instead to defend the purport of Nicea's teaching while avoiding the novel expression. The striking character of incipient development is begrudgingly acknowledged in another treatise, *On the Decree of Nicea* (c. 351–355). There Athanasius found the authority of the formula in the sense of its teaching, so that the formula's acknowledged novelty diminished before the sense's purported continuity with the biblical writings, in which it was admittedly not found:

> Therefore if they [opponents of Arius yet concerned about the novelty of the conciliar formula], as the others, make an excuse that the terms are strange, let them consider the sense in which the Council so wrote, and anathematize what the Council anathematized; and then if they can, let them find fault with the expressions. But I well know that, if they hold the sense of the Council, they will fully accept the terms in which it is conveyed. . . . This then

was the reason of these expressions; but if they still complain that such are not scriptural, that very complaint is a reason why they should be cast out, as talking idly and disordered in mind. . . . However, if a person is interested in the question, let him know, that, even if the expressions are not in so many words in the Scriptures, yet, as was said before, they contain the sense of the Scriptures, and expressing it, they convey it to those who have their hearing unimpaired for religious doctrine.[10]

In a later work, *On the Synods* (359), Athanasius was less confrontational with and more accepting of those who trouble about the novelty of the *homoousion* formula. As long as such believers "accept everything else that was defined at Nicaea, and doubt only about the Coessential [*homoousios*]," they "must not be treated as enemies" but "as brothers." "For, confessing that the Son is from the essence of the Father," he continued, "and not from other subsistence, and that He is not a creature nor work, but his genuine and natural offspring, and that He is eternally with the Father as being His Word and Wisdom, they are not far from accepting even the phrase, 'Coessential' [*homoousios*]."[11]

This same concession to the novelty of the formula is found in a still later work, *Letter to the African Bishops* (c. 369). Athanasius admitted that those who may very well be allies in the Nicene cause can be "alarmed at the phrase 'coessential' [*homoousios*]." He urged his fellow bishops to assure the faithful that the phrase possesses a meaning no different from the conciliar condemnation of those who regard the Son as a creature. Yet Athanasius did not understand the *homoousion* formula to be an optional expression of the faith, devoid of real authority. Neither did he regard the formula to be entirely contingent on the conciliar anathema. Building on his earlier claim that its true sense if not its actual phrasing is biblical, he now argued to the African bishops that the fathers at Nicea were "not inventing phrases for themselves but learning in their turn . . . from the Fathers who had been before them."[12] Although his earlier strategy of commending the sense and not the letter of the *homoousion* formula conceded its novelty as an expression, Athanasius now insisted on the place of the formula in tradition to such a degree that he attributed the alarm at its reception to the pretense of ignorance on the part of those who questioned its authority.[13]

Here, then, in the emergence of a nonsubordinationist christology and of the *homoousion* formula to convey the definitiveness of this belief, one finds a double example of tradition that has developed incipiently. The authority that the teaching of Nicea came to possess in the course of the next generation or two of believers, and then throughout the subsequent tradition, is lucid evidence that its incipient development achieved the status not only of second-sense but also of first-sense tradition. The *homoousion* formula shares in this same development by virtue of its inclusion in a creed that was reaffirmed by the Councils of Constantinople (381) and Chalcedon (451) and, of course, throughout the subsequent tradition. Indeed, the Chalcedonian Decree, which taught the complete divinity and the complete humanity of the incarnate Christ, further evinces the development of the *homoousion* formula from incipience to second- and first-sense tradition. According to the decree, the incarnate Christ is "*homoousion* with the Father in divinity, *homoousion* with us in humanity, like us in every respect except for sin,"[14] an extension of the *homoousion* formula to a second and unprecedented application to Christ's share in humanity that was possible only through the secured authority of the formula's first use.

Recall at this point that early christology illustrates an incipient development that every Christian belief and practice undergoes whenever it first appears. Incipient development can be identified with relative ease in the past from the vantage point of the present. When present-day believers look to their own times and places to discern and to represent tradition that is incipiently developing, their task is far more difficult. Claims for incipiently developing belief or practice may prove with the passing of time to be no more than ephemeral custom and no tradition at all. Or such claims could, in time, be configured in a traditional continuity extending back to the apostolic age. Present claims for incipiently developing belief or practice may share richly in traditional truth, as did the *homoousion* formula, or may be completely outside of it, as christological subordinationism proved to be. Clearly, the traditional stakes are high for claims on behalf of the fourth sense, especially if one recalls that such claims carry the power of traditional renewal. Let us turn to three possible candidates for incipiently-developing tradition, appreciating by their analysis the ambiguity that attends any contemporary claim on behalf of the fourth sense.

God as Parent

The first candidate for incipiently developing tradition can be found in contemporary belief that poses a wider understanding of the parenthood of God than is offered in the traditional understanding of God as Father. The belief in God as Father is as old as Christian belief, and probably as old as the preaching of Jesus himself, so at home is this representation of the divine in the language of the New Testament. Christian belief was faithful to its Jewish heritage in ascribing personal existence to God and in imaging the mutuality inherent in such existence in terms of the parent-child relationship, an expected consequence of belief in a creator God lovingly involved in the lives of creatures. Moreover, the most basic Christian claims regarding the divine sonship of Jesus Christ and the expectation that discipleship involved conformity to the life of Christ and thus to Christ's filial relationship to God intensified the significance of a parental understanding of God on the part of believers.

That this parental relationship was conceived as a relationship to a male parent so that God typically was portrayed as Father can be attributed to cultural assumptions regarding the power, privilege, and relative freedom of males in families of the ancient Mediterranean world—assumptions that have been prevalent in Christianity's history in Western and Byzantine cultures, as well as in world cultures throughout history. The fatherhood of God could be parsed in different ways in the early tradition as Christians faced challenges that called for different emphases on the divine paternity. But whether Christians stressed the identity of the divine Father as creator against the Gnostics or the importance of the divine fatherhood for an orthodox christology,[15] claims for the fatherhood of God were made with remarkable consistency. The name "Father" appeared in the New Testament, early liturgy, and creeds as a synonym for "God"[16] and, while still retaining this earliest meaning, later became the proper designation for the first person of the Trinity.

In the past several decades, theologians have found the critical perspectives of the so-called second wave of the feminist movement to be an important resource for understanding, criticizing, and reconstructing the Christian tradition. Appealing to the authority of women's experience and prophetically decrying the injustice of discrimination toward women, feminist approaches to theology have transformed its disciplinary landscape by their critical attention to a host of issues—christology, anthropology, ecclesiology, and the doctrine of creation among them. No issue, though, has been more central to a feminist critique of the Christian tradition than has the doctrine of God, particularly the traditional understanding of God as Father. One would be hard-pressed to name a feminist theologian who has not placed this doctrine first on the theological agenda, a priority that follows the order of the creed much more than it follows individual decision. Belief in God is so basic to Christian faith that its constitution is reflected in virtually every other traditional belief and practice. The doctrine of God literally permeates the tradition. In recognition of its priority and influence, feminist theologians have sought to delineate the consequences of belief in God as Father on the Christian heritage and on culture at large.

No brief summary could possibly do justice to the many nuanced ways in which feminist theologians have addressed what they judge to be the limitations of the traditional doctrine of God as Father. Often, however, feminist theological reflection involves two distinguishable and yet inseparable stages: a moment of critique and a moment of reconstruction. A feminist critique of the doctrine of God attempts to expose patriarchal assumptions, prejudices, and practices in the workings of the doctrine's history, use, and authority. Feminist theologians usually begin this analysis by showing the susceptibility of religious symbols to co-option and distortion by the power relationships at work in the broader culture in which they hold meaning. Claims for the fatherhood of God not only convey but also reify cultural patriarchy, as the supremacy of the divine Father is invoked—even if unconsciously—to justify male supremacy in the family, in political and economic life, and in the arts and sciences. Sallie McFague, for example, has noted that the divine paternity is readily expressed in imagery connected to male power in ancient (and modern) societies, so that the God of the tradition has typically been portrayed as a king who remains distant from "his" subjects who are encouraged by the metaphor to conceive themselves as powerless before "him."[17] Anne E. Carr articulated one of the most prevalent and basic feminist critiques in her judgment that despite "the long theological tradition that maintains that God transcends sexuality, . . . both popular and theological language suggest that God is 'somehow masculine,' that God is 'he.' "[18] This literalism, which brings the symbol in thrall to patriarchy, is considered by many feminist theologians to be a manifestation of idolatry that yet manages to masquerade insidiously as the tradition itself.[19]

Feminist theological reconstruction of the doctrine of God informed by the critical moment takes many forms and moves in many directions. Whereas some theologians have argued that the traditional symbolism has been corrupted beyond rescue by its long misuse in an inescapably patriarchal setting, others have proposed strategies for understanding the parenthood of God in a way that counters this patriarchal symbolism. Feminist theologians often point out that the attribution of maleness to God stems from a deficient anthropology, itself an expression of patriarchal values, in which maleness is defined as normative for understanding the human. From the assumptions of ancient biology to contemporary hiring practices in corporate America, the ascription of priority to maleness in thinking about what makes for the fullness of a human person relegates femaleness to the status of second or supplement, absence or lack. Feminist theologians such as Rosemary Radford Ruether reconstruct a more adequate doctrine of God by reconstructing a more adequate anthropology, one that is at least inclusive and, more, appreciates the distinctiveness of women's experience in configuring the human.[20] An anthropology that repudiates the inferiority of women has implications for every dimension of personal existence otherwise warped by the prejudice of patriarchy, including our understanding of parenthood and the Christian attribution of parenthood to God.

A feminist anthropology challenges any understanding of parenthood that supports the ancient Roman model of paterfamilias in which the father possesses absolute authority over spouse and children. Moreover, such an anthropology calls to task any understanding of parenthood that would pose a binary opposition between fatherhood and motherhood in which the duties, effectiveness, and finally the value itself of parenting would reside far more in paternity than in maternity. Claims for an egalitarian understanding of parenting need not be reductive, as though there were no differences at all between men and women, or between this man and this woman, and so between fathers and mothers. Yet, although most feminists readily acknowledge actual differences between the sexes—and some even legitimate differences in how gender might be culturally constructed—most, if not all, feminists would be suspicious of difference that carries the weight of priority and privilege. History suggests that difference so weighted would tilt toward misogyny and its terrible effects on women.

Feminist theologians who seek to recover the doctrine of God by drawing on these insights argue for the importance of appreciating how God is Mother as much as Father and of carrying this appreciation for the divine life into theological representation. Carr notes that, by attending to such a neglected emphasis on divine motherhood "as a source for symbolizing parenthood in God, theology is opened to rich perceptions of authority as life giving and of power as enablement of the autonomy of others, as gentle persuasion, as patient love and encouragement, themes consonant with the biblical descriptions of God."[21] Following different constructive paths, Elizabeth Schüssler Fiorenza and Elizabeth Johnson have found a common biblical resource for the divine maternity in the *sophia* tradition that runs through the Old and the New Testaments. *Sophia*, the wisdom of God, is personified in their writings as the feminine divine whose maternal traits inform the economy of salvation and, in the Rahnerian commitments of Johnson's work, the Trinitarian life of God itself.[22] Like all who have benefited from the work of feminist historians, Johnson knows that the maternal imagery for God proposed by contemporary theologians has precedence in the tradition.[23] But in her judgment, "the maternal relationship as a pointer to the divine has been actively derogated and consciously erased from the repertoire of suitable images," a situation that can be remedied by a new appreciation for the imaging of God as "Holy Wisdom . . . the mother of the universe" whose "creative maternal love is the generating matrix of the universe, matter, spirit, and embodied spirit alike."[24] Dorothee Sölle insists that "speaking of God our father and God our mother can be liberating,"[25] for inclusive language itself has the power to challenge patriarchical assumptions and, in this case, to support a richer understanding of God as person and parent.

Claims for a broader, inclusive understanding of God as parent have not been contained in academic circles but have spilled out into the community of the faithful as a sensibility shared by many, though certainly by a relatively small minority in the Church. In spite of their minority status, such claims have found their renewing power to evince the genuine work of the Spirit in need of recognition by the whole Church if God's presence to its continuous tradition is to be fully known and appreciated. Yet the whole Church does not recognize the legitimacy of this novel claim. Moreover, many in the Church, even those who have found feminist insights to be religiously significant in other respects, have judged this claim for incipient development to be no sense of tradition at all and, more, the utter lack of such sense. A single illustration of this disagreement will suffice.

The feminist critique of noninclusive language has influenced the practice of speech in many cultures, a change in the habits of language that reflects and to some degree has caused social change, however modest, toward the equality of women. This has been especially true in Western industrial societies where the feminist movement has flourished in spite of an environment often hostile to its growth. The value of inclusive speech as a guard against discriminatory assumptions, conceptions, and behaviors has been recognized by the U.S. National Conference of Catholic Bishops, which in 1992 approved a proposal for an inclusive-language lectionary for liturgical use. This proposal, however, was not sanctioned by the Vatican, reportedly because of concern about the appropriateness of inclusive language in the new lectionary's translations of scripture. Yet the U.S. bishops' proposed revision of the lectionary opted for inclusive language only "horizontally," in reference to human persons, refraining from proposing inclusive language "vertically," in reference to God.[26]

In a February 27, 1997 lecture, Bishop Donald Trautman—then immediate past-president of the U.S. Bishops' Committee on the Liturgy—contemplated the still-undetermined fate of the inclusive-language lectionary by noting that it "will be a sad day for Catholic biblical scholarship and even a sadder day for the pastoral life of the church in the U.S. if the new Lectionary does not incorporate the principles of gender-inclusive language."[27] While championing horizontally inclusive language, however, Bishop Trautman adamantly rejected linguistic representation of the belief cited here as a possible candidate for incipiently developing tradition:

> Bad inclusive language also exists. The Oxford University Press recently published *The New Testament and Psalms: An Inclusive Version*. This is a most irresponsible translation that offends the doctrine of the church and revealed truths. This translation eliminates all references to God the Father. The Lord's Prayer begins "Our Father-Mother in heaven." . . . In my opinion, this biblical version is not so much a translation as a rewrite based on contemporary political and social ideologies.[28]

It is difficult to know whether Bishop Trautman's remarks simply make the laudable hermeneutical point that translation needs to balance faithfulness to the original and intelligibility in a new context and judge that this particular example fails to do so or whether the statement makes a judgment as well on the orthodoxy of the belief offered as an example. In any case, two points are worthy of note. First, the example cited does not eliminate reference to God the Father as he states but speaks of God as "Father-Mother." Second, many in the Church would criticize Bishop Trautman's ardent support for horizontally inclusive language in the lectionary for the same reason that he criticizes vertically inclusive language in biblical translation—that it is no more than a "rewrite" of the sacred Word "based on contemporary political and social ideologies." If this criticism does not invalidate the inclusive-language lectionary proposal of the U.S. National Conference of Catholic Bishops, as the bishops almost certainly have argued to the Vatican, then it is difficult to see why this criticism in principle would rule out the acceptability of belief in God as an inclusive parent and why one could not judge the expression of this belief in scriptural translation to be an authentic balancing of traditional faithfulness and contemporary meaningfulness.

The issue at stake for the Church is not whether contemporary political and social ideologies should be at play in tradition, since they always and inescapably are. Rather, the issue is whether the Spirit of God can be at work in a particular political or social ideology in a way that can inform, and even be claimed as, Christian tradition. Those in the Church who profess the Catholic legitimacy of an inclusive understanding of God as parent see, no doubt, the workings of the Spirit in a theological appropriation of feminist insights. Yet Bishop Trautman speaks for many in the Church—and no doubt a majority—who would judge this claim to be contrary to the literal sense of tradition and, for this reason, false. As relatively few believers profess this faith and the Christian practice it implies, they make a claim on behalf of tradition's fourth sense. Only time will tell whether such a claim for incipient development can be upheld, for its proof lies in the claim's affirmation as first- or second-sense tradition by the whole Church. But if proof comes in the receptive judgment of a future Church that finds both renewal *and* continuity in what was once a claim for incipient development, the fourth-sense claim affirmed as the truthful tradition now by only a few certainly must be so, even if most in the Church now are not clear enough in their vision of the *sensus fidei* to recognize it as such.

Preferential Option for the Poor

The second candidate for incipiently developing tradition is the claim of some in the Church that has come to be known as the "preferential option for the poor." In many respects, a Christian concern for the poor is as old as the tradition. It is so consistently presented in the New Testament as the message of Jesus that even the most rigorous historical-critical reader would have a difficult time attributing this concern only to the early Church and not to Jesus himself. Moreover, this concern for the poor has been prevalent throughout the tradition in common understandings of the authentic life of discipleship, especially as modeled in the life of the great saints, such as Francis of Assisi, and in the importance of almsgiving as a virtuous practice. In our own time, however, a certain interpretation of this literal sense of tradition has appeared that qualifies as an example of incipient development.

In the late 1960s a number of Latin American Christians, from bishops to laity, found that the insights of a new orientation in theology elucidated the plight of the poor in Third World countries such as theirs, where a large majority of the population finds itself beset by the harsh realities of economic and political injustice, by hunger and violence—in short, by the systemic presence of death in daily life. The Peruvian theologian Gustavo Gutiérrez articulated these sensibilities in a July 1968 lecture entitled "Toward a Theology of Liberation," which coined a name for the new theological perspective. Appealing to the authority of the biblical prophetic tradition, Gutiérrez argued that the peace promised in God's kingdom "supposes the establishment of justice, the defense of the *rights of the poor*, the punishment of oppressors, a life without the fear of being enslaved by others." According to Gutiérrez, the coming of God's kingdom demands an active concern for the poor and their situation that risks nothing less than the transformation of injustice and the social conditions in which it is rooted. "An intimate relationship exists," he claimed, "between the kingdom and the elimination of poverty and misery," for the "kingdom comes to suppress injustice."[29] Gutiérrez elaborated these judgments in his later and major work, *A Theology of Liberation* (1971). The Christian life appropriately lived is one that takes a stand with the poor as a witness against the scandal, indignity, and injustice of the sinful structures that oppress so many in the human family. This testimony must take practical shape "in specific action, a style of life." The witness of "solidarity with the poor," Gutiérrez insisted, is not an embrace of poverty "for its own sake" but "as an authentic imitation of Christ," as "a protest against poverty" that aspires "to liberate humanity from sin and all its consequences."[30]

These sensibilities—which, in Gutiérrez's judgment, represent not one of many ways of being Christian but the heart of the gospel itself—found expression in two meetings of the Latin American bishops, at Medellín, Colombia, in 1968 and at Puebla de los Angeles, Mexico, in 1979. According to the Latin American bishops at Medellín:

> We ought to sharpen the awareness of our duty of solidarity with the poor, to which charity leads us. This solidarity means that we make ours their problems and their struggles, that we know how to speak with them. This has to be concretized in criticism of injustice and oppression, in the struggle against the intolerable situation that a poor person often has to tolerate, in the willingness to dialogue with the groups responsible for that situation in order to make them understand their obligations.[31]

At the Puebla conference, nearly eleven years later, the bishops followed the lead of Medellín in decrying a false choice between what they now called the ideologies of liberal capitalist and Marxist collectivist economic systems, as though these exhausted the possible resources for a Christian response to the plight of the economically oppressed. Solidarity with the poor, they insisted, must be based on the gospel and on the Church's social teaching, which transcend the limitations of any ideology.[32] The conference's final document now described that solidarity, the same urged by Medellín, in a particular way:

> With renewed hope in the vivifying power of the Spirit, we are going to take up once again the position of . . . Medellín, which adopted a clear and prophetic option expressing preference for, and solidarity with, the poor. We do this despite the distortions and interpretations of some, who vitiate the spirit of Medellín, and despite the disregard and even hostility of others. . . . We affirm the need for conversion on the part of the whole church to a preferential option for the poor, an option aimed at their integral liberation.[33]

Gutiérrez commented on Puebla's phrasing of the belief in a recent writing. "Preferential" should be understood in a way that "precludes any exclusivity; it simply points to who ought to be the first—not the only—objects of our solidarity." The word "option" denotes "the free commitment of a decision." And this decision entails "a deep, ongoing solidarity, a voluntary daily involvement with the world of the poor."[34]

In the words of the Latin American bishops at Puebla can be seen traits of the incipiently developing sense. On one hand, the bishops claimed belief in the preferential option for the poor as the universal tradition to which the whole Church should be responsible. On the other hand, it is a universal truth to which the Church needs to be, and so is not now, converted; a belief that not only has failed to receive wide acceptance but also has been misunderstood, distorted, and vitiated—and by many *within* the Church, before and after Puebla, who reject the claim that the preferential option deserves recognition as Catholic tradition.

The theologian Michael Novak, for example, has spoken for many in arguing that the class analysis important to liberation theologians such as Gutiérrez reflects a final commitment on their part to Marxist ideology. Touting the advantages of capitalism for Third World development, Novak's analysis regards the phrase "opting for the poor" as an expression of Marxist sensibilities that define the poor as a social class set in opposition to the affluent and that overlook the role of individuals in changing their economic plight and the poverty of nations.[35] A concern for the influence of Marxism on liberation theology, the intellectual matrix for the claim of the preferential option, was also expressed by Pope John Paul II in his opening address at the Puebla conference and in a CDF "Instruction on Certain Aspects of the 'Theology of Liberation' " (August 6, 1984). While acknowledging the scandal of poverty, an abiding concern for the poor in the Church's teaching, and the desire for liberation among the "disinherited classes" as one of the "signs of the times" that must be interpreted in light of the gospel, the "Instruction" yet finds the interpretive orientation of liberation theology to be guilty of a "historical immanentism" that reduces the Kingdom of God to history and history to "a process of the self-redemption of man by means of the class struggle."[36] In this "purely temporal messianism," "faith, hope, and charity are given a new content: They become 'fidelity to history,' 'confidence in the future,' and 'option for the poor.' "[37] This judgment on the false novelty of the preferential option was followed by an attempt to correct the formula in a second CDF teaching on this theme, "Instruction on Christian Freedom and Liberation" (1986). Here the formula "love of preference for the poor" is put forward as a traditionally faithful alternative to the possibly materialistic and exclusivistic decision of the "option" called for at Puebla.[38]

Yet, for a significant minority in the Church, the claim on behalf of the preferential option for the poor is a belief that expresses a new consciousness about the meaning of the gospel that deserves recognition as eccesial tradition. That minority includes believers in ecclesial base communities who live out the preferential option in daily life, Latin American bishops who contemplate the meaning of tradition in the face of the endemic poverty of their congregations, the bishops of the United States who in their 1986 Pastoral Letter on the U.S. economy cited the authority of the preferential option for the poor,[39] and economically advantaged First and Second World Christians who recognize the truth of the novel belief and wrestle with its implications for their lives. This minority professes the incipient development of the preferential option by claiming its renewing power and its truthful constancy, however unrecognized, as tradition.

The ambiguity of this belief as an instance of incipient development is perhaps best exemplified in the encyclical of John Paul II *Sollicitudo rei socialis* (December 30, 1987). Even though this papal teaching appeared more than a year after the second CDF "Instruction" on liberation theology, it still included the language of "preferential option" alongside the hitherto magisterially preferred "preferential love." "Here," the Pope noted, "I would like to indicate [one theme of the magisterium commended in recent years]: the option or love of preference for the poor. This is an option or a special form of primacy in the exercise of Christian charity to which the whole tradition of the church bears witness."[40] This dual portrait of the belief as "option or love" both endorses the incipiently developing belief that originated in the Latin American Church only twenty years earlier and voices the ambivalence that such novelty, with its susceptibility to misunderstanding, can meet in a Church that measures the authority of tradition by an ecclesial assent that usually coalesces over long periods of time. In the midst of the papal ambivalence, however, it is interesting to observe the novel formula—even in the company of its qualification—claimed as the age-old Catholic tradition.

The Restriction of Priestly Ministry to Men as Divine Revelation

The final example of a possible candidate for incipiently developing tradition is a claim put forward recently by the magisterium, by some theologians, and subsequently by many in the Church in defense of the traditional practice of restricting priestly ordination to men.

Only in the past several decades has there been a need in the Church to defend the practice of ordaining only men to the priesthood, a need addressed formally and for the first time by the magisterium in the CDF's *Inter insigniores* (1976). This document makes the point that the Church in the past had condemned heretical groups such as the Gnostics that extended priestly ordination to women. But these condemnations were made principally for other reasons, for the heretics' violation of the Church's ancient "rule of faith," which did not include the practice of ordination. As the Vatican document acknowledges:

> The church's tradition in the matter [of ordination] has thus been so firm in the course of the centuries that the magisterium has not felt the need to intervene in order to formulate a principle which was not attacked, or to defend a law which was not challenged. But each time that this tradition had the occasion to manifest itself, it witnessed to the church's desire to conform to the model left to her by the Lord.[41]

These last words present a new way of justifying a practice long held but lately questioned by many in the Church, as illustrated in the previous chapter. The traditional practice of ordaining only men is now ascribed in *Inter insigniores* to the intention of Christ to which the Church has the resolved obligation of fidelity. The Church is not free to act on its own judgment in this matter, the document states, but "is bound by Christ's manner of acting." The normative practice, "based on Christ's example, has been and is still observed because it is considered to conform to God's plan for his church."[42] John Paul II reiterates this claim of the 1976 CDF teaching in *Ordinatio sac-*

erdotalis (1994) by observing that "the Gospels and the Acts of the Apostles attest that this call [of only men as apostles and so as priests] was made in accordance with God's eternal plan."[43] In other words, the restriction of priestly ordination to men is judged to be divine revelation itself, though divine revelation only recently seen and appreciated in scripture and tradition in the face of calls for the ordination of women.

Within what for centuries had been a literal-sense practice of tradition, one witnesses the unfolding of a fourth-sense claim never before made and now vying for recognition as the Church's authoritative tradition. In an April 10, 1997 lecture at Fordham University—where he holds the title Distinguished University Professor—Avery Dulles, S.J. defended this position by citing evidence from scripture, tradition, theological reasoning, and the teaching of the magisterium, in short, the same evidence presented in *Inter insigniores*.

Although Dulles conceded to supporters of the ordination of women that this matter cannot "be definitively settled by Scripture alone," he concluded that "[a]ll the biblical evidence we have about priestly office in the primitive church tends to confirm its exclusively masculine character."[44] Magisterial teaching obliges a reading of the New Testament in which Jesus ordained his apostles to the ministerial priesthood. And even though Jesus could have broken with the Jewish customs of his time, as he often did—in this case by ordaining women—he chose not to do so. For Dulles, it is a simple matter of history that the consistent practice of the Church regarding ordination was maintained throughout the centuries and sometimes in the face of practice to the contrary on the part of heretical groups. The christological argument "from representation" explored in the previous chapter is invoked as a defense of the current practice from theological reasoning, though Dulles's focus is on the use of the traditional spousal metaphor by *Inter insigniores* as the most effective way to make this argument. Only males can be ordained, according to Dulles, because they must represent Christ, whose maleness is theologically significant for his spousal relationship to the Church—he as the bridegroom to the Church as the bride. "In order for Christ himself to be the bridegroom of the church, as God had been bridegroom of Israel," Dulles has concluded, "he had to be a man."[45] Dulles's view seems to be that the ordination only of men serves the symbolic role of the priesthood by representing this spousal character of the incarnation itself. Finally, Dulles has claimed, the magisterium has held to the validity of the current practice with utter clarity, especially in John Paul II's *Ordinatio sacerdotalis*, which taught that the Church has no authority to confer priestly ordination on women and that this judgment is to be definitively held by all the faithful.

For Dulles, this fourfold evidence—from scripture, tradition, theological reasoning, and magisterial teaching—leads inescapably to the judgment that this practice and the beliefs it reflects are nothing less than divine revelation. With his usual care and appreciation for nuanced theological distinction, Dulles has observed that the magisterium has not called for an "act of divine or theological faith" regarding its teaching on the practice. And yet, according to Dulles, "inasmuch as this assent is to be given to a teaching contained in the deposit of faith, it seems hardly distinguishable from an act of faith,"[46] an act required before divine revelation. The Church's defense of its classical heritage, for Dulles, is the truly prophetic element in tradition and not the current call for the ordination of women that derives from "the pressures of public opinion and political correctness to which the Church may not yield." "Continuing to uphold the revelation given to it in Christ and the Scriptures, as handed down in sacred tradition," Dulles has insisted, "the church must be prepared to risk unpopularity and become, if necessary, a 'sign of contradiction.' "[47]

Here, then, in this recent justification for the authority of an ancient practice, is a possible candidate for incipiently developing tradition—one that rivals both the possible incipient development of tradition in the claim that women may be ordained to priestly ministry and its attending claim for dramatic development that the restriction of priestly ordination to men is losing traditional authority as it moves toward its eventual obsolescence.[48] The fourth-sense claim taught by the magisterium, defended theologically by Dulles, and held in belief by many in the Church may very well with the passing of time show itself to be the universal tradition as the whole Church ascribes the practice of ordaining only men to priestly ministry to the revealed will of God. But the current rivalry between fourth-sense claims on this practice, claims for tradition that are mutually exclusive in their ability to prove truthful, means that the ascription of revelatory authority to the ancient practice is not now a second- or first-sense claim.

The Regionality of Fourth-Sense Claims

The examples just cited illustrate several noteworthy traits of incipient development. As fourth-sense claims are made by a minority in the Church, they engender dispute. Their novelty calls for a shift in previously established configurations of tradition, particularly the pattern of the literal sense in which the Church invests the highest degree of authority. The authority claimed by the fourth sense is often regarded as no authority at all but rather as pretense or heresy, depending on the seriousness with which its claim is taken by those who judge it false. The fourth sense is prophetic in its cry for a traditional change of heart that yet presents itself as true faithfulness to tradition. And even though this change rarely takes the form of denial or reversal but more typically takes the form of fuller realization and renewal, it shows the literal sense to be capable of a movement to which it is often thought impervious. In the example of priestly ordination, the prophetic call for change supports the literal sense to the greatest possible degree. The novelty of the justification of the age-old practice as divine revelation is thus minimized to the same degree. Usually, however, fourth-sense claims offer a striking contrast to the literal sense, as can be seen in the examples of divine parenthood and the preferential option. Here the prophetic call for change is made in a critical tone and in the imperative mood, ways of speaking that are out of sorts with the literal sense's calm and measured cadence. However much these fourth-sense claims beckon the Church's regard as authentic tradition, their novelty is at a premium and makes their authority at least questionable and at most dismissable, much in the manner of the *homoousion* formula in the immediate aftermath of Nicea.

The sense of incipient development is striking because its claim to traditional authority flourishes in a span of time that is extraordinarily compact when set against the long temporal continuity mapped by the first and second senses. That the fourth sense by nature is exercised by few in apparent opposition to the *sensus fidei* would be enough to disturb the sensibilities of those abiding completely in the traditional consensus, unmoved if not untouched by the novel insight. But that the new sensibility occurs in the short time of years, and not centuries, and that its beginnings can often be traced to a very specific time, and perhaps even to a certain moment, makes its claims for traditional authority all the more precarious. The tenuous character of the fourth sense is compounded further by the compactness of the locality from which its claims issue. Whereas first- and second-sense representations of the *sensus fidei* as tradition proceed from the Church in every place, fourth-sense beliefs and practices arise in determinate places—such as the United States and Europe in the example of the maternal dimensions of the divine, Latin America in the example of the preferential option, and Vatican City in the example of the revelatory authority of ordination practice. Space, like time, shrinks to the greatest possible degree as the brief lineage of the fourth-sense claim can be traced back to the abode of a single voice prophetically beckoning the Church to a different understanding of its tradition. Limited space, like limited time, is often perceived as a scandal by the first and second senses, even if some limited spaces traditionally incite scandal less than others.

These characteristics of the fourth sense bespeak the thick regionality of the act of faith by which it claims to discern the truthful movement of tradition. As illustrated in chapter 2, the regionality of faith should not be understood in a way that makes faith a solitary or individual act rather than the communal commitment it truly is. But faith does possess more particular dimensions through which the universal faith of the whole Church is sedimented in local communities and even in the smallest reaches of the individual's encounter with God. Prospective conceptions of tradition, whether classical or modern, are inclined to imagine the universality of the Church's common faith as an originary given, trickling down from the Great Church through the local churches into the life of every believer and informing the ever smaller times and places of ecclesial experience with an infallibility as grand as it is fixed. But the sense of incipient development occurs as an act of faith that finds a previously unnoticed truth of the living Word in the immediate particularity of culture and time. The fourth sense judges this local encounter to have more than local significance. However particular its circumstances or the faithful response it engenders, this truthful encounter is affirmed as being of universal significance that deserves the status of Catholic tradition. If this local find is real, Catholic belief expects this sensibility for the novel to broaden from the insight of one, to the faith of a few, to the claims of a local community, to the claims of more communities still. Along this path, these claims continue to express the sense of incipient development as an increasingly significant minority of believers posit the catholicity of an originally local claim and continue to generate, as well, disagreement about its legitimacy as the Church's tradition. This disagreement will gradually abate as the fourth-sense claim approximates the second-sense claim, finally to become it, though this discord will usually intensify as the ecclesial minority making the fourth-sense claim increases in size.[49]

If this is an accurate rendition of how incipient development occurs, then it describes as well how the universality affirmed as second- and first-sense tradition takes shape and continues to be reconfigured by new regional claims for tradition's universal truth. If this rendition is accurate, then it also suggests that the "upward" development of fourth-sense claims, from the faith of a single believer through an ever- increasing number of local communities, takes place in the context of an established catholicity that informs the encounter with tradition at every regional level. Novel ecclesial experience is never utterly novel but only relatively so, as all the examples given here attest. The fourth sense has no integrity of its own apart from its relationship to the senses that represent the faith of the whole Church. By the same token, the constancy treasured by the first and second senses originates in and is constantly renewed by the novel claims of the fourth sense. Tradition is ever incipient.

If this study's rendition of the workings of incipient development is accurate, then it also sheds light on the historical workings of the Spirit of God to whom Catholic belief attributes the movement of tradition. The rootedness of universal tradition in regional claims means that the activity of the Spirit must be attended in local ecclesial experience, as well as in the *sensus fidei* shared by the whole Church. Although the postconciliar Church has appreciated the local power of the Spirit in the proliferation of lay ministries, in the value of inculturation, in a growing pluralism of spiritualities, and in the principle of subsidiarity, this appreciation has rarely extended as far as tradition itself. There is a penchant in Catholic assumptions to think of the reliable presence of the Spirit to tradition only when the constancy of doctrine and practice has been manifest for long periods of time and only where this constancy truly has achieved catholic proportions in space. There is a Catholic comfort in affirming the first and second, but not the fourth (to say nothing of the third!), senses of tradition as the work of the Spirit. No doubt, prospective prejudices about the abiding, once-and-for-all givenness of a finished, traditional truth account for Catholic discomfort about the local proclivities of the fourth sense. But there are other reasons that cannot be discounted.

The constancy prized by the first two senses may be the palest reflection of the timelessness attributed to the Spirit of God, but it is, nonetheless and however faint, a reflection that can be understood to mirror the divine eternity. The sense of incipient development calls on believers to imagine the workings of the Spirit in a temporal moment so regional that its point of origin can be marked out and even identified with the new insights of a particular community or the latest work of a particular theologian. That determinateness seems to rule out the possibility of traditional constancy, even though fourth-sense claims include constancy as an attribute of the novel belief or practice they urge upon the Church. How can the activity of the Spirit "begin" now, in such a temporally regional manner, in a tradition of such duration? Moreover, the catholicity prized by the first two senses may be the smallest instantiation of the omnipresence attributed to the Spirit of God, but it nonetheless can be understood as a reflection—however diminutive—of the Spirit's pervasive presence to all creation. The sense of incipient development calls on believers to imagine the workings of the Spirit in a place so regional that its boundaries delineate only a nation, a parish, an office, or, metaphorically, the boundaries of a single, creative act of faith. That spatial particularity threatens the catholicity regarded as the Spirit's proper traditional dwelling. For a tradition that finds the assurance of the Spirit in its constancy and catholicity, the fourth-sense expectation for the graceful activity of the Spirit in regional time and place seems strange at best and contradictory at worst. The sign of contradiction appears again as one recalls that the fourth-sense is not an alternative to the first or second senses but appears along with them as a call and impetus for their renewal. If the fourth sense truly discerns the presence of the Spirit in the novel and the local, then how can this presence be different at all from the truthful divine presence the whole Church discerns in the constancy and catholicity of the first and second senses?

The holistic approach to tradition pursued in the discussion of the previous three senses can inform one's understanding of the fourth, and its often precarious, relationship to the Catholic heritage. Each of the senses of tradition, when discerning well, is an exercise of the *sensus fidei*, the Church's communal act of faith that yet fathoms, affirms, and represents tradition discriminately and in some respects individually through the four senses. The unity of tradition is properly conceived as the unity of the four senses in the communal act of faith whose mystery they extend meaningfully in different ways to times and places capable of tradition's embrace. Often, however, the unity of tradition is conceived more reductively as the literal sense, or as the classical deposit of faith, or as a content that abides amid developing form. However it is conceived, this reduction accords an untoward priority to the constancy and catholicity of tradition. Measured against this imbalance, which severs constancy and catholicity from the power of traditional renewal, the fourth sense finds its affirmation of "beginning" and "local" truth as tradition to be judged thoroughly inconsistent. But there is no inconsistency in principle within the holism of the senses. The incipience of tradition is a function of time, and the inevitably local character of tradition's origins is a function of space. Time and space, the created conditions of history, are just as much the created conditions of the *sensus fidei* and its exercise as the four senses of tradition that together weave time and space into a pattern of the Spirit's graceful presence to history.

Of the senses of tradition, it is the fourth that is especially attuned to the fine particularities of time and space and the continual workings of the Spirit even then and there. Although all four senses affirm tradition from the present moment, the first two seek it in the grander sweep of time and space. Their shared orientation becomes problematic only when it is regarded as exclusive and normative, as though only the senses bent on constancy possess legitimacy. Constancy and renewal, as values of a single tradition, are as holistically related as the four senses that all frame their relationship in one way or another. Without the contributions of the fourth sense to the integrity of tradition that all the senses have a hand in making, tradition would languish in an unrenewed constancy and, in such a state, which is only abstractly imaginable, would be no tradition at all.

The Fourth Sense and the Future of Tradition

It is the responsibility of the fourth sense to seek the Spirit of God in the smallest times and places of everyday life that might show themselves to be tradition and to pose its findings to believers as a presentiment of what that tradition might be when it is finally reconfigured in a pattern of development-in-continuity. The fourth sense anticipates the movement of tradition by claiming to apprehend an authentic movement of the Spirit of God that is "new" to history and "new" when viewed against the backdrop of tradition's most recent portrayal of continuity. But this novelty, as already seen, is relative to what precedes it. Fourth-sense claims are always already informed by the constant tradition they hope to develop anew. Novel workings of the Spirit can be identified only by virtue of the Church's continuous witness to the Spirit. A fourth-sense claim is not true in principle. Any claim for tradition might show itself with the passing of time, or even immediately, to be so at odds with customary representations of the Spirit's presence to history that an initial reception by an ecclesial minority is not sustained or reception by more than a few believers is never garnered. Neither is there a reason in principle for the novelty of fourth-sense claims to be regarded as utterly strange or foreign to tradition, for the renewing assimilation of such claims as those of the second or first sense shows that the novelty of any present claim may be truthfully relative to, eventually compatible with, and finally attested as the universal and Catholic tradition.

Fourth-sense claims are also relative to time. This sort of relativity characterizes all of the senses, if only because faith is faith in history. Tradition is a way of valuing time religiously. The framing of tradition as constant by the first and second senses, however, can suggest—albeit wrongly—that real tradition is timeless, a judgment that works to alienate the blatant novelty of fourth-sense claims from the tradition they purport to renew. Appreciating the relativity of the fourth sense to time, and through it the other senses, can do much to mitigate the prejudiced imbalance of constancy and renewal.

In an extended meditation on time as the measure of creatureliness, Barth has made the remark, simple and yet rich in possible nuance, that God gives us time.[50] If fourth-sense claims are relative to time, then it is important to begin even a brief reflection on this relativity by noting with Barth that time is a divine gift. Within the unfolding of the present from the past, and the anticipation of the future in the present, one encounters a duration marked in experience by memory, immediacy, and expectancy; in language by "now" and "then"; and in tradition by "always," "still," and "will be." However this duration is imbued with meaning, it stands as the condition of eventfulness. Occurrence happens in time that can be rendered as short or long, depending on how beginnings and endings are positioned or envisioned. "Morning," "today," "my life," and "Catholic tradition" are all relative ways of fixing temporal boundaries so that a duration and the occurrences that fill it can be appreciated and meaningfully negotiated. Just as time is God's gift in creation, so, too, are the eventful durations through which time's cosmic duration nestles its way existentially into our social and personal histories. Christian faith expects that this extraordinary gift never completely leaves the hands of the giver, not because God finally withholds the gift or qualifies the act of giving but because the divine giver remains fully present to the gift. God is present to time and perhaps, one might conjecture, most fully present to the durations in which one actually meets time, and thus the power, goodness, and truth of the divine presence.

Tradition is such a gratuitous duration, as are the smaller durations that tradition comprises. And yet the integrity of these durations as tradition frequently goes unappreciated. The ecclesial investment in constancy often leads to the eclipse of the "still" of the present and the "will be" of the future by the "always" of the past. This is particularly true of the traditional duration that extends from the present through the open future. Prospective conceptions of tradition, whether classical or modern, make the shape of the religiously meaningful future predictable with regard to at least an assured content and at most an assured form. Prolepsis here becomes inexorable. Even when envisaged in terms of this study's categories, the possibility of development that the future offers tradition can present itself as a threat to the "always" of a literal sense wrenched from its holistic relation to the other senses. The traditional future's "will be," then, is claimed by an anxious and falsely hypostatized literal sense as inevitability governed by the authoritative past. The future duration of "will be," however, is better understood in terms of possibility as "might be." The contingency of such a future does indeed seem threatening to Catholic sensibilities, as though its apparent randomness were out of joint with the continuity one expects of religiously valued time. It suggests a sheer, temporal openness, an unending duration utterly resistant to tradition's patterning of time—in George Steiner's provocative phrase, a "Satanic chaos."[51] But if one recalls that time in all its durations is a divine gift to which the giver remains ever present, then the contingency of the future belongs not to Satan but to the Spirit. Possibility in grace shows itself to be providence. The duration of "might be" becomes as well the promise of yet unrealized constancy and catholicity.

Along the lines of the *Genesis* account, one might imagine the Spirit of God hovering over the chaos of time, creatively shaping it into tradition in and through the human agency of the four senses. The analogy holds in the sense that this tradition-building creativity is exercised in duration. The analogy breaks down in that the divine rest has yet to come. An eye only for tradition's grand duration, an inability to see the divine work on each of its "days," can lead to the judgment that the novel claims of the fourth sense cannot be truthfully consistent with the Spirit's attested presence to the Church's established, universal tradition. But this judgment rests on the assumption that tradition's time is a single duration and thus really no duration at all, a time that is always "always." It assumes, too, that the Spirit is bound by the Church's testimony to the literal sense, as though the literal sense were a "letter" capable of immobilizing the Spirit's presence to time. However the "might be" of tradition's possible and yet providential future enters the present life of the Church, it does so as a fourth-sense claim for constancy and catholicity whose desire to renew attests to its conceivable consistency with what tradition is and has been.

The grand duration of traditional constancy not only tends to eclipse the durations of present and future but also, and as a consequence, can foster an impatience with truth that appears novel when measured against its older claims and that shows itself to be developing now from an incipience that is precisely definable in both time and place. It is this impatience that is quick to make the charge of truthful inconsistency in the face of fourth-sense claims. The Spirit's presence to all the durations of time and thus to all the durations of tradition undermines the legitimacy of this charge—though the expanse of that presence over time may very well mean that the truthful presence of the Spirit to one duration is relatively clear, whereas the Spirit's presence to another duration is relatively obscure. But even in their obscurity, fourth-sense claims—as claims for constancy and catholicity—attest to their veridical consistency with traditional precedence, even if the constancy and catholicity they claim calls for the retrospective reconfiguration of continuity with the past.

The sense of incipient development is tradition's authentic prospectivity, its legitimacy defined by the stance it takes from the present moment of faith turned toward the future. Unlike prospective conceptions of tradition, the fourth sense does not claim all durations as its own from the position of an idealized past. Rather, it looks forward to the future from a present into which the future ever spills. There, at the intersection of present and future, possible occasions for the renewal of tradition offer themselves to the judgment of the Church, which is itself judged by those occasions that are truly the work of the Spirit. In this regard, the sense of incipient development exercises its discernment as a power of reception, much in the manner of the second sense. Unlike the second sense, however, the fourth sense receives not the traditional past but the traditional future, the renewal of "will be" rather than the constancy of "always" and "still." Believers committed to time instilled with the value of tradition are ready to acknowledge their responsibility to the past. But responsibility to the future is important too if traditional time possesses the unity of all durations,[52] and the traditional renewal that issues from the duration of present to future is appreciated for its capacity to make that unity at once tighter and richer. The fourth sense attends particularly to this traditional duration, just as the first sense attends particularly to the duration of "always" and the second sense to the duration of "still." The fourth sense's attention to the future may require it to engage tradition with considerably less evidence and considerably more imagination than do the other senses. And yet its proven claims, though having their provenance in the meeting of present and future, in time do much to make tradition what it has been and is.

Incipience in the Narrative of Tradition

Much of late-twentieth-century theology has appreciated the extent to which the openness of the future offers the opportunity of openness to God and, more, stands before us as God's very openness to history.[53] Theological portrayals of tradition have appreciated this insight less, no doubt because their typical prospectivity envelops the future in the apostolic past. In this conflation, the future becomes as finished as the revelation bequeathed tradition in the apostolic age, its openness reduced to the possibility of historical forms for timeless content in the modern conceptualization or virtually denied in the premodern conceptualization, which sees the future as a multitude of yet-to-appear hands to pass on the ancient deposit. Theologies of tradition would do well to let the future possess the integrity it does, not merely as the locus of development or handing down but as a veiled, though ever unveiling, duration that is God's very openness to tradition. The sense of incipient development is an awareness of this integrity of the future as God's and of God's donation to tradition at the moment the future intersects the present. Fourth-sense acts of reception, oriented as they are toward the future, seek the gift of tradition, are moved by the gift and the continuing presence of the giver, and insist on the placement of the gift in the history of graciousness that tradition is.

This placement is not without its difficulties, as the examples considered herein illustrate. Claims for the traditional authority of the novel have been problematic in principle. These claims often require argument in order to justify their authority. The dissension that argument highlights has its source in fourth-sense desire for truthful recognition and is often regarded as proof of fourth-sense falsity by those who expect to find tradition only in the harmonious, untroubled accord of the literal sense. Claims for the novel, especially in recent times, often present themselves through the genre of criticism whose testy tone and *via negativa* into established tradition stand in marked contrast to the ready assent of faithful consensus and to negation only in the pronouncements of anathema that comfortably foist the condemned outside established tradition. The most formidable difficulty that faces the traditional placement of fourth-sense claims, though, concerns the status of revelation in relation to such claims. The very idea of the authoritatively novel being recognized and welcomed at the threshold of long-standing tradition seems to suggest that the new arrival, a stranger who claims to be one of the family, goes by the heretical name of Montanism. According to this ancient belief, rightly rejected by the Catholic tradition as early as the third century, God's revelation to the world has not been finally given in the apostolic age but remains open to new, postapostolic installments. To those suspicious of the holistic relationship between the old and new in the model of tradition proposed here, the fourth-sense might seem to be a Montanist sensibility and its insights pretenders to a new revelation. This is not a negligible concern; it is one that should be taken seriously. The earlier consideration of second-sense tradition as postmodern allegory can help frame a response.

As has been shown, the understanding of development-in-continuity that informs all the senses of tradition proposed in these pages might be likened to ancient scriptural allegory, though its narrative resemblance is qualified by its commitment to historicity, its historical-critical awareness, the value it places on a pragmatics of use, and its willingness to respect the retrospective coherence of tradition's narrative—in short, by the postmodern character of the story it tells. If tradition can be conceived as postmodern allegory, then its narrative plots the Church's faithful efforts to negotiate and renegotiate the literal sense in each of its present reconfigurations of continuity. This ongoing process of negotiation develops the tradition, usually staidly as a continuity that largely reaffirms the literal sense, occasionally dramatically in the loss of traditional authority that requires the redefinition of continuity, but always novelly as the renewing power of the fourth sense provides an impetus to any development at all. The contributions of the fourth sense provide a narrative energy to this plot, an energy in which believing fourth-sense discerners share but that is finally attributed to the power of the Holy Spirit. The modern theological tradition has grown accustomed to the idea that the narrative of tradition develops by virtue of this Spirit-filled élan, and that the Spirit's authorial talent constructs this narrative deliberately, the most recent eventualities in traditional plot carefully signaled and anticipated in all that has come before. But the modern theological tradition, to say nothing of the abiding presence of the classical in our midst, has not grown accustomed to the idea that the narrative's plot can have unexpected twists and turns that seem to deviate surprisingly from what has preceded and that, if truly tradition, require a new understanding of the authoritative plot that has unfolded thus far if they are to be embraced by it.

In many respects, the claims of the sense of incipient development present what might be called a narrative "shock" that disturbs the expectations formed in the story of tradition as it has unfolded thus far. Whether or not one encounters this shock and its effects as corrupt in principle or as potentially beneficial depends entirely on one's assumptions about what a narrative should be. Whereas the ancient literary genre of the epic, for example, mitigates narrative shock to the greatest degree by presenting expectation in plot as something to be predictably and undisturbedly fulfilled, the modern literary genre of the novel appreciates the shocking value of the unanticipated and its capacity to create meaning by transforming and even reversing expectations formed earlier in the narrative.[54] Suspicion of the truthful value of narrative shock in Christian tradition often conveys the assumption that its narrative is properly an epic, whether classical or Romantic. This study's proposal that tradition be conceived as postmodern allegory judges that tradition is better understood as a novel in which the narrative shock stirred by the new can be and often is truthfully productive, as any reader of the genre knows.

The openness of narrative in such an understanding can be regarded as traditionally anomic, since it raises the spectre of Montanism, of an intra-Christian supersessionism in which the narrative coherence of what has authoritatively transpired is rendered obsolete by the most recent claims to authority. Admitting the transformative force of the new suggests a boundlessness of possibility that seems to vitiate the more limited possibility of real narrative, and thus traditional, coherence. Yet the possibilities that newness presents to tradition are never boundless or sheer, however shocking their newness yet may be. The newness of tradition's futurity is bound to a faith located in a present shaped largely by a religious past. Indeed, tradition's narrative shock is a reaction that can be elicited only from a faith firmly committed to the value of constancy shared by the first and second senses. The issue for a theology of tradition is not whether shock can be stirred in the tradition's authoritative narrative, since the history of Christian doctrine and practice offers many testimonies to its appearance as new claims thickened the traditional plot. Rather, the issue for a theology of tradition, to say nothing of tradition itself, is how newness can find narrative coherence amid the old, how narrative shock with the passing of time can become delightful and eager surprise and eventually the calm of the traditionally accustomed, an ecclesial mood primed to be renewed once again by the sort of narrative shock in which it emerged long ago.

Here, again, the literary genre of the novel can be instructive. The traditional novel's twisting plot need not, and when well executed does not, vitiate narrative coherence as set out to the point of shocked expectations. The shocking eventuality, discovery, realization, conversion, or manifestation achieves its narrative power only against the backdrop of an established coherence. The appearance of the new does not discard that coherence but redefines it now in light of the new, enriching and extending the order of plot in ways that could not be anticipated before. The novelist's unexpected negotiation of a plot's previous coherence, its literal sense as it were, can be a helpful analogy for understanding the initial juxtaposition of fourth-sense claims and tradition's coherent narrative. The novelty of fourth-sense claims may initially cause shock to the sensibilities of constancy. And that shock may be conveyed as displeasure with the new or awe in the face of an undeniably veridical power. No matter whether the new is first judged ill or well, if the Spirit is the author of this unexpected turn in tradition's plot, then the effect of incipient development on its narrative coherence will not be corrosive but enriching and solidifying as coherence is defined anew by the second sense. Through the claims of the fourth sense, tradition will not be made new in a "form" distinguishable from "content" and certainly not in a "content" distinguishable from "form" but as a particular configuration of tradition's narrative coherence as the whole Church tells its story, retrospectively and from this present moment in its unfolding plot.

At this point, however, analogy with the narrative genre of the novel may seem to break down. The novel's narrative coherence is finally judged within its covers as the story moves through climax and dénouement and reaches an end. Tradition's plot is an extended dénouement following the narrative climax of the life, death, and resurrection of Jesus Christ. Its ending is never reached in time. Its story continually measures all stories because none follow it. Its pages of belief, doctrine, and practice are bound between the covers of creation and eschaton. This inability to close the book of tradition within history, to make some final judgment in time on the finished coherence of its plot, would seem to undercut the fruitfulness of comparing the narrative workings of tradition with the novel. And yet the novel can be instructive for tradition even in light of this difference. Tradition's narrative coherence is like the coherence of the novel's narrative structure at any point short of its conclusion. At any such point, the reader has formed a certain understanding of coherence that the author vitiates at any future moment in the plot at the terrible cost of loss of narrative meaning and betrayal of the reader. Still, the story's coherence is ever being reshaped as the plot unfolds, sometimes most meaningfully through narrative shock. The tradition's narrative coherence is configured through the workings of the fourth sense in much the same way, in the ongoing course of its narrative development this side of an eschatological ending. The truthful contributions of the fourth sense to tradition may initially be shocking to the community of faith, but, as the work of the divine author, they can never vitiate the previous coherence of tradition's narrative even as they reconfigure it—and in a way that the Church eventually will judge to be more coherent.

The sense of incipient development stirs narrative expectations that have changed in the course of the tradition. The early Church's imminent sense of an ending made a distinction between the fourth and the first senses virtually impossible. Incipience very quickly became the rule of faith in anticipation of the immediate fulfillment of Christian hope in the return of the Lord. As the centuries have passed, though, and as the eschaton has retreated into the more distant future, the fourth and the first senses have become quite distinguishable as the time in which their reconciliation may occur has lengthened. This lengthier time should mold the Church's narrative expectations accordingly. If there is no reason to think that the eschatological end of tradition is near, then the senses of tradition must expect that their discernment of the Spirit will be relative to the divine gift of duration through which tradition's narrative coherence will gradually show itself. In the light of such durable expectations, the Church is obliged to exercise patience with fourth-sense claims—respecting the time it may take to assume their place in narrative coherence—and to remember that what is called the apostolic tradition possesses a dimension of obscurity at any moment in time that can become clearer and more coherent in the future.

5

Discerning the Senses
of Tradition

The senses of tradition might be understood as a taxonomy of Catholic belief, doctrine, and practice. This understanding is possible because each sense of tradition presents a traditional type distinguishable from the other three by its particular traits—the measure of its authority, its stability in the tradition, its capacity for development, its ability to garner the faithful allegiance of local communities or of the whole Church, its balancing of the values of constancy and renewal. Taxonomies of tradition have appeared more lately in Christian history. Within the settled and homogeneous authority of medieval tradition, a taxonomy of belief, doctrine, and practice was unnecessary. Medieval propagators of tradition distinguished only disjunctively between its uniform orthodoxy and heretical pretenders to it. The Christian practice of presenting tradition taxonomically is a response to the pluralism of the postmedieval world—that is, to the crisis and controversy occasioned by this pluralism's threat to ecclesial unity. A taxonomy of tradition attempts to negotiate this pluralism by showing where the unity of the Church truly lies and how this unity stands within its own diversity of beliefs, doctrines, and practices, as well as within the even wider diversity of time and place, the conditions of historicity in which tradition moves.

Amid the splintering factions of a burgeoning Protestantism, the sixteenth-century Lutheran Reformer Philip Melanchthon, for example, invoked the ancient Stoic category of *adiaphora* to refer to matters of doctrinal indifference that should not cause divisiveness among the Protestant confessions. By doing so, he implicitly proposed a simple taxonomy of essential and unessential doctrine and practice, the essential defined in classical Reformation fashion by the divine Word alone.[1] Responding to the dizzingly complex pluralism of modernity and its deleterious effects on Christian integrity, the contemporary Lutheran theologian George Lindbeck has proposed an explicit taxonomy that categorizes doctrines as unconditionally necessary, conditionally permanent, and conditionally temporary. Lindbeck's classification intends to foster the unity of Christian faith by showing how its basic beliefs and practices, its "grammar" as he has called it, abides within the changing colloquialisms of its own religious language and the many strange tongues it encounters in the modern age.[2] A Roman Catholicism struggling to define its relationship to the modern world offered a taxonomy of tradition in Vatican II's teaching on the hierarchy of truths. That the council taught only the fact of a taxonomy that remains undifferentiated by any classificatory schema is testimony, perhaps, to the tentativeness with which the Church has begun to face its own pluralism, to say nothing of the modern world's. Since the Second Vatican Council, many Catholic theologians have invoked what amounts to a taxonomic classification of infallible and noninfallible doctrine and practice, a distinction that has been embraced recently by the CDF.[3]

The senses of tradition also sketch a Catholic taxonomy of belief, doctrine, and practice, though one more explicit and differentiated than any other latter-day Catholic classification. Each of the four senses details a type of tradition under which any number of particular examples might be ranked. The taxonomy of the four senses provides a classification, though not one in which categories are rigidly fixed. Rather, this taxonomy accentuates the fluidity of traditional types within the holistic unity of a developing tradition. Like all the other examples of taxonomy, the four senses are a response to Catholic Christianity's difficult reconciliation of its own values of constancy and renewal in a pluralistic age and within a Church that is itself increasingly pluralistic. Indeed, the four senses are ways of naming tradition's pluralism within its own affirmed catholicity.

But the senses of tradition offer more than a taxonomy of belief, doctrine, and practice. As *senses* of tradition, they dwell in the life of the Church as its distinctive experience. As dimensions of the *sensus fidei*, they are ways of apprehending the truthfulness of the Spirit in history. And if the senses of tradition are exercised subjectively in the most regional of times and places, as has been argued previously, then they are ways in which even the personal act of faith itself receives, seeks, finds, integrates, and makes its commitment to the developing continuity of the apostolic tradition. The senses of tradition function at both the communal level of the *sensus fidei* and in its individual appropriation in the act of faith. And yet, as has been shown, the individual and communal workings of the senses are integrally related. There is no communal discernment of the universal pattern of tradition that does not have its origin in the discernments of the third and fourth senses. There is no individual or locally communal discernment of dramatically or incipiently developing tradition that is not measured or informed by the first and second senses. The discernments of all four senses together continually shape, and by doing so develop, the unity of tradition. Even though the senses of tradition can be understood and appreciated as a second-order classification of holistically related types of tradition, they thrive in the Church more basically as the constancy and renewal of its discerning faith.

How, though, does a discernment of tradition meaningfully take place? How can its truthfulness be fathomed? What criteria can be invoked to measure its authenticity? How do the discernments of the four senses coalesce to form a single discernment on the integrity and unity of tradition? How does one gauge the responsibility inherent in any claim to apprehend the proper relationship between tradition's constancy and renewal? This chapter wrestles with the difficult issues that these questions elicit and many more questions that the issues prompt one to ask.

Theological Responsibility

Posing the question of the responsibility inherent in the discernment of authentic tradition leads to a deeper consideration of a refrain often repeated throughout this study. The delineation of the four senses in the previous chapters insists that each sense apprehends, makes claims about, and represents the presence of the Holy Spirit to history or, better, to the close detail of times, places, and lives—the fabric of historicity into which the Spirit's presence is finely woven. The discernment of tradition is nothing other than, and simply, an apprehension of the Spirit purposefully at work in the Church and in the world. Claims for the community's need to recognize this apprehension's truthfulness are claims for the validity of a discernment of tradition. The representation of the Church's tradition as the myriad relationships of constancy and renewal is a representation of the various kinds of discernment that together take shape as a universally communal discernment of the Spirit's patterned activity. Tradition, in all of its dimensions, emerges in the discernment of the Spirit. And because tradition's authenticity has no standing apart from this measure of faithfulness, traditional responsibility is responsibility to the Spirit. The authority of any discernment, its power to sustain and to renew tradition, derives from this theocentric responsibility. The host of discernments in which tradition is subjectively grasped, objectively claimed, and communally represented are discernments responsible to God.

Conceiving authority in this way is at odds with customary cultural assumptions. Since we live in a world in which the exercise of authority often involves an exercise of penal power, it is easy to think that all forms of authority—including the authority of discernment—function in this way. Even Christian history offers its own examples. The exile of heretics in the fourth-century Constantinian church, the terrible power of the Inquisition in early modern Europe, and the censuring of present-day theologians remind one that authority in the Church has been and always can be exercised as the power of correction, punishment, or exclusion. The Catholic Church may have a divine commission, but it is still a human institution that works in some ways as the world does. Even when the ecclesial exercise of power in correction, punishment, and exclusion is just, it exhibits many of the traits of human fallenness, if only in its presumed need. What makes the Church different from the world is that its most basic understanding of authority is not juridical but theological. Authority in the Church derives from the responsibility of believers to God.

This theocentric orientation of authority in the Church can be easily forgotten as one attends one-sidedly to its juridical exercise. Perhaps such factors as the visible dimensions of the Church, the association of authority with hierarchy, the Church's regulation by its own canonical legal system, and a quick tendency to explain the exercise of authority solely in political terms account for a preoccupation with the juridical side of ecclesial authority. This tendency is encouraged by life in the media age, in which Church authority is often portrayed in news reports and commentaries as a power struggle for ascendancy between rival camps—be they liberals and conservatives; the magisterium and theologians; or Rome and other local regions, such as Latin America (over the issue of liberation theology), Asia and Africa (over the issue of inculturation), and the United States (over the issue of liberal values). Yet these shortcomings should not finally prevent us from recognizing that authority in the Church has to do most fundamentally with the Church's responsibility to God and thus, too, with the individual believer's responsibility to God.

The English word "authority" derives from the Latin word *auctoritas*, which means "source" or "origination," and more derivatively still from the Latin word *auctor*, which means "originator," "author," or "founder." This etymological lineage can prove instructive for understanding the workings of authority, including the authority that derives from relationship to God. One speaks of people's possession of authority in civil society, for example, when they are conduits to the sources or original principles on which civil society is founded, such as a constitution or a system of laws. To the degree that elected officials, trustees, military and police officers, and citizens in unofficial positions are responsible to the civil sources of authority not only in position or word but also, and more important, in deed, they are all—albeit in different ways—authorities. Authority exists as a relational power that unfolds in an enacted faithfulness to the sources professed as true, just, or good. Faithlessness to the sources dissolves authority. Authority, of course, can be measured in a juridical fashion by attention to the formal conditions in which power is legitimately exercised. But even this juridical approach to authority is constantly measured by practiced faithfulness to the sources through which the practitioner proves authority by enactment. Office, position, oath, and duty demonstrate their authority, though not necessarily their power, in and through practice faithfully responsible to the sources.

Even though the Church cannot be confused with civil society, these same general principles on enacted authority apply as much to the Church as they do to civil society. But the profound difference is that the source of the Church's authority is the God who is recognized as the source of all and who cannot rightly be relegated to one among many sources aptly deserving of authoritative faithfulness. However the secondary objects of ecclesially faithful responsibility are defined—as the ancient teachings of the Church, the more recent teachings of the magisterium, or the guidance of pastors—all members of the Church, and all structures within the Church, derive their authority from their responsibility to God. This authority exists as a power that unfolds in enacted faithfulness to God, even when that faithfulness is practiced in particular offices, such as the papacy or the episcopate, in which the more precise expectations of this responsibility are more sharply defined.

This, of course, is an obvious point in a theological setting. To maintain another position, that authority in the Church is not responsibility to God, would be to take an idolatrous stance, however sophisticated or roundabout its expression. This most basic Christian view, though, does become more nuanced when one considers the means rather than the object of authoritative responsibility. Authority in the Church is the power of responsibility to God. But how is that responsibility practiced? How does the believer, and how do all believers together, enact the faithfulness to God that establishes any and all Christian authority? These questions do not possess a single answer with regard to Christian practice in particular circumstances. Practice remains context dependent to some degree, even when measured by the one, divine will. Yet, the question of the "how" of Christian responsibility, of its means, does admit of a single, albeit general, answer if considered theologically in light of the God who is the source of all authority.

The God to whom believers are responsible is the God who is present to history in Christ and the Spirit. Since the earliest apostolic witness to the resurrection, Christians have believed that Jesus' life and death offer the perfect model of authoritative responsibility to God. Certainly the evangelists wrote their gospels as testimonies of faith to his authoritative life and death. All the evangelists state that Jesus acted with authority (Mark 1:22, Matthew 21:23–27, Luke 4:36, John 5:27) and assume that his authority derives its power from his relationship to God. The evangelists portray Jesus' authoritative life and death as the criterion of discipleship, as the measure of aspiring Christian character and thus of the authority that any person might possess, in some measure, through relationship to God. Matthew (28:18) presents the Risen Lord as the one on whom God has bestowed full authority in heaven and on earth, suggesting that the authority of Jesus' life and death, indeed his very identity as a person, reaches its fullest expression in his resurrection from the dead.[4] The authority of Jesus, then, lies in what he is (the Risen Lord) as well as in what he does (live and die in utter faithfulness to God), and both his being and his doing are distinctive by virtue of their relationship to God.

The scriptures offer a portrait of Jesus' authoritative life, death, and resurrection for later generations of Christians that allows them to practice his life in theirs. But an adequate notion of authority in the Church would not speak of faithfulness to God through Jesus only as the imitation of a literary account, even acknowledging that account's truth as God's own inspired Word. Only through the power of the Holy Spirit, the very Spirit of God poured out on the Church at Pentecost and promised to the Church as the power of its sanctification from generation to generation, could the scriptures be written, believed, and practiced at all. In the living reality of God's Spirit, the faithful relationship to God that is authority in the Church meets believers as the gift of God's grace that engenders their response. Authority in the Church may be observable in lives lived in Christ-like responsibility to God. The Spirit, however, empowers such faithfulness as the very presence of God in these very same lives. The believer's relationship to God who is the source of all, and to God who became incarnate, flourishes in the living encounter with God who is present to creation and history as the Spirit. Authority in the Church is faithfulness to God, and Jesus' life fully images that faithfulness. But as Christians share their lives with others, they meet the power of that authority and the possibilities of its concrete enactment in the presence of the Holy Spirit.

God's own trinitarian being, economically disposed toward the world for salvation's sake, then, establishes a framework for considering *how* believers are responsible to God. If the presence of the Holy Spirit to creation is both the mode of encounter with God, who is Father and Son, and the graceful power itself of enacted faithfulness, then authority in the Church is mediated by the Spirit who, as both divine communication and the power of believers' commitment, *is* the "how" of responsibility to God. In other words, how authority dwells in the Church, how it is exercised, and how it is evaluated and questioned are in large measure a matter of determining how believers are responsible to the Spirit who enables their belief and action.

This theological perspective on the issue of authority lends perspective to any specific concerns about what belief, what teaching, what life, or what action is truly authoritative in and for the Church. Making such judgments is the work of the four senses of tradition, and these judgments are discernments that attempt to name the presence of the divine as tradition. As acts of discernment, the four senses aspire to authority but not to an authority measured by any created source of truth, justice, goodness, or beauty. Rather, the four senses aspire to an authority that derives from their responsibility to the trinitarian God. Their discerning authority lies not in what is old or what is new, not in what is stable or what is changing, not in what is constant or in what renews. Their discerning authority lies in the Spirit, the "how" of God's immanence to history, to the Church, and to the most regionally bound act of faith in which claims for tradition begin. The discernments of the four senses do not garner their authority simply from the believer's rightful aspiration to be responsible to God. Like all forms of authority, the authority of the discerning senses is gained through practice that witnesses to their enacted faithfulness to the source of their authority. Simply put, discernments are judged true as they prove themselves faithful to the economy of the divine life that unfolds in creation, incarnation, and sanctification.

Criteria for Traditional Discernment

Portraying the authority of traditional discernment as responsibility to the Spirit might seem to be a choice for one particular theological style over another and, in the judgment of some, a poor or at least a limited choice at that. The orientation pursued here and throughout this study might be judged to be pneumatological at the expense of the christological and, because of this one-sided approach, so committed to the experiential that it overlooks the value of the sacramental, so preoccupied with discerning the senses that it fails to respect the givenness of tradition in all its tangibility. Any theology of tradition guilty of such a skewed orientation that played off pneumatology against christology and perpetuated this opposition in all its possible variations would deserve criticism. The intention of this study is to keep from committing this error. These pages have spoken, throughout, of tradition as the work of the Spirit and of the movement of the Spirit in history as the objectively truthful measure of the configuration of tradition as the four senses. This attention to the Spirit, however, has presupposed the most basic claims of an orthodox trinitarian theology—that Father, Son, and Spirit are one in being and economically one in activity. The work of the Spirit in which the Church seeks its truth is not different from, but the completion of, the work of the Father and the Son. Although, with the tradition, one may distinguish the particular work of the Spirit and do so particularly with an eye to its value for a theology of tradition, one may do so adequately only by remembering with Gregory of Nyssa that in the life of God "one certain motion and disposition of goodwill occurs, proceeding from the Father through the Son to the Spirit."[5]

The attention to the Spirit in these pages does take seriously the Spirit's mediating role in the post-Pentecost Church. The Spirit is the continuing presence of God to creation, to time and space, and even to the small durations and places of historicity. And as the continuing presence of God to history, as the abiding testimony of God's promise of eternal life kept once and for all in the resurrection of Jesus from the dead, the Spirit has been— and continues to be—an important theme, focal point, and veridical standard for theologies of tradition. But the Spirit's continuing presence is neither spiritual at the expense of the physical nor pneumatological in a way that prescinds from the incarnational.[6] A presence of the Spirit to history that did not communicate the presence of Father and Son could not be a real presence. A discernment of the Spirit as tradition that was not deeply sacramental, that did not fathom God's incarnational presence to a created world, good yet fallen, fallen yet redeemed, could not be a truthful discernment. This trinitarianly inclusive understanding of the Spirit's normativity in and for a theology of tradition can be appreciated more fully by considering the criteria that might be invoked in discerning the senses of tradition.

Being responsible to the Spirit in promulgating the tradition through proper discernment is a concern as old as Christianity—and one that found expression in the New Testament. Paul's well-known commendation that the Spirit itself be recognized as the power of prayer that calls God *Abba* (Romans 8: 15–16) beckons believers to the most elementary of Christian discernments, one that presumes the confession of the Holy Spirit as the Spirit of truth (1 John 5:6). Identifying the Holy Spirit as the discernible truth of Christ in the midst of the believing community immediately raises the issue of the authenticity of this discernment. Even if the presence of the Spirit is so graciously universal that its absence is never finally possible, a purported and well-intentioned discernment of the Spirit may yet be false, as are insidious claims that masquerade as the Spirit's truth. Paul exhorted the community in Thessalonica to embrace the task of right discernment so that it "not quench the Spirit," urging its members to "test everything; hold fast to what is good; abstain from every form of evil" (1 Thessalonians 5:19, 21–22). The Johannine writer, sounding a more cautionary tone, warned faithful readers "not

[to] believe every spirit, but [to] test the spirits to see whether they are from God" (1 John 4: 1) And no doubt addressing a concrete instance of false belief facing the community, the same writer offered one of the earliest criteria for truthful discernment: "By this you know the Spirit of God: every spirit that confesses that Jesus Christ has come in the flesh is from God, and every spirit that does not confess Jesus is not from God" (1 John 4:2–3).

The early Christian centuries offered their own versions of criteria for discerning tradition. Apologists such as Justin Martyr, Irenaeus, and Tertullian rendered orthodox belief in the terse exposition of the *regula fidei*, which defined credal criteria for distinguishing Christian tradition from its heretical distortion. Lindbeck has called attention to the way that Christianity's early doctrinal tradition put in place a set of rules that governed the right interpretation of the biblical narrative and that provided an authoritative framework for Christian speaking and acting. Lindbeck's tendency has been to think of these rules as the early creeds and formulae of ecumenical councils through which the early communities together set parameters for orthodox belief and practice—its "grammar" in Lindbeck's cultural-linguistic metaphor—and, by doing so, ruled out belief and practice at odds with this basic grammatical structure. Although Lindbeck has not discussed these credal rules as criteria for the discernment of tradition, to do so would be not only consistent with his cultural-linguistic rule theory but also an interesting way of appreciating how the authoritative teachings of the early Church set norms for judging the presence of the Spirit. Understood in this way, the rules for the discernment of tradition in the premodern Church were established tradition itself, unsurprisingly reflexive criteria for a theological culture in which tradition is conceived mimetically and its promulgation is conceived as uncorrupted, hand-to-hand transmission.

The modern notion of developing tradition did not displace the premodern criteria for discernment. Creed and conciliar teaching remain as authoritative for the modern and postmodern Church as they were for premodern believers. The modern notion of a developing tradition, however, complicates the task of discerning the Spirit in history. Since the modern presumption of tradition's development introduces an obscurity into its workings that far surpasses any ambiguity in the premodern traditioning process, criteria for judging the presence of the Spirit to history become valuable and even necessary aids for framing the ongoing discernment of the Church. The seven "notes" that Newman sketches in *An Essay on the Development of Christian Doctrine* are an interesting and certainly the best-known example of a modern criteriology. On the face of it, the notes provide a heuristic for distinguishing legitimate doctrinal development from its corruption or falsity. And yet, if one assumes with Newman that the Holy Spirit is the source of all genuine development, then the notes offer something like criteria for discerning the Spirit at work in the Church. According to Newman, the Spirit can be discerned in developing tradition that retains its type, principles, and organization, whose beginnings anticipate its subsequent phases, whose later phenomena protect and subserve its earlier, and that possesses both a power of assimilation and a vigorous action from beginning to end.[7] These criteria for discerning tradition are more elaborate than, say, the ancient Vincentian canon, itself a simple, premodern criterion of discernment. Their comprehensiveness is a formal response to the more complicated task of modern discernment. And yet, like their ancient counterparts, Newman's criteria stress the concrete givenness of tradition as the consistent norm to which the Church appeals in discerning the presence of the Spirit, an emphasis that proves instructive for considering criteria for the four senses of tradition.

Newman's more extensive criteria for discernment, such as the ancient creeds and conciliar pronouncements, show that tradition's pneumatological source of authority is also incarnational. This is so not only because the Spirit is the Spirit of Christ but also because the task of discernment takes place only through the mediatorial embodiment of the divine through worldly things, countless instances of which achieve their mediatorial worth as reflections of the Incarnation's own sacred tangibility and its continuing, real eucharistic presence. The criteria for discerning tradition, both premodern and modern, presuppose tradition's concrete objectivity in proven discernments of the Spirit against which the authority of the most recent handing down or development can be measured. These ancient and modern criteria may differ in their respective inattention or attention to the assumption of traditional development, but they differ not at all in their high regard for the steadfastness of the Spirit's presence to tradition, a presence manifested in and through the physical and discernible by appeal to objectifiable norms.

This incarnational dimension of tradition is an indispensable standard in the discernment of all four senses of tradition, but especially the first and the second. In the high value they place on traditional constancy, the literal sense and the sense of development-in-continuity look to the concreteness and tangibility of what manifestly has garnered authority in the tradition in order to identify the Spirit's abiding presence. First and foremost, God's self-revelation in Jesus Christ—his life, death, and resurrection—offers an insuperable criterion to the Church of any age, by which it measures the ongoing life of Christ in its midst. For Christian faith, the entire biblical story gives account of the meaning of this life, rendered with greatest clarity and in finest detail in the narratives of the four gospels. If the creeds and teachings of the great councils can be judged as criteria for the discernment of tradition, it is only because they provide tangible flesh to the invisible spirit of communal faith and in this regard provide a literal witness, relatively explicit and clear, to an ecclesial understanding of the life of Jesus and its inspired biblical record. Tradition is primarily faithfulness to scripture, for scripture is tradition's surest way of drawing close to its own incarnational truth.[8]

The constancy prized most of all by the first two senses of tradition, and finally by all four, is a constancy that derives principally from tradition's developing continuity with the life and message of Jesus in its narrative portrayal. But this incarnational constancy permeates the tradition in innumerable ways, all of which present themselves as established criteria for discerning the Spirit and thus the authentic movement of tradition. Liturgical practice, sacramental devotion, the visibility of the Church as an institution, the Church's great communal prayers, the Church's pastoral offices, the lives of the saints, the charismatic teaching of the magisterium, the order of the Church calendar, and Christianity's sacred places are all among the criteria of traditional discernment whose normativeness appears in the same concrete mode as God's incarnational immanence. The four senses of tradition, but especially the first two, invoke these criteria and many others that are just as sacramentally palpable in order to discern the Spirit's traditional presence. As these criteria shape the judgments of the first two senses, they configure tradition's constancy with regard to tangible signs, persons, events, doctrines, and practices that are judged within the Church to be obvious manifestations of the Spirit's presence. This configuration of constancy itself, as the literal sense of tradition, takes on criteriological significance with respect to the other senses. The literal sense is the Church's trusted lineage of meaning that binds the Incarnation to the Spirit's contemporary rustlings in the life of the Church. It lies at the heart of the sense of development-in-continuity, fixing a steady norm for continuing fidelity to the gospel from time to time and place to place. This same steadfastness, even when disturbed, highlights and questions the alternative claims of the third sense. When challenged by novelty that yet claims authority, it stands as the measure, stolid and yet revisable, of the fourth sense's aspiring constancy.

The literal sense is, of course, a *sense* of the Church. Its experience and its claims are not timelessly fixed; rather, they are continually affirmed in every historical moment. This recurring affirmation sustains the literal sense, as the Church professes its ongoing faith in the Spirit's presence gauged by its most reliable incarnational markers. The literal sense is authoritative for the Church, and for the other senses of tradition, not by status or privilege but by virtue of its enacted faithfulness to its divine source. The communal act of faith in which the literal sense is affirmed and by which the universal pattern of tradition is represented proves itself again and again in the life of the Church by what it does. And what it does is remain faithful to the tradition's most basic claims sedimented in the uncountable affirmations of continuity with the past made throughout the centuries. This faithfulness is enacted from moment to moment, and any one of these enactments might configure the apostolic tradition in a somewhat different way from previous first-sense enactments. Even so, the incarnational criteria for the literal sense ensure that its ongoing enactment of responsibility to the Spirit will be unsurprising in any historical moment not only because these criteria frame the present in terms of a tangible past but also because the literal sense of tradition affirms what the Church already believes. Since the literal sense is itself a traditional criterion for the Spirit's constancy, the same expectation characterizes the second sense, which makes literal-sense constancy the basis for its developing claims.

The same criteriological clarity does not exist for discernments of the third and fourth senses. Recall that the third and fourth senses of tradition do stand in measured relationship to the literal sense. In some respect, the literal sense even functions as a contrapuntal criterion for the third and fourth senses. The way in which the present configuration of the literal sense stands at odds with the third sense highlights its striking claims for dramatic development and its implicit vision of a literal sense differently configured. The fourth sense always meets the literal sense as disapproving judge, even when the judge's ecclesial conscience is tweaked by fourth-sense claims for an overlooked constancy that deserves to be tradition. This contrapuntal relationship between the literal sense, on one hand, and the third and fourth senses, on the other, calls attention to a lack of criteriological clarity for discerning the more controversial senses of tradition. The literal sense can be invoked in order to make judgments on the authority of third- and fourth-sense claims. Since third- and fourth-sense discernments are not at all true in principle, the literal sense is the basis for the Church's judgment of their falsity, whenever that judgment is eventually and rightly made. Moreover, third- and fourth-sense discernments that eventually prove truthful, and by doing so reconfigure the literal sense, find themselves negotiated by and integrated into the long history of first-sense claims that are presently affirmed in a particular pattern of the apostolic tradition. The incarnational dimensions of the literal sense always accompany third- and fourth-sense discernments, if not as direct then as indirect criteria.[9] Yet, by their very nature, third- and fourth-sense discernments of the Spirit pose an alternative to the present configuration of the literal sense. And for this reason, the criteria they may invoke are far more pneumatological than those to which the literal sense appeals, since present-day understandings of the tradition's incarnational markers are so closely associated with the current configuration of the literal sense.

The senses of dramatic and incipient development, like the first two senses, are responsible to the Spirit. But the criteria by which they discern the Spirit's renewing power are so set by the Spirit's power itself that they are far less clear, far more nebulous, or—to use ecclesial language that speaks properly of criteria for the Spirit's presence—far more mysterious than the proven criteria for the first and second senses.[10] Whereas the first and second senses garner their authority by enacted faithfulness to the Spirit that occurs in a long history of such enactment, the third and fourth senses garner their authority by enacted faithfulness to the Spirit that takes place without clear precedent. Though the tradition's incarnational markers remain for third- and fourth-sense discernments, their focused authority for first-sense judgment blurs as the senses of renewal anticipate a different traditional future and imagine the incarnational markers refocused in a new light. The third and fourth senses cannot appeal to a criteriological constancy in the manner of the first and second senses—the third sense because its claims for renewal involve a loss within the previous configuration of constancy, the fourth sense because its novel claims for constancy suggest the incompleteness of constancy's accepted pattern. In both cases, literal-sense criteria for the discernment of tradition prove inadequate.

What criteria there are for discerning the third and fourth senses of tradition lie in the local settings of duration and place in which the Spirit begins the work of striking renewal—and particularly in the experiential appropriation of the local that takes place in the act of faith. Let us proceed by considering some insights of the modern theology of faith that can enhance our appreciation for the task of discerning all the senses of tradition—particularly the third and fourth.

Discernment and the Act of Faith

In the late nineteenth and early twentieth centuries, Catholic thinkers found themselves challenged as they never before had been to reflect on the act of faith.[11] Faced with the unhappy options of the Enlightenment critique of reasoning, which shook traditional claims for the content of a positive revelation; an ineffective Catholic apologetics, which upheld the natural reasonableness of the miracles and signs affirmed in faith; and the limitations of a Neo-Scholastic Thomism, which tended to isolate the natural and supernatural dimensions of faith; theologians sought new ways to conceive the act of faith that would be adequate to the day and do justice to the most basic claims of the tradition. To detail all the subtle nuances in their various constructive responses would be to go far afield from the immediate task of exploring the more ambiguous criteria for third- and fourth-sense discernments. Instead, three important currents in the modern theology of faith, each considered in turn, serve this study as historical background and constructive resource for this issue: faith's contextuality, its supernaturality, and its personal character.

Newman's 1870 *Essay in Aid of a Grammar of Assent* is a philosophical study of the nature of faith that possesses interesting theological implications. Apologetical in tone and execution, Newman's work skirts any narrow focus on religious commitment as a special case entirely different from other forms of belief and responsible to rules peculiar to its own brand of theological assent. Instead, the book analyzes the phenomenon of belief, religious or otherwise, in the broader spectrum of human experience in order to account for the warrants that might be called upon to support the various kinds of assent and in order to explore the role of reasoning, inference, and judgment in making the claims of faith. This last task, which is addressed in the text's long second and final section, is a familiar one in classical Catholic theology, one that is typically accomplished by demonstrating the compatibility of faith and reason. Newman's work follows this classical direction in the sense that the book, along with the tradition, acknowledges the priority of a faith based on revelation for real assent to the divine mysteries and yet values reason's probative discipleship to faith, its capacity to complement faith's assent with logical inference that augments the scope of its certitude. Surprisingly, though, some of Newman's most memorable and influential reflections on the act of faith take their point of departure not from the act of faith itself but from the power of reasonable judgment, an activity that can be explained adequately only by appeal to the rather numinous category of the illative sense.

Newman's *Essay in Aid of a Grammar of Assent* regards certitude as a "mental state" not passively impressed upon the mind from without but engendered by an "active recognition of propositions as true," an awareness exercised "at the bidding of reason." The act of inference that may lead to certitude in a concrete situation is a mental operation. It stems only from the "personal action of the ratiocinative faculty" and cannot be reduced to words or syllogistic construction. "Everyone who reasons," Newman insists, "is his own centre; and no expedient for attaining a common measure of minds can reverse this truth."[12] The particular traits of personal character, one might say, set the ambiance for reasoning confident in its attainment of the truth.[13] This particularity of character accounts for the diversity in philosophical, moral, and religious claims for certitude that rely on reasoning in making and presenting their claims, but the same particularity also raises the question of consistency and uniformity of rational standard. Is there any criterion, Newman has asked, for the validity of inference and thus for the certainty that reason bids when recognizing such validity? For Newman, the only criterion that may be invoked lies within the "perfection or virtue" of the reasoning faculty that he has named the "Illative Sense."[14]

The illative sense is nothing more than "right judgment in ratiocination."[15] No objective measure or rule can ensure judgment's rightness and the certitude that accompanies it. Rather, the illative sense is, so to speak, its own rule, though one redefined by every concrete instance in which it fashions empirical evidence and logic into a judgment that it itself judges to be apt. The illative sense is an architectonic faculty of reasoning. And yet one can identify counterparts to its specifically reasonable sphere of operation in all activities that require practical sense. Buying and selling, arranging contracts, speaking, working, and recreating, for example, all require talents that do not mature "by mere rule, but by personal skill and sagacity."[16] They are activities whose excellent conduct can be explained only by *phronesis*, by a skillful wisdom defined by circumstance and not by abstract principles. If there is a general law that bears upon the workings of this skillful wisdom, it is the ironic postulate that the practical sense owes nothing to general laws. And why, Newman has rhetorically asked, should ratiocination "be an exception to a general law which attaches to the intellectual exercises of the mind?"[17] The illative sense is the source of constructive originality. Supplementing the "logic of language" with the "more subtle and elastic logic of thought,"[18] it manifests itself in genius as well as in the most ordinary operations of reasoning to sound judgment. Surpassing the "methodical processes of inference," the illative sense is a "living *organon*" that gives reasoning and imagination "a sense beyond their letter, and which, while acting through them, reaches to conclusions beyond and above them."[19] In "no class of concrete reasonings, whether in experimental science, historical research, or theology," according to Newman, "is there any ultimate test of truth and error in our inferences besides the trustworthiness of the Illative Sense that gives them its sanction."[20]

Newman's portrait of the illative sense is informed, no doubt, by the growing significance accorded to the creative power of imagination in the Western intellectual tradition throughout the eighteenth and nineteenth centuries. But one should not overlook the degree to which this Romantic influence is itself shaped by Newman's commitment to a Catholic understanding of reason's relationship to faith. Just as the Catholic tradition holds that reasoning is elevated to a higher exercise by the grace that illumines faith, so, too, does Newman's work hold that inferential reasoning is raised above its formal, rule-bound use by the higher wisdom of the illative sense. Just as the Catholic tradition finds reason to achieve a richer meaning in the context of faith, so, too, does Newman's work regard the illative sense as the proper context for reason—and one in which reason comes to its fullest realization. And just as the Catholic tradition judges faith to supply its own nondiscursive rule to the workings of reason so that reason is judged by faith and not faith by reason, so, too, does Newman's work regard the illative faculty of judgment as a nondiscursive rule, "a rule to itself" as Newman has put it,[21] that supplies the ratiocinative insight for which discursive reasoning can only strive. The illative sense is, to be sure, a faculty of reasoning—specifically the power of right judgment—and not the experience of faith, to say nothing of Christian faith. And yet Newman has introduced the illative sense to the pages of his *Essay in Aid of a Grammar of Assent* in order to explain the nature of assent and, in doing so, has ascribed the graceful qualities of faith to the illative sense and its relationship to inferential reasoning.

If this interpretation has merit, then Newman's analysis is interesting for its insistence that the traditional qualities of faith, and not the traditional qualities of reason, provide a context within which all manner of assent—religious, philosophical, or commonsensical—might finally be understood.[22] The theology of faith in the twentieth century typically has not directly made use of Newman's notion of the illative sense, since—as a faculty of reasoning—its explanatory advantage, when perceived, is more naturally put to the service of an epistemologically concerned philosophy of religion. But Newman's treatment of assent has been influential on the modern theology of faith, which has recognized both the apologetical advantage of claiming faith as the proper context for an otherwise critical reasoning and the consistency of this modern explanation with the tradition's classical belief on the priority of faith for an adequate knowledge of God. This same concern for the contextuality of faith can be seen in arguments for faith's supernaturality at the turn of the twentieth century.

Of all the works on the modern Catholic theology of faith, Pierre Rousselot's 1910 *The Eyes of Faith* deserves pride of place for its imaginative account of the act of faith itself—one that manages faithfulness to the teaching of Vatican I on the compatibility of faith and reason while transcending the insufficiencies of contemporary Neo-Scholastic interpretations of the nineteenth-century conciliar position. In response to advocates of a "scientific faith"—

such as the Gregorian professor and later Cardinal Ludovico Billot, who understood Vatican I's teaching to mean that "reason can discover the specification of the truths of faith by itself"[23]—Rousselot has touted the indispensability of grace for all of faith's credibility. And yet his work shows his awareness that unnuanced appeals to faith's graceful source run the same risk of divorcing nature and grace that characterized the approach of scientific faith. Whether the diremption of nature and grace takes its point of departure from the former or the latter, the result is a theology of faith that cannot adequately account for either faith's reasonableness or its freedom, its naturalism or its supernaturalism.[24] The difficulty shared by each one-sided emphasis on nature or grace, Rousselot has argued, is that its account of the act of faith proceeds analytically and thus represents faith conceptually by marking out distinctions in the believer's conscious states that separate faith's discrete natural and supernatural aspects. Rousselot has proposed a more integrated account by attending to "the *synthetic activity of the intelligence, whether natural or supernaturalized*"[25] in the act of faith.

Within this synthetic activity of the intelligence from which faith proceeds, there is no longer a need to distinguish a reasonable moment after or before the graceful moment of belief in which the believer, committed or soon to be, makes a rational judgment of credibility as a distinct act. "Perception of credibility and belief in truth," according to Rousselot, "are identically the same act."[26] This unity of credible perception and belief is possible because faith is a "supernatural cognitive activity,"[27] a particular way of seeing reality that Rousselot has explained by invoking the Thomistic doctrine of the "light of faith." This divine illumination bathes the act of faith in a clarity that holds together every otherwise separable representation of its natural and supernatural dimensions into "*one* selfsame *certitude.*"[28] Moreover, the light of faith, no different from the divine love, presupposes a supernatural faculty, the metaphorical "eyes of faith" of Rousselot's title, to which grace can bring "the perfection of seeing."[29] In the "complex and indissoluble whole that is the act of faith," the natural and the supernatural can "be neither *opposed* nor *disparate.*" Rather, the "one must encompass and transcend the other, deepening and perfecting it from within."[30] Like Maurice Blondel before him, Rousselot has always accounted for the nature of faith under the auspices of the supernatural, although, unlike Blondel, Rousselot has located faith's synthetic activity primarily in the intellect rather than in the will.[31]

The reasonableness of the act of faith, then, "derives from its very supernaturality,"[32] its credibility illuminated by the light of faith itself. Here in Rousselot's insightful explanation, which exerted a profound influence on transcendental Thomism and Henri DeLubac's midcentury *ressourcement* studies on the supernatural, one meets a variation on the theme of the contextuality of faith. Like Newman, Rousselot has insisted that the character of faith supplies the conditions for its own meaningfulness, although, unlike Newman, Rousselot has portrayed faith's contextuality in classical theological categories and the centuries-old debate on the relationship between nature and grace. By presenting the supernaturality of the act of faith as "natural being, but elevated,"[33] Rousselot has maintained that every created dimension of the act of faith achieves its intelligibility only in faith's own light and thus only in the mystery of God's love. Admittedly, according to Rousselot, within this mystery theological explanation possesses a circularity defined by the mutually interpretive unity of faith's reasonableness and freedom.[34] But it is a benign circularity shaped by the prevalent activity of grace—and one wrongly perceived as vicious only in the dim light of natural reasoning.

In illustrating the intimacy with which faith judges the internal conditions of its evidence, Rousselot has found examples from the sphere of personal relations to be particularly apt. A convert's explanation of his conversion to an uncomprehending acquaintance, a parishioner's recognition of his or her pastor's holiness, a lover's wordless familiarity in the beloved's physical presence, all appear in *The Eyes of Faith* as analogies from ordinary experience for the supernaturality—and thus particularity—of faith's apprehension. This attention to the personal character of faith blossomed in the twentieth century, especially through the influence of *I and Thou*, the 1923 mystical meditation on dialogical relationship by the Jewish philosopher Martin Buber. This work proved to be so consequential for the modern theology of faith, and for the many existentialist philosophies to which theology looked for interpretive insight, that its categories quickly became the twentieth century's common coin for portraying the relationship between the believer and God. A host of works, then, could illustrate the hermeneutical role of personalism in the modern theology of faith. An interesting Catholic contribution to this broad genre, one that was much read in its day and that now serves the purpose of this study, is Jean Mouroux's 1938 *I Believe in You: The Personal Structure of Faith*.[35]

Mouroux understood his study to be a reading of Aquinas on the act of faith and happily embraced Aquinas's authority throughout his presentation. And yet Mouroux was intent on placing all the issues at stake in the traditional consideration of his topic in the framework of personalist categories. The first and essential object of faith, he claimed, "is not an abstract truth, but God, a personal Being." The first truth is "Someone."[36] The same, though, must be said for the subject of faith, the believer, who always stands in personal relationship to the divine person. "It follows," Mouroux asserted, "that in its essence faith will be the response of the human person to the personal God and therefore *the meeting of two persons*."[37] The very reality of faith unfolds in the dialogue, the word-laden reciprocity, that ensues between these persons. "God speaks," Mouroux declared with striking simplicity, and in this speaking testifies to the eventfulness of God's own saving truth in a way that "inserts itself ordinarily into the concrete psychology of the human being." These humanly accessible means are, above all, Jesus Christ, himself a "human person," and the Church, which "extends and represents the witness of Christ at the heart of humanity."[38] The faith of the believer is a witness to this personal God, a "dynamic perception"[39] that entrusts its adherence, commitment, and desire to the words of a God who speaks. Faith is a free response, a human overture in the mutuality that this saving dialogue requires. It is a personal witness to the personal witness God has made in revelation.

This appeal to personalist categories led Mouroux to attend more closely to the eventful dimension of faith often overlooked by the scholastics of the early century. The act of faith, he reminded his readers, is "not only a personal act but also a *personalizing* one."[40] The highest human values, such as courage, humility, and fidelity, are all "immanent to the act of faith" and, through faith's "personalizing force," develop toward their perfection.[41] Faith brings the believer to a maturity in spiritual character as much as it effects the believer's eternal salvation. The language of personalization does not simply name a psychological event, one that can be explained entirely within the scope of human mental states and action. In traditional fashion, Mouroux attributed the power of personal development to a divine grace whose efficacy, however, can no longer be conveyed sufficiently by traditional Aristotelian categories. God illuminates and draws the believer to God's own personal self through a grace informed by the same traits as the act of faith it stirs. Grace is itself both personal and personalizing: personal because it is "addressed to each soul in its own difference," personalizing because it "destines the soul to realize its unique vocation."[42] God, Mouroux continued, is the "sole agent" of grace and its effects in the life of the believer, a causality that led Mouroux's theology to the inescapable and comforting conclusion that God's own being is both personal and personalizing.

This attention to faith's personalism leads to an interesting nuance in the modern theology of faith that extends beyond the reconstruction of classical categories. If personal encounter is an appropriate model for faith, then all of the ambiguous vagaries of personal relationship, as well as its moments of clarity and fulfillment, must be acknowledged as aspects of faith. By focusing on faith as a process of personal transformation, Mouroux felt obliged, as do so many other modern theologians who conduct their business in the currency of personalism, to acknowledge this ambiguity inherent in the act of faith. With the classical Catholic tradition, Mouroux made much of the certitude of faith and followed Rousselot in using the time-honored metaphors of illumination and visual clarity to convey certitude's subjective confidence. But the act of faith, he held, also possesses an obscurity that derives from the very nature of its relationship. Faith in God is obscure "because it is the revelation of a *divine* person through a *human* testimony,"[43] an immeasurable inequality that casts the shadow of divine transcendence over what certitude faith does indeed possess. The Neo-Scholastic theology that Mouroux reinterpreted had spoken of this sort of obscurity as a dimension of faith,[44] though not with the resonance of Mouroux's existentialist voice. Faith's obscurity, he claimed, is the human encounter with the mystery of God's impenetrable darkness, which stirs in faith a sense for the hiddenness of God to its own creaturely fallenness and before which reason boldly, though wrongly, declares God's absence.[45] But Mouroux's personalism allowed him to take this theme a step further. The act of faith, he proposed, is obscure "first of all because in it [one] reveals oneself to another, and because this always remains obscure to discursive reason."[46] Whereas reason meets its object in analytic abstraction, faith meets a person in the profound concreteness of consciousness and conscience. The obscurity of faith in this sense lies in the mystery of self and other that arises in any transformative encounter, for Mouroux finally the mystery of personal love whose unfathomable depths reason cannot fathom and through which God works salvation.[47]

Mouroux's acknowledgment of obscurity as a dimension of the experience of faith itself was not, as has been shown, without precedent in the tradition. Indeed, Mouroux enlisted the most famous purveyor of this motif, Saint John of the Cross, as an authority on the stages of spiritual progress in faith. The sixteenth-century mystic is instructive, Mouroux believed, in showing how faith must pass through a "dark night of the soul" before it can be confirmed in its own centeredness.[48] And yet, even though Mouroux attributed great importance to John's mystical path as a paradigm for faith, his contribution to the modern theology of faith is based much more in showing how obscurity lies in faith's ordinary, personal conditions and not just in a purgative moment in the extraordinary journey toward mystical union with God. By presenting obscurity as a necessary complement to faith's certainty, as an abiding accompaniment to its divine light, and as a trait of the love binding believer and God, Mouroux offered an understanding of the personal dimensions of faith that allowed for the consideration of faith as a paradoxical experience whose commitment could embrace its own ambiguity. For the many theologians of the twentieth century who took up the personalist orientation that Mouroux illustrated so well, faith exhibits all the complexity of personal relationship in which fulfillment and alienation, knowledge and doubt, and intimacy and distance tensively coexist.

These three traits of faith—its contextuality, its supernaturality, and its personal character—are clearly interrelated, as my analysis has suggested. Each of these traits might be seen as a way of understanding the other two, all the expression of a homology defined by their common representation of the mysteriousness of faith. This homology has interesting implications for the concerns of this chapter. All three traits of faith highlight the degree to which faith's evidence garners its intelligibility within faith's own nondiscursive experience. The evidence of faith is internalized in a manner that places any consideration of its credibility under the auspices of faith itself. Faith's experiential ambiance, one might say, provides an environment within which faith's own testimony verifies its vision of reality. Reason may evince what faith believes—but only on faith's terms, which bring a deeper meaning to reason that eludes its ordinary workings. Given the supernaturality of faith, this ambiance is itself the mystery of divine being, a mystery not only acknowledged by faith but also communicated in grace to the act of faith itself. Faith, in Rousselot's telling phrase, is "natural being, but [natural being] elevated" into the mysterious supernaturality of God's unfathomable being. Acknowledging faith's personal character allows one to appreciate and respect this mystery further by recognizing God's profound obscurity as not only the transcendent object of faith but also an immanent aspect of faith's own commitment.

This attention to the mystery of the act of faith—in its consummation of rationality in fidelity, in its sharing in the incomprehensible divine life, and in the inherent obscurity of its encounter with the personal God—did much to foster the importance of the theme of discernment in contemporary theology. Discernment, of course, becomes a more pressing need as the mysteriousness of the act of faith is accentuated. Fulfilling this need, though, also has important consequences for the practice of discernment. If the discernment of tradition is the work of faith, and if what discernment discerns is the presence of God to the faith of the Church—a faith that is rooted as much in individual acts as they are rooted in its communal sharing—then the currents of twentieth-century theology examined herein suggest that discernment is always exercised in the mystery of the act of faith and, more, *as* the mystery of that act. The act of faith, to be sure, relies on God's revelation for its content. Its commitment is measured by incarnational markers that offer a tangibility and concreteness to the claims of faith as they are made individually and communally. But even the meaningfulness of these incarnational markers—how they are affirmed, how they are understood, how they are emphasized so that their many possible interrelationships are patterned this way or that—always proceeds from an act of faith that participates in the divine mystery. Faith's discernment of this mystery issues from the mystery itself. Its subjectivity is the condition for the intelligibility of every objectivity that tradition poses for faith's guidance. Discerning tradition, one might say, is as pneumatological a practice as it is an incarnational one. And since it is the Spirit who, through acts of faith made here and now, testifies to the Lordship of Jesus (1 Corinthians 12:3), one could rightly say that the discernment of tradition is incarnational in and through the pneumatological character of its exercise.[49]

This observation applies to the criteriology of the senses of tradition discussed earlier. However much the tradition's incarnational markers serve as palpable criteria for the discernments of the senses of tradition, their objectivity achieves its clarity in the light of grace and through the eyes of faith. The tradition's incarnational criteria may measure the literal sense and the sense of development-in-continuity in a way that aligns these judgments of constancy with the tradition's authoritative corporeality, bringing to them a certain obviousness so important to the communication of tradition across the expanse of time and place. But whatever conspicuousness these discernments of constancy possess manifests itself only in and through the mystery of faith.[50] This same point holds even more strongly for discernments of the sense of dramatic development and the sense of incipient development. These senses claim the truth of their discernments by appeal to the same incarnational criteria invoked by the first and second senses. And yet, because the third and fourth senses discern the renewal of tradition in a far more striking way than do the first two senses, their relationships to these criteria seem strained, especially in light of the normativeness accorded to discernments of constancy. Moreover, a third- or fourth-sense discernment first appears without precedent in the tradition and may consequently claim to satisfy its incarnational criteria only by posing, in however slight a way and usually to the chagrin of the first two senses, a new understanding of how those criteria function and what they measure. Though they remain completely, and yet ambiguously, responsible to the tradition's incarnational criteria, third- and fourth-sense discernments initially measure their truthfulness much more by reference to pneumatological criteria thoroughly immersed in the act of faith.

Here, however, within the act of faith, distinguishing criteria for discernment becomes difficult. The physical sacramentality of the tradition's incarnational markers allows for the discreteness of multiple criteria, even if their plurality does presuppose and evince the unity of the Incarnation. This plurality of criteria enhances the clarity of discernment's judgment, allowing its soundness to be tested from various quarters. But to the degree that the act of faith finally settles on evidence internal to its experience, and to the degree that this evidence is the self-communication of the divine mystery itself, discernment understood as the act of faith measures its authenticity by appeal to the invisibility of grace, to the immanence of the Holy Spirit, and thus to the single criterion of the presence of the Spirit to subjectivity.

Third- and fourth-sense discernments especially fathom the renewal of the Spirit as acts of faith that carry the Spirit's own authority as both the source and the measure of their experience and of their claims for the reconfiguration of tradition. Authentic discernments of striking renewal, of course, are not vapidly self-referential. They reach into the regionality of time and place to find the presence of the Spirit in the concreteness of persons, communities, and events. The physical terrain of the unfolding future surveyed by third- and fourth-sense discernments, however, is far less familiar than the landscape of established Catholic tradition across which first- and second-sense discernments knowingly trek. Its smaller durations and spaces do not provide an aesthetic for the Spirit's presence that is universal, like the grand time and space in which the tradition's acknowledged sacramentality is set. Its concreteness, though claimed as the manifestation of the Spirit's work and will, does not possess the time-honored authority of the incarnational markers and indeed may seem far removed from their sacred tangibility. The finally Spirit-referential character of these discernments of the "new" and the "regional" means that they seek their authority even more profoundly within the very act of faith that they as discernments are. In doing so, these discernments of striking renewal place the ecclesially obscure evidence of local time, place, and circumstance in the context of a regional act of faith whose criterion of truth can be only the subtle whisper of the Spirit not yet heard by the Church at large.

The rich particularity of third- and fourth-sense discernments intensifies the mystery in which they abide and that they, as discernments of the unpredictable movement of tradition, attempt to apprehend for the sake of tradition's renewal. Their pneumatological orientation eludes differentiated, and thus relatively clear, criteria for their authenticity. The very nature of third-

and fourth-sense discernments means that their authority, though acquired through their responsibility to the Spirit, will remain fairly ambiguous for the Church unless they come to be assimilated into the tradition as first-or second-sense claims. Like any discernment, however, these discernments of striking renewal prove themselves to be true not only in the subjectivity of the act of faith but also in the objectivity of faith's acts in Church and world. Enacted faithfulness is the means by which third- and fourth-sense discernments show their authority. And through the demonstrative power of enacted faithfulness, third-and fourth-sense discernments become less and less regional as their veridical testimony arises in an increasing number of individual acts of faith, discernments that—in their growing community of commitment and practice—begin to gain authority as the faith and tradition of the universal Church.

Discernment and the *Sensus Fidei*

Discernment takes place in somewhat different ways in the four senses. Each of the four senses exhibits a sensitivity to a particular aspect of how the Spirit moves in history. Each represents the significance of its insights for a tradition shaped by the values of constancy and renewal. Each contributes in its own way to the traditioning that leads to tradition, the communal faith of the universal Church. This communal faith, as has been shown, is represented by the first and second senses. Tradition presupposes communal acknowledgment of universal proportions that one finds only in the literal sense and the sense of development-in-continuity. Discernments of the third and fourth senses may prove worthy of the claims of tradition in some future time when they are embraced and claimed by the first two senses; while they are still affirmed only in individual or regionally communal acts of faith, however, they are not yet tradition. And yet, as illustrated in the previous chapter, the truthfulness of ecclesial discernment is not exhausted in the universally communal discernment of tradition. Wherever and whenever the Spirit of God is discerned truly, there and then the Church has the truth that it eventually and with some measure of confidence communally affirms as tradition. Discernments of striking renewal may not qualify as tradition, which is and remains a judgment of the whole Church. But their truthfulness is measured only by their faithfulness to the Spirit, whose reality is both the object and graceful enabler of any truthful discernment in and through any of the four senses.

As different as the four senses of tradition are and however limited any sense's recognition of the truth may be at any particular moment or however opposed to another's one sense's discernment may seem to be, they possess a unity in the truth that runs through each and all of the senses in the course of their traditional development. This veridical unity has its basis in the Spirit who is truly discerned. But how can the fourfold multiplicity of the traditional senses finally align themselves with the unity of this truthful objectivity, even if the truth of any sense's particular discernment is the truth of the Spirit? How, in other words, can the discernments of the four senses coalesce to form a single discernment on the integrity and unity of tradition? One can begin to answer this question by following Rousselot's lead. The act of faithful discernment can be conceived as a unitive assimilation by which the objectivity of the Spirit's truth is subjectively apprehended by the believer and then, through the believer, by the Church.

The discerning power of the four senses has its teleology in their common yearning for the Spirit's truth that tradition preserves and esteems anew. One would do well to conceive of this yearning common to the four senses as the *sensus fidei*, the Church's supernatural sense for the Spirit's infallible truth. Although this sense is often portrayed theologically as an "instinct" or "charism" or "habitus," such depictions run the risk of understanding the *sensus fidei* as an indwelling, self-contained capacity that reflects, by its recognition, only the economy of the Spirit.[51] The *sensus fidei* does indeed recognize manifestations of the Spirit's truth. Its responsibility presupposes the givenness of an authoritative source that makes the passivity of acknowledgment and obedience appropriate responses, especially if the authoritative source is the divine. One would do well, though, to conceive the *sensus fidei* also as an active faculty, as a yearning or desire for the Spirit's truth.[52] In this regard, the *sensus fidei* can be appreciated more fully as the energy of the act of faith that seeks the Spirit's truth by reaching into all the dimensions of time and place in which that truth might be fathomed. Although graceful empowerment must finally account for this activity, as it does for all virtuous exertion, its endeavor is testimony to its incompleteness and thus to its human freedom and active responsibility, proven in how its search is enacted.

It is through the senses of tradition that the *sensus fidei* conducts this search. The four senses stand in holistic relationship because they are all ways of exercising the *sensus fidei*. They are the discerning means by which its desire for the Spirit's truthful presence to tradition comes to fulfillment. But more, the unity of this desire for infallible truth itself might be understood as the basis for every comprehensive discernment of tradition in which the discernment of each sense is synthesized into a single truthful vision of what has been, what is, what has been but no longer will be, and what will be tradition. The *sensus fidei* so conceived, one might say, is unwilling to leave truth scattered among the senses of tradition, as though particular discernments of stolid constancy or striking renewal offer alternatives from which the faithful—inclined toward one or the other—might choose. Rather, its consistent desire for the Spirit's truth apprehended in all the senses of tradition compels the believer to make a discernment comprising all the discernments and in which the senses' shared responsibility to the Spirit is put on display.[53]

Comprehensive discernments are a function of a developing tradition and especially of a developing tradition differentiated in the fourfold sense proposed here. The assumption that tradition develops highlights the value of renewal in a way that requires repeated comprehensive discernments to reconcile the alignment of renewal and constancy. The finer detail of constancy and renewal within the four senses of tradition heightens the need for such comprehensive discernments, lest the values of tradition remain disparate and devoid of unity. The comprehensive discernment not only satisfies faith's desire for the unity of the Spirit's truth but also tests the integrity of each sense's discernment as it is assessed in the context of faith's singular judgment and measured by all the pneumatological and incarnational criteria at its disposal. Any such comprehensive discernment of all four senses will possess an inevitable tentativeness and uncertainty, for its overarching stand on tradition will embrace judgments of the third and fourth senses that, by definition, are not shared by the whole Church. Comprehensive discernments are made by individuals or regional communities struggling to understand the faith of the universal Church in relationship to discernments of striking renewal. They are not judgments of the whole Church. This tentativeness is increased as any particular comprehensive discernment encounters other regional comprehensive discernments, judging some to be deficient in spite of their similar claims to authority and others to complete its own, now exposed, deficiency. Uncertainty thus arises in the face of competing comprehensive discernments that blend constancy and renewal in different ways, while yet purporting to experience and represent the same presence of the Spirit.

It may seem odd to speak of the tentativeness and uncertainty of comprehensive discernments of tradition if such discernments are attributed to the unifying desire of the *sensus fidei*, an ecclesial sense to which the teaching of Vatican II ascribes the power of infallible discernment.[54] Perhaps this seeming inconsistency, though, stems from the assumption that the Church's infallibility, wherever it exists, is manifest and apparent to all the faithful—an assumption that does not hold up under scrutiny. This assumption can be tested by considering the *sensus fidei* in terms of the customary distinction between the *fides quae*, the faith that is believed, and the *fides qua*, the faith that believes.

As the tradition's *fides quae*, the *sensus fidei* is better understood and more accurately designated as the *consensus fidelium* and is represented as the tradition's literal sense. This expressed literal sense conveys the Church's common belief and practice, its first-sense tradition, within which infallibility can be professed in the clarity of explicit dogmatic definition. And yet explicit infallible definitions are relatively rare instances in the tradition that do not exhaust the scope of its infallible truth, even within the literal sense. Although expressed literal-sense tradition does present a field in which the Church can more confidently recognize and identify the Spirit's infallible truth, much of that infallibility remains undefined. And even the relative clarity of explicit infallible definitions, one might say, derives from the light that such definitions cast on the profound mysteries they frame for the believing community. The sense of the faith, then, envisaged in its objectivity as the Church's *fides quae*, offers few represented discernments that set the Spirit's infallible truth in relief from its supernatural hiddenness. However universal they may be, nearly all these represented discernments express the claims of first-sense tradition within which infallibility *may* dwell. Infallibility is first and foremost a quality of the Spirit's truth and, as such, is not a function of the Church's recognition of that truth.

Understood as the *fides qua*, the sense of the faith shares all the characteristics of the act of faith considered earlier in this chapter. The *sensus fidei*, as the Church's universal act of faith, indeed discerns the Spirit's infallibility, as *Lumen gentium* teaches. But that universal act is itself drawn from regionally communal acts of faith, which in turn are affirmed through individual acts of faith. The *sensus fidei*, therefore, arises in the experience of the Church in the same contextuality, with the same supernaturality, and through the same encounter with the personal God that characterize the individual act of faith. The sense of the faith as the *fides qua* weighs evidence that is already its own testimony. Its createdness as human experience is elevated by grace to a supernatural participation in the being of the Spirit whose truth it desires. The certainty affirmed in its relationship to the divine personal other is laced with an obscurity that is not extraneous to but inherent in the conditions of this relationship and its experience. The *sensus fidei* and its discernment of infallibility, in other words, are thoroughly immersed in the mysteriousness of the act of faith that Newman, Rousselot, and Mouroux described so well.

This mysteriousness can be appreciated by considering the simple theological criterion invoked to measure the universality of a first- or second-sense discernment in which the Spirit's infallible truth more surely dwells—that it be believed "by the whole Church." This universally communal act of faith is the *sensus fidei* as the *fides qua*. But how does "the whole Church" make a universal discernment? What does the phrase "by the whole Church" mean? The phrase cannot refer to the gathering that *Lumen gentium* names the "Church of Christ,"[55] the Church in its widest earthly and eschatological dimensions, for, in its largely unthematic and supernatural reaches, explicit discernments of tradition are not made. The phrase cannot refer to "all baptized" or even "all baptized into the Roman Catholic Church," for all the baptized—the lapsed, for example—do not participate in making what the Church considers to be universal discernments. The phrase cannot refer to those faithful in belief to all the teachings of the magisterium, unless one assumes a Church small in number, whose constituency shifts with the dramatic development of some magisterial teachings. The magisterium is itself bound by the *sensus fidei* to the same degree that it offers it guidance. The phrase cannot refer to all sincere reciters of the Nicene Creed, for certainly among that number there are some who, even in their sincerity, attribute to their words a meaning objectively different from that of the universal Church. The very expectation of the phrase as a theological description of real universality seems to rule out the possibility of explaining its referent as a simple majority, even if that explanation would make sociological sense. To say that the phrase "the whole Church" refers to those who truly discern the Spirit's presence begs the question of its status as a criterion if those true discerners cannot be identified universally. The universality claimed as the measure of infallibility is a mystery that defies analytic explanation, as does the universality of the communal act of faith by which this authoritative catholicity makes its mark on the Church.[56]

The *sensus fidei*, as both the communal *fides quae* and the communal *fides qua*, does indeed discern infallible truth whenever it discerns the Spirit's presence. But that infallibility nearly always remains hidden in the Spirit's own presence to tradition and to the act of faith that is the communal discernment itself. Even when believers discern infallible truth communally and universally, they discern it as the mystery it is—and usually with a tentativeness and uncertainty that are the appropriate responses to its hiddenness. And if this tentativeness and uncertainty always accompany discernments of the first and second senses, it should not be surprising that these same traits of ambiguity always accompany regional comprehensive discernments that judge just how the discernments of the four senses coalesce into a single discernment of the Spirit's constancy and renewal, in all their complex interrelationships. The *sensus fidei*, in its activity as an individual or regionally communal act of faith, makes such comprehensive discernments. And even though no comprehensive discernment as such can ever can be affirmed by the whole Church and thus as first-or second-sense tradition, such discernments are extraordinarily important in the traditioning process for the contributions some make to configuring the universal tradition.

In discerning comprehensively, the *sensus fidei* as the regional *fides qua* searches for the Spirit's infallible truth in familiar and unfamiliar times and places. Its supernatural appreciation for the rich unity of that truth, manifested in tradition's past and appearing in surprising ways only now at the cusp of present and future, enables it to look beyond the apparent clashes between and among the discernments of the four senses and to fashion a single judgment about how the Spirit's presence extends throughout reality. Such comprehensive discernments encourage the Church to imagine a thicker unity to tradition, even if the unity of any particular discernment proves with the passing of time not to be influential on the unity of established tradition affirmed by the whole Church. The apparent tentativeness and uncertainty of comprehensive discernments reminds the faithful that the *sensus fidei* probes for the Spirit's infallibility on this side of the eschaton with a reserve and sense for the incompleteness of its task, proper dispositions toward an apostolic tradition that has not yet run its course in time but is always discerned and represented in a passing present moment.

Like all discernments, comprehensive discernments of the *sensus fidei* that unify all four senses of tradition have a host of incarnational and pneumatological criteria that measure their authenticity. And yet, like all discernments, comprehensive discernments follow no rules that specify their practice.[57] Like all discernments, they prove themselves by practice, by an enacted faithfulness that gains authority by showing how the power of renewal bolsters the tradition's constancy and how the tradition's constancy extends as far as and into discernments of striking renewal.[58] Although this authority remains ambiguous as tradition continues to unfold—and although this ambiguity can be disconcerting to some in the community of the faithful who are inclined to think of the Spirit's infallible truth dwelling only in those times, places, persons, and events in which faithfulness already has been enacted—its ambiguity is rightly named the mystery of the Spirit's presence, the source and the means of all authority that truthful discernments in search of tradition might possess.

6

Tradition and Theology

The previous chapter concluded by noting that comprehensive discernments, through which individuals and local communities configure the relationships among the four senses of tradition, encourage the Church to imagine a thicker unity to tradition—one that extends beyond tradition's acknowledged catholicity to its more questionable, though perhaps yet infallibly truthful, anticipation in local times and places, persons and events. Comprehensive discernments require no special qualifications or knowledge in order to be made. And they certainly require no study of the four senses of tradition presented here. Comprehensive discernments are as old as the tradition, and this study's theoretical account of the four senses is a recent, and no doubt controversial, arrival in the long tradition of thinking about tradition.

Comprehensive discernments occur in the most simple act of faith as the *sensus fidei* seeks out and gathers together historical instantiations of the Spirit's constancy and renewal. These discernments occur as apprehensions of the Christian inner life, though they usually find their way to expression in the most ordinary faith-filled conversations about where the Spirit presently is and is not. Comprehensive discernments, however, can also be made by those in the Church who are more learned in the nuances of tradition's past and whose discourse articulating the purport of such discernments exhibits informed, critical, and even systematic reflection. When comprehensive discernments are made and expressed in such a self-consciously informed, critical, and even systematic fashion, the result is a theology, an interpretation of the Spirit's presence to history, culture, and tradition.

Understanding theology as the informed, critical, and even systematic articulation of comprehensive discernments is a fine way of conceiving its disciplinary task in a Catholic setting or, for that matter, in the setting of any Christian confession that values the authoritative role of tradition in *some* way. With regard to Catholic theology, it is important to remember not only that a comprehensive discernment of tradition embraces scripture but also that tradition comprehensively discerned cannot be reduced to the reception of scripture. Comprehensive discernments are time- and place-bound experiences of the meaning of divine revelation, dwelling as that meaning does in what Jürgen Moltmann has called the "interlaced times of history."[1] Envisaged as acts of theological reflection, comprehensive discernments configure the truth of scripture and tradition in an ordered, albeit tentative, unity in which the established authority of the first and second senses and the disputed authority of the third and fourth senses together have a share. Theological reflection and its representation, like the comprehensive discernment they convey, are the work of individuals or a local community of like-minded individuals committed to the theological vision of a certain comprehensive discernment. Theology is never the work of the universal Church. To the degree that its reflection and representation proceed from a comprehensive discernment of tradition, theology always weaves local judgments about and claims for the Spirit's truth into the fabric of the Church's universal faith. Its insights into the Spirit's historical presence are narrower in scope than the Church's universal faith, though, even in this more limited range, they may correspond to the Spirit's infallible truth.

By definition, a comprehensive discernment of tradition involves an apprehension of the Spirit's presence that goes beyond tradition's literal sense as all the senses of constancy and renewal are accounted for, positively or negatively, in its discerning judgment. If theology is conceived as the representation of a comprehensive discernment, then any theology must give account of the relationships among all four senses of tradition. This comprehensive theological portrait, however, need not be, and usually is not, explicit in delineating these relationships. Any theology might choose to focus on a particular theme, issue, or topic that leads it to attend more to one sense than to another. A feminist critique of the current practice of priestly ordination, for example, will address the sense of dramatic development in a pointed way, just as an ecological theology will make much of the sense of incipient development and a *ressourcement* theology will look especially to the constancy highlighted in the first or second senses. But, in each case, the primary attention a theology gives to a particular sense of tradition will entail the negotiation of the other senses in one way or another, even if only negatively. A feminist theology judging the current practice of ordination to be an instance of dramatic development not only takes a stand on the insufficiency of the literal sense but also makes incipient claims for a future practice that imagines a new configuration of development-in-continuity. An ecological theology makes incipient claims for a reconstruction of the God-world relationship that criticizes the literal sense, possibly, though not necessarily, to the point of claims for dramatic development and in a way that imagines a new configuration of development-in-continuity. A *ressourcement* theology will proceed from the authority of the literal sense, perhaps eschewing the possibility of dramatic development, conceiving incipience only as the finer manifestation of the literally given and understanding the development that laces the continuity of the second sense as the stolid reception of the classical sources.

This chapter considers the relationship between tradition and theology in order to appreciate how the Church conducts the business of interpreting the senses of tradition in a formal way. Tradition, according to Catholic belief, receives its most authoritative interpretation by the magisterium through the authentic teaching of the Pope and the bishops. It would be incorrect to think, however, that the magisterium's most authoritative interpretation of tradition exhausts the possibilities for ecclesial interpretation. Experience is not prior to interpretation but is itself a mode of interpretation; therefore, the discernment of any of the senses or all of them together amounts to an interpretation of tradition of which any believer is capable. Interpreted experience enters the symbolic world as representation and may occur through any of the means a culture, or a specifically ecclesial culture, has to offer. Theology involves a particular kind of interpretive experience and representation that has a special place in the history of the Church. As a disciplinary mode of interpretation, it conducts its task in an informed, critical, and even systematic fashion through self-conscious reflection on the intersecting meanings of scripture, tradition, and experience. To the degree that the theologian's discernments are informed by a knowledge of the history of ecclesial interpretation and tempered by a critical awareness of hermeneutical possibilities and limitations, the Church expects more from the theologian's interpretive creativity in configuring the Spirit's traditional presence. These higher expectations also stem from the realization that theology as representation has made profound contributions to the development of the Church's tradition throughout the centuries. The faithful promulgation of the deposit of faith, tradition's literal sense, is the principal responsibility of the magisterium. And discharging that responsibility presupposes the magisterium's authority to interpret the deposit of faith authentically.[2] But what the magisterium (to say nothing of the whole Church) believes the deposit to be and how the magisterium engages in the deposit's authentic interpretation draw in no small measure on the procedures and results of theological interpretation from ancient times to the present. Theology remains an extremely important mode of ecclesial interpretation not only for representing the senses comprehensively but also for discerning them meaningfully.

The close analysis of examples such as the few just offered would be one way of exploring the relationships between the senses of tradition and theology. A better path to follow, however, would be the consideration of the senses of tradition in relationship to general styles of theology in the modern period. The reflective rubrics that theologians have adopted by their practice as available options for interpreting scripture and tradition are the styles of narrative, hermeneutical, and critical theologies. As has been illustrated, any theology represents a comprehensive discernment of tradition. No matter how a theology's choice of focus may narrow its interpretive attention, any theology must explicitly or implicitly negotiate all four senses of tradition. And yet a particular style of theology negotiates all four senses by taking its point of departure from one, by according one of the senses an emphasis within tradition's complementary meanings that issues either in a narrative, a hermeneutical, or a critical approach to theology. The task in this chapter is twofold: to examine how each of these three theological styles fosters a particular understanding of tradition and to appreciate how this pluralism of theological styles offers more than a range of options from which a theologian might choose. This range offers a disciplinary spectrum that in its entirety aids the Church in its ongoing efforts to discern comprehensively the Spirit at work in tradition.

The Style of Narrative Theology and the Literal Sense

What we are accustomed to call narrative theology today is a style of interpretation that often takes its point of departure from an influential thesis advanced by Hans W. Frei. In his important 1974 tome *The Eclipse of Biblical Narrative* Frei argued that the inherently narrative quality of biblical revelation was vitiated in modern times by historical-critical approaches to scripture whose assumptions increasingly and wrongly came to be embraced by the most ardent believers. Prior to the eighteenth century, Christians read the biblical plot in a realistic or "history-like" manner. In such a premodern and, Frei would judge, consistently Christian reading, the narrative's theme and subject matter, its characters, their motivations and actions, and the circumstances in which these unfold are inextricably tied to natural and social environments and related in ordinary language—all these elements "fitly" rendering each other in a simple, literal meaning.[3] This literal reading can also proceed figurally, as a figural understanding stretches the Bible's literal sense throughout the canonical books so that—with the Old Testament conformed to the New and the New to the Old—the scriptural plot possesses a realistic coherence from Genesis to Apocalypse. Simply put, realistic readings, whether literal or figural, proceed on the assumption that the biblical narrative as narrative presents an ostensible meaning, which is to say that it establishes its meaning in an indispensably narrative way.

This narrative approach was supplanted in post-Enlightenment exegesis as modern readers, initially those who were hostile to the biblical claims and eventually those who were not, separated the biblical message from its embeddedness in narrative and took the abstracted message to refer to something other than its scriptural plain sense. The traditional bearing of the Bible's realistic or history-like quality on its meaning and interpretation "was immediately transposed into the quite different issue of whether or not the realistic narrative was historical."[4] Since modern readers assumed that many biblical events could not possibly have occurred as portrayed in the text, realistic narrative was now reconceived as metaphor. Whereas premodern readers took the biblical narrative to mean what it said, modern readers—first in the academy and soon in the churches—located the referent of biblical meaning outside the narrative in an idea or law of nature or moral truth or psychological state, any or all now touted as what the bible "really" means. Frei showed how this shift, neatly depicted in his title as the eclipse of biblical narrative, gained ground through the interpretive practice of eighteenth- and nineteenth-century hermeneutics and came to reside in the assumptions of modernity itself.[5]

Frei's account of the modern plight of the plain sense has been appreciated by a host of theologians—Lindbeck, Thiemann, Hauerwas, and Wood among them[6]—who have found his historical arguments compelling and replete with implications for the theologian's interpretive task. Following Frei—albeit in different ways—these theologians have all insisted on the responsibility of interpretation to, in Thiemann's phrase, the gospel's narrated promise. All have insisted that the biblical "good news" is revealed in a storied way that avails itself to Christian understanding when its literal sense is given priority. All, consequently, have been suspicious of rival interpretive priorities to the literal sense, especially as these appear in extrabiblical theoretical constructs that promise to elucidate some deeper, and finally unbiblical, meaning to scripture's narrated promise. All have conceived theological creativity as a skill in extending the narrative's literal sense to the infinitely possible reaches of human experience and thus as an unbounded exercise in figural interpretation through which, in Lindbeck's phrase, the text absorbs the world.

Clearly, the style of narrative theology as it has appeared in the work of Frei and his followers is distinctly Protestant in its commitments. Its nonfoundational approach to theological interpretation grants exclusive authority to the plain sense of the biblical Word. Its denunciation of historical-critical readings of scripture as an aberrant modern allegorization that betrays the literal sense might well be understood as a Protestant polemic advancing a postmodern version of *sola scriptura*. Although the banner of a narrative style has been carried into the late twentieth century by the Protestant theologians considered here—all admirers of the pride of place accorded narrative in the work of Barth—there is no reason to think that the same theological style is incapable of Catholic appropriation. How, though, in principle, might a Catholic theology embrace a narrative approach? Simple Christian faith in God's biblical revelation makes the interpretive approach of the Word's close, descriptive reading commended by the Protestant nonfoundationalists an acceptable narrative style for any Christian confession. A more distinctively Catholic narrative theology, however, would be more inclined to understand its narrative, and thus the responsibilities of theological narration, in terms of Catholic belief in the communication of God's inspired Word in scripture *and* tradition. Like its Protestant counterpart, a Catholic narrative theology would attend especially to the literal sense, though to the literal sense of tradition.

Scripture is often described as a narrative. But calling tradition a narrative introduces an analogy that should be explored at this point. Tradition, after all, need not be considered a narrative. Tradition is more usually understood, as it is in the New Testament and in the teaching of Trent, as the handing down of a fixed teaching. From this perspective, tradition is a catechetics, an instruction that preserves the purity of a truth once given. Or tradition might be conceived more statically, à la Denzinger, as the collection of all authoritative pronouncements of the magisterium throughout the ages. Or tradition might be portrayed as it is in modern conceptualization as a prospective development in which the apostolic truth gradually manifests itself in the life of the Church. All these conceptions of tradition have flourished in the Church at one time or another, and all flourish still in the Church today. None of these examples invokes the analogy of narrative to convey its understanding of tradition, though all could admit of narrative interpretation, albeit in different ways. What justification is there for applying the analogy of narrative to a Catholic understanding of tradition?

First, to the extent that the Tridentine Decree and Vatican II's *Dei verbum* reject a *partim . . . partim* regard for revelation in which saving truth is parceled out partially in scripture and partially in tradition, it is theologically justifiable to conceive the unity of God's revelation to be so inclusive that that unity appears at the level of genre. As Lash reminds us, "[N]ot all the texts of the New Testament are stories but, taken together, they 'tell the story' of Jesus and the first Christian communities."[7] Lash's observation can be applied to the Bible as a whole, as canonical readings suppose, and in light of Catholic belief, one could propose, to God's revelation in scripture and tradition. In other words, the revelational unity of scripture and tradition as conveyors of the one truth of Christ might engender one's greater appreciation were one to extend that unity even to genre—and in this case to the genre of narrative. Second, and more pragmatically, the analogy of narrative serves Catholic belief well, a point that might be made by way of comparison with another of Frei's works that constructively advances his historical thesis.

In his remarkable book *The Identity of Jesus Christ*, Frei offered what he has called an "identity description" of Jesus Christ in the gospels. Contrary to the expectations of modernity that would have the meaning of the Bible lie outside itself in some symbol or moral, the gospels, Frei has argued, are rightly read by Christians as a "realistic narrative" that is history-like "in its language as well as its depiction of a common public world . . . , in the close interaction of character and incident, and in the non-symbolic quality of the relation between the story and what the story is about."[8] The gospels "literally mean what they say."[9] According to Frei, a narrative theology is one that sets itself the task of describing the gospel story's main character, Jesus, by attending to the storied presentation of what Frei has called Jesus' "enacted intentions." The identity of any person, he has noted, "is the self-referral, or ascription to him, of his physical and personal states, properties, characteristics, and actions."[10] Eschewing Romantic preoccupation with Jesus' inner life or idealistic construction of a represented meaning that takes flight from Jesus' actual character, Frei has looked for Jesus' identity, as he would any person's, in how Jesus' self is manifested in action and circumstance. Narrative interpretation seeks the meaning of revelation in the identity that Jesus enacts in the course of the story, an identity that Frei has located in Jesus' obedience to God's will, in his powerlessness before his passion and death, and in his enacted acceptance of God's plan to save humanity through his resurrection from the dead. Indeed, Jesus becomes so much himself in the resurrection, Frei has claimed, "that his nonresurrection becomes inconceivable."[11]

The manner of Frei's narrative interpretation exhibits a profound faithfulness to the Reformation scripture principle in the particular circumstances of its encounter with modernity. To the degree that a narrative approach to theology is identified with Frei's proposal and the manner in which it has been adopted and adapted in the work of such theologians as Lindbeck, Thiemann, Hauerwas, and Wood, there is some natural reluctance on the part of many Catholic theologians to tread their interpretive path. Taking note of how Frei's theological approach is so nonfoundationally faithful to his confessional commitments, though, should evoke an awareness on the part of Catholic theologians that they, mutatis mutandis, share the same responsibility and might exercise that responsibility through a narrative theology.

Were a Catholic theology to regard tradition as its narrative, could that tradition be understood as a *realistic* narrative in any sense comparable to Frei's? This question may be answered affirmatively with some important qualifications. For Frei, a realistic or history-like reading can be theologically normative because the gospels offer a literal portrayal of a person in circumstances that demonstrate his character. The realism of the narrative derives from the realism of its central character rendered in the midst of realistic circumstances—in Frei's provocative description, Jesus in his powerful powerlessness. Any Christian, of course, would agree with Frei that Jesus is the central character in the biblical story. And any Christian biblical theology intent on portraying the entire Bible as a single narrative would do so by making Jesus Christ the main character, as well as the line of narrative unity running through the various persons, events, and genres of scripture. The realistic Jesus of the gospels also remains the core of the central character of the Catholic narrative, though now—in the more pluralistic setting of tradition—the central character of the narrative becomes more multifaceted, complex, and nuanced in its fuller development. Or, to make the point in a way that subverts any risk of threat to Christic authority, the central character of tradition is a less-focused character than is Jesus, though one that can, in certain respects, be rendered realistically.

This central character is, of course, the apostolic deposit of faith as it is embraced in all the times, places, persons, practices, and events that the Church values as sacred tradition. Were one to name this character more personally, one might be tempted to identify it as the Holy Spirit, for in Catholic belief the Spirit of God is the graceful agency of tradition. The same Catholic belief, however, would insist that the Spirit's intentions become enacted in tradition through the graceful cooperation of human agency. In line with this belief, it would be better to name the central character in the narrative of tradition "Spirit-in-reception." By this I mean the written and unwritten truth of Christ proclaimed in the apostolic preaching and embraced, as the presence of the Holy Spirit, in the lives of the faithful through the ages. Identifying the central character of the Catholic narrative of tradition as "Spirit-in-reception" immediately suggests some telling divergences between Frei's narrative theology and what one might expect the general style of a Catholic narrative theology to be.

First, if the character of "Spirit-in-reception" is a less focused character than is Jesus of Nazareth, it is not only because the pneumatological and the incarnational instantiate themselves in the created order differently but also because the narrative of circumstances through which tradition unfolds and in which the character of "Spirit-in-reception" is rendered is far less determinate, far more extended and open-ended than the narrative of circumstances offered in the gospels or even in all of canonical scripture, which renders more particularly the character of Jesus. The unfinished quality of a narrative continuing to unfold in actual time makes the identity of its central character in the latest moment of narrative sequence more ambiguous than the identity of a character in a narrative brought to some formal closure.[12] Expressed in terms of a conclusion already reached in our study, what the Church calls the apostolic tradition is always to some degree in a state of revision. Second, whereas, for Frei, talk about the identity of Jesus is properly prior to talk about the manner of his presence to believers—since "who" Jesus is as the divine and risen Lord determines the "how" of his presence[13]—the reverse is the case for the character of "Spirit-in-reception." The narrative of tradition does provide occasions for the identity of the apostolic tradition to achieve a greater clarity, but the relative clarity of this identity reflects the relative clarity with which the Church continues to discern the presence of the Spirit to history, a presence that is pneumatological and always measured against the greater clarity of the tradition's incarnational markers. Third, although the literal sense stands alone in Frei's narrative theology as the conveyor of meaning, the literal sense is but one of the senses of tradition in a Catholic narrative theology. Because the central character of the Catholic narrative of tradition is not simply the Holy Spirit but Spirit-in-reception, it is a character that embraces both the unity and plurality of ecclesial life constituted by the lives of every Christian in every time and place. Whereas Frei could portray the character of Jesus as a literally manifested personal identity, which seems largely undifferentiated even amid the fourfold pluralism of the gospel accounts, the character of Spirit-in-reception would be more adequately portrayed in a Catholic narrative theology as a historically manifested identity-in-difference, as a unity dwelling and developing amid the various meaningful senses that together constitute a comprehensive discernment of tradition.[14]

Given these differences, a Catholic style of narrative theology would seem to offer small prospect for narrative realism. Such, however, is not the case. The realistic character of the narrative of tradition lies in tradition's literal sense, the Church's uncontroversial understanding of the Spirit's presence to its past times and places. Here—one might say, paraphrasing Frei—the character of Spirit-in-reception, in its close ties to the created and ecclesial environments, is rendered through the fine details of moment and culture that take narrative shape as tradition's plain meaning. A Catholic narrative style would take its point of departure from tradition's literal sense, making much of the constancy strongly affirmed in the first sense and interpreting tradition as a unity marked by the traits of authority, identity, and permanence. Although a Catholic narrative style's account of tradition would acknowledge in some way the role of the other senses, it would find in the literal sense a continuity that runs from tradition's beginning to its latest moment—a continuity absorbing any striking instance of incipient development into the cadence of its literal description or standing against any instance of striking renewal resistant to domestication on terms set by the literal sense.

This continuity provides a narrative line in which the identity of Spirit-in-reception is literally manifested in the consistent course of apostolic tradition. A Catholic style in this theological approach rightly resists the temptation to portray the narrative of tradition prospectively, as though the identity of Spirit-in-reception were originally given and could be rendered apart from the realism of unfolding historical circumstance. Presence is properly prior to identity in a Catholic narrative theology that seeks the Spirit's truth in tradition. As character and circumstance fitly render each other under the auspices of the Spirit's presence, the narrative consequence is character identity defined by a long and authoritative past, circumstances imbued with sacred import, and a story of faithful witness stretched canonically from Jesus to the contemporary Church and, in faith's anticipation, brought to closure only at the Second Coming. This canonical narrative would draw little of its storied coherence from a propositional account of doctrinal tradition, for—though the Church's sentences of belief offer elements capable of narrative appropriation as sentences are placed in a more developed exposition and the exposition in turn takes on the contours of ecclesial story—they, as propositions, do not offer a realistic context within which character and circumstance can be mutually interpretive.

A Catholic style of narrative theology would highlight the value of tradition's literal sense, interpreting the first sense by delineating the narrative structures of the tradition's most basic beliefs, doctrines, and practices. My consideration of this theological style has proceeded in conversation with the work of Frei, which has brought some specificity to the theological category of narrative used so widely in the contemporary discussion. Were one to seek an actual Catholic example of a theology that interprets tradition as a narrative cohering in its literal sense, the work of von Balthasar would serve best of all. Von Balthasar has offered a narrative style of theology in nearly all of his writings, but especially in the voluminous trilogy that comprises *The Glory of the Lord*, *Theo-Drama*, and *Theo-logic* and, of these, most directly in *Theo-Drama*, which explicitly looks to the narrative form of the play as an interpretive context for the traditional themes of creation, sin, redemption, and discipleship.[15] Given the constraints of space and this study's illustrative interest in von Balthasar's work, discussion here is limited to the first entry in his trilogy.

Like Frei's, von Balthasar's narrative theology serves a genealogy of modernity that accounts for the post-Enlightenment dissolution of Christian meaning. Moderns, von Balthasar has maintained, have lost the ability to "see the form" of God's revelation, a loss depicted in aesthetic terms as a lack of spiritual taste for the theologically beautiful but that might also be understood in the categories of this study as an incapacity to discern the iconic dimensions of tradition's literal sense. The theological aesthetics that von Balthasar has developed in *The Glory of the Lord* purports to restore the classical power of the "eyes of faith" through a close description of revelation's misapprehended but ever-graceful form, mediated above all in the Incarnation but also in scripture, tradition, and the Church. Revelation's objectivity, what might be called its literal sense in the very givenness of its manifestation, provides a constancy to tradition that is inherently beautiful and, to the degree that each of the transcendentals implicates the others, is good and true as well.

This revelational beauty requires an acknowledgment in faith's humble appreciation of traditional form.[16] The narrative of von Balthasar's aesthetics charts this abiding appreciation in patristic and medieval theologies, examples of what he has called "clerical styles" for which the fluent apprehension of revelation's beauty was a common ecclesial sensibility. And it charts this appreciation in the lonely, alienated aesthetic enactment of such figures as Dante, Blaise Pascal, Gerard Manley Hopkins, and Charles Pierre Péguy, representatives of "lay styles" intent on describing the beauty of revelation in and to a postclassical age aesthetically fractured and removed from truly Christian sensibilities.[17] *The Glory of the Lord* extends this typology of theology's fall and expulsion from the interpretive garden to an account of philosophy's complicity in obscuring the beauty of the divine dispensation by either identifying this beauty too closely with the world's in the manner of ancient myth or severing revelational beauty from creation's in the manner of Nominalism.[18] This great work reaches a crescendo in a canonical reading of the Old and New Testaments that finds in the unity of scripture a proclamation of Christ-centered glory to which the beauty of traditional form testifies in all of its appearances.[19]

Even in this embarrassingly brief sketch of a profoundly rich and erudite work, one meets the main features of a Catholic narrative style of theology, and perhaps in such a way that von Balthasar's work can be said to define the genre, at least as a post-Enlightenment interpretive option. Von Balthasar's *The Glory of the Lord* understands the narrative structure of revelation to extend through scripture and tradition and to cohere in a literal sense conceived sacramentally as the beauty of the Incarnation instantiated in all the words, doctrines, devotions, perspectives, and practices that scripture and tradition have to offer.[20] In this single narrative of scripture and tradition, the character of Spirit-in-reception appears in the proper enactment and reenactment of tradition, as the informing of experience by divine grace and the conforming response of human subjectivity to the revelational object depicted in von Balthasar's well-known discussion of Christian attunement.[21] This submission to an aesthetically conceived literal sense, exemplified so well in saintly enactment, unfolds in tradition's realistic circumstances, in the fine detail of faithful beliefs, writings, events, and deeds that render the character of apostolic truth as they, in turn, are rendered meaningful by its character. While attending always to the unity of apostolic character, and thus to the identity of tradition, von Balthasar's Catholic regard for the pluralism of tradition has led him to portray the character of Spirit-in-reception as an identity-in-difference in which the single impress of revelational form can be received in clerical and lay styles and in representative figures as varied as Irenaeus, Pseudo-Dionysius, Bonaventure, Georg Johann Hamann, and Vladimir Soloviev.[22] Theological interpretation narratively conducted offers a dramatic rendition of tradition's literal sense and, given the indeterminacy of tradition's narrative features in comparison with scripture's far greater determinacy, a dramatic rendition that is—as von Balthasar's own alternate, however complementary, efforts in *Theo-Drama* and *Theo-logic* demonstrate—one version among many possible versions.

The company of Catholic narrativists who interpret with close attention to tradition's literal sense is small.[23] Perhaps this can be explained by the fact that, since the First Vatican Council, Neo-Scholastic theologies have nearly exhausted the Catholic possibilities for making the literal sense of tradition interpretively preeminent and that, since the midtwentieth century, Neo-Scholastic approaches have fallen into disfavor. Von Balthasar's theological style conveys a dissatisfaction with Neo-Scholastic approaches, while affirming the value of the traditionally literal. Indeed, the particularly Catholic genius of his work may lie in its valorization of tradition's literal sense even as it engages in mystical speculation, as it does trinitarianly in *Theo-logic* or christologically in *Heart of the World* and *Mysterium Pascale*.[24] Even if any Catholic narrative style has precedence in Augustine's *Confessions* and *City of God*, and even if von Balthasar's theological style exhibits the influence of Barth, on whom he published an important study in his early years,[25] his work is highly original—arguably the most impressive Catholic contribution to the narrative genre—and offers a late modern alternative to the hermeneutical and critical styles that most Catholic theologians have found to be better alternatives to the limitations of Neo-Scholasticism.

The Style of Hermeneutical Theology and the Sense of Development-in-Continuity

Throughout its history, Catholic theology has always appreciated the value of faith-filled speculation as an avenue, a *via positiva* or *negativa*, to the divine mysteries. Catholic theology in modernity and postmodernity has taken up this traditionally speculative approach not by making the Neo-Platonic hierarchy of being its reflective road to God but by accepting the Kantian critique of metaphysical knowledge and finding in epistemology a range of issues to be negotiated in order for theological insight and reflection to prove meaningful. This, broadly speaking, hermeneutical style of theology makes the concerns of able interpretation a paradigm for theological understanding. It attends closely to the historicity of experience as an indispensable context for knowledge of God, Christ, and the Church and defines the theological task as the right representation of a finite set of the infinitely possible meaningful relationships that ensue between and among scripture, tradition, and experience. As Lonergan has noted, theology so conceived in an empirical culture is an ongoing process within which questions of method become especially important.[26] Methodological issues always accompany theologies in the hermeneutical style, for their interpretive forays acknowledge the complexity of adequate understanding amid the perspectives, preunderstandings, prejudices, and distortions of both experience and text—a complexity to which method brings the order of systematic reflection and criticism. The concern for method in hermeneutical theologies bespeaks a concern for the pluralism of theology's sources in scripture, tradition, and experience.

Theologies in a hermeneutical style are apologetical in orientation. Accepting the integrity of a modern standard of reasonable intelligibility, if not the Enlightenment exclusion of all things religious from the truly reasonable, they construct theological knowledge with an eye to its reception outside the Church in the culture at large. Tracy has spoken of this receptive breadth by identifying the academy and society as audiences for theology in addition to its traditional audience of the Church, the responsibility of the theologian to all three issuing in a theology as public as it is ecclesial.[27] This public sensibility of the hermeneutical style rests on the double assumption that sacred scripture and tradition have truth to offer the culture at large just as the culture at large offers a worldly wisdom to revelation that enhances its relevance to time and culture. The hermeneutical style of theological interpretation regards the juxtaposition of the Word and worldly wisdom as but a moment transcended in a creative interweaving of the two that makes sacred text inseparable from worldly context and makes worldly text inseparable from sacred context. *Blessed Rage for Order*, Tracy's earlier work, portrays this hermeneutical task as the "critical correlation" of the texts of the Christian tradition, on one hand, and common human experience and language, on the other. This somewhat generic description of both Word and world is presented with greater nuance in *The Analogical Imagination*, Tracy's later work in which Gadamer's discussion of traditional understanding as the "fusion of horizons" yields a more integrated and less bipolar conception of the correlational task.[28]

Catholic correlationists draw on a remarkable variety of theoretical resources in order to achieve meaningful interpretive results. Although Tracy's early writings rely more on the methodological insights of Lonergan and the later writings more on the interpretation theory of Gadamer, his work yet stands consistently in a Catholic approach to hermeneutics as correlation that stems from a dissatisfaction with Neo-Scholasticism and its rather static conception of tradition's literal sense. Advocates of a transcendental understanding of experience and its construction as knowledge, such as Joseph Maréchal, Rahner, and Lonergan, sought a more eventful conception of traditional truth in a productive dialogue between Thomistic metaphysics and Kantian criticism.[29] Rahner, the twentieth century's most influential theologian in the hermeneutical style, broadened this dialogue to include the phenomenological-existentialist trajectory in modern philosophy represented best by Heidegger—a trajectory continued in Gadamer's hermeneutics of "effective-historical consciousness" so important for Tracy's depiction of correlative understanding as the enduring power of the Christian classic.[30]

Correlation can also be accomplished by appeal to intellectual traditions outside the Continental heritage. Francis Schüssler Fiorenza, for example, has drawn on the insights of American pragmatism and the work of such philosophers as Quine, Sellars, and Rorty to offer a more nuanced understanding of theological correlation as "reconstructive hermeneutics." Typically modern approaches to fundamental theology in the hermeneutical style, Fiorenza has argued, always run the risk of foundationalism—in this case, the reductive error of hypostatizing one of the poles in the correlative dynamic so that either the divine Word or worldly wisdom is taken as an immediately justified belief resistant to interpretation and in control of, by virtue of its apparent truthfulness, what is now a skewed interpretive process. In what amounts to a critique of literalist tendencies in the method of correlation itself, Fiorenza has insisted on a nonfoundationalist approach to fundamental theology that appreciates how thoroughly hermeneutical—that is, subject to ongoing interpretation—experience and its construction are. Such an approach takes shape in a foundational theology seeking an ever-redefined equilibrium among the hermeneutical reconstruction of tradition, the variety of tradition's warrants and their criticism, and background theories inherent in tradition's claims and their contemporary experience.[31]

However the hermeneutical style of correlation is framed—whether as the transcendental method of Rahner and Lonergan, as the bipolar model of Tracy's early work, or as Fiorenza's holistic approach—it conceives the theological task in a revisionist fashion. The correlationist project never ceases. The experience that enters into critical conversation with the Christian tradition in all its manifestations is always in time and capable of representation in more or less determinate ways. Its contemporaneousness reappears in each new moment. Its regionality unfolds in a spectrum that traverses countless possibilities short of the universal. Hermeneutical theologies are tireless in their efforts to discern, construct, and reconstruct the meaningfulness of tradition within this experiential pluralism. The correlational method in any of its variations seeks a balance between sacred and worldly meanings, a balance whose point of equilibrium is ever reconstituted, subject as it is to the historicity of experience the method ever pursues.

The sense of tradition that hermeneutical theologies value above all is the sense of development-in-continuity, for, of all the senses, the second sense discerns most pointedly the very aspects of tradition that theological correlation unites in any of its constructive revisions. The constancy of established tradition discerned by the second sense is the same communal understanding of the revelatory Word that hermeneutical theologies regard as authoritative in the correlated interpretation. The renewal of tradition in the present moment of faithful re-reception is the same contemporary experience of the community that hermeneutical theologies regard as the relevance that able correlation achieves. The coinherence of tradition's constancy and renewal in

second-sense discernments is the object of correlation. As hermeneutical theologies represent this coinherence of traditional constancy and renewal, they
offer to the Church's judgment an interpretation of how tradition should currently be configured and, in so doing, contribute to the Church's traditional
self-understanding and thus to tradition itself.

Theologies in the hermeneutical style attend to the second sense in a special
way but not to the exclusion of the other senses and the theological styles
particularly attendant to them. Correlational interpretation draws on first-
sense constancy and its representation in the narrative style, just as it draws
on the senses of striking renewal and their representation in the critical style
of theology considered in chapter 4 and further in this chapter's following
section. In setting the traditional values of constancy and renewal in a relative
balance, any hermeneutical theology may fix its point of equilibrium more
on the side of constancy or more on the side of renewal. It may offer an
interpretation of development-in-continuity that places greater emphasis on
tradition's literal sense and its narrative quality or that gives a more careful
account of the re-receptive moment and its capacity to reconfigure previous
receptions of the literal sense. In any case, a correlative interpretation will
purport to be faithful to the development-in-continuity of tradition. The community of believers will judge whether a particular correlation of constancy
and renewal represents its current discernment and confession of the Spirit's
presence or anticipates what it should now discern and confess as that presence to a historicity of faith continually developing.

In its efforts to represent the second sense, the hermeneutical style will find
its highest accomplishment in interpretations that refuse to distinguish between theological form and content. Just as what might be distinguished as
continuity and development are actually the same in the retrospective affirmation of a particular configuration of tradition, so, too, correlational attempts to represent the second sense will faithfully recognize that what might
be distinguished in methodological abstraction as the content of the revelatory
Word and the form of worldly wisdom are actually the same in interpretation.
In making claims about tradition's current stage of development, hermeneutical theologies risk not merely a translation of Word into worldly wisdom or
worldly wisdom into Word, a reductionism of which Protestant narrativists
sometimes accuse them.[32] Rather, the indistinguishability of form and content
in correlation means that the interpretation that any hermeneutical theology
offers to the Church for its judgment is nothing less than a representation of
tradition—one that holistically presents the Word within the full range of its
historicity so that, as tradition, the Word properly may no longer be abstracted from its historicization and historicization may no longer be abstracted from the Word. The indistinguishability of form and content in correlational results means that, in the interpretive moment, the methodological
concerns of hermeneutical theologies and all their abstractive efforts to do
justice to the complexity of Word and world are eclipsed by an actual interpretation which, in faith and for the Church's faith, ventures a representation
of developing tradition.[33]

Although hermeneutical theologies may devote themselves to a particular locus—issuing in interpretations that speak more of God or Christ or Spirit or Church or, as in the case of the present study, tradition—their contributions are always made to a broader narrative defined by the biblical story of God and the Christ and the traditional story of the Spirit of God at work in the Church. Hermeneutical theologies can be, and usually are, the source of valuable insights into the many ways in which the Catholic narrative unfolds in our own time, as worldly wisdom of all sorts is welcomed into the narrative world and has a role in shaping its central character, the Spirit-in-reception. Hermeneutical theologies aid the Church in understanding better not only how the plot of traditional narrative moves now as Christians struggle to discern the workings of the Spirit in their lives but also how the plot has moved at critical junctures in its story. In both of these respects, hermeneutical theologies, in their attention to interpretive development, contingency, and pluralism, are indispensable aids in guarding against a Catholic narrative theology's particular temptation to regard its narrative of scripture and tradition—in Bakhtin's telling distinction—only as an epic and not at all as a novel, only as a finished story of distant events impossible to change, rethink, or reevaluate and not at all as an ongoing story in which unfinished characters are developed in local settings, amid a plurality of voices, and in the realism of creativity and even laughter.[34]

The traditionally historicized Word, though, can possess narrative dimensions even in the hermeneutical style. In this regard, hermeneutical theologies do not aid the narrative style merely by clarifying character-forming moments in its grand story but may actually construct a narrative framework for tradition correlationally and with particular attention to the second sense. Tracy's appeal to the interpretive workings of the classic as a model for traditional understanding and its representation in systematic theology is a good example of correlation finding interpretive resource in narrative, as is Terrence W. Tilley's account of the tasks of a narrative theology in *Story Theology*.[35]

Still another example, whose aptness I leave to the reader's judgment, is the presentation of tradition in this study as a narrative in the manner of a postmodern allegory. This analogy correlates features of ancient allegory as a functional negotiation of the literal sense and a postmodern commitment to the believer's present faith retrospectively configuring the coherence of tradition. The result is a narrative portrayal of tradition attuned to the sense of development-in-continuity as an ever-redefined variation on tradition's literal sense. The narrative coherence of this allegory unfolds retrospectively as the present faith of the community looks back across the ages and universally affirms a developed continuity, a plot, that runs from the contemporary moment to the apostolic age. This retrospective narrative, this story told backward, is neither subject to chronological time nor completely explainable by historical-critical sensibilities that make chronological time their analytical ambiance. In this regard, the memory of the Church from which this narrative proceeds works much like the memories of its members, which offer another analogy from experience for theological correlation. An individual construes personal narrative by finding coherence in a selective concatenation of life's meaningful words, deeds, events, and relationships and may frame this coherence as a genealogy from present to past. And in this same way the ecclesial community may configure tradition as a meaningful plot stretching from present to past and in which the present affirmation of continuity embraces a selective host, nearly all but in any particular present moment not necessarily all, of the tradition's previously affirmed continuities.

The narrative of tradition can also be correlationally constructed from past to present, from apostolic age to contemporary ecclesial life. The experience of reading within a novel's plot, short of its conclusion, presented an analogy of revisable narrative coherence that allowed the conception of the apostolic deposit of faith in a manner consistent with the evidence of history, the Church's orthodox faith, and a retrospective account of tradition. The novel reader's ability to reconcile a commitment to the author's plot as it has unfolded so far with an openness to the next narrative moment resembles the stance of present-day believers who affirm the truth of tradition's received past within the continued unfolding of its truth in the present. The capacity of the novel's next narrative moment to modify, and not vitiate, one's understanding of previous narrative coherence offers insight into how believers in the Church can conceptualize development-in-continuity from beginning to relative end, while avoiding the prospectivity inherent in premodern and modern conceptualizations of tradition.

Like theologies in the narrative style, hermeneutical construals of narrative may avail themselves of the full range of narrative categories in order to understand the workings of tradition more fully. Catholic narrative theologies such as von Balthasar's find typological or figural readings of scripture and tradition especially appealing, for typology provides an overarching meaning to a literal sense that extends over areas of page and time otherwise too vast to offer an apparent narrative unity. Literal readings of scripture throughout Christian history have often invoked the typology of promise/fulfillment in order to weave the biblical canon into a single story. Von Balthasar's theological aesthetics reads the literal sense of tradition in terms of the typology of loss/recovery. Modern conceptualizations of the development of doctrine also invoke typologies in order to foster a narrative unity to tradition. When placed in a narrative framework, distinctions such as Tradition/traditions, infallible/noninfallible, and content/form become modern typologies for speaking of the unity and stability of tradition amid the plurality and contingency encountered in the course of its development. Such modern typologies are equally committed to the formation of narratives in which tradition's potentially hegemonic power is checked by the resourceful presence of plurality and contingency in every moment of development.

These typologies all construe the narrative of scripture and tradition from past to present and in this regard all exhibit prospective traits, if not full-blown prospective commitments. Were the correlationally constructed narrative of postmodern allegory explained typologically, none of these typologies would suffice. Postmodern allegory is formed retrospectively as the contemporary community of faith binds the continuities affirmed in the ecclesial past into a particular shape that finds continuity from present to apostolic past. This study has portrayed this traditional configuration as a way of telling the Church's inspired story; it has portrayed the story as an allegory to the degree that, like ancient allegory, it negotiates a given, literal sense in the face of possible conflicts of meaning, and it has portrayed the allegory as postmodern in its refusal, unlike ancient and modern allegory, to regard the story as a metaphor that does not literally mean what it says. Since this postmodern allegory tells the story of tradition's ever-renewed constancy, it can also be understood typologically, though through a typology that sets narrative unity as a sequence from present to past rather than from past to present. The typology binding together this narrative in the hermeneutical style might be described as affirmation/attestation, with affirmation understood as the present community's commitment in faith to a particular retrospective configuration of tradition and attestation as the real witness of past continuities that form narrative lines of retrospective meaning back to the apostolic age. This typology offers a way of conceiving tradition's narrative unity across the ages as faith's current affirmation of tradition's construal to which a particular understanding of the past testifies.

If tradition understood as postmodern allegory can be regarded typologically as well, it is because a theological construction in the hermeneutical style invokes whatever analogy it can, whether from resources inside or outside the tradition, in order to elucidate the truth of God's revelation. Finally, however, the integrity of the analogy depends on how it serves revelation. Correlation is a means to an end and not an end in itself. The same can be said for the means of critical analysis on which narrative and hermeneutical styles draw but that, when highlighted in the theological task, can appear as a distinct interpretive style.

The Style of Critical Theology and the Senses of Incipient and Dramatic Development

Naming the third style of theology "critical" might suggest that this interpretive approach exclusively lays claim to the analytical traits, the careful scrutiny of evidence, the acumen in judgment, and the respect for the limitations of knowledge that characterize the intellect's critical sensibility. And such an exclusive identification of the critical style of theology with the critical sensibility might suggest further that narrative and hermeneutical styles of theology are uncritical as interpretive exercises. This, of course, is not so. All three theological styles depend on the intellect's critical faculties in order to advance interpretations adequate to their goal of representing tradition well. All, too, require creative insight that can focus an interpretive vision of tradition's four senses, even if each style highlights one or another. Above all, all three theological styles rely on divine grace as the agency of critical and creative interpretation, for, when the analytic and synthetic powers of the intellect are enlisted in the service of theology, they serve faith. In and through faith, the intellect's critical and creative powers are able to pursue dimensions of the truth that otherwise would lie beyond their recognition.

The third theological style is critical in a determinate way that justifies the designation of this genre by a trait indispensable to any theological reflection. Critical theologies take their point of departure from the restlessness of faith in local circumstances. Closely bound in interpretive sensibility to regional time and place, critical theologies highlight the implications of traditional development in its finest detail. They eschew the relatively generic descriptions of Word and human situation that hermeneutical theologies typically make the ingredients of correlation. Correlational theologies attend to the second sense of tradition and thus to the universal claims for tradition made by the whole Church, a universality reflected not only in their theological claims but also in how these theologies represent the Word and worldly wisdom brought into interpretive dialogue. Critical theologies are suspicious of the universalizing tendencies of hermeneutical constructions, however tempered they might be by nuance and qualification. In the judgment of the critical style, claims for theological universality often show themselves to be pretenders, the claims of some but not all in the Church whose representativeness is exaggerated in order to promote a narrow interest, established power relations, the hypostatization of a certain time or place, and finally an understanding of tradition's literal sense that is not true to the experience of the whole Church. This suspicion extends to any claim for first- or second-sense tradition—the language of liturgy, creed, or doctrine—which, under the gaze of the critical style, may show itself to be guilty of the same false universalizing.

And yet, in spite of their reservations about the hermeneutical style, critical theologies are deeply correlational. The worldly wisdom they enlist into dialogical partnership with the Word, though, does not venture a general account of the human situation, a metaphysics, however historicized, of one sort or another. Worldly wisdom here appears rather as a critique of any such universalized construction. Critical theologies appreciate that what might be generically described as "the human situation" actually stands in a pluralism so thorough as to defy such representation. Its temporality, its spatiality, its culture, and its situation in gender, race, and class remain so differentiated that overarching constructions fail to correspond to the remarkably diverse situations in which remarkably diverse persons actually live their lives.

In order to account for this pluralism, critical theologies turn to theories that criticize the universalizing tendencies of constructive reflection and find in these theories more adequate resources for correlation. Ideology-critique, feminist criticism, class analysis, social theory, and deconstructionist criticism of binary oppositions in which power is capriciously privileged and usurped are all examples of theories that lead—in the judgment of the critical style—to a more realistic interpretive result. Images of synthesis, balance, or fusion that depict hermeneutical correlation do not account well for correlation in the critical style. Pluralistically conscious theories enter into a mutually critical relationship with scripture and tradition in which the Word prophetically informs worldly wisdom and worldly wisdom makes the Word itself a critical target, exposing not only the immersion of the modes of divine revelation themselves in the limited interests of ideology and prejudice but also the lacunae and absences in revelation's communication of the truth. Whereas hermeneutical correlation is apologetical and eager to embrace Enlightenment assumptions in however religiously qualified a manner, correlation in the critical style involves a hermeneutics of suspicion that turns the Enlightenment's assault on revelation back upon its own assumptions and their reasonable construction as a philosophical anthropology.

Theologies in the critical style are especially attendant to the third and fourth senses of tradition. These senses discern in the contemporary movement of the Spirit a development of tradition that challenges the literal sense, calling for its modification through the renewing claims of incipient and dramatic development. The third and fourth senses themselves might be described as critical powers of the *sensus fidei* by which it seeks the Spirit in the most particular reaches of the human situation and struggles to dispel any complacency that would regard the literal sense in its latest reception as impervious to renewal—even renewal prompted by the loss of a long-established configuration of the literal sense. The senses of striking renewal are exercised as a faith laced with the hope that the Spirit's inspiration of tradition will continue in ways strong enough to be thoroughly surprising. This same hope entails the doubt that tradition as it has unfolded thus far is adequate to the new life the Spirit ever breathes into history so that the future's cascade into the present can be charged with sacred meaning.

The senses of striking renewal find their claims to be disturbing to a tradition that strongly values first- and second-sense constancy and that frames that constancy by looking to the past. And, in the same way, critical theologies find their construction of third- and fourth-sense discernments to be regarded by many in the Church as untruthful deviations from the Spirit's acknowledged reception. Theologies in the critical style, however, appreciate that the Spirit's truth is not exhausted in acknowledged reception. Indeed, acknowledged reception becomes continually possible only through the renewing contributions of the third and fourth senses. Whether a critical theology reflects on a fourth-sense discernment that offers tradition an incipient development to be added to its understanding of its constancy or reflects on a third-sense discernment that calls for a shocking redefinition of constancy, its reflections chasten the universal faith of the Church, though for the sake of its more particularistic attunement to the Spirit's traditional presence.

The critical style is the latest arrival in the history of theological interpretation. It emerged in politically conscious variations on the hermeneutical style that were leery of the transcendental method as an adequate rendition of correlation. In the Catholic tradition, Johann Baptist Metz's political theology understood itself as an explicit challenge to Rahner's transcendental orientation. Metz's critical approach to correlation interprets the human sit-

uation with a careful regard for its sociopolitical dimensions and the susceptibility of the Church to market forces that shape ecclesial life into the idolatry
of bourgeois religion. This same critical perspective has led Metz to represent
the Word as the prophetic "dangerous memory" of Jesus, a liberating recollection that "oppresses and questions the present because it reminds us not
of some open future, but precisely [God's] future and because it compels Christians constantly to change themselves so that they are able to take this future
into account."[36] Latin American theologians such as Gutiérrez, Juan Luis
Segundo, and Jon Sobrino, have emphasized the need for a critical theology
of praxis, one that understands Jesus' liberating life, death, and resurrection
not only as the promise of life to come but also as God's work in a history
fraught with economic injustice and political oppression often encouraged by
false readings of the gospel. These theologians regard the Christian life as a
cooperation in this divine, liberating work through faithful solidarity with the
poor and—in accordance with Jesus' example—as action to address, both
individually and structurally, the needy cries of the socially disenfranchised.[37]

Feminist theologies also embrace the critical style in a hermeneutics of
suspicion directed toward Word and world. Like Latin American liberationists,
feminist theologians criticize the Enlightenment's failure to live up to its promise of universal social liberation and see injustice particularly in discriminatory practices toward women. Even more important, this exercise in ideology-
critique is directed toward scripture and tradition whose teachings not only
represent an authoritative source for correlative interpretation but also have
offered a powerful reification for the patriarchy of society at large. Whether
feminist theologians proceed as Elizabeth Schüssler Fiorenza does by recov-
ering a lost discipleship of equals in early Christianity, as Carr does by judging
the current practice of priestly ordination to be a symbol of the lack of
women's presence in the official life of the Church, or as Ruether does by
seeking alternatives to biblical God-language, all criticize the current shape
of tradition's literal sense in the name of third- and fourth-sense discernments
that emerge in the particularities, and not the universality, of ecclesial experience.[38] These particularities, considered in their full and rich spectrum,
yield a wide array of renewing insights that appear in the more particular
histories of peoples and cultures and in their representation as African-
American, Hispanic, and Asian theologies of liberation.[39]

This critical version of the method of correlation also produces constructive
results, much in the manner of hermeneutical correlation. Theological criticism of traditional understandings of constancy is not an end itself, as though
theologians in the critical style could be counted in the ranks of Christianity's
modern cultured despisers. Rather, the third- and fourth-sense discernments
highlighted in the critical style are themselves claims for constancy, albeit a
constancy that calls for the reconstruction of what the Church thus far has
judged to abide. Criticism expresses dissatisfaction with tradition's status quo.
But it is a dissatisfaction prompted by the desire for tradition, albeit a tradition
that needs to be imagined in accordance with the Church's developing ex-

perience of the Spirit's presence. Critical theologies serve this need for tradition's reimagining by offering criticism that leads to the construction of third- and fourth-sense insights as novel portrayals of traditional possibilities. Gutiérrez's insistence on solidarity with the poor as the liberating message of the gospel, Johnson's recovery of the *sophia* tradition as a resource for an inclusive doctrine of the Trinity, and Elizabeth Schüssler Fiorenza's appeal to the same ancient tradition as a resource for new understandings of Mary and Church are all examples of how the critical style of theology finally takes shape in constructive directions.[40]

Whether any of these critical constructions comes to be embraced as the Church's universal tradition depends on the communal judgment of believers as a graceful agency in cooperation with the Spirit's historical work. This judgment requires time, and time requires patience so that the imaginative constructions of critical theologies can be subjected to the same criticism they advocate and the truthfulness of any particular claim can be measured against a tradition that, understood correctly, is always open to the novel as a function of the Spirit's omnipresence to unfolding time.

The constructive possibilities of correlation in the critical style demonstrate what has already been illustrated in this study's analysis of the narrative and hermeneutical styles—that no theological style is completely divorced from the others in the way it offers an interpretation of tradition. Critical theologies may take their point of departure from the ecclesially regional, but the construction that their criticism prompts always ventures beyond the particular as a claim for the notice of the whole Church. Such critical construction learns much from the hermeneutical style, however chastened its universal-izing of Word and world may be in critical appropriation. Aspects of the narrative style, even if not narrative commitment to the literal sense, are also capable of critical embrace. Like hermeneutical theologies, critical theologies always go about their reflective business by interpreting the biblical narrative of God and the Christ and the ecclesial narrative of the Spirit of God in history. In framing this narrative, broadly understood as the story of tradition, critical theologies often offer fresh perspectives on its central character, Spirit-in-reception, and the traditional circumstances in which its identity is formed. Tradition, narratively arranged in the critical style, often appears as a *Bildungsroman* that plots the fall of Spirit-in-reception from an early innocence or inescapable guilt to the new or continuing corruption of anti-Judaism, misogyny, imperial politics, or Eurocentrism, needing and seeking redemption in and through the traditional differences that its literally configured identity is inclined to deny.[41] One sees this construal of narrative circumstance and its character-forming power particularly in Latin American and feminist liberation theologies, which present traditional plot as a context for Spirit-in-reception's struggles to achieve a faithful identity that embraces difference not as alienation from but *as* its authentic ecclesial self.

This narrative dimension of the critical style testifies to a holism in the theological enterprise that deserves appreciation not only in the ways that the other stylistic traits accompany any particular style but also comprehensively in the manner that all the styles together contribute to the Church's understanding of tradition.

Tradition in the Spectrum of Theological Styles

Theology's tasks typically have been parceled out in the modern period among the subdisciplines of fundamental, systematic, and practical theologies. And these have been concerned, respectively, with the issues of the intelligibility of revelation, the coherence of faith, and the application of doctrine to life. The theological styles explored in this chapter cannot be aligned neatly with these subdisciplines. There are ways of conducting each of the disciplinary tasks in any one of the theological styles. The hermeneutical style, for example, can be a venue for the task of fundamental, or systematic, or practical theology, as can the narrative and the critical styles. The theological styles are not set by specific disciplinary tasks but, instead, by their orientation toward one or another of the senses of tradition. Since the theological styles are oriented toward certain kinds of discernments of the Spirit's truth, they are more basic to the theological enterprise than the disciplinary tasks, which are defined by the anthropological concerns of understanding, believing, and acting. The theological styles, one might say, are closer to the workings of tradition than are the disciplinary tasks that are *in* tradition as dimensions of theology's modern heritage but not consistently *of* it as are the senses of tradition.

Any theological style attends particularly to one of the senses of tradition. And yet, as this study's consideration of the styles has shown, each may draw on the others in order to represent what is finally the distinctiveness of its own perspective. A theological style may advance its interpretive insights by marking its distinctiveness as exclusivity, eschewing constructive relationship to the other styles, and even regarding them as spurious options for tradition's representation. Certainly this is an error to which the narrative and critical styles are most susceptible. The narrative style can become enamored of the tried and the familiar, reduce tradition to what has been, and regard claims for the new only as deviations from an epic-like account of the ecclesial narrative. The critical style can be seduced by claims for the new that reduce tradition to a contemporary moment cut loose from its moorings in the authoritative past and set adrift in a history charted by local caprice and accommodation rather than by the faith of the whole Church. Although the hermeneutical style of theology, like all things human, may err in its execution, its wide interpretive embrace can be instructive to the other styles in appreciating the breadth of both tradition and theological reflection upon it.

If the discipline of theology is entrusted by the Church with representing tradition well, then it can do so only by offering a faithful account of the *sensus fidei* in all its dimensions. It has been shown that this supernatural sense of the faith cannot be conceived only as the discernment of what the whole Church confesses as its literal sense. Rather, the *sensus fidei* is an act of faith made in both universal and regional settings and through which all four senses of tradition discern the truth of the Spirit. This fourfold discernment will eventually be drawn into the unity of a comprehensive discernment. Any theology will attempt to account for such a comprehensive discernment by focusing its attention on one of the four senses but will attend, in any case, to the relationships between and among all four. And to the degree that all four senses together constitute a comprehensive discernment represented theologically, each interpretive style may contribute in some way to the understanding that any theology seeks. Although one style will most likely predominate in the theological interpretation presented to the Church for its developing understanding, any interpretation—even if its commitment to a predominating style leads it to obscure its appeal to other stylistic resources—is likely to be pluralistic in its style.

This stylistic holism within a theological interpretation reflects the holism of the four senses of tradition in their apperceptive unity in the *sensus fidei*. This unity dwells in, but not only in, the subjectivity of the act of faith, for finally the unity of the four senses in the *sensus fidei* rests on the unity of the Spirit's truth, the objectivity of tradition that extends through time and place. The Spirit may be discerned truly in tradition's literal sense, the sense of development-in-continuity, and the senses of dramatic and incipient development. For this reason, theology may appear in a particular style that expresses a theologian's judgment on when and where and how the Spirit is compellingly present—and in a way that demands the Church's attention. Yet were a theology to advance an interpretation in a stylistically narrow fashion, it could no more give satisfactory account of the Spirit's traditional presence than could any one of the four senses artifically abstracted from the others.

The pluralism of theological styles even within a stylistically particular interpretation conveys the pluralism of the senses of tradition, which convey, in turn, the many times, places, persons, and events to which the Spirit is traditionally present. This layered pluralism admits of layered unities, from the unity of the Spirit in the Godhead, to the unity of tradition, to the unity of the senses, to the unity of a single sense and its representation in a particular theological style. In the unity and plurality that coinhere in God, in tradition, in the act of faith, in the discerning senses, and in their theological interpretation, believers encounter the continuing mystery of Pentecost in which the one Spirit came to rest on each of the Twelve and was promised "to everyone whom the Lord our God calls" (*Acts* 2:3, 39).

This situatedness of any particular theological interpretation in the pluralism of the traditional senses applies as well to all the theological styles available as interpretive options in the modern period and considered together as ecclesial ways of configuring what has been, is, and will be tradition. Narrative, hermeneutical, and critical theologies together form a literary trove that aids the Church in understanding the constancy and renewal of the apostolic tradition. Theologies written in one or another of these styles advance their claims in the confidence that a particular style best captures a dimension of tradition that the Church should heed. It would not be inaccurate to describe this stylistic predilection of any theology as an agenda. Theologies may have different agendas, as long as any agenda falls within tradition's concerns. Unfortunately, however, theological difference frequently is seen as a sign of contradiction. Advocates of particular styles often regard each other as rivals for the Spirit's truth. Proceeding from the false assumption that tradition may be done justice only narratively or hermeneutically or critically, any one style may regard its own perspective as privileged. Such exclusivism, of course, rests on the judgment that the Spirit's truth dwells only in the sense to which the privileged style is aligned. The expectation that good theology can be found in only one of the theological styles finally stems from the reduction of traditional truth to one of the four senses.

Although the Church articulates its universal tradition in first- and second-sense claims, the Spirit's truth appears in all four senses of tradition. Theology's contribution to tradition and the life of the Church lies in its reflective pursuit of this truth that all believers seek and discern, even if not in theology's informed, critical, and even systematic manner. Theology is responsible to the historical mediation of God's truth, whose veridical power cannot be contained only within universal confessions of faith, the consistency of liturgy, and time-honored practice. It is a common error to confuse theology with established doctrine, as though theology were solely the articulation of the Church's established first- or second-sense judgment on the Spirit's traditional presence. But theology is, and needs to be, a speculative enterprise that risks interpretation beyond tradition's constancy. Any theology represents a comprehensive discernment of tradition in which a certain, though always questionable, relationship is affirmed between and among the four senses. A theological representation of a comprehensive discernment takes a stand on the historical dimensions of constancy and renewal in the Spirit's truth. The different theological styles represent different comprehensive discernments—at least in the emphasis given to one sense in its relationship to the others and probably, too, in the actual configuration of all four senses as what tradition has been, is, and will be.

On this side of the eschaton, tradition is not finished. It is always being configured. Its continuity is always developing. In the spectrum of theological styles, the Church meets a pluralism in the kinds of comprehensive discernments that the faithful make on how this development unfolds. Instead of viewing the styles as competing claims for the constancy and renewal of tradition, the Church would do better to regard all the styles together as the host of ecclesial claims on how and when and where the Spirit is truly present to the created order, to the community of believers, and to every receptive life. All the styles together offer not a representation of this or that theologian's comprehensive discernment of tradition but a collective representation of the Church's comprehensive discernments from which, with the passing of time, faithful witness will be sifted and, with the passing of time, will be renewed stolidly or strikingly. In the interpretive holism of all the styles, the Church encounters ever-recurring opportunities to consider, criticize, and configure the fourfold senses as a faithful rendition of the Spirit's eventful presence, as the tradition that it treasures.

Notes

Introduction

1. "Dogmatic Constitution on Divine Revelation" (*Dei verbum*), in *Vatican Council II: The Conciliar and Postconciliar Documents*, ed. A. Flannery, O.P. (Northport, N.Y.: Costello, 1987), 755, no. 10.

2. Discussions of the nature and task of theological interpretation are nearly as numerous as discrete theological writings, since hermeneutical issues have become woven into the fabric of theological thinking itself. For Catholic contributions to the genre of interpretive method, see David Tracy, *The Analogical Imagination: Christian Theology and the Culture of Pluralism* (New York: Crossroad, 1981); Tracy, *Plurality and Ambiguity: Hermeneutics, Religion, Hope* (San Francisco: Harper and Row, 1987); Francis Schüssler Fiorenza, *Foundational Theology: Jesus and the Church* (New York: Crossroad, 1986); Claude Geffré, *The Risk of Interpretation: On Being Faithful to the Christian Tradition in a Non-Christian Age*, trans. D. Smith (New York: Paulist Press, 1987); Werner G. Jeanrond, *Text and Interpretation as Categories of Theological Thinking*, trans. T. Wilson (New York: Crossroad, 1988); Jeanrond, *Theological Hermeneutics: Development and Significance* (New York: Crossroad, 1991).

3. Hans-Georg Gadamer, *Truth and Method*, trans. G. Barden and J. Cumming (New York: Crossroad, 1975); Paul Ricoeur, *The Symbolism of Evil*, trans. E. Buchanan (Boston: Beacon Press, 1967), 347–57; Wolfgang Iser, *The Act of Reading: A Theory of Aesthetic Response* (Baltimore, Md.: Johns Hopkins University Press, 1978).

4. For Derrida's critique of the literal sense, which can be found in nearly all his works, see especially Jacques Derrida, "White Mythology: Metaphor in the Text of Philosophy," in *Margins of Philosophy*, trans. A. Bass (Chicago: University of Chicago Press, 1982), 207–71. For his discussion of the literal sense as the signifier and its dissociation from the signified in the age of the Book, see Derrida, *Of Grammatology*, trans. G. Spivak (Baltimore, Md.: Johns Hopkins University Press, 1976), 6–26.

5. For overviews of early Christian interpretive practices, see Robert M. Grant and David Tracy, *A Short History of the Interpretation of the Bible*, 2d ed. (Philadelphia: Fortress Press, 1984); James Barr, *Old and New in Interpretation: A Study of the Two Testaments* (London: SCM Press, 1966); P. R. Ackroyd and C. F. Evans, eds., *The Cambridge History of the Bible*, vol. 1, *From the Beginnings to Jerome* (New York: Cambridge University. Press, 1970).

6. Origen, *On First Principles*, trans. G. Butterworth (Gloucester, Mass: Smith, 1973), 275–87.

7. For Tyconius, see Maureen A. Tilley, *The Bible in Christian North Africa: The Donatist World* (Minneapolis: Fortress Press, 1997), 112–28. In his own reflections on scriptural interpretation, Augustine made Tyconius's hermeneutical rules his

guide. Augustine, *On Christian Doctrine*, trans. D. W. Robertson Jr. (New York: Bobbs-Merrill, 1958).

8. See John Cassian, *The Conferences*, trans. B. Ramsey, O.P. (New York: Paulist Press, 1997), 509–11 (XIV, 8). The most extensive study of the four senses is Henri DeLubac, *Exégèse médiévale: Les quatre sens de l'écriture*, 2 vols. (Paris: Aubier, 1959–1961). DeLubac examined each the four senses systematically in vol. 1/2, 425–681.

9. James Samuel Preus, *From Shadow to Promise: Old Testament Interpretation from Augustine to the Young Luther* (Cambridge, Mass.: Harvard University. Press, 1969), 13–16. Augustine's understanding of the productive capacity of the literal sense can be seen clearly in *De Genesi ad Litteram*, where he defined the literal sense as "a faithful record of what happened" (*The Literal Meaning of Genesis*, vol. 1, trans. J. Taylor, S.J. [New York: Newman Press, 1982], 19 [I, 1]). In Augustine's judgment, though, the occurrences that the literal sense records are not merely events in history; they are the supernatural events of God's creation of the heavens and the earth, events that other ancient exegetes, such as Origen, sought through the more speculative apprehensions of the allegorical sense.

10. See Beryl Smalley, *The Study of the Bible in the Middle Ages* (Oxford: Blackwell, 1952).

11. Thomas Aquinas, *Summa Theologiae*, I, 1, 10.

12. Henricus Denzinger-Adolfus Schönmetzer, *Enchiridion Symbolorum Definitionum et Declarationum de Rebus Fidei et Morum*, 34th ed. (Freiburg im Breisgau, Germany: Herder, 1965), 365, nos. 1502–03. Some might judge the Denzinger collection to function as a canonical listing of tradition, but this possibility fails on three counts: Denzinger's compilation includes only doctrinal tradition and not the tradition of Christian practice; the compilation is incomplete even in its presentation of the doctrinal tradition; and, unlike Trent's enumeration of the inspired biblical books, the Denzinger compilation possesses no authority as a listing, in spite of the acknowledged authority of the doctrines it lists.

13. See, for example, Gerhard Ebeling, " 'Sola Scriptura' and Tradition," in *The Word of God and Tradition*, trans. S. Hooke (Philadelphia: Fortress Press, 1968), 102–47.

14. Twentieth-century interpretations of the Council of Trent commonly distinguish between the apostolic tradition and ecclesial traditions. Trent, the common interpretive wisdom holds, defines the authority of the former and not the latter. Peter Lengsfeld, summarizing the respected views, has named five characteristics of teachings or practices that mark the apostolic tradition in the minds of the fathers at Trent: (1) they possess a divine origin through Christ or the Holy Spirit; (2) they have been passed on and received since the time of the apostles; (3) they possess a relevance for faith and morals and thus for the life of discipleship; (4) they have been continually preserved in the Church to the present time; and (5) unlike scripture, they were not committed to writing in the apostolic age. "Tradition und heilige Schrift: Ihr Verhältnis," in *Mysterium Salutis*, vol. 1, *Die Grundlagen heilsgeschichtlicher Dogmatik*, ed. J. Feiner and M. Löhrer (Einsiedeln, Switzerland: Benziger Verlag, 1965), 473. We would do well to note two further characteristics of the apostolic tradition that were not explicitly articulated by the Tridentine fathers: Teachings and practices of the apostolic tradition that were committed to writing after the apostolic age, and—as previously noted—teachings and practices that faithfully complement, as well as interpret, biblical teaching. See the discussion of Trent's teaching on tradition that follows.

15. Cf. Josef Rupert Geiselmann, *The Meaning of Tradition* (Quaestiones Disputatae, 15), trans. W. J. O'Hara (Freiburg, Germany: Herder; London: Burns and Oates, 1966), 9.

16. Hans von Campenhausen, *The Formation of the Christian Bible*, trans. J. A. Baker (Philadelphia: Fortress Press, 1972), 269.

17. Yves M.-J. Congar, O.P., *La Tradition et les traditions*, vol. 1, *Essai historique* (Paris: Librairie Arthème Fayard, 1960), 64–66.

18. See Irenaeus of Lyons, *Against Heresies*, in *The Ante-Nicene Fathers*, vol. 1, ed. A. Roberts and J. Donaldson (Grand Rapids, Mich.: Eerdmans, 1977), 347 (I, 22). For versions of the rule of faith in Tertullian and Origen, see Tertullian, *On Prescription Against Heretics*, in *The Ante-Nicene Fathers*, vol. 3, ed. A. Roberts and J. Donaldson (Buffalo, N.Y.: Christian Literature, 1887), 251–52 (19); Origen, *On First Principles*, 2–5 (I, Preface, 4).

19. Congar, *La Tradition et les traditions*, vol. 1, 157–59.

20. On this classical understanding of authorship, see John E. Thiel, *Imagination and Authority: Theological Authorship in the Modern Tradition* (Minneapolis, Minn.: Fortress Press, 1991), 14–19.

21. George H. Tavard, *Holy Writ or Holy Church: The Crisis of the Protestant Reformation* (New York: Harper and Brothers, 1959), 7.

22. "Tradition, then, was the overflow of the Word outside Sacred Scripture. It was neither separate from nor identical with Holy Writ. Its contents were the 'other scriptures' through which the Word made himself known" (*ibid.*, 8). Cf. Congar, *La Tradition et les traditions*, vol. 1, 193.

23. Congar, *La Tradition et les traditions*, vol. 1, 124, 127.

24. Tavard, *Holy Writ or Holy Church*, 22–43.

25. Martin Luther, "On the Councils and the Church (1539)," in *Luther's Works*, vol. 41, ed. E. Gritsch, trans. C. Jacobs (Philadelphia: Fortress Press, 1966), 123. Luther, "Against Hanswurst (1541)," trans. E. Gritsch, in *ibid., 223*.

26. Martin Luther, "To the Christian Nobility of the German Nation concerning the Reform of the Christian Estate (1520)," in *Luther's Works*, vol. 44, ed. J. Atkinson, trans. C. Jacobs (Philadelphia: Fortress Press, 1966), 134.

27. Martin Luther, "Avoiding the Doctrines of Men (1522)," in *Luther's Works*, vol. 35, ed. E. Bachmann, trans. W. Lambert (Philadelphia: Fortress Press, 1960), 146.

28. Luther, "To the Christian Nobility of the German Nation," 205.

29. Martin Luther, "Against the Thirty-Two Articles of the Louvain Theologists (1545)," in *Luther's Works*, vol. 34, ed. and trans. L. Spitz (Philadelphia: Muhlenburg Press, 1960), 358–59.

30. For Zwingli's and Calvin's assessments of tradition, see Huldrych Zwingli, "Of the Clarity and Certainty of the Word of God (1522)," in *Zwingli and Bullinger* (The Library of Christian Classics), ed. and trans. G. Bromiley (Philadelphia: Westminster Press, 1953), 86–88; John Calvin, *Institutes of the Christian Religion* (The Library of Christian Classics), vol. 2, ed. J. McNeill, trans. F. L. Battles (Philadelphia: Westminster Press, 1977), 1179–1210 (IV, 10); John Calvin, "Reply to Sadoleto (1539)," in *A Reformation Debate: John Calvin and Jacobo Sadoleto*, ed. J. Olin (Grand Rapids, Mich.: Baker Book House, 1990), 62, 82.

31. For Prierias, see David V. N. Bagchi, *Luther's Earliest Opponents: Catholic Controversialists, 1518–1525* (Minneapolis, Minn.: Fortress Press, 1991), 27–29, 59–60; for Cochläus and Schatzgeyer, see Tavard, *Holy Writ or Holy Church*, 124–30; 173–79, respectively.

32. Denzinger-Schönmetzer, *Enchiridion Symbolorum*, 364–65, no. 1501. The English translation is from J. F. Clarkson, S.J., et al., eds. and trans., *The Church Teaches: Documents of the Church in English Translation* (St. Louis, Mo.: Herder, 1955), 44–45.

33. Hubert Jedin, *A History of the Council of Trent*, vol. 2, trans. D. Graf, O.S.B. (St. Louis, Mo.: Herder, 1961), 55–57.

34. Quoted in Edmond Ortigues, "Écritures et traditions apostoliques au Concile de Trente," *Recherches de science religieuse* 36 (1949): 272–73.

35. Quoted in *ibid.*, 279.

36. See *ibid.*, 283, 277; Jedin, *History of the Council of Trent*, 74–75; 64–65.

37. Tavard has noted that the language of "*partim . . . partim*" appears in Thomas More's *Responsio ad Convitia* (1523), a commentary on Henry VIII's *Assertio Septem Sacramentorum* (1521) (*Holy Writ or Holy Church*, 132–35). Jedin has pointed to the use of the same formula in Johannes Eck's 1526 work on the Mass (*A History of the Council of Trent*, 75). The idea of "*partim . . . partim*" appeared in the works of many of the early sixteenth-century Catholic apologists. See Tavard, *Holy Writ or Holy Church*, 131–50.

38. J. R. Geiselmann, "Un malentendu éclairci: La relation 'Écriture-Tradition' dans la théologie catholique," *Istina* (1958): 204.

39. Ortigues, "Écritures et traditions apostoliques au Concile de Trente," 286.

40. Congar, *La Tradition et les traditions*, vol. 1, 215, 227–28 n. 40.

41. *Ibid.*, 195. The specificities of Congar's description, of course, should suggest neither that the Reformers lacked their own understanding of the plenitude of the apostolic witness nor that the Catholic Church lacked its own understanding of an apostolic heritage of purity.

42. Geiselmann, "Un malentendu éclairci," 207. For another view of the religious perspective of the Baroque, one that sees it as an alternative to the currents of modernity flowing from the assumptions of Nominalism, see Louis Dupré, *Passage to Modernity: An Essay in the Hermeneutics of Nature and Culture* (New Haven Conn.: Yale University Press, 1993), 237–48.

43. For statistics on pontificates from Benedict XIV (1740–1758) to Paul VI (to 1968), see Arthur Peiffer, *Die Enzykliken und ihr Formaler Wert für die dogmatische Methode: Ein Beitrag zur theologischen Erkenntnislehre* (Freiburg, Germany: Universitätsverlag, 1968), 52–56.

44. Of these works, Franzelin's was the most influential. See Johannes Baptist Franzelin, *Tractatus de divina traditione et scriptura*, 4th ed. (Rome: Typographia Polyglotta, 1896). Franzelin's fifth thesis is the clearest expression of the tendency in post-Vatican I theology to identify tradition with the magisterium: "Vivens magisterium demonstratur perpetuum organon Traditionis Christianae ex disertis verbis evangelicis et apostolicis" (ibid., 28). Walter Burghardt, S.J., has found a less-restrictive understanding of tradition in Franzelin, calling attention instead to Franzelin's conception of the magisterium as "living," a focus that seems to appreciate the developmental character of tradition ("The Catholic Concept of Tradition in Light of Modern Theological Thought," *Proceedings of the Sixth Annual Convention of the Catholic Theological Society of America* 6 [1951], 59–60). For a discussion of the identification of tradition and the magisterium in Neo-Scholastic theology, see J. P. Mackey, *The Modern Theology of Tradition* (New York: Herder and Herder, 1963), 1–52. For the theology of tradition in the nineteenth-century Roman School, see Walter Kasper, *Die Lehre von der Tradition in der Römischen Schule* (Freiburg, Germany: Herder, 1962).

45. See Joseph Ratzinger, "The Transmission of Divine Revelation," in *Commentary on the Documents of Vatican II*, ed. H. Vorgrimler, trans. W. Glen-Doepel et al. (New York: Herder and Herder, 1969), 190–96.

46. "Dogmatic Constitution on Divine Revelation" (*Dei verbum*), 755, no. 9.

47. Josef Rupert Geiselmann, *Die Heilige Schrift und die Tradition* (Freiburg, Germany: Herder, 1962), 91–107, 274–82.

48. Karl Rahner, "Scripture and Tradition," in *Theological Investigations*, vol. 6, trans. K. -H. Kruger and B. Kruger (New York: Seabury Press, 1974), 107–112.

49. David Tracy, "On Reading the Scriptures Theologically," in *Theology and Dialogue: Essays in Conversation with George Lindbeck*, ed. B. Marshall (Notre Dame, Ind.: University of Notre Dame Press, 1990), 37–38.

50. Cf. Gabriel Moran, *Scripture and Tradition: A Survey of the Controversy* (New York: Herder and Herder, 1963), 17–28.

51. Peter Lengsfeld has expressed the Scylla and Charybdis of this hermeneutical negotiation as follows: "Wer dem Trienter Dekret folgt und es theologisch auswerten will, braucht deshalb nicht einer Aufteilung der Offenbarungswahrheiten auf die Schrift einerseits und die Tradition andererseits im Sinne der nachtridentinischen partim-partim-Lehre zuzustimmen" (*Überlieferung: Tradition und Schrift in der evangelischen und katholischen Theologie der Gegenwart* [Paderborn, Germany: Verlag Bonifacius, 1960], 126).

52. Cf. ibid., 19. Congar has made this same distinction by using the word "Tradition" in the singular to refer to the traditioning process and "traditions" in the plural to refer to the objects of tradition. Yves Congar, O.P., *The Meaning of Tradition*, trans. A. Woodrow (New York: Hawthorn Books, 1964), 46. There is another way of understanding the active-passive distinction found in the work of Franzelin and his disciples. Here "active" tradition refers to the teaching of the magisterium and "passive" or "objective" tradition to its proper reception by the faithful, a distinction that assumes the substantive identification of tradition with the magisterium. See Franzelin, *Tractatus de divina traditione et scriptura*, 11–12, 19–21. Cf. Avery Dulles, *The Craft of Theology: From Symbol to System* (New York: Crossroad, 1992), 91.

53. Maurice Bénevot, S.J., "*Traditiones* in the Council of Trent," *Heythrop Journal* 4 (1963): 333–47.

Chapter 1

1. Nicholas Lash, "Performing the Scriptures," in *Theology on the Way to Emmaus* (London: SCM Press, 1986), 37.

2. This concern for the integrity of an abiding meaning is threatened most dramatically by what I call here a hermeneutics of erasure. But even what I call a hermeneutics of sublation raises this threat in the minds of those inclined to acribe meaning to the fact of literality itself.

3. Raphael Loewe, "The 'Plain' Meaning of Scripture in Early Jewish Exegesis," *Papers of the Institute of Jewish Studies London*, vol. 1, ed. J. G. Weiss (Jerusalem: Magnes Press [Hebrew University], 1964), 141.

4. Ibid., 141–42.

5. Ibid., 181.

6. Brevard S. Childs, "The Sensus Literalis of Scripture: An Ancient and Modern Problem," in *Beiträge zur alttestamentlichen Theologie: Festschrift für Walther Zim-*

merli zur 70. Geburtstag, ed. H. Donner et al. (Göttingen: Germany: Vandenhoeck and Ruprecht, 1977), 80–93.

7. Ibid., 92.

8. Ibid.

9. Ibid.

10. Ibid., 93.

11. Kathryn E. Tanner, "Theology and the Plain Sense," in *Scriptural Authority and Narrative Interpretation,* ed. G. Green (Philadelphia: Fortress Press, 1987), 62, 63. Charles M. Wood has made this same point on the literal or the plain sense, regarding it as an orientation of communal Christian understanding; see *The Formation of Christian Understanding: An Essay in Theological Hermeneutics* (Philadelphia: Westminster Press, 1981). Childs, Tanner, and Wood have developed the insights of Hans W. Frei on the plight of the plain sense in modernity and the insights of David H. Kelsey on a functionalist reading of scripture. See Hans W. Frei, *The Eclipse of Biblical Narrative: A Study in Eighteenth and Nineteenth Century Hermeneutics* (New Haven, Conn.: Yale University. Press, 1974), and see his essays "Theology and the Interpretation of Narrative: Some Hermeneutical Considerations" and "The 'Literal Reading' of Biblical Narrative in the Christian Tradition: Does It Stretch or Will It Break?" in *Theology and Narrative: Selected Essays,* ed. G. Hunsinger and W. Placher (New York: Oxford University Press, 1993), 94–116, 117–52. See also David H. Kelsey, *The Uses of Scripture in Recent Theology* (Philadelphia: Fortress Press, 1975). Tracy's reflections on the plain sense call attention to how "obvious" readings of scripture will be motivated by confessional commitments. See David Tracy, "On Reading the Scriptures Theologically," in *Theology and Dialogue: Essays in Conversation with George Lindbeck,* ed. B. Marshall (Notre Dame, Ind.: University of Notre Dame Press, 1990), 35–68.

12. Tanner, "Theology and the Plain Sense," 63.

13. Ibid., 72.

14. Ibid., 64.

15. "Dogmatic Constitution on the Church" (*Lumen gentium*), in *Vatican Council II: The Conciliar and Postconciliar Documents,* ed. A. Flannery, O.P. (Northport, N.Y.: Costello 1987), 363, no. 12.

16. Athanasius, "Letter XXXIX," in *St. Athanasius: Select Writings and Letters* (Nicene and Post-Nicene Fathers of the Christian Church), vol. 4, ed. A. Robertson (Grand Rapids, Mich.: Eerdmans Publishing Company, 1978), 551–52. For this sketch, I relied on Raymond F. Collins, "Canonicity," in *The New Jerome Biblical Commentary,* ed. R. Brown, et al. (Englewood Cliffs, N.J.: Prentice-Hall, 1990), 1035.

17. James A. Sanders, *Torah and Canon* (Philadelphia: Fortress Press, 1972), 91–92.

18. Hans von Campenhausen, *The Formation of the Christian Bible,* trans. J. A. Baker (Philadelphia: Fortress Press, 1972), 327.

19. The narrative identity of the canon does not preclude the recognition and even valorizing of narrative difference. Joseph Blenkinsopp, for example, has argued that the inclusion of prophecy in the canon results in the abiding criticism of canon from within its bounds: "Prophecy is necessary if only to show up the precarious nature of all fixed orders and the claims to legitimacy which sustain them" (*Prophecy and Canon* [Notre Dame, Ind.: University of Notre Dame Press, 1977], 152). And yet, because in Blenkinsopp's own judgment "prophecy alone cannot build a lasting community" (ibid.), narrative difference finally points back again to the canon's narrative identity, even at the prophetic moment at which

difference is most accentuated. Cf. Ronald E. Clements, "Patterns in the Prophetic Canon," in *Canon and Authority: Essays in Old Testament Religion and Theology*, ed. G. Coats and B. Long (Philadelphia: Fortress Press, 1977), 42–55.

20. David G. Meade, *Pseudonymity and Canon: An Investigation into the Relationship of Authorship and Authority in Jewish and Earliest Christian Tradition* (Grand Rapids, Mich.: Eerdmans, 1987), 217. There is some value, no doubt, in Robert B. Laurin's observation that canonization emerges in a situation of "radical political and psychological threat," but his inference from this pychosocial perspective that "the continuing work of the Spirit was forgotten in the attempt to find theological security" through canonization is one that fails to appreciate how rooted canonicity can be in the vitality of tradition ("Tradition and Canon," in *Tradition and Theology in the Old Testament*, ed. D. Knight [Philadelphia: Fortress Press, 1977], 272).

21. Of course, another way of accounting for the authority of the canonical writings, and thus explaining the authority of the canon as a whole, is to say that they, and it, serve the Church's "rule of faith." See Joseph T. Leinhard, *The Bible, the Church, and Authority: The Canon of the Christian Bible in History and Theology* (Collegeville, Minn.: Liturgical Press, 1995), 40–41.

22. "Dogmatic Constitution on Divine Revelation" (*Dei verbum*), in *Vatican Council II*, 755, no. 8.

23. Ibid., no. 9.

24. Ibid., 754–55, no. 8.

25. Ibid., 755, no. 9.

26. In a reflection on the workings of a literary canon, Mary McClintock Fulkerson has observed that collections of authoritative writings are not formed on the basis of abstract or formal rules. A canon, she has noted, "is a set of norms, or a stabilization of meaning, that is not identical with explicit doctrine or belief but must be viewed as inseparable from social practices" (*Changing the Subject: Women's Discourses and Feminist Theology* [Minneapolis, Minn.: Fortress Press, 1994], 168). McClintock Fulkerson's functionalist perspective on canon formation and canonical authority applies especially well to the extension of the notion of the canon to the Catholic understanding of tradition as advanced here, for the canon of tradition is a collection of authoritative practices as well as a collection of authoritative writings. In this sort of canon, more than in an ostensibly literary canon, it is particularly clear that texts and practices mutually inform their shared canonical authority. Anthony Godzieba, too, has made this point well; see "Method and Interpretation: The New Testament's Heretical Hermeneutic (Prelude and Fugue)," *Heythrop Journal* 36 (1995): 286–306.

27. Delwin Brown has employed the category of "canon" to name the " 'spaces' . . . within which and with which the [cultural] negotiation [of tradition] is conducted" (*Boundaries of Our Habitations: Tradition and Theological Construction* [Albany: State University of New York Press, 1994], 90). Whereas the present study finds an analogy with the biblical canon in order to understand the workings of tradition's literal sense (in traditional language, the apostolic deposit of faith), Brown has drawn on philosophical and anthropological theory in order to understand canon as a hermeneutical arena in which order and chaos challenge and remake each other. Brown's theory of tradition is a good example of what the next chapter calls a "dialectical" model of development.

28. Denzinger-Schönmetzer, *Enchiridion Symbolorum Definitionum et Declarationum de Rebus Fidei et Morum* (Freiburg im Breisgau, Germany: Herder, 1965),

601, no. 1839. The English translation is from J. F. Clarkson, S.J., et al., eds. and trans., *The Church Teaches: Documents of the Church in English Translation* (St. Louis, Mo.: Herder, 1955), 102.

29. Avery Dulles has described this as an institutional model of the Church; see *Models of the Church* (Garden City, N.Y.: Doubleday, 1974), 39–50.

30. Perhaps the clarity of succinctness that is often typical of the doctrinal tradition encourages this isolated propositionalist regard for the infallibility of particular doctrines. Yet even such compendia as Denzinger's or the new *Cathechism of the Catholic Church* in which clarity of succinctness is heightened to the greatest degree can be, and properly are, understood holistically. The very idea of a compilation of authoritative propositions or paragraphs presupposes a judgment about how authority is shared by all the entries not only as particular propositions but also in their interrelationship to one another.

The Second Vatican Council's teaching on the "hierarchy of truths" holds that there is a gradation of authority among the beliefs, doctrines, and practices of Catholic tradition. This might suggest that some doctrines and not others possess a clear and distinguishable authority, for according to the "Decree on Ecumenism," doctrines "vary in their relation to the foundation of the Christian faith" ("Decree on Ecumenism" [*Unitatis redintegratio*], in *Vatican Council II*, 462, no. 11). Yet the document never names the precise foundation of faith and its dogmatic expression by which the authority of other doctrines are to be measured. Even though the teaching on the "hierarchy of truths" presents an image that suggests the clear distinguishability of doctrinal authority, the actual practice of judging the authority—and even the unerring authority—of doctrine actually takes place holistically within the setting in which the "Decree on Ecumenism" envisages doctrines being compared with one another within the hierarchy. Any number of interpretations of the "hierarchy of truths" is consistent with this holistic understanding of its teaching. For a review of the various interpretations, see William Henn, "The Hierarchy of Truths Twenty Years Later," *Theological Studies* 48 (1987): 439–71.

31. In the context of a balanced discussion of the responsibilities of the magisterium, theologians, and all the faithful in the ongoing reception of tradition, Patrick Granfield has cautioned against this temptation to magisterial authority; see *The Limits of the Papacy: Authority and Autonomy in the Church* (New York: Crossroad, 1987), 163–64.

32. For example, Hans Küng, *Infallible? An Inquiry*, trans. E. Quinn (Garden City, N.Y.: Image Books, 1972), 90.

33. Yves Congar, "A Brief History of the Forms of the Magisterium and Its Relations with Scholars," in *Readings in Moral Theology No. 3: The Magisterium and Morality*, ed. C. Curran and R. McCormick (New York: Paulist Press, 1982), 323.

34. See, for example, Francis A. Sullivan, S.J., *Magisterium: Teaching Authority in the Catholic Church* (New York: Paulist Press, 1983), 153–73.

35. For a history of the formulation of the power of the ordinary universal magisterium, see John P. Boyle, *Church Teaching Authority: Historical and Theological Studies* (Notre Dame, Ind.: University of Notre Dame Press, 1995), 10–42. See also Richard R. Gaillardetz, *Witnesses to the Faith: Community, Infallibility, and the Ordinary Magisterium of Bishops* (New York: Paulist Press, 1992), 18–35.

36. On the prophetic role of the magisterium, see Boyle, *Church Teaching Authority*, 62. See also Hermann J. Pottmeyer, "Rezeption und Gehorsam—Aktuelle Aspekte der wiederentdeckten Realität 'Rezeption,' " in *Glaube als Zustimmung: Zur*

Interpretation kirchlicher Rezeptionsvorgänge (Quaestiones Disputatae, 131), ed. W. Beinert (Freiburg, Germany: Herder, 1991), 77–79.

37. My attention to the literal sense as a context for understanding infallibility in the Church might be seen as another perspective on the contemporary theological concern for detailing the limits of infallibility. Granfield, for example, sketches these limits by speaking of the various constituencies in the Church that share in its unerring truth and by considering how these constituencies (the bishops, the Catholic faithful, believing Christians) and their relations (primacy, collegiality, connections between the local and universal churches) set the power of the papacy in relief. See Granfield, *Limits of the Papacy*. Peter Chirico often speaks of the limitations of infallibility by presenting the finite conditions of understanding and the contingency of interpretation as inescapable settings within which the gifts of ecclesial and papal infallibility stand and by which they are always at least indirectly touched; see *Infallibility: The Crossroads of Doctrine* (Kansas City: Sheed Andrews and McMeel, 1976). The advantage of speaking of the literal sense as a context for and limit on infallibility is that it speaks of limitation in terms set by the tradition of the Church itself. In this regard, the reflections offered here are closer in orientation to Granfield's presentation than to Chirico's.

38. For this discussion, I have relied on the treatment of universality in John E. Thiel, "Pluralism in Theological Truth," in *Why Theology?* (Concilium/Fundamental Theology: 1994/6), ed. C. Geffré and W. Jeanrond (London: SCM Press; Maryknoll, N.Y.: Orbis Books, 1994), 57–69.

39. For a careful discussion of this ecclesiology and its criticism, see Paul Lakeland, *Theology and Critical Theory: The Discourse of the Church* (Nashville, Tenn.: Abingdon Press, 1990), 105–37.

Chapter 2

1. The literature on doctrinal development is extensive. Representative works are Henri DeLubac, S.J., "Le problème du développement du dogme," *Recherches de science religieuse* 35 (1948): 130–60; Owen Chadwick, *From Bousset to Newman: The Idea of Doctrinal Development* (Cambridge: Cambridge University Press, 1957); Herbert Hammans, *Die neueren katholischen Erklärungen der Dogmenentwicklung* (Essen, Germany: Ludgerus-Verlag Hubert Wingen, 1965); Jaroslav Pelikan, *Development of Christian Doctrine: Some Historical Prolegomena* (New Haven, Conn.: Yale University Press, 1969); Nicholas Lash, *Change in Focus: A Study of Doctrinal Change and Continuity* (London: Sheed and Ward, 1973); Jan Hendrik Walgrave, *Unfolding Revelation: The Nature of Doctrinal Development* (Philadelphia: Westminster Press, 1972); Bradford E. Hinze, "Narrative Contexts, Doctrinal Reform," *Theological Studies* 51 (1990): 417–33.

2. Magisterial teaching acknowledged the development of doctrine for the first time in the Second Vatican Council's "Dogmatic Constitution on Divine Revelation" (*Dei verbum*), in *Vatican Council II: The Conciliar and Postconciliar Documents*, ed. A. Flannery, O.P. (Northport, N.Y.: Costello, 1987), 754, no. 8.

3. Johannes Stöhr, "Modellvorstellungen im Verständnis der Dogmenentwicklung," in *Reformata Reformanda: Festgabe für Hubert Jedin zum 17, Juni 1965*, vol. 2, ed. E. Iserloh and K. Repgen (Münster Westfalen, Germany: Verlag Aschendorff, 1965), 595–630.

4. Catholic theologians, especially in the twentieth century, have preferred the term "development of dogma" for the historical unfolding of Church teaching.

This terminology, however, suggests that the historical development of faith and its expression occurs only with regard to what has reached, or what eventually will reach, the status of explicit, authoritative, and long-established teaching in the Church—that is, dogma. Throughout this study, I use the term "doctrinal development" or the "development of doctrine" to refer to not only doctrine that has achieved the status of dogma but also doctrine that, although it is the teaching of the Church, has not reached—and perhaps will never reach—the status of dogma. Dogma, in other words, has a more particular referent than doctrine. Moreover, I assume that "doctrine" in the phrase "development of doctrine" refers not simply to literarily articulated teaching but also to the Church's beliefs and practices. For a comprehensive study of the various understandings of tradition in recent Catholic thought, see Jean-Georges Boeglin, *La question de la tradition dans la théologie catholique contemporaine* (Paris: Éditions du Cerf, 1998).

5. Stöhr, "Modellvorstellungen im Verständnis der Dogmenentwicklung," 627–30.

6. Although Drey's entire theological career can be understood as an exercise in apologetical theology, the major work of his considerable literary corpus is, in fact, a specific contribution to this theological genre. Johann Sebastian Drey, *Die Apologetik als wissenschaftliche Nachweisung der Göttlichkeit des Christenthums in seiner Erscheinung*, 3 vols. (1838, 1843, 1847; reprint, Frankfurt, Germany: Minerva G.M.B.H., 1967). For an excellent study of Drey's apologetical theology, see Abraham Peter Kustermann, *Die Apologetik Johann Sebastian Dreys (1777–1853): Kritische, historische und systematische Untersuchungen zu Forschungsgeschichte, Programmentwickelung, Status und Gehalt* (Tübingen: Mohr [Paul Siebeck], 1988).

7. For Drey's use of "essence of Christianity" (and more specifically, "essence of Catholicism") argumentation, see Johann Sebastian Drey, "Vom Geist und Wesen des Katholizismus," in *Geist des Christentums und des Katholizismus: Ausgewählte Schriften katholischer Theologie im Zeitalter des deutschen Idealismus und der Romantik*, ed. J. R. Geiselmann (Mainz, Germany: Matthias-Grünewald, 1940), 195–234.

8. For discussions of Drey on doctrinal development, see Bradford E. Hinze, *Narrating History, Developing Doctrine: Friedrich Schleiermacher and Johann Sebastian Drey* (Atlanta: Scholars Press, 1993); John E. Thiel, *Imagination and Authority: Theological Authorship in the Modern Tradition* (Minneapolis, Minn.: Fortress Press, 1991), 63–94; Thiel, "Naming the Heterodox: Interconfessional Polemics as a Context for Drey's Theology," in *Revision der Theologie—Reform der Kirche: Die Bedeutung des Tübinger Theologen Johann Sebastian Drey (1777–1853) in Geschichte und Gegenwart*, ed. A. Kustermann (Würzburg, Germany: Echter Verlag, 1994), 114–39; Thiel, "The Universal in the Particular: Johann Sebastian Drey on the Hermeneutics of Tradition," in *The Legacy of the Tübingen School: The Relevance of Nineteenth-Century Theology for the Twenty-First Century*, ed. D. Dietrich and M. Himes (New York: Crossroad, 1997), 56–74.

9. Eberhard Tiefensee, " 'Erläuterung aus dem Beispiel der Naturgeschichte unserer Erde': Naturphilosophische Wurzeln des Entwicklungsbegriffs Dreys," in *Revision der Theologie—Reform der Kirche*, 229–45; Bradford E. Hinze, "Johann Sebastian Drey on Narrating Tradition," in ibid., 185–203.

10. Consider, for example, Drey's use of vitalistic imagery and mechanical or thanatological imagery, respectively, to convey salutary and pathological historical periods in Christian tradition and theology in his first published work, originally published in 1812, "Revision des gegenwärtigen Zustandes der Theologie,"

in *Revision von Kirche und Theologie: Drei Aufsätze*, ed. F. Schupp (Darmstadt, Germany: Wissenschaftliche Buchgesellschaft, 1971), 3–26. Consider, too, the prevalence of biological imagery in Drey's unpublished 1812–1813 sketch "Ideen zur Geschichte des katholischen Dogmensystems," in *Geist des Christentums und des Katholizismus*, 235–331.

11. For Schleiermacher's understanding of doctrinal development, see Friedrich Schleiermacher, *Kurze Darstellung des theologischen Studiums zum Behuf einleitender Vorlesungen*, ed. H. Scholz (Leipzig, Germany: Deichert'sche Verlagsbuchhandlung, 1910; reprint, Darmstadt, Germany: Wissenschaftliche Buchgesellschaft, 1973), 77–79 par. 201–8.

12. Johann Sebastian Drey, *Kurze Einleitung in das Studium der Theologie mit Rücksicht auf den wissenschaftlichen Standpunct und das katholische System*, ed. F. Schupp (1819; reprint, Darmstadt, Germany: Wissenschaftliche Buchgesellschaft, 1971), 170 par. 256.

13. Ibid., 171 par. 258.

14. Ibid., par. 257.

15. Ibid., 170–71 par. 256.

16. Ibid., 171–72 par. 258.

17. Ibid., 173 par. 260.

18. Ibid.

19. Ibid., 172 par. 259. Cf. Schleiermacher, *Kurze Darstellung*, 76 par. 199.

20. Drey, *Kurze Einleitung*, 66 par. 99.

21. Johann Adam Möhler, "Die Tradition als Quelle des Kirchenrechts," in *Geist des Christentums und des Katholizismus*, 399.

22. Ibid.

23. Geiselmann has noted that tradition functioned in two ways in Möhler's earliest conception: as the norm of faith and as a source of theological proof. In both cases, the fixed quality of tradition is emphasized. Josef Rupert Geiselmann, *Lebendiger Glaube aus geheiligter Überlieferung: Der Grundgedanke der Theologie Johann Adam Möhlers und der katholischen Tübinger Schule*, 2d ed. (Basel, Switzerland, and Vienna: Herder Freiburg, 1966), 309–10.

24. Johann Adam Möhler, *Die Einheit in der Kirche oder das Prinzip des Katholizismus dargestellt im Geiste der Kirchenväter der drei ersten Jahrhunderte*, ed. J. R. Geiselmann (Darmstadt, Germany: Wissenschaftliche Buchgesellschaft, 1957), 6.

25. Ibid., 7.

26. Ibid., 8–9.

27. Ibid., 8, 11.

28. Ibid., 50–51.

29. Ibid., 29.

30. Ibid., 43.

31. Ibid., 43–44.

32. Ibid., 44.

33. For a discussion of these modifications in Möhler's understanding of developing tradition, see Josef Rupert Geiselmann, *Lebendiger Glaube aus geheiligter Überlieferung*, 428–35. Geiselmann identified a pattern in which the organic model of development is not abandoned but expressed with new emphases on the objectivity, authority, and christocentric character of tradition. In his writings after *Die Einheit in der Kirche*, Möhler increasingly attributed development to the conceptual reception of established doctrine rather than to the mystical workings of the Spirit

in history. See Geiselmann, *Die katholische Tübinger Schule: Ihre theologische Eigenart* (Freiburg, Germany: Herder, 1964), 79–91. See also Bradford E. Hinze, "The Holy Spirit and the Catholic Tradition: The Legacy of Johann Adam Möhler," in *Legacy of the Tübingen School*, 75–94.

34. Möhler, *Die Einheit in der Kirche*, 114, 31.

35. Ibid., 32–33.

36. Ibid., 33, 63.

37. Ibid., 98.

38. John Henry Newman, *An Essay on the Development of Christian Doctrine* (Notre Dame, Id.: University of Notre Dame Press, 1989), 29. Citations are from the second edition, originally published in 1878.

39. For a thorough discussion of the probability of influence, see Henry Tristram, "J. A. Moehler et J. H. Newman: La pensée allemande et la renaissance catholique en Angleterre," *Revue des sciences philosophiques et théologiques* 27 (1938): 184–204.

40. Newman, *Essay on the Development of Christian Doctrine*, 2d ed., 34.

41. Ibid., 35.

42. Ibid., 36.

43. Ibid., 37–38.

44. Ibid., 38.

45. Ibid., 75.

46. Ibid., 68.

47. Nicholas Lash, *Newman on Development: The Search for an Explanation in History* (Sheperdstown, W.V.: Patmos Press, 1975), 38–41.

48. Ibid., 65.

49. Newman, *Essay on the Development of Christian Doctrine*, 2d ed., 65.

50. Ibid., 169.

51. For Newman's account of the seven notes, see ibid., 171–206.

52. To some extent, Newman's arrangement of the *Essay*'s subject matter in the second edition of 1878 obscures the degree to which the seven notes serve the noetic analogy. In the second edition, the presentation and historical illustration of the notes are placed in a second part of the work devoted to "doctrinal developments viewed relatively to doctrinal corruptions," which follows a first part devoted to "doctrinal developments viewed in themselves" in which Newman offered his theory of ideas as a propaedeutic to the entire work. The first edition of 1845 does not offer a bipartite division of the subject matter, and it delineates together the theory of ideas and the seven notes, there called "tests," in the *Essay*'s very first chapter. See John Henry Newman, *Essay on the Development of Christian Doctrine* (London: Toovey, 1845), 30–93.

53. Newman, *Essay on the Development of Christian Doctrine*, 2d ed., 206.

54. Later in his career, in writings through the 1870s to the 1877 edition of the *Via Media*, Newman did recognize the contributions of the *schola theologorum* to the Church. But he tended to think of theological insight in this classically corporate form and not as an individual, creative act. On this point, see Paul Misner, *Papacy and Development: Newman and the Primacy of the Pope* (Leiden: Brill, 1976), 158–73; Avery Dulles, "Newman on Infallibility," *Theological Studies* 51 (1990): 443; Thiel, *Imagination and Authority*, 116–17 n. 39.

55. Yves Congar, "La 'réception' comme réalité ecclésiologique," *Revue des sciences philosophiques et théologiques* 56 (1972): 369–403.

56. Ibid., 375.

57. The Second Vatican Council's "Dogmatic Constitution on Divine Revelation" (*Dei verbum*) gives the most authoritative support for reception understood as growth (*Vatican Council II*, 754, no. 8.):

> The Tradition that comes from the apostles makes progress in the Church, with the help of the Holy Spirit. There is a growth in insight into the realities and words that are being passed on. This comes about in various ways. It comes through the contemplation and study of believers who ponder these things in their hearts. . . . It comes from the intimate sense of spiritual realities which they experience. And it comes from the preaching of those who have received, along with their right of succession in the episcopate, the sure charism of truth. Thus, as the centuries go by, the Church is always advancing towards the plenitude of divine truth, until eventually the words of God are fulfilled in her.

58. Pope John XXIII, "Opening Address to the Council," in *The Documents of Vatican II*, ed. W. Abbott, S.J. (New York: America Press, 1966), 715.

59. "Finally, even though the truths which the Church intends to teach through her dogmatic formulas are distinct from the changeable conceptions of a given epoch and can be expressed without them, nevertheless it can sometimes happen that these truths may be enunciated by the Sacred Magisterium in terms that bear traces of such conceptions" ("In Defense of Catholic Doctrine" [*Mysterium ecclesiae*, June 24, 1973], *Origins* 3 [July 19, 1973]: 110–11).

60. The form-content distinction typically has been invoked in influential twentieth-century Catholic accounts of the development of doctrine to explain how continuity can abide within historicity. Thus, Rahner has stated that "if the [traditional] concepts are allowed to keep their plain, original simple meaning, we are bound to say that an explication of what is formally implicit in a revealed proposition is present only when the new proposition really states the *same thing* as the old one in other words, has the same content as the old one, however useful and necessary it may be for various reasons to formulate the new proposition" (Karl Rahner, S.J., "The Development of Dogma," in *Theological Investigations*, vol. 1, trans. C. Ernst [London: Darton, Longman and Todd, 1961], 59). Cf. this same position theologically detailed in Rahner, "Considerations of the Development of Dogma," in *Theological Investigations*, vol. 4, trans. K. Smyth (Baltimore, Md.: Helicon Press, 1966), 18–20; and Rahner, "Basic Observations on the Subject of Changeable and Unchangeable Factors in the Church," in *Theological Investigations*, vol. 14, trans. D. Bourke (New York: Seabury Press, 1976), 3–23. Bernard J. F. Lonergan, S.J. has made the form-content distinction by noting that the 'permanence of the dogmas . . . results from the fact that they express revealed mysteries. Their historicity, on the other hand, results from the facts that (1) statements have meanings only in their contexts and (2) contexts are ongoing and ongoing contexts are multiple" (*Method in Theology* [New York: Herder and Herder, 1972], 326). Edward Schillebeeckx, O.P., has portrayed an orthodox position on the reinterpretation of dogma as one in which "the aim . . . is to purify our insights into faith of their earlier, and now obsolete, forms of expression." In this approach, "what was originally intended through the use of this older form of representation will remain inviolably true" (*Revelation and Theology*, vol. 2, trans. N. D. Smith [New York: Sheed and Ward, 1968], 27).

61. See Thomas F. O'Meara, O.P., *Romantic Idealism: Schelling and the Theologians* (Notre Dame, Ind.: University of Notre Dame Press, 1982), 94–108.

62. Hans Urs von Balthasar, *Theo-Drama: Theological Dramatic Theory*, vol. 4, *The Action*, trans. G. Harrison (San Francisco: Ignatius Press, 1994), 455.

63. For a study of the ambivalent regard for creativity in the history of modern theology, see Thiel, *Imagination and Authority*.

64. It is worth noting that the principal trait of the organic model—its conceptualization of development as a homogeneous growth from earlier to later periods in tradition—is a valued trait of all four models and became the most basic assumption for the orthodoxy of subsequent models of development—from the reflections of the nineteenth-century Roman School, to the scholastic presentation of F. Marín-Sola, to the popular writing of Karl Adam, to the representations of development in the contemporary theologies of Joseph Ratzinger, Karl Rahner, Bernard Lonergan, and Edward Schillebeeckx. See Walter Kasper, *Die Lehre von der Tradition in der Römischen Schule* (Freiburg im Breisgau, Germany: Herder, 1962); F. Marín-Sola, O.P., *L'Évolution homogène du dogme catholique*, 2 vols. (Fribourg, Switzerland: Saint-Paul, 1924); Karl Adam, *The Spirit of Catholicism*, trans. J. McCann (New York: Macmillan, 1941); Joseph Cardinal Ratzinger, *Principles of Catholic Theology: Building Stones for a Catholic Fundamental Theology*, trans. M. F. McCarthy (San Francisco: Ignatius Press, 1987), esp. 85–190; For Rahner, Lonergan, and Schillebeeckx, see note 60.

65. Jean-Pierre Jossua has described what I call "prospectivity" not as a human's divine perspective but as one that is as humanly unnatural—that is, as the timeless gaze of a human observer in flight across centuries; see "Immutabilité, progrès ou structurations multiples des doctrines chrétiennes?" *Revue des sciences philosophiques et théologiques* 52 (1968): 180. In his study of doctrinal development, Lash has voiced his wariness of prospectivity, disavowing what he has called a " 'bird's eye view' of the historical process" (*Change in Focus*, 148).

66. It is worth recalling that even in Drey's dialectical model, the fixity of dogma in doctrinal development derives from its conceptual conformity to the eternal idea of the Kingdom of God. See Karl-Heinz Menke, "Definition und spekulative Grundlegung des Begriffes 'Dogma' im Werke Johann Sebastian von Dreys (1777–1853)," *Theologie und Philosophie* 52 (1977): 23–56, 182–214. Cf. Max Seckler, "Das Reich Gottes Idee als 'höchste Idee des Christentums' in der Theologie Johann Sebastian Dreys," in *Revision der Theologie—Reform der Kirche*, 292–308, esp. 299.

67. Richard Rorty has shown how ocular imagery has shaped epistemological assumptions in the history of Western philosophy; see *Philosophy and the Mirror of Nature* (Princeton, N.J.: Princeton University Press, 1979). For Rorty, visual metaphors put to the service of epistemology have ironically obscured philosophy's proper task, and so their use has been misleading. I follow Rorty's lead with regard to the negative judgments expressed here about the prospective conception of tradition. But the retrospective conception of tradition that I present in the pages that follow offers benign ocular imagery that realistically corrects the prospective conception's visual flights of fancy.

68. Martin Buber, *I and Thou*, trans. R. G. Smith (New York: Scribner's Sons, 1958).

69. The understanding of tradition developed here is sketched briefly in John E. Thiel, "Pluralism in Theological Truth," in *Why Theology?* (Concilium/Funda-

mental Theology: 1994/6), ed. C. Geffré and W. Jeanrond (London: SCM Press; Maryknoll, N.Y.: Orbis Books, 1994), 57–69, esp. 66–69. For a theory of tradition that shares many of these same concerns, see Kathryn Tanner, *Theories of Culture: A New Agenda for Theology* (Minneapolis, Minn.: Fortress Press, 1997), 128–38.

70. Raymond E. Brown has detailed this tension between the Johannine community and others in *The Community of the Beloved Disciple* (New York: Paulist Press, 1979).

71. E.g., E. D. Hirsch Jr., *The Aims of Interpretation* (Chicago: University of Chicago Press, 1976), esp. 50–73.

72. Thomas G. Guarino has marshaled the most ardent theological defense of the content-form distinction, arguing that the distinction is necessary in order to protect the truth of divine revelation, which is placed, of course, on the side of content. Guarino seems convinced that blurring the distinction involves the eclipsing of content by form and the concomitant loss of revelation's timeless truth to a historicity of sheer relativism in which change can never possess the patterned order of development—an order supplied, it would seem, by a separable content; see *Revelation and Truth: Unity and Plurality in Contemporary Theology* (Scranton, Pa.: University of Scranton Press, 1993). Moreover, in several articles, Guarino has pressed his case by claiming that theological interpretations of divine revelation must avoid what he has sweepingly called "postmodern" or "nonfoundational" philosophies as the "form" to express the "content" of divine revelation. These positions (he seems to refer to historicist-phenomenological philosophies in the Heideggerian trajectory) lack a metaphysical ontology and thus a correspondence theory of truth—both of which are requisites, he has assumed, for a theological "form" consistent with the ontological and epistemological assumptions of revelation's content. See Guarino, "Between Foundationalism and Nihilism: Is *Phronesis* the *Via Media* for Theology?" *Theological Studies* 54 (1993): 37–54; Guarino, " 'Spoils from Egypt': Contemporary Theology and Non-Foundationalist Thought," *Laval théologique et philosophique* 51 (1995): 573–87; Guarino, "Postmodernity and Five Fundamental Theological Issues," *Theological Studies* 57 (1996): 654–89.

Guarino's position appears to be deficient on two, related counts. First, it does not seem to consider that philosophies can be, and indeed throughout history have been, used theologically in discriminating ways, in ad hoc fashion, so that reasonable constructions themselves at odds with the claims of faith can be understood in ways that serve those claims. Second, it fails to consider that in such cases of truly theological interpretation in which a theologian speaks of faith well—even while employing categories and language that, prior to their interpretation, were at least faithless and possibly even hostile to the claims of faith—the distinction between content and form evaporates as a way of accounting for the integrity of tradition. What remains is theological interpretation judged to be true by the present community because it is deemed continuous with, while at the same time it renews, past theological interpretations.

It would be interesting to read the 1989 publication of the International Theological Commission "On the Interpretation of Dogmas" as a statement of dissatisfaction with the form-content distinction. The text does invoke the distinction, claiming that dogmas "are the doctrinal form whose content is God's own word and truth" (*Origins* 20 [May 17, 1990]: 10). Yet it condemns "naive realism" (ibid., 3) in the interpretation of dogmas and proposes that such interpretation can presuppose "no clear-cut separation . . . between the content and form of the [dogmatic] statement" (ibid., 12).

73. Donald Davidson, "What Metaphors Mean," in *Inquiries into Truth and Interpretation* (Oxford: Clarendon Press, 1984), 246.

74. Ibid., 262.

75. Ibid., 246.

76. In other words, claims for the continuity of tradition are particularist beliefs *made* as universal claims that renounce relativism. See Gene Outka, "The Particularist Turn in Theological and Philosophical Ethics," in *Christian Ethics: Problems and Prospects*, ed. L. S. Cahill and J. Childress (Cleveland, Ohio: Pilgrim Press, 1996), 112–13.

77. *Catechism of the Catholic Church* (New York: Catholic Book Publishing 1994), 227, no. 857.

78. Jaroslav Pelikan, *The Christian Tradition: A History of the Development of Doctrine*, vol. 1. *The Emergence of the Catholic Tradition (100–600)* (Chicago: University of Chicago Press, 1971), 108–20.

79. Henricus Denzinger-Adolfus Schönmetzer, *Enchiridion Symbolorum Definitionum et Declarationum de Rebus Fidei et Morum*, 34th ed. (Freiburg im Breisgau, Germany: Herder, 1965), 364–65, no. 1501. The English translation is from J. F. Clarkson, S.J., et al., eds. and trans., *The Church Teaches: Documents of the Church in English Translation* (St. Louis, Mo.: Herder, 1955), 44–45.

80. Newman expressed this modern, developmental understanding of prospectivity well in recounting his thoughts prior to the publication of the *Essay*: "I am very far more sure that England is in schism, than that the Roman additions to the Primitive Creed may not be developments, arising out of a keen and vivid realizing of the Divine Depositum of Faith" (John Henry Newman, *Apologia Pro Vita Sua*, ed. D. DeLaura [New York: Norton, 1968], 163).

81. On this point, see Karl Rahner, "Scripture and Tradition," in *Theological Investigations*, vol. 6, trans. K.-H. Kruger and B. Kruger (New York: Seabury Press, 1974), 106.

82. Denzinger-Schönmetzer, *Enchiridion Symbolorum*, 562, no. 2803; *Church Teaches*, 208.

83. Thomas Aquinas, *Summa Theologiae*, IIIa, 27, 3.

84. For careful studies of the history of the dogma, see the contributions by Georges Jouassard, Carlo Balić, Wenceslaus Sebastian, and René Laurentin in *The Dogma of the Immaculate Conception: History and Significance*, ed. E. O'Connor (Notre Dame, Ind.: University of Notre Dame Press, 1958).

85. For a valuable account of the various theological implications of postmodernity, see Paul Lakeland, *Postmodernity: Christian Identity in a Fragmented Age* (Minneapolis, Minn.: Fortress Press, 1997).

86. David Dawson, *Allegorical Readers and Cultural Revision in Ancient Alexandria* (Berkeley and Los Angeles: University of California Press, 1992).

87. Ibid., 1.

88. Ibid., 2.

89. Ibid., 10.

90. Ibid., 2.

91. George A. Lindbeck, *The Nature of Doctrine: Religion and Theology in a Postliberal Age* (Philadelphia: Westminster Press, 1984).

Chapter 3

1. In this chapter, I use a technical version of the word "authentic" according to its use in magisterial documents, where it means "authoritative," referring specifically to the authority that bishops possess when they teach the doctrine of Christ in accordance with the responsibility of their office. See Francis A. Sullivan, S.J., *Magisterium: Teaching Authority in the Catholic Church* (New York: Paulist Press, 1983), 26–28.

2. Martin Heidegger, *Being and Time*, trans. J. Macquarrie and E. Robinson (Oxford: Blackwell, 1967), 102–7.

3. John T. Noonan Jr., "Development in Moral Doctrine," *Theological Studies* 54 (1993): 662.

4. Ibid., 664.

5. Ibid., 666.

6. Ibid., 667.

7. Ibid., 667–68. Cf. "Declaration on Religious Liberty" (*Dignitatis humanae*), in *Vatican Council II: The Conciliar and Postconciliar Documents*, ed. A. Flannery, O.P. (Northport, N.Y.: Costello, 1987), 809, no. 12. Noonan's fourth example is an unusual exercise of papal authority in 1924, which altered "the meaning of the commandment against adultery." Pius XI authorized the marriage of the unbaptized Charles Marsh and the Catholic Lulu La Hood by dissolving Marsh's previous non-Catholic marriage that had ended in divorce. This uncustomary assertion of papal jurisdiction over a non-Catholic marriage allowed Marsh and La Hood to marry without incurring, in the moral judgment of the Church, the bigamy of Marsh and the adultery of La Hood. Noonan argued that this action departed from the age-old teaching "that marriage was indissoluble except in the special case of the conversion of an unbeliever" ("Development in Moral Doctrine," 664). Although this is clearly an example of the development of moral doctrine, it seems not to exemplify dramatic development for two reasons. First, Pius XI's exception to the age-old teaching did not render it obsolete. Second, it is arguable that Pius XI exercised a prerogative on marital jurisdiction implicit in papal powers, in which case the 1924 exception represented a change in actual practice that caused no loss of tradition.

8. Pius XII, *Mystici corporis Christi* (June 29, 1943), in *The Papal Encyclicals: 1939–1958*, ed. C. Carlen (Raleigh, N.C.: McGrath, 1981), 48, no. 57.

9. Rahner highlights the connection between the issue of membership in the Church in *Mystici corporis Christi* and the ancient teaching on the Church as the only means of salvation. See Karl Rahner, "Membership of the Church according to the Teaching of Pius XII's Encyclical 'Mystici Corporis Christi,' " in *Theological Investigations*, vol. 2, trans. K.-H. Kruger (Baltimore, Md.: Helicon Press, 1963), 1–88, esp. 36–64.

10. See Walter Principe, "When 'Authentic' Teachings Change," *The Ecumenist* 25 (1987): 70–73; John H. Wright, S.J., "That All Doubt May Be Removed," *America* 171 (July 30, 1994): 18–19.

11. "Decree on Ecumenism" (*Unitatis redintegratio*), in *Vatican Council II*, 455, no. 3.

12. "Dogmatic Constitution on the Church" (*Lumen gentium*), in *Vatican Council II*, 357, no. 8.

13. Pius XII, *Mystici corporis Christi*, 50, no. 65.

14. "Dogmatic Constitution on the Church" (*Lumen gentium*), 367, no. 16. Cf. "Declaration on the Relation of the Church to Non-Christian Religions" (*Nostra aetate*), in *Vatican Council II*, 738–42.

15. "Dogmatic Constitution on Divine Revelation" (*Dei verbum*), in *Vatican Council II*, 754, 755, nos. 8, 10.

16. "Dogmatic Constitution on the Church" (*Lumen gentium*), 363, no. 12.

17. Ibid.

18. Franz Jozef van Beeck makes this point well, while sounding the same caution previously noted with regard to the authority of theologians; see *God Encountered: A Contemporary Catholic Systematic Theology*, vol. 2/1: *The Revelation of the Glory: Fundamental Theology* (Collegeville, Minn.: Liturgical Press, 1993), 4–5.

19. Henricus Denzinger-Adolfus Schönmetzer, *Enchiridion Symbolorum Definitionum et Declarationum de Rebus Fidei et Morum* (Freiburg im Breisgau, Germany: Herder, 1965), 102–4, nos. 290–95. English translation of the complete text is in E. Hardy, ed., *Christology of the Later Fathers* (Philadelphia: Westminster Press, 1954), 360–70.

20. Comparisons of magisterial practice across centuries must yet acknowledge the different understandings of teaching authority that have flourished in the Church. See Yves Congar, O.P., "A Semantic History of the Term 'Magisterium,' " in *Readings in Moral Theology No. 3: The Magisterium and Morality*, ed. C. Curran and R. McCormick (New York: Paulist Press, 1982), 306–10.

21. For an interesting discussion of logical mediation in religious doctrinal traditions, see William A. Christian Sr., *Doctrines of Religious Communities: A Philosophical Study* (New Haven, Conn.: Yale University Press, 1987), esp. 12–114.

22. Pius XI, *Casti connubii* (December 31, 1930), in *The Papal Encyclicals: 1903–1939*, ed. C. Carlen (Raleigh, N.C.: McGrath, 1981), 399, no. 54. For a thorough discussion of the history of the teaching, see John T. Noonan Jr., *Contraception: A History of Its Treatment by the Catholic Theologians and Canonists* (Cambridge, Mass.: Harvard University Press, 1965).

23. Paul VI, *Humanae vitae* (July 25, 1968), in *The Papal Encyclicals: 1958–1981*, ed. C. Carlen (Raleigh, N.C.: McGrath, 1981), 227, no. 14.

24. Ibid., 226, no. 14.

25. Ibid.

26. A typical statistic is offered in a recent Gallup poll, which found that 84 percent of American Catholics believed they "should be allowed to practice artificial means of birth control," whereas 13 percent believed they should not be allowed (*The Gallup Poll: Public Opinion 1993* [Wilmington, DE: Scholarly Resources, 1994], 145). A 1994 *New York Times*/CBS News poll found that 98 percent of American Catholics eighteen to twenty-nine years of age practice artificial birth control, as do 91 percent of those thirty to forty-four, 85 percent of those forty-five to sixty-four, and 72 percent of those sixty-five and older (*New York Times* [June 1, 1994], B8).

27. Paul VI, *Humanae vitae*, 223, no. 2.

28. Ibid., 225, no. 9.

29. Ibid., 226, no. 12.

30. Ibid., no. 10.

31. Ibid., no. 11.

32. Ibid., 223–24, nos. 1–3.

33. Ibid., 228, no. 18.

34. Charles E. Curran, "Natural Law and Contemporary Moral Theology," in *Contraception: Authority and Dissent*, ed. C. Curran (New York: Herder and Herder, 1969), 159–60. Cf. Charles E. Curran, *Transition and Tradition in Moral Theology* (Notre Dame, Ind.: University of Notre Dame Press, 1979), 30–31.

35. Joseph A. Komonchak, "*Humanae Vitae* and Its Reception: Ecclesiological Reflections," *Theological Studies* 39 (1978): 252.

36. Karl Rahner, "On the Encyclical 'Humanae Vitae,' " in *Theological Investigations*, vol. 9, trans. D. Bourke (New York: Seabury Press, 1974), 276–77.

37. The 1977 Gallup poll is cited in Leonard Swidler, "Roma Locuta, Causa Finita?" in *Women Priests: A Catholic Commentary on the Vatican Declaration*, ed. L. Swidler and A. Swidler (New York: Paulist Press, 1977), 3. A 1993 Gallup poll found that 33 percent of Catholic respondents "strongly agreed" and 30 percent "moderately agreed" that it would be "a good thing if women were allowed to be ordained as priests" (*Gallup Poll*, 144). A 1994 *New York Times*/CBS News poll found that 59 percent of American Catholics favored the ordination of women to the priesthood (*New York Times* [June 1, 1994], B8).

38. See Swidler, "Roma Locuta, Causa Finita?" 3.

39. "Vatican Declaration: Women in the Ministerial Priesthood" (*Inter insigniores*, October 15, 1976), *Origins* 6 (February 3, 1977): 517–19, nos. 1, 3, 4.

40. Ibid., 519, no. 6.

41. Ibid., 519–20, no. 10.

42. Ibid., 520–21, nos. 14–17.

43. Ibid., 522, no. 25.

44. Ibid., no. 26.

45. Ibid., nos. 28, 30.

46. See, e.g., Elizabeth Schüssler Fiorenza, "The Twelve," and "The Apostleship of Women in Early Christianity," in *Women Priests*, 114–22, 135–40. Anne E. Carr has pointed out that making Jesus' practice normative for the Church's practice of ordination cannot in principle sift from the other traits involved in his choice the fact that he chose only males for the Twelve: "[I]f the practice of Jesus were followed in all aspects, married men would have to be eligible for ordination—and only converted Jews could be ordained!" (*Transforming Grace: Christian Tradition and Women's Experience* [San Francisco: HarperCollins, 1988], 55). John H. Wright, S.J., has examined the citation of patristic teaching in the argument of *Inter insigniores* and has concluded that such evidence only supports the position "that women by nature, temperament, and social status are inferior to men," a teaching of the fathers that "the Second Vatican Council reversed" ("Patristic Testimony on Women's Ordination in *Inter Insigniores*," *Theological Studies* 58 [1997]: 526).

47. Elizabeth A. Johnson, *She Who Is: The Mystery of God in Feminist Theological Discourse* (New York: Crossroad, 1992), 153.

48. Ibid.

49. Paul VI, *Humanae vitae*, 231, no. 28.

50. John Paul II, *Ordinatio sacerdotalis*, *Origins* 24 no. 4 (June 9, 1994), 50–52, no. 4.

51. On October 28, 1995, the CDF, with papal approval, issued a *responsum* to the *dubium* on the teaching of *Ordinatio sacerdotalis*, which stated that the teaching "requires definitive assent, since, founded on the written word of God and from the beginning constantly preserved and applied in the tradition of the church, it has been set forth infallibly by the ordinary and universal magisterium" and must

be regarded as "belonging to the deposit of the faith" ("Inadmissibility of Women to Ministerial Priesthood," *Origins* 25 [November 30, 1995]: 402). The Catholic Theological Society of America (CTSA) responded to the teachings of *Inter insigniores*, *Ordinatio sacerdotalis*, and the 1995 *dubium* in a position paper entitled "Tradition and the Ordination of Women," which was approved as a resolution by an overwhelming majority of those in attendance at the June 5, 1997 meeting of the CTSA. For the text of the position paper, which is an extended criticism of, and counterargument to, the magisterial arguments on this issue, see *Origins* 27 (June 19, 1997): 75–79.

52. Ibid.

53. "Instruction on the Ecclesial Vocation of the Theologian" (*Donum veritatis*), *Origins* 20 (July 5, 1990) 118–26, no. 28.

54. Ibid., no. 34.

55. Ibid., no. 29.

56. Ibid., no. 30.

57. Ibid., no. 31. Emphasis mine. John P. Boyle has noted that the diction of *Donum veritatis* places "emphasis on the contemplative rather than the analytic side of theology" (*Church Teaching Authority: Historical and Theological Studies* [Notre Dame, Ind.: University of Notre Dame Press, 1995], 144).

58. For the discussion that follows I have relied on the presentation of nonfoundationalist philosophies in John E. Thiel, *Nonfoundationalism* (Minneapolis, Minn.: Fortress Press, 1994), 1–37.

59. Richard Rorty, *Philosophy and the Mirror of Nature* (Princeton, N.J.: Princeton, University Press, 1979), 157.

60. Richard J. Bernstein, *Beyond Objectivism and Relativism: Science, Hermeneutics, and Praxis* (Philadelphia: University of Pennsylvania Press, 1983), 16–20.

61. Wilfrid Sellars, "Empiricism and the Philosophy of Mind," in *Science, Perception and Reality* (New York: Humanities Press, 1963), 140.

62. Ibid. 170.

63. W. V. Quine, "Natural Kinds," in *Ontological Relativity and Other Essays* (New York: Columbia University Press, 1969), 126–27.

64. W. V. Quine, "Use and Its Place in Meaning," in *Theories and Things* (Cambridge, Mass.: Harvard University Press, 1981), 45.

65. Willard Van Orman Quine, *From a Logical Point of View* (Cambridge, Mass.: Harvard University Press, 1964), 41.

66. W. V. Quine, "On Empirically Equivalent Systems of the World," *Erkenntnis* 9 (1975): 313.

67. Michael Williams, *Groundless Belief: An Essay on the Possibility of Epistemology* (New Haven, Conn.: Yale University Press, 1977), 89.

68. The distinction introduced here between "weak" and "strong" versions of foundationalist argumentation parallels a distinction sometimes made in the philosophical literature between "weak" and "strong" foundations for knowledge. See, e.g., William P. Alston, "Has Foundationalism Been Refuted?" *Philosophical Studies* 29 (1976): 290–91; Ernest Sosa, "The Raft and the Pyramid: Coherence versus Foundations in the Theory of Knowledge," *Midwest Studies in Philosophy* 5 (1980): 14–15.

69. E.g., Francis Schüssler Fiorenza, *Foundational Theology: Jesus and the Church* (New York: Crossroad, 1986); Nicholas Lash, *Easter in Ordinary: Reflections on Human Experience and the Knowledge of God* (Notre Dame, Ind.: University of Notre

Dame Press, 1990); James J. Buckley, *Seeking the Humanity of God: Practices, Doctrines, and Catholic Theology* (Collegeville, Minn.: Liturgical Press, 1992).

70. See, e.g., George A. Lindbeck, *The Nature of Doctrine: Religion and Theology in a Postliberal Age* (Philadelphia: Westminster Press, 1984), 38; Ronald F. Thiemann, *Revelation and Theology: The Gospel as Narrated Promise* (Notre Dame, Ind.: University of Notre Dame Press, 1985), 6.

71. Denzinger-Schönmetzer, *Enchiridion Symbolorum*, 591, 592, nos. 1797, 1799. This teaching is expanded in a recent papal encyclical. See John Paul II, *Fides et ratio* (October 15, 1998), *Origins* 28 (October 22, 1998): 318–47.

72. One convincing model for a dialogical ecclesiology is presented in Paul Lakeland, *Theology and Critical Theory: The Discourse of the Church* (Nashville, Tenn.: Abingdon Press, 1990).

73. In this regard, I should offer a coda on Jan Walgrave's well-known distinction between "logical" and "theological" theories of development. "Logical" theories refer to explanations that attribute the development of tradition to the formal deduction of reasonable implications from the premises of official Church teaching. Historically, this understanding of development was typical of the Catholic scholastic tradition. "Theological" theories refer to post-Enlightenment explanations that anchor development in the historical workings of the Holy Spirit. The four modern models, and the retrospective model, of development sketched in the previous chapter could all serve as examples of Walgrave's "theological" type; see *Unfolding Revelation: The Nature of Doctrinal Development* (Philadelphia: Westminster Press, 1972), 135–78, 278–347. Although one can appreciate Walgrave's distinction, his typology—if only in its distinguishing labels—separates the logical and the theological too sharply. This study's discussion of reason's role in identifying dramatically developing doctrine and in configuring tradition presupposes the congruence of the logical and the theological in a comprehensive theory of development presented as the four senses of tradition.

74. I should note that even dramatically developed doctrines and practices remain in the *history* of the Church as matters of fact, even if their traditional values of constancy and renewal have been lost. Their obsolescence serves present-day affirmations of tradition as a contrapuntal record of what the Church once, but no longer, affirms as true, and in this regard their obsolescence can have both an instructive and a constructive effect on the development of tradition.

Chapter 4

1. For expressions of the typical premodern judgment, see Beryl Smalley, "Ecclesiastical Attitudes to Novelty c. 1100–c. 1250," in *Studies in Medieval Thought and Learning: From Abelard to Wyclif* (London: Hambleton Press, 1981), 97–115.

2. "The Creed of the Synod of Nicaea (June 19, 325)," in *The Trinitarian Controversy*, ed. and trans. W. Rusch (Philadelphia: Fortress Press, 1980), 49. The original text appears in Henricus Denzinger-Adolfus Schönmetzer, *Enchiridion Symbolorum Definitionum et Declarationum de Rebus Fidei et Morum*, 34th ed. (Freiburg im Breisgau, Germany: Herder, 1965), 52–53, nos. 125–26. For Arius's statement of his position, see "Arius's 'Letter to Eusebius of Nicomedia' " and "Arius's 'Letter to Alexander of Alexandria,' " in *Trinitarian Controversy*, 29–32.

3. Maurice F. Wiles, "In Defence of Arius," *Journal of Theological Studies* 13 (1962): 339–47; Robert C. Gregg and Dennis E. Groh, *Early Arianism—A View of Salvation* (Philadelphia: Fortress Press, 1981); Rowan Williams, *Arius: Heresy and Tradition* (London: Darton, Longman and Todd, 1987), 16–22.

4. For Justin, see Richard A. Norris, *God and World in Early Christian Theology: A Study in Justin Martyr, Irenaeus, Tertullian and Origen* (London: Black, 1965), 48–56; Aloys Grillmeier, S.J., *Christ in Christian Tradition*, vol. 1, *From the Apostolic Age to Chalcedon (451)*, trans. J. Bowden (Atlanta, Ga.: John Knox Press, 1975), 110–11. For Theophilus, see Robert M. Grant, *Jesus after the Gospels: The Christ of the Second Century* (Louisville, Ky.: Westminster Press; Atlanta, Ga.: John Knox Press, 1990), 68–82. For Tertullian, see Norris, *God and World in Early Christian Theology*, 93–97. For Origen, see Jaroslav Pelikan, *The Christian Tradition: A History of the Development of Doctrine*. vol. 1, *The Emergence of the Catholic Tradition (100–600)* (Chicago: University of Chicago Press, 1971), 191; Henri Crouzel, *Origen*, trans. A. Worrall (San Francisco: Harper and Row, 1989), 186–92.

5. For Athenagoras, see J. N. D. Kelly, *Early Christian Doctrines* (San Francisco: Harper and Row, 1978), 99–100. For Irenaeus, see Dennis Minns, O.P., *Irenaeus* (Washington, D.C.: Georgetown University Press, 1994), 50.

6. The text is presented in Grillmeier, *Christ in Christian Tradition*, 234–35. Grillmeier argues that Arius might well have written his *Thalia* in point-by-point opposition to Gregory's *Expositio Fidei* (ibid., 235–38).

7. For a discussion of this temporal terminus ad quem, see John C. Cavadini, *The Last Christology of the West: Adoptionism in Spain and Gaul, 785–820* (Philadelphia: University of Pennsylvania Press, 1993). It would be more correct to locate the shift from fourth- to second-sense development earlier in this span of time rather than later, in which case the eighth-century Spanish adoptionism explored in Cavadini's excellent study represents more a deviation from an established tradition than a still viable traditional claim.

8. "The Letter of Eusebius of Caesarea Describing the Council of Nicaea," in *Christology of the Later Fathers*, ed. E. Hardy (Philadelphia: Westminster Press, 1954), 336–38. Cf. Robert M. Grant, *Augustus to Constantine: The Rise and Triumph of Christianity in the Roman World* (San Francisco: Harper and Row, 1990), 241.

9. Frances M. Young, *From Nicaea to Chalcedon: A Guide to the Literature and its Background* (Philadelphia: Fortress Press, 1983), 75.

10. Athanasius, "De Decretis," in *St. Athanasius: Select Works and Letters* (Nicene and Post-Nicene Fathers of the Christian Church, second series), vol. 4, ed. A. Robertson (Grand Rapids, Mich.:Eerdmans, 1978), 164, no. 21.

11. Athanasius, "De Synodis," in *St. Athanasius*, 472, no. 41.

12. Athanasius, "Ad Afros Epistola Synodica," in *St. Athanasius*, 493, no. 9.

13. According to the 369 letter, "[T]hey pretend as if in ignorance to be alarmed at the phrase" (ibid.). For a study of Athanasius's negotiation of the formula in the divisive aftermath of Nicea, see Timothy D. Barnes, *Athanasius and Constantius: Theology and Politics in the Constantinian Empire* (Cambridge, Mass.: Harvard University Press, 1993).

14. Denzinger-Schönmetzer, *Enchiridion Symbolorum*, 108, no. 301. The English translation is from J. F. Clarkson, S.J., et al., eds. and trans., *The Church Teaches: Documents of the Church in English Translation* (St. Louis, Mo.: Herder, 1955), 172.

15. See the discussion throughout Peter Widdicombe, *The Fatherhood of God from Origen to Athanasius* (Oxford: Clarendon Press, 1994).

16. Catherine Mowry LaCugna, *God for Us: The Trinity and Christian Life* (San Francisco: HarperCollins, 1991), 33.

17. Sallie McFague, *Models of God: Theology for an Ecological, Nuclear Age* (Philadelphia: Fortress Press, 1987), 63–69. Cf. Elizabeth A. Johnson, C.S.J., "Does God Play Dice? Divine Providence and Chance," *Theological Studies* 57 (1996): 8–9.

18. Anne E. Carr, *Transforming Grace: Christian Tradition and Women's Experience* (San Francisco: HarperCollins, 1988), 35.

19. Rosemary Radford Ruether, *Sexism and God-Talk: Toward a Feminist Theology* (Boston: Beacon Press, 1983), 66–67. Cf. Mary McClintock Fulkerson, *Changing the Subject: Women's Discourses and Feminist Theology* (Minneapolis, Minn.: Fortress Press, 1994), 22–23.

20. Ruether, *Sexism and God-Talk,* 93–115.

21. Carr, *Transforming Grace,* 145.

22. Elizabeth Schüssler Fiorenza, *Jesus. Miriam's Child, Sophia's Prophet: Critical Issues in Feminist Christology* (New York: Continuum, 1995), esp. 131–62; Elizabeth A. Johnson, *She Who Is: The Mystery of God in Feminist Theological Discourse* (New York: Crossroad, 1992), esp. 124–87.

23. Among many possible illustrations, see Caroline Walker Bynum, " '. . . And Woman His Humanity': Female Imagery in the Religious Writing of the Later Middle Ages," in *Fragmentation and Redemption: Essays on Gender and the Human Body in Medieval Religion* (New York: Zone Books, 1991), 151–79; Bynum, *Jesus as Mother: Studies in the Spirituality of the High Middle Ages* (Berkeley and Los Angeles: University of California Press, 1982); Joan M. Nuth, *Wisdom's Daughter: The Theology of Julian of Norwich* (New York: Crossroad, 1991). Nuth claims that "Julian is unique [in the Middle Ages] in considering motherhood an essential attribute of God" (*Wisdom's Daughter,* 94).

24. Johnson, *She Who Is,* 173, 179.

25. Dorothee Sölle, "Paternalistic Religion as Experienced by Women," in *God as Father?* (Concilium, 143), ed. J. B. Metz and E. Schillebeeckx (New York: Seabury Press, 1981), 74.

26. For accounts of the proposal and the process, see William Cardinal-designate Keeler, "The NRSV, the Revised NAB and the Liturgy," *Origins* 24 (November 10, 1994): 376–77; "On File," *Origins* 24 (February 2, 1995): 546; "On File," *Origins* 25 (September 7, 1995): 186.

27. Bishop Donald Trautman, "Inclusive Language and Revised Liturgical Books," *Origins* 26 (April 10, 1997): 690.

28. Ibid., 689. For a coincident judgment on the new belief, see Francis Martin, *The Feminist Question: Feminist Theology in the Light of Christian Tradition* (Grand Rapids, Mich.: Eerdmans, 1994), esp. 221–92.

29. Gustavo Gutiérrez, "Toward a Theology of Liberation (July 1968)," in *Liberation Theology: A Documentary History,* ed. A. Hennelly, S.J. (Maryknoll, N.Y.: Orbis Books, 1990), 72, 73.

30. Gustavo Gutiérrez, *A Theology of Liberation: History, Politics, and Salvation,* trans. C. Inda and J. Eagleson (Maryknoll, N.Y.: Orbis Books, 1988), 172.

31. "Second General Conference of Latin American Bishops: 'The Church in the Present-Day Transformation of Latin America in the Light of the Council' (August 26–September 6, 1968)," in *Liberation Theology,* 116–17.

32. "Third General Conference of the Latin American Bishops: 'Evangelization in Latin America's Present and Future' (Puebla de los Angeles, Mexico, January 27–February 13, 1979)," in *Liberation Theology,* 243–47.

33. Ibid., 254.

34. Gustavo Gutiérrez, "Option for the Poor," in *Systematic Theology: Perspectives from Liberation Theology,* ed. J. Sobrino and I. Ellacuría (Maryknoll, N.Y.: Orbis Books, 1996), 26. Gutiérrez also noted that this expression "had already begun to be used in the theological reflection of that time in Latin America" and that the "Puebla Conference bestowed a powerful endorsement" on it (ibid.).

35. Michael Novak, *Will It Liberate?: Questions about Liberation Theology* (New York: Paulist Press, 1986), 148–49.

36. Congregation for the Doctrine of the Faith, "Instruction on Certain Aspects of the 'Theology of Liberation' " (August 6, 1984), *Origins* 14 (September 13, 1984): 201, no. 11, 3.

37. Ibid., 201, no. 9, 4, 5.

38. Congregation for the Doctrine of the Faith, "Instruction on Christian Freedom and Liberation" (March 22, 1986), *Origins* 15 (April 17, 1986): 722–23, nos. 66–70. Especially worthy of note is the following passage:

> The special option for the poor, far from being a sign of particularism or sectarianism, manifests the universality of the church's being and mission. This option excludes no one.
>
> This is the reason why the church cannot express this option by means of reductive sociological and ideological categories which would make this preference a partisan choice and a source of conflict.

Ibid., 723, no. 68.

39. "Economic Justice for All: Catholic Social Teaching and the U.S. Economy," *Origins* 16 (November 27, 1986): 437, no. 260.

40. John Paul II, *Sollicitudo rei socialis* (December 30, 1987), *Origins* 17 (March 3, 1988): 656, no. 42.

41. Congregation for the Doctrine of the Faith, "Vatican Declaration: Women in the Ministerial Priesthood" (*Inter insigniores,* October 15, 1976), *Origins* 6 (February 3, 1977): 519, no. 10.

42. Ibid., 522, no. 15.

43. John Paul II, "Apostolic Letter on Ordination and Women" (*Ordinatio sacerdotalis,* May 22, 1994), *Origins* 24 (June 9, 1994), 51, no. 2.

44. Avery Dulles, S.J., "Gender and Priesthood: Examining the Teaching," *Origins* 26 (1996): 779, no. 2.

45. Ibid., 781, no. 6. Cf. Avery Dulles, S.J., *The Priestly Office: A Theological Reflection* (New York: Paulist Press, 1997), 41–42.

46. Ibid., 782, no. 10.

47. Ibid., 783, no. 10. For theological arguments that run counter to Dulles's, see the 1997 CTSA position paper, "Tradition and the Ordination of Women," *Origins,* 27 (June 19, 1997): 75–79.

48. Sara Butler, M.S.B.T., has proposed that several doctrinal developments in the teaching of the Second Vatican Council support the traditional practice of ordaining only men to the ministerial priesthood. When taken together, she has argued, the council's teachings on the "difference in kind between the common and the ministerial priesthood, the sacramentality of the episcopate, and the collegial structure of the Church as rooted in the apostolic college" all "reinforce the plausibility" that the ministerial priesthood should be "identifiable by some visible sign," which Butler in turn identifies with the maleness of the original Twelve whom Jesus chose, presumably as a reflection of his own maleness ("Women's

Ordination and the Development of Doctrine," *The Thomist* 61 [1997]: 522). Her argument is a good example of what I have called a claim for incipient development.

49. These fourth-sense dynamics of discord and harmony may seem to apply only to those beliefs and practices that appeared against the backdrop of a previously established literal sense of tradition. Nearly all beliefs and practices would fit into this category, though a few of the earliest, such as the resurrection of Jesus from the dead, would not. The belief in Jesus' resurrection is an example of an incipience so radical that its development as a basic claim instantly became the literal sense of Christian tradition. Even this extraordinary incipience, though, engendered discord with the formative Judaism from which the earliest belief in the resurrection arose, especially in the early Christian regard for the resurrection of *this* person, Jesus of Nazareth, as God's fulfillment of Israel.

50. Karl Barth, *Church Dogmatics*, III/2, trans. H. Knight et al. (Edinburgh: Clark, 1960), 525.

51. George Steiner, *Real Presences* (Chicago: University of Chicago Press, 1989), 44.

52. Cardinal Ratzinger has spoken of the Church's responsibility to the future. Even though he has conceived this responsibility largely in prospective terms, his appreciation for differentiation within the unity of traditional time reads much like the analysis presented here:

> [T]radition properly understood is, in effect, the transcendence of today in both directions. The past can be discovered as something to be preserved only if the future is regarded as a duty; discovery of the future and discovery of the past are inseparably connected, and it is this discovery of the indivisibility of time that actually makes tradition. The emphasis may vary, but tradition can evolve only if the whole of time has been discovered.

Joseph Cardinal Ratzinger, *Principles of Catholic Theology: Building Stones for a Fundamental Theology*, trans. M. F. McCarthy, S.N.D. (San Francisco: Ignatius Press, 1987), 87.

53. There are many examples, but the best and most influential is found in the writings of Jürgen Moltmann. Cf. his *Theology of Hope*, trans. J. Leitch (San Francisco: HarperCollins, 1991) and the recent collection of Concilium essays in Johann-Baptist Metz and Jürgen Moltmann, *Faith and the Future: Essays on Theology, Solidarity, and Modernity* (Maryknoll, N.Y.: Orbis Books, 1995).

54. I rely here on the genre analysis advanced by Mikhail Bakhtin. See, especially, his "Epic and Novel: Toward a Methodology for the Study of the Novel," in *The Dialogic Imagination: Four Essays*, ed. M. Holquist, trans. C. Emerson and M. Holquist (Austin: University of Texas Press, 1981), 3–40.

Chapter 5

1. Phillip Melanchthon, "Apology of the Augsburg Confession," in *The Book of Concord: The Confessions of the Evangelical Lutheran Church*, trans. T. Tappert (Philadelphia: Fortress Press, 1959), 222 art. 15; 273–74 art. 27. Cf. "Formula of Concord," in Ibid., 492–94 art. 10.

2. George A. Lindbeck, *The Nature of Doctrine: Religion and Theology in a Postliberal Age* (Philadelphia: Westminster Press, 1984), 84–88.

3. The 1990 teaching of the CDF's *Donum veritatis* concedes the existence of "non-infallible teaching of the magisterium," while deploring a theological mind-set that would regard such teaching as devoid of authority. The "Instruction" also speaks of "non-irreformable magisterial teaching" ("Instruction on the Ecclesial Vocation of the Theologian" [*Donum veritatis*], *Origins* 20 [July 5, 1990]: 124, no. 33; 123, no. 28). Another contemporary rhetorical and conceptual version of this taxonomy distinguishes between dogma and doctrine in order to identify, respectively, what does not and what does admit of change in tradition.

4. Frei has made this point cogently in *The Identity of Jesus Christ: The Hermeneutical Bases of Dogmatic Theology* (Philadelphia: Fortress Press, 1967), 139–52.

5. Gregory of Nyssa, "Concerning We Should Think of Saying That There Are Not Three Gods," in *The Trinitarian Controversy*, ed. and trans. W. Rusch (Philadelphia: Fortress Press, 1980), 155.

6. On this point, see Louis-Marie Chauvet, *Symbol and Sacrament: A Sacramental Reinterpretation of Christian Existence*, trans. P. Madigan, S.J., and M. Beaumont (Collegeville, Minn.: Liturgical Press, 1995), esp. 453–89. Congar has referred to this incarnational dimension of tradition as the "monuments of tradition." See Yves M.-J. Congar, O.P., *La Tradition et les traditions*, vol. 2, *Essai théologique* (Paris: Librairie Arthème Fayard, 1963), 181–213.

7. John Henry Newman, *An Essay on the Development of Christian Doctrine* (Notre Dame, Ind.: University of Notre Dame Press, 1989), 171.

8. Cf. David H. Kelsey, *To Understand God Truly: What's Theological about a Theological School* (Louisville, Ky.: Westminster Press; Atlanta, Ga.: John Knox Press, 1992), 170.

9. On this relationship between the local and the universal in the configuration of tradition, see Robert J. Schreiter, *Constructing Local Theologies* (Maryknoll, N.Y.: Orbis Books, 1985), 31–38.

10. Nevertheless, Christopher Morse has delineated a list of criteria for testing doctrinal faithfulness that offers an interesting complement to Newman's. In addition to criteria for constancy, such as "continuity with apostolic tradition," "congruence with scripture," and "catholicity," Morse includes criteria for renewal, such as "consonance with experience," "conformity with conscience," and "cruciality" in the present situation. See Christopher Morse, *Not Every Spirit: A Dogmatics of Christian Disbelief* (Valley Forge, Pa.: Trinity Press International, 1994), 45–70.

11. The most comprehensive study of this period is Roger Aubert, *Le problème de l'acte de foi: Données traditionnelles et résultats des controverses récentes*, 2d ed. (Louvain, Belgium: Publications Universitaires de Louvain, 1950). See also, Avery Dulles, S.J., *The Assurance of Things Hoped For: A Theology of Christian Faith* (New York: Oxford University Press, 1994), 96–115.

12. John Henry Newman, *An Essay in Aid of a Grammar of Assent* (Notre Dame, Ind.: University of Notre Dame Press, 1979), 271.

13. "Thus in concrete reasonings we are in great measure thrown back into that condition, from which logic proposed to rescue us. We judge for ourselves, by our own lights, and on our own principles; and our criterion of truth is not so much the manipulation of propositions, as the intellectual and moral character of the person maintaining them, and the ultimate silent effect of his arguments or conclusions upon our mind" (ibid., 240).

14. Ibid., 271.

15. Ibid., 269.

16. Ibid., 280.

17. Ibid.

18. Ibid., 281.

19. Ibid., 250.

20. Ibid., 281.

21. Ibid., 283.

22. Cf. Aidan Nichols, "John Henry Newman and the Illative Sense: A Re-Consideration," *Scottish Journal of Theology* 38 (1985): 364: "One illuminating way to see Newman's concept of illation is to view it as a transposition into a philosophical key of the sacramentalism of the English religious tradition. The illative sense actualises our capacity to uncover, by a searching and subtle attention to experience in its complexity, the sacramental transparence of the world to God." My proposed transposition looks more to the Roman religious tradition on faith and reason to account for the workings of the illative sense, though Nichols's interpretation and mine both attend to the influence of a graced view of nature on Newman's *Essay in Aid of a Grammar of Assent*.

23. Pierre Rousselot, S.J., *The Eyes of Faith*, trans. J. Donceel, S.J. (New York: Fordham University Press, 1990), 23. Rousselot's judgment is based on a reading of Billot on reason's place amid the supernatural virtues. See Ludovico Billot, S.J., *De virtutibus infusis: Commentarius in secundam partem S. Thomae* (Rome: Joseph, 1905), 64–94. For a discussion of Billot and other advocates of "scientific faith," see Aubert, *Le problème de l'acte de foi*, 241–55.

24. Cf. Gerald A. McCool, S.J., *From Unity to Pluralism: The Internal Evolution of Thomism* (New York: Fordham University Press, 1992), 76.

25. Rousselot, *Eyes of Faith*, 26.

26. Ibid., 31.

27. Ibid., 29.

28. Ibid., 27.

29. Ibid., 60; cf. 64–65.

30. Ibid., 45, 34.

31. This difference can be observed, however, with the hasty qualification that, for Rousselot as for Blondel, faith is an act, even if one that is not initially at least practical. See Maurice Blondel, *Action (1893): Essay on a Critique of Life and a Science of Practice*, trans. O. Blanchette (Notre Dame, Ind: University of Notre Dame Press, 1984), 363–88, esp. 375, 378.

32. Rousselot, *Eyes of Faith*, 45.

33. Ibid., 34.

34. Ibid., 31.

35. Jean Mouroux, *Je crois en toi: Structure personnelle de la foi*, 2d ed. (Paris: Éditions du Cerf, 1948). The content of this short book originally appeared as an article in the journal *Recherches de science religieuse* in 1938. For discussion of Mouroux's theology of faith, see Aubert, *Le problème de l'acte de foi*, 615–22. Aubert has identified the existentialist phenomenology of Gabriel Marcel as the most direct influence on Mouroux. See also Dulles, *Assurance of Things Hoped For*, 137–38.

36. Mouroux, *Je crois en toi*, 15, 17.

37. Ibid., 45.

38. Ibid., 25, 41.

39. Ibid., 18.

40. Ibid., 67.

41. Ibid., 68.

42. Ibid., 25.

43. Ibid., 56.

44. See, for example, Billot, *De virtutibus infusis*, 318: "Tres sunt principales actus fidei theologicae proprietates.—Prima est obscuritas, quae tota derivat ex hoc quod materiale obiectum de non apparentibus est, formale autem non in aliqua evidentia, etiam mere extrinseca consistit, sed in sola auctoritate revelantis." The other aspects of faith Billot delineated are "libertas" and "certitudo."

45. Mouroux, *Je crois en toi*, 56–58.

46. Ibid., 54.

47. "Or c'est là [dans une existence spirituelle] que se situe l'acte de foi et, par suite, il se place de lui-même sur un plan obscur et irritant pour la pure raison: l'univers des personnes est un monde où l'on n'entre vraiment que par l'amour" (ibid., 56).

48. Ibid., 82–97.

49. Cf. John Paul II, "Lord and Giver of Life (May 30, 1986)" (*Dominum et vivificantem*) (Washington, D.C.: U.S. Catholic Conference, 1986), 94–96, nos. 50–51.

50. On this point, one must recall Rahner's insistence on the incomprehensibility of God, even and especially in God's self-communication: "Grace does not imply the promise and the beginning of the elimination of the mystery, but the radical possibility of the absolute proximity of the mystery, which is not eliminated by its proximity, but really presented as mystery" (Karl Rahner, "The Concept of Mystery in Catholic Theology," in *Theological Investigations*, vol. 4, trans. K. Smyth [Baltimore, Md.: Helicon Press, 1966], 55).

51. Wolfgang Beinert, "Bedeutung und Begründung des Glaubenssinnes (Sensus Fidei) als eines dogmatischen Erkenntniskriteriums," *Catholica* 25 (1971): 292–93. In another writing, Beinert has referred to this conceptualization of the *sensus fidei* as the " 'Echo-Modell' " ("Der Glaubenssinn der Gläubigen in Theologie- und Dogmengeschichte," in *Der Glaubenssinn des Gottesvolkes—Konkurrent oder Partner des Lehramts?* ed. D. Wiederkehr [Freiburg, Germany: Herder, 1994], 92).

52. For a discussion of the proper understanding of the *sensus fidei* as both passive and active, see William M. Thompson, "Sensus Fidelium and Infallibility," *American Ecclesiastical Review* 167 (1973): 479–84.

53. Congar has made the point that the very nature of tradition is synthetic. Congar, *La Tradition et les traditions*, 164.

54. "Dogmatic Constitution on the Church" (*Lumen gentium*), in *Vatican Council II: The Conciliar and Postconciliar Documents*, ed. A. Flannery, O.P. (Northport, N.Y.: Costello, 1987), 363, no. 12.

55. Ibid., 357, no. 8.

56. On the practical problem of establishing the *sensus fidei*, see Karl Lehmann, "Verbindliche Lehraussagen und Geschichtlichkeit des Lebens der Kirche," *Una Sancta* 31 (1976): 293–94.

57. The best-known rules for discernment are those that Ignatius of Loyola catalogued in his *Spiritual Exercises*. Ignatius offered advice to the director in discerning the states of consolation and desolation in the spiritual life of the exercitant as he or she moves through the first and second weeks of the Exercises. See Ignatius of Loyola, *The Spiritual Exercises of St. Ignatius*, trans. A. Mottola (Garden City, N.Y.: Doubleday, 1964), 129–34. It is important to note that these are rules

for the discernment of "spirits" and not for the discernment of the Spirit. See W. A. M. Peters, "Ignatius of Loyola and 'Discernment of Spirits,' " in *Discernment of the Spirit and of Spirits* (*Concilium*, 119), ed. C. Floristán and C. Duquoc (New York: Seabury Press, 1979), 27–33. And even though the Spirit is certainly at work among the "spirits" for whose discernment Ignatius gave ruled direction, and even though one might be able to imagine the movement of tradition as subject to comparable dynamics of consolation and desolation, these similarities do not justify the view that the discernment of the Spirit by the *sensus fidei* is rule bound. As noted earlier in this chapter, the Spirit itself is the "how" of ecclesial responsibility and thus of responsibility exercised as discernment. Judging the discernment of tradition to transcend Ignatian-like rules, however, should not suggest that discernment in the Ignatian tradition cannot be theologically informative and resourceful. See, for example, Christoph Theobald, S.J., "Une manière ignatienne de faire de la théologie: La théologie comme discernement de la vie authentique," *Nouvelle revue théologique* 119 (1997): 375–96.

58. Beinert has made this point well: "Der Glaubenssinn ist . . . stets praxisbezogen," and it is love that impels its practice ("Der Glaubenssinn der Gläubigen in Theologie- und Dogmengeschichte," 114).

Chapter 6

1. Jürgen Moltmann, *God in Creation*, trans. M. Kohl (San Francisco: Harper-Collins, 1991), 124–39.

2. "Dogmatic Constitution on Divine Revelation" (*Dei verbum*), in *Vatican Council II: The Conciliar and Postconciliar Documents*, ed. A. Flannery, O.P. (Northport, N.Y.: Costello, 1987), 755, no. 10.

3. Hans W. Frei, *The Eclipse of Biblical Narrative: A Study in Eighteenth and Nineteenth Century Hermeneutics* (New Haven, Conn.: Yale University Press, 1974), 13–14.

4. Ibid., 16.

5. For other presentations of Frei's thesis and its theological implications, see his "Remarks in Connection with a Theological Proposal," "Theology and the Interpretation of Narrative: Some Hermeneutical Considerations," and "The 'Literal Reading' of Biblical Narrative in the Christian Tradition: Does It Stretch or Will It Break?" in *Theology and Narrative: Selected Essays*, ed. G. Hunsinger and W. Placher (New York: Oxford University Press, 1993), 26–44, 94–116, 117–52.

6. Representative works are George A. Lindbeck, *The Nature of Doctrine: Religion and Theology in a Postliberal Age* (Philadelphia: Westminster Press, 1984); Ronald F. Thiemann, *Revelation and Theology: The Gospel as Narrated Promise* (Notre Dame, Ind.: University of Notre Dame Press, 1985); Stanley Hauerwas, *A Community of Character: Toward a Constructive Christian Social Ethic* (Notre Dame, Ind: University of Notre Dame Press, 1981); Charles M. Wood, *The Formation of Christian Understanding: An Essay in Theological Hermeneutics* (Philadelphia: Westminster Press, 1981).

7. Nicholas Lash, *Theology on the Way to Emmaus* (London: SCM Press, 1986), 42.

8. Hans W. Frei, *The Identity of Jesus Christ: The Hermeneutical Bases of Dogmatic Theology* (Philadelphia: Fortress Press, 1975), xiii–xiv.

9. Ibid., xiv.

10. Ibid., 38.

11. Ibid., 145.

12. It is important to note that Frei extended the presence of the resurrected Christ into ecclesial tradition to the present moment, and thus there is a qualified sense in which the narrative also remains unfinished in his treatment, even acknowledging the canonical completeness of the scriptural story. The same nuanced judgment appears in a Catholic narrative style in the concession that, though historically unfinished, tradition offers no new revelation.

13. Frei, *Identity of Jesus Christ*, 5.

14. I have found Ricoeur's analysis of narrative identity to be a helpful guide in portraying the character of Catholic tradition in this way. See Paul Ricoeur, *Oneself as Another*, trans. K. Blamey (Chicago: University of Chicago Press, 1992), 113–68.

15. Hans Urs von Balthasar, *Theo-Drama: Theological Dramatic Theory*, 5 vols., trans. G. Harrison et al. (San Francisco: Ignatius Press, 1988–1998).

16. These themes are developed in detail in Hans Urs von Balthasar, *The Glory of the Lord: A Theological Aesthetics*, vol. 1, *Seeing the Form*, trans. E. Leiva-Merikakis (San Francisco: Ignatius Press, 1982). Cf. Louis Dupré, "Hans Urs von Balthasar's Theology of Aesthetic Form," *Theological Studies* 49 (1988): 299–318.

17. Hans Urs von Balthasar, *The Glory of the Lord: A Theological Aesthetics*, vol. 2, *Studies in Theological Style: Clerical Styles*, trans. A. Louth et al. (San Francisco: Ignatius Press, 1984); Von Balthasar, *The Glory of the Lord: A Theological Aesthetics*, vol. 3, *Studies in Theological Style: Lay Styles*, trans. A. Louth et al. (San Francisco: Ignatius Press, 1986).

18. Hans Urs von Balthasar, *The Glory of the Lord: A Theological Aesthetics*, vol. 4, *The Realm of Metaphysics in Antiquity*, trans. B. McNeil, C. R. V., et al. (San Francisco: Ignatius Press, 1989); Von Balthasar, *The Glory of the Lord: A Theological Aesthetics*, vol. 5, *The Realm of Metaphysics in the Modern Age*, trans. O. Davies et al. (San Francisco: Ignatius Press, 1991).

19. Hans Urs von Balthasar, *The Glory of the Lord: A Theological Aesthetics*, vol. 6, *Theology: The New Covenant*, trans. B. McNeil, C.R.V., and E. Leiva-Merikakis (San Francisco: Ignatius Press, 1991); Von Balthasar, *The Glory of the Lord: A Theological Aesthetics*, vol. 7, *Theology: The New Covenant*, trans. B. McNeil, C.R.V., et al. (San Francisco: Ignatius Press, 1989). For studies of von Balthasar's project, see John J. O'Donnell, S.J., *Hans Urs von Balthasar* (Collegeville, Minn.: Liturgical Press, 1992); Edward T. Oakes, *Pattern of Redemption: The Theology of Hans Urs von Balthasar* (New York: Continuum, 1994).

20. "[W]hile Scripture does indeed have a form, this form is of theological relevance only in so far as it is an indication and a testimony of the form of revelation of God in Christ through the Holy Spirit. . . . For this very reason Scripture cannot claim for itself a form which can be understood and apprehended in itself" (von Balthasar, *Glory of the Lord*, vol. 1, 546). Gerard Loughlin's work enlists von Balthasar in the cause of a narrative style for theology but seems not to recognize von Balthasar's difference from Protestant narrativists on the issue of the traditional character of the narrative. See Gerard Loughlin, *Telling God's Story: Bible, Church and Narrative Theology* (Cambridge: Cambridge University Press, 1996), 201–2.

21. Von Balthasar, *Glory of the Lord*, vol. 1, 241–57.

22. The issue of the unity and plurality of tradition is considered pointedly in Hans Urs von Balthasar, *The Truth is Symphonic: Aspects of Christian Pluralism*, trans. G. Harrison (San Francisco: Ignatius Press, 1987).

23. Besides von Balthasar, DeLubac and Ratzinger—respectively, pre- and postconciliar *ressourcement* theologians—might be included in this small society. Frans Josef van Beeck, S.J., and James J. Buckley also attribute great importance to the narrative quality of tradition's literal sense—van Beeck by attending to the roles of liturgical practice and the "Great Tradition" in framing an authoritative story to which theological interpretation is responsible and Buckley by reading the teachings of the Second Vatican Council as a narrative within which the Church finds direction in its contemporary search for God. Franz Josef van Beeck, S.J., *God Encountered: A Contemporary Catholic Systematic Theology,* vol. 1 (San Francisco: Harper and Row, 1989); vol. 2 (Collegeville, Minn.: Liturgical Press, 1993). James J. Buckley, *Seeking the Humanity of God: Practices, Doctrines, and Catholic Theology* (Collegeville, Minn.: Liturgical Press, 1992).

24. Hans Urs von Balthasar, *Theologik,* 3 vols. (Einseideln, Switzerland: Johannes Verlag, 1985–1987); von Balthasar, *Heart of the World,* trans. E. Leiva (San Francisco: Ignatius Press, 1979); von Balthasar, *Mysterium Pascale: The Mystery of Easter,* trans. A. Nichols, O.P. (Edinburgh: Clark, 1990).

25. Hans Urs von Balthasar, *The Theology of Karl Barth,* trans. J. Drury (Garden City, N.Y.: Doubleday, 1972).

26. Bernard J. F. Lonergan, S.J., *Method in Theology* (New York: Herder and Herder, 1972), xi.

27. David Tracy, *The Analogical Imagination: Christian Theology and the Culture of Pluralism* (New York: Crossroad, 1981), 3–31.

28. David Tracy, *Blessed Rage for Order: The New Pluralism in Theology* (Minneapolis, Minn.: Seabury Press, 1975), 43–56; Tracy, *Analogical Imagination,* esp. 99–192.

29. Joseph Maréchal, *Le point de départ de la métaphysique,* 5 vols. (Paris: Desclee de Brouwer; Brussels, Belgium: Édition Universelle, 1927–49); Bernard J. Lonergan, S.J., *Verbum: Word and Idea in Aquinas,* ed. D. Burrell, C.S.C. (Notre Dame, Ind.: University of Notre Dame Press, 1967); Karl Rahner, *Spirit in the World,* trans. W. Dych, S.J. (London: Sheed and Ward, 1968).

30. Variations on the phenomenological-existentialist approach to the hermeneutical style are legion. Hans Küng, for example, pursues this approach methodologically by consistent application of historical criticism; Schillebeeckx by appreciating the contrasting value of particularistic and negative experiences within a universal horizon of meaning; Piet Schoonenberg by insisting on the creatureliness of any interpretive act; and Heinrich Fries by understanding faith within the general openness of human experience to meaning. See Hans Küng, *On Being a Christian,* trans. E. Quinn (Garden City, N.Y.: Doubleday, 1976); Edward Schillebeeckx, *Jesus: An Experiment in Christology,* trans. H. Hoskins (New York: Seabury Press, 1979), esp. 591–625; Piet Schoonenberg, *Auf Gott hin Denken: Deutschsprachige Schriften zur Theologie,* ed. W. Zauner (Vienna: Herder, 1986), 15–17; Heinrich Fries, *Fundamental Theology,* trans. R. Daly, S.J. (Washington, D.C.: Catholic University of America Press, 1996), esp. 11–34.

31. Francis Schüssler Fiorenza, *Foundational Theology: Jesus and the Church* (New York: Crossroad, 1986), esp. 251–321. Another example of correlation outside the Continental heritage is Joseph A. Bracken, *The Triune Symbol: Persons, Process, and Community* (Lanham, Md.: University Press of America, 1985), which enlists a Whiteheadian metaphysics of process as the term of worldly wisdom.

32. The locus classicus for the charge is Lindbeck, *Nature of Doctrine,* 112–35. Cf. George Lindbeck, "The Gospel's Uniqueness: Election and Untranslatability,"

Modern Theology 13 (1997): 423–50. For Catholic responses to the charge, see David Tracy, "Lindbeck's New Program for Theology: A Reflection," *The Thomist* 49 (1985): 460–72; Tracy, "The Uneasy Alliance Reconceived: Catholic Theological Method, Modernity, and Postmodernity," *Theological Studies* 50 (1989): 548–70; John E. Thiel, *Imagination and Authority: Theological Authorship in the Modern Tradition* (Minneapolis, Minn.: Fortress Press, 1991), 167–200; Thiel, "Schleiermacher as 'Catholic': A Charge in the Rhetoric of Modern Theology," *Heythrop Journal* 37 (1996): 61–82.

33. Robert M. Doran has criticized the method of correlation by arguing that its abstractive distinction between Word and worldly wisdom as the terms of correlation fails to recognize that worldly wisdom is always already theologically interpreted so that "tradition and situation are not as disparate as a pure method of correlation would insinuate" (*Theology and the Dialectics of History* [Toronto, Canada: University of Toronto Press, 1990], 454). Cf. Neil Ormerod, "Quarrels with the Method of Correlation," *Theological Studies* 57 (1996): 707–19. One cannot but agree with Doran that a mediating method needs to be sophisticated enough to acknowledge where its epistemic loyalties finally lie and the extent to which these loyalties have a hand in any interpretive act. By defining his object of criticism as he has done, Doran seems to judge a "pure" method of correlation to be interpretively naïve. Since Doran has cited no example of a pure correlationist, it is difficult to know whom he would count an offender under this negative rubric. One can concede to Doran that some descriptions of correlation can appear naïve when simplicity in definition is the methodologist's goal. Tracy's account of the method in *Blessed Rage for Order* (but not in *The Analogical Imagination*) and Roger Haight's account in *Dynamics of Theology* come to mind. But even the terse, abstract definitions of correlation in these works are explained in sufficiently nuanced detail to keep them from being charged fairly with the sort of "purity" Doran has decried. See Tracy, *Blessed Rage for Order*, 43–87. Roger Haight, S.J., *Dynamics of Theology* (New York: Paulist Press, 1990), 189–212.

34. Mikhail Bakhtin, "Epic and Novel: Toward a Methodology for the Study of the Novel," in *The Dialogic Imagination: Four Essays*, ed. M. Holquist, trans. C. Emerson and M. Holquist (Austin: University of Texas Press, 1981), 17, 23.

35. Terrence W. Tilley, *Story Theology* (Wilmington, Del.: Glazier, 1985), 11–16.

36. Johann Baptist Metz, *Faith in History and Society: Toward a Practical Fundamental Theology*, trans. D. Smith (New York: Seabury Press, 1980), 90. Cf. Metz, *Theology of the World*, trans. W. Glen-Doepel (New York: Herder and Herder, 1971); Metz, *The Emergent Church: The Future of Christianity in a Postbourgeois World* (London: SCM Press, 1981). Political theology has drawn especially on the critical social theory of Jürgen Habermas. See Helmut Peukert, *Science, Action, and Fundamental Theology: Toward a Theology of Communicative Action*, trans. J. Bohman (Cambridge, Mass.: MIT Press, 1984); Matthew L. Lamb, *Solidarity with Victims: Toward a Theology of Social Transformation* (New York: Crossroad, 1982); Paul Lakeland, *Theology and Critical Theory: The Discourse of the Church* (Nashville, Tenn.: Abingdon Press, 1990); Edmund Arens, *Christopraxis: A Theology of Action*, trans. J. Hoffmeyer (Minneapolis, Minn.: Fortress Press, 1995). Worthy of note, too, are approaches to political theology that seek the contextualization of Christian meaning in national histories and through a negotiation of their own particular ideologies and social problems. See, for example, Gregory Baum, *Theology and Society*

(New York: Paulist Press, 1987); John A. Coleman, *An American Strategic Theology* (New York: Paulist Press, 1982).

37. See Gustavo Gutiérrez, *A Theology of Liberation: History, Politics, and Salvation*, trans. C. Inda and J. Eagleson (Maryknoll, N.Y.: Orbis Books, 1988). See also the references to Gutiérrez's work in chapter 4 of this volume. Cf. Juan Luis Segundo, *The Liberation of Theology*, trans. J. Drury (London: Gill and Macmillan, 1977); Segundo, *Faith and Ideologies*, trans. J. Drury (Maryknoll, N.Y.: Orbis Books, 1984); Jon Sobrino, S.J., *Christology at the Crossroads: A Latin American Approach*, trans. J. Drury (Maryknoll, N.Y.: Orbis Books, 1978); Leonardo Boff and Clodovis Boff, *Salvation and Liberation: In Search of a Balance between Faith and Politics*, trans. R. Barr (Maryknoll, N.Y.: Orbis Books, 1984).

38. Elizabeth Schüssler Fiorenza, *In Memory of Her: A Feminist Theological Reconstruction of Christian Origins* (New York: Crossroad, 1989); Anne E. Carr, *Transforming Grace: Christian Tradition and Women's Experience* (San Francisco: HarperCollins, 1988); Rosemary Radford Ruether, *Sexism and God-Talk: Toward a Feminist Theology* (Boston: Beacon Press, 1983).

39. Among the many examples are Diana L. Hayes, *And Still We Rise: An Introduction to Black Liberation Theology* (New York: Paulist Press, 1996); Virgilio P. Elizondo, *Galilean Journey: The Mexican-American Promise* (Maryknoll, N.Y.: Orbis Books, 1983); Ada María Isasi-Díaz, *En la Lucha: Elaborating a Mujerista Theology* (Minneapolis, Minn.: Fortress Press, 1993); Aloysius Pieris, S.J., *An Asian Theology of Liberation* (Maryknoll, N.Y.: Orbis Books, 1988).

40. For Gutiérrez, see the references in chapter 4 of this volume; Elizabeth A. Johnson, *She Who Is: The Mystery of God in Feminist Theological Discourse* (New York: Crossroad, 1992); Elizabeth Schüssler Fiorenza, *Jesus. Miriam's Child, Sophia's Prophet: Critical Issues in Feminist Christology* (New York: Continuum, 1995).

41. For a critical version of traditional narrative with attention to the corrupting circumstances of anti-Judaism, see Darrell J. Fasching, *Narrative Theology after Auschwitz: From Alienation to Ethics* (Minneapolis, Minn.: Fortress Press, 1992).

Index of Names

Index of Subjects